Napoleon's Navigation System

A STUDY OF TRADE CONTROL DURING
THE CONTINENTAL BLOCKADE

BY

FRANK EDGAR MELVIN

AMS PRESS
NEW YORK

Reprinted from the edition of 1919, New York
First AMS EDITION published 1970
Manufactured in the United States of America

International Standard Book Number: 0-404-04288-0

Library of Congress Number: 79-135721

AMS PRESS INC.
NEW YORK, N.Y. 10003

A THESIS

Presented to the Faculty of the Graduate School in
Partial Fulfillment of the Requirements for
the Degree of Doctor of Philosophy

CONTENTS

FOREWORD..Page

Factors determining the nature and emphasis of this study. Main theses developed: (a) Napoleon's Navigation System and the economic struggle with England was the prime factor in the growth of the Napoleonic Empire, therefore the policies and institutions of the System afford a good test of Napoleon's statesmanship. (b) The determining factor in the economic strife of Napoleon with England was the position of the United States as the chief neutral, demonstrating the decisive function of a strong neutrality in every contest between land-power and sea-power.

INTRODUCTORY CHAPTER

THE SIGNIFICANCE OF THE NAVIGATION SYSTEM..Page 1

Changing historical appraisals of the Napoleonic regime. The influence of the British Navigation Acts during the century before the French Revolution. Navigation Acts of Frence during the Revolution. Character of Napoleon's commercial policies prior to the adoption of the Continental System

CHAPTER I

THE FORMATION OF THE CONTINENTAL SYSTEM..Page 6

A—*The Land Blockade*: The Berlin decree, its character and origin initial problems of execution. The British retort: Orders in Council of January and February, 1807. The treaties of Tilsit: demonstration of the military value of the System; Continental acceptance of the Blockade and the elimination of land neutrals.

B—*The Real Intent of the System*: Plans for economic expansion. The British attack upon Copenhagen. Rigorous closure measures.

C—*The Maritime Interdict*: The status of the neutral carrier and his vessels. British Orders in Council, November 1807. Napoleon's decrees of Fontainebleau and Milan, Nov.-Dec. 1807. Consequences.

CHAPTER II

AMELIORATIVE EXPERIMENTS...Page 48

Consequences for France of the elimination of the neutral carrier. The new Council of the Interior: its efforts to remedy the situation in February, 1808. Measures to protect French *cabotage*. The colonies and colonial

v

trade problems. The American Embargo of December 1807 leads to the retaliatory "Bayonne decision" of April 1808. Futile expedients in aid of French trade: subsidized *armements en aventurier*; use of national ships for colonial trade; government insurance; grant of protection-papers for the Barbary trade. The provision of quinine without a deviation from the Blockade. Abortive efforts for a *rapprochement* with the United States.

CHAPTER III

TRADE BY EXCEPTION..Page 77

The Napoleonic System at the beginning of 1809. The international situation: Spain; Austria; America. The agricultural crisis in the West Loyseau's petition for the right to export grain leads to a licence trade. Criticism of this action. Napoleon's personal responsibility. Initial problems and measures. Selection and protection of licenced ships: neutralizations and simulations. Status of American shipping. New negotiations for a *rapprochement* with the United States.

The Non-Intercourse Act and its European effect. The Erskine agreement and its disavowal by England. Napoleon's Altenberg offer of 22 August 1809. The detection of fraud in licence petitions.

CHAPTER IV

THE LICENSE EXPERIMENT..Page 109

Development of licenced trade, March 1809-May 1810. Policies of Cretet, Fouché, and Montalivet. Growth of the trade. Changes in commercial regulations. Consideration of results. Influences and arguments for and against a continuance of the licence policy. Fauchat's reports.

CHAPTER V

INTERNATIONAL SIGNIFICANCE OF THE LICENCE EXPERIMENT........Page 139

European interest in the imperial licence policy. Requests to participate. Attitude of Russia. Dutch violations of the Continental System. Neapolitan evasions and Murat's knavery. Relation of Spain, Italy, North Germany, and Denmark to the Blockade and the licence trade. Legal status of the licences. Fraud and trickery in the traffic. Americans involved. Opposition of the United States. Franco-American relations, August 1809 to March 1810. Armstrong's manoeuvres. Crisis of December 1809 for Napoleon and his systems. Negotiations to modify the Blockade. The "great affair" of American relations. Futility of Napoleon's secret negotiations. His revenge on Holland and America.

CHAPTER VI

THE ABANDONMENT OF EXCLUSION..Page 160

Factors leading to a change of system. The final crisis in Dutch relations. Fouche's intrigues and disgrace. Napoleon's remarriage. The tour of the North. Effect upon his economic policies. The establishment of the *Conseil du Commerce*: its character and program. Crisis in American relations. The Rambouillet decree: its actual history and effect. American "Commercial Intercourse Act": news of it in France and Napoleon's first reaction. His American *permit* scheme. Its nature and American attitude toward it. Efforts to alter it. Further results of the repeal of Non-Intercourse. Explanation of Armstrong's course. Cadore's note of 5 August on the revocation of the Berlin-Milan decrees. Its actual history and significance. Reasons for American acceptance of it.

CHAPTER VII

THE NEW ACTS OF NAVIGATION..Page 187

Initial shifts in Napoleon's commercial regulations, June-July 1810: (1) The restriction of grain exportation. (2) The police of fisheries. (3) The supervision of licenced smuggling and its dramatic significance. (4) The reconstruction of the system. Imperial decree for Licenced Navigation, St Cloud, 3 July: Its origin, provisions and significance. Connection with the American crisis. Supplementary licence decrees of July 1810.

CHAPTER VIII

THE CONTINENTAL ZOLLVEREIN..Page 211

Tariff revision necessitated by the substitution of Licenced Navigation for Continental Closure. Legislative history of the new tariff system: the export decree of 31 July; the "Trianon decree" of 5 August the "St. Cloud decree", the colonial tariff regulations. Negotiations for a Continental adoption of the Trianon tariff policy: results. Measures to enforce the new tariff system. The "Fontainebleau decree": prevotal courts and destruction of proscribed articles. Efforts for Continental adoption of these measures. The economic crisis of 1810. The Russian ukase. Ultimate consequences of these measures.

CHAPTER IX

LICENCED NAVIGATION: THE "NOUVEAU SYSTÈME"..........................Page 235

Scope and significance of the new economic program. Inauguration of the system of July 1810. Elaboration of policies and regulations. "*licences simples*" and "*licences diverses*" for the French Empire. The "American permits." "Hanseatic licences" and their availability for Baltic countries generally. The "continentalizing" of the new "Navigation System." International use of licences. The "Italian licence" decree for Mediterranean trade and its complementary measures. "Ottoman permits." Colonial licences. Licences for Holland. General character of the new system.

CHAPTER X

THE NOUVEAU SYSTÈME IN OPERATION..Page 256

French duplicity in regard to the promised repeal of the blockade decrees. American protests. Modifications in the licence system. Regions and commodities affected. Efforts to aid various economic activities through the the licences. Commercial co-operation between the French and English governments. Secret negotiations of July–September 1810 with the British Board of Trade and with Spanish-American revolutionaries. Administrative problems of the licence system, and their solution (a) correspondence with England; (b) evaluation of cargoes; (c) certificates of origin; (d) evasions and frauds.

CHAPTER XI

LICENCED NAVIGATION: THE GRAND SYSTEM..Page 284

Factors tending toward a revision of the commercial system at the close of 1811. The new American minister and his instructions. Commercial aspects of Napoleon's inspection tour in the North. nventory of results of the Navigation System. Prospects and projects. Economic crisis in Great Britain induces concessions for trade with France. Scheme for an exchange of sugar for wine. News reaches Paris at a favorable moment. Investigations and negotiations. The Conseil du Commerce of 13 January: Napoleon outlines a "Grand System" for the trade of the Continent, and vaunts the triumph of his policy over Britain's commercial tyranny. Creation of a Ministry of Manufactures and Commerce to inaugurate the "Grand System."

CHAPTER XII

THE BARRIERS CRASH...Page 311

A—An Equivocal Reversal of Systems. Divergent views of the wine-sugar deal. Napoleon's triumph too belated. Food shortage in France. Diplomatic *impasse* with Russia. America disputes Napoleon's boasted victory over England. Unexpected virility of the American stand brings both belligerents to terms. France offers public proof of the repeal of the Blockade decrees. Negotiations opened for reparations and a trade treaty. The British Opposition forces the sacrifice of the Order in Council System in order to placate America. Concessions made too late to prevent the War of 1812 and the Invasion of Russia.

B—The Experiment of the Grand System. British-French regulations for their co-operative licence-trade. Disastrous effects of the Moscow campaign upon economic conditions. Barlow's death prevents settlement of the American demands.

C—The Outcome of Napoleon's System. Statistics of the results of licenced navigation. Basic alterations in the System in order to finance Napoleon's last campaigns. The System crumbles. Economic crash coincident with the fall of the Empire. Restored Bourbons hasten to demolish the Napoleonic Navigation System, but the Navigation Acts of 1793 still survive: Results of the Napoleonic System, also are enduring.

CHAPTER XIII

ADMINISTRATION OF NAPOLEON'S NAVIGATION SYSTEM..........................Page 347

Importance of the institutional developments of the System. Administrative ramifications of the System. Ministries concerned and their connections with the System. Modifications evolved in the administrative organization. New institutions created: their history and functions. The human element in the system. The historical view of Napoleon's Navigation System.

BIBLIOGRAPHICAL ESSAY...Page 378

    A—Explanatory note.
    B—Bibliographical aids.
    C—Manuscript Sources:
        I—Archives; (a) Paris; (b) London; (c) Washington.
        II—Special Collections.
    D—Printed Sources:
        I—Legal, diplomatic, and administrative: (a) France; (b) Holland; (c) England; (d) United States; (e) Russia.
        II—Correspondence and related writings.
        III—Memoires of contemporaries.
        IV—Contemporary periodicals.
        V—Contemporary books and pamphlets.
    E—Secondary Writings:
        I—Special Studies of the Continental System.
        II—Writings of a more general nature.

FOREWORD

Napoleon's Navigation System, which comprehends as one of its elements his famous "continental blockade," was preëminently a controlling factor in his career. Historical interest in the investigation of the System is challenged at once, therefore, by a threefold appeal—by the inherent importance of the whole subject, and by its institutional and by its international aspects. The general appeal of so significant a subject is self-evident. It is also obvious that a study of the most ambitious and best sustained program of the First Empire offers a unique opportunity for tracing the genesis of the policies and institutions most typical of Napoleonic statesmanship. Similarly the mere mention of a continental blockade is immediately suggestive of momentous international consequences. Indeed a recognition of the real significance of these special aspects of the problem was the primary incentive for the present study. Its chief emphasis therefore is institutional. But particular emphasish as been laid, also, upon those international aspects of the subject which have so pertinent an interest at a time when the herculean forces of another world conflict between land-power and sea-power have been reproducing with marvellous fidelity the problems and expedients of a century ago. The realization of this latter significance of the subject necessarily has deepened steadily with the progress of the investigation. For such foreshadowings of the recurrence of an economic blockade, like that of the Napoleonic era, as were discernible at the outset of the writer's researches in Europe—at the moment of the Agadir crisis in 1911—have become realities, big with meaning, as the old warfare of blockade and interdict, danger-zone and *seesperre*, has been revived and waged with an intensified ruthlessness, and as sometimes it has seemed that America, almost with the halting yet uncanny precision of the blind, might be retreading the paths of 1806 to 1812, oblivious to old lessons and to the true meaning of present issues. But while growing recognition of their new pertinency has led to the placing of greater stress upon the international phases of Napolon's System, especially as it affected neutrals, yet this stress has only been incidental to the main task of portraying the evolution of the system itself. For, above all, it is this history of its actual evolution that affords the basis for a new interpretation of Napoleon's "continental blockade," and related measures, as a broadly conceived European Navigation System—which is the fundamental thesis of the present monograph.

The investigation of which this monograph is an outgrowth was begun at the University of Illinois, at the instance of Professor Guy Stanton Ford, as a study primarily of the licenced and illicit trade in violation of the Continental System. For it was hoped that such a study of the actual effectiveness of the continental blockade might not only throw new light upon its real value as a war-weapon, but might also make it possible to guage the actual responsibility of the System for the downfall of the Napoleonic regime. Hope of really solving these questions propounded at the inception of the investigation was, indeed, later abandoned. Nevertheless certain conclusions have been reached with regard to the licence-trade problems, which, though treated incidentally throughout the monograph, are necessarily so subordinated to the broadened scope of the thesis, that they may well be particularly summarized here. Thus it is the opinion of the investigator that, while his researches have shown the impossibility of determining the extent of infractions of the blockade, yet they have demonstrated pretty clearly:

(a) That the failure of the Continental System was not necessarily due to the policy of licenced navigation;

(b) That, although the downfall of the Continental System was inseparable from the fall of the Napoleonic regime, the Empire was doomed regardless of the System;

(c) That the Napoleonic Navigation System, and the continental blockade as a part thereof, failed in the very hour of apparent triumph because of Napoleon's own temperamental impatience, rather than by reason of vices inherent in the System;

(d) That, in fine, the results of the Napoleonic experiment are not a final, trustworthy test of the strategic possibilities of an economic blockade.

The modification of the problems and the scope of the research, referred to, was due not merely to the impossibility of finding certain essential data, but also—and more particularly—to the discovery of other significant evidence making possible a reinterpretation of the Continental System. Thus it was speedily realized—and this has been amply confirmed with the progress of the study—that published sources were quite inadequate for the purposes of the investigation. Moreover the initial examinations of British and French manuscript sources, while revealing much material of interest, also indicated that the records were not sufficiently complete for the original purposes of the research. On the other hand, a large body of economic records for the Napoleonic period, at the French National Archives, proved to have been practically unexploited. What is more, the exploration of these papers kindled a real—though frankly reluctant—admiration for the Emperor Napoleon. For with the stray bits of information picked up here and there from the dust-heaps of worm-riddled routine papers, or scarcely decipherable minutes endorsed with the nervous scrawl of the Emperor's "N . . .", it has been possible to piece together a mosaic which portrays the growth and meaning of the Continental System. Thus is revealed Napoleon's concept of his Navigation System: a truly comprehensive program for the economic reconstruction of France and the Continent. It also shows his peculiar genius for organization, his kaleidoscopic interests, his sure mastery of varied details, his remarkably keen sense of values—illustrated by his alert comprehension in digesting tedious ministerial reports, and his quick responsiveness to ideas from any source—effectively employed in the formation of institutions needed for the operations of his System. Nor has the search merely demonstrated afresh the abilities of Napoleon himself, for it has revealed his very real indebtedness for the aid of men whose names "history" neglects. The course of these researches placed me under obligations to various persons. Thus my thanks are due to Mr. Hubert Hall, of the Royal Manuscripts Commission, for words of introduction which were for me the open sesame to English repositories of documents. Indeed his services, and the special research facilities afforded me by officials and clerks of the Public Record Office, the Privy Council, and elsewhere, deepen my regrets that I have been unable, in the present monograph, to present more evidences of my profits from their courtesies. Likewise in my labors at Paris I was grateful for courtesies extended me by M. Charles Schmidt and other officials of the Archives Nationales. I was also under peculiar obligations for the kindness and services of Mr. Waldo G. Leland, in charge of the Carnegie Institution's historical researches in France, and for the ready aid of his assistants, M. Abel Doysié and Mlle. Rouyer. Moreover I would make mention here of later obligations to Mr. Leland, as well as to Professor William E. Lingelbach of the University of Pennsylvania, for the use of notes from the archives of the Ministère des Affaires Étrangères, which I had not examined in Paris in view of Dr. Lingelbach's own plans for the study of diplomatic aspects of the Continental System. A mutual redelimitation of fields was made, however, when the development of my study, under his sponsorship, made it evident that an indispensable key to the changes in Napoleon's Navigation System was held by the United States government, and that, on the other hand, the clue to unsolved riddles of Franco-American relations between 1806 and 1815 was supplied by my findings regarding the Napoleonic System. This circumstance, moreover, led to subsequent researches in Washington, and elsewhere, only part of the results of which it has been deemed practicable to embody in the present study. Yet enough has been included to prove the vital significance of the rôle—heretofore too largely unrecognized—which was played by the United States in the great international crisis of a century ago.

The final preparation of this monograph, under the auspices of Professor Lingelbach, as a University of Pennsylvania dissertation, has been a part of his plan for a series of related studies covering commercial and industrial aspects of the Revolutionary and Napoleonic era, several of which have been completed or are now in hand. It has been both pleasurable and profitable to be in touch with these co-workers. Elsewhere recognition is made of the work of two of them, Dr. Peter Hoekstra and Dr. F. L. Nussbaum. To the members of the History faculty at Pennsylvania in 1912 to 1915—the years of may service as Harrison Fellow and Research Fellow in History—I render sincere acknowledgments for helpful interest by no means limited to that period. Nor am I forgetful of what I owe to the continued interest of other former teachers, notably Professor Frank H. Hodder for his aid during the preparation of the manuscript for publication. Lastly recognition is heartily tendered to that friend of research in French history, Mr. Joseph G. Rosengarten of Philadelphia, to whose interest is largely due the appearance of this present volume in the University of Pennsylvania Historical Studies.

University of Kansas   FRANK E. MELVIN.
Lawrence, May 1918.

INTRODUCTORY CHAPTER
THE SIGNIFICANCE OF A NAVIGATION SYSTEM

Historians, romancers, and tacticians for a century have been telling of the meteoric career of the Corsican and the generalship of the Little Corporal. Disproportionately little attention has been given, meanwhile, to studying the many-sided statesmanship of Bonaparte, the First Consul, and of Napoleon, Emperor of the French. Happily recent years have seen a growing tendency to a juster emphasis upon the governmental policies and institutional developments of the Napoleonic régime. Particularly is this true of the manifold aspects of social and economic polity. Rare indeed, and like voices crying in the wilderness, had been they who spoke with authority upon such topics prior to 1890. Then came the work of men like Admiral Mahan in America, J. Holland Rose in England, Lumbroso in Italy, and especially scholars like M. Charles Schmidt of the French National Archives, and Prof. Paul Darmstaedter of Germany, to whose pioneering labors are due numerous investigations in the field during the past decade.

The significance of this newer view-point was recognized by Sorel who, when choosing a title for the notable seventh volume of his *Europe et la Revolution Français*, called it, "Le Système Continental, Le Grand Empire." This title strikingly voices the essential agreement of recent scholarship with Napoleon's contemporaries in signalizing the importance of his most famous economic policy. It recognizes that this policy was at once not only the creative force but the nemesis of the "grand empire." For, to re-echo the epigrammatic phrase of Kiesselbach, "Der Sturz der Continentalsperre ist Napoleon's Sturz."[1] This Continen-

[1] Kiesselbach, *Die Continentalsperre* (Tübingen 1850). In thus recording the consensus of judgment I do so with reservations for I am not convinced that the System was the failure it is usually deemed, or that it was primarily responsible for the Spanish revolt, the Russian invasion, or the War of Liberation in Germany.

tal System which was so strikingly linked with the heyday and fall of the Empire was vitally related to the "Napoleonic Navigation System." The two systems were not, however, identical. For the term "navigation system" implies not merely or necessarily a program of Continental Closure, but rather the policy, legislation and administrative measures devised by a nation to control for its own interests its sea-borne trade.

Since the period of Edward III and the Hundred Years' War, England had utilized "navigation acts," protective—and offensive—tariffs, and special trade treaties, with allied measures, to build up her own economic power and curb that of her rivals. The apparent effectiveness of this system, particularly after the legislation of Cromwell and the restored Stuarts, had deeply impressed the world. Britons counted it the palladium of their national welfare. Other states regarded it as a world menace; a most effective device for gaining commercial dominance by the economic ruin of their neighbors, and the very secret of that system of credit—the source of unfailing subsidies—by which England used her allies to crush her rivals.

When even today, decades after the collapse and abandonment of this navigation system, nations are still obsessed with spectral visions of British commercial tyranny it should not be difficult to conceive of the world's attitude toward the system in the days of its vigor. Already France in the eighteenth century, like Holland in the seventeenth, had felt the virulence of its attack. Being fully persuaded that it had been a large factor in the loss of their colonial empire, having but just secured a costly revenge by aiding the American revolt against the same throttling economic system, it was but natural that many Frenchmen viewed with jealous fear Lord Auckland's skill in the commercial negotiations of 1786, seeing therein a vital thrust at the economic welfare of France itself.[2] In sooth the unequal Convention of Versailles was as

[2] For an account of this convention—the so-called "Eden treaty"—see F. Dumas, *Étude sur le Traité de Commerce de 1786 entre la France et l'Angleterre*. This study, however, has not used all the sources, nor does it adequately show

salt upon open wounds—and at a critical moment. For such an injury could scarcely be forgotten by revolutionists bent on asserting in every way their national destiny. And, being alert experimenters as well as theorists, the statesmen of the Revolution found in the British navigation acts not only an attack to be resisted but also a method of counter-attack. That this project of fighting fire by fire was largely inspired by American influence seems very probable,[3] but if so it was readily adopted by France where such an idea was fostered by agitators and pamphleteers who, in an age of economic theorizing, could not fail to discuss the bases of Britain's supremacy. The result of the outcry was the French Navigation Act of 1793, which reinforced or modified by later measures became a notable feature of the war of Revolutionary France against her maritime foe.[4]

When Napoleon Bonaparte became First Consul he inherited the navigation acts and kindred measures against English trade in the execution of which he had been active under the Directory. A continuance of this policy was supported by the influence

---

the historical influence of the treaty. The most famous contemporary French protest was by the Chamber of Commerce of Normandy. See bibliography for references on the treaty.

[3] Aside from any possible influence of the American trade policy there is evidence that Joel Barlow about 1792 was advocating a joint commercial attack on England by France and the United States. See the Barlow MSS. II, 20, (in Harvard Library). But the most direct influence was the work of Ducher— the real author of the French navigation act reported by Barère, for Ducher had just returned from consular service in the United States strongly affected by American ideas. (See his articles in the *Moniteur* during 1793-4.) His career is the theme of a study by Mr. F. L. Nussbaum (Univ. of Pa. MSS. diss. 1915).

[4] See 6 Duvergier 221 (act of 21 September); *Ibid.*, 292 (decree of 27 vendémiaire An II = 18 October 1793); *Ibid.*, 267 (decree of 18 vendémiaire An II); also, 10 Duvergier 214 (29 nivose An VI = 18 January 1798); and *Ibid.*, 391 (5 fructidor An VI = 22 August 1798); etc. Also see Lepec, *Bulletin annoté*, II, 351-5 and notes; IV, 421-2, 438-9, 473-4, 489; VII, 444. For tracing the commercial policy and regulations of the Revolution the *Bulletin d'histoire économique*, année 1912, is indispensable. For debates and public discussion see especially the *Archives Parlementaires, Moniteur, Journal des Débats*, etc.

of the Armed Neutrality in 1800-1801, and thereafter by the fresh outcries against a revival of the Eden treaty, which were evoked by the negotiation of the Peace of Amiens.[5] During the brief truce that followed this treaty the original Navigation Act of 1793, without the later modifications in favor of neutrals and the special measures against English goods, continued in force.[6] The renewal of the war brought fresh modifications of the navigation policy, particularly with respect to the neutral trader and the prohibition of intercourse with England.[7] These were further supplemented during the following three years by a long succession of edicts, executive orders, and diplomatic agreements, as section by section came the closure of the coasts of the continent against English commerce.

Besides the line of modifications of the navigation system which grew out of the decree of 18 vendémiaire An II (9 October 1793), specially directed against English goods, there was a second line of *tariff* legislation supplementary to the Navigation Act of 1793. This militant tariff policy was also inherited by the Consulate and continued with various modifications throughout the Napoleonic règime.[8] Most of the tariff changes made by Napoleon affected a limited number of articles and chiefly those of colonial

[5] See the *Moniteur*, 1801-3, also Peuchet, *Bibliothèque Commerciale*, vols. 1-6. For Napoleon's favorable attitude toward the protests against a revival of the "Eden treaty" see his note of 1 March 1801 to Lebrun regarding the Rabasse memoir (*Cor. de Nap.*, 7:53, no. 5423). Cf. too, Thibaudeau, *Memoires sur le Consulat*, 402; Goldsmith, *Recueil de decrets*, I, 523; Redhead-Yorke, *Letters of 1802*, pp. 241-4; Pinkerton, *Recollections of Paris . . . 1802-5*, II, chs. 3, 4, etc.

[6] Peuchet, *Bibliothèque Commerciale*, 1:138 ff., and 14 Duvergier 12 and 27, laws of 12 vendèmiaire and 27 frimaire An XI (4 October and 18 December 1802).

[7] Especially the law of 1 messidor An XI (20 June 1803), 14 Duvergier 335. Cf. also 14 Duvergier 355, 1 thermidor An XI (20 July 1803), and *ibid.*, 403, 4e jour complémentaire (21 September 1803).

[8] See Lepec, *Bulletin annoté*, VIII, historical notes on the law of 12 nivose An VI, Peuchet, *Bibliothèque Commerciale*, and Duvergier, *Lois*, for the tariff acts themselves and contemporary views upon them. For later discussions

origin. In most cases, such revisions struck at English commercial rivalry as truly as did the avowed exclusion laws. One of the most significant instances of this is found in the customs legislation of 1806. During the winter of 1805 a series of petitions and deputations from manufacturers, workmen, and commercial organizations besought the Emperor for further protection of the cotton industry against actual or anticipated British competition.[9] The result was the tariff decrees of 22 February and 4 March developed as the *loi des douanes* of 30 April 1806.[10]

It was during a ministerial discussion of these measures on 4 March that the Emperor is reported to have said: "forty-eight hours after peace with England, I shall proscribe foreign products and shall promulgate a navigation act which will permit the entry of our ports only to French ships constructed from French timber, manned by a crew two-thirds French. Even coal and English milords can land only under the French flag. There will be a great outcry because commerce in France has a bad spirit, but six years afterward there will be the greatest prosperity."[11]

But Napoleon did not wait for peace to inaugurate his new navigation act. Before the end of the year he had taken a notable step toward the end in view by proclaiming a system of Continental Closure. This act was the culmination of the navigation program of the Revolution. It was also the point from which was to be developed the new Napoleonic navigation system which before its own fall not only was to avenge, at last, the treaty of 1786, but even to fore-doom that palladium of English prosperity, the British navigation system itself. The story of this evolution becomes now the theme of our study.

---

of the system see Amé, *Étude sur les tariffs de douane et sur les traités de commerce*, I, ch. 3, and Gouraud, *Histoire de la politique commerciale de la France*, II, livre VIII.

[9] AF^{IV} 1318, pieces 10-12, and Peuchet, *Bibliothèque Commerciale*, 12:1-4.

[10] 15 Duvergier 415 ff.

[11] Pelet de La Lozère, *Opinions de Napoléon*, p. 238.

CHAPTER I

THE FORMATION OF THE CONTINENTAL SYSTEM

A—*The Land Blockade*

It was on 21 November 1806 that Napoleon issued from Berlin that momentous edict which formally inaugurated his Continental System. Though an adept in the creation of dramatic scenes, he staged few with so impressive a background of place or time as was afforded by the great Frederick's capital in the hour of Prussia's deepest abasement.[1] Verily such a scene was well calculated to convince a marvelling world that Jena had answered Trafalgar. That this was distinctly in the Emperor's mind may be divined from his explanatory declaration to his brother Louis: "Vous avez vu, par mon message au senat et par mon décret que je veux conquêrir la mer par la puissance de la terre."[2]

The Berlin decree is prefaced by a statement of causes—a detailed arraignment of England's disregard for the accepted rules of naval warfare.[3] The object of this maritime usurpation being, forsooth, to raise English trade upon the ruins of that of the Continent, the preamble of the decree declares that whoever upon the Continent deals in English wares becomes thereby an accomplice in the English plot. England's policy having aided her to the hurt of all other nations, the injured nations have a right of retaliation in kind. In virtue thereof France adopts this decree which shall be "a fundamental principle of the Empire until England shall acknowledge the principles of international law, that there is the same law of war for the sea as for the land, which

[1] Cf. Napoleon to Cadore, 7 October 1810. *Cor. de Nap.*, 21:197.
[2] *Cor. de Nap.*, 14:28, no. 11379. To Louis, 3 December 1806. Cf. also no. 11378, "C'est le seul moyen de porter coup à l'Angleterre et de l'obliger à le paix"; and also see *Cor. de Nap.*, nos. 11010, 11064, 11093, 11217, 11271, etc.
[3] *Cor. de Nap.*, 13:556-7, no. 11283; *Moniteur*, 5 December 1806. For judicial interpretations, and for precedents for the decree see Lepec, *Bulletin annoté*, XI, 75-7.

cannot be extended to private goods or non-combatants, and that blockades must be limited to fortified places invested with competent force." The decree proper then declares (1) that the British Isles are in a state of blockade. (2) Trade and intercourse therewith are forbidden, and English mail shall be seized. (3) All Englishmen in the Empire or allied states are to be arrested as prisoners of war. (4) English warehouses and merchandise and all property of English origin or ownership shall be seized as good prize. (5) Half the product of the confiscations thus ordained shall go to indemnify merchants for losses sustained through captures by English cruisers. (6) No vessel coming direct from England or her colonies or having been there subsequent to this decree shall be received in any port. (7) Any vessel contravening this provision by making a false declaration shall be seized as if it were English. (8) The Prize Court at Paris for the Empire, or occupied countries, that at Milan for the kingdom of Italy, shall have final cognizance of such cases. (9) The Minister of Exterior Relations is to communicate the decree to the kings of Spain, Naples, Holland and Etruria who are like sufferers with the Emperor. (10) Execution is vested in the ministers of Exterior Relations, War, Marine, Finance and of Police, and the Director General of Posts.

Prolific formulator of great edicts that he was, Napoleon fulminated scarcely another so portentous as this: banning English men, English goods and English intercourse from the Continent of Europe—in short, laying the British Isles under a commercial interdict, and calling the nations to join a Holy League, "une croisade contre le sucre et le café, contre les percales et les mousselines."[4] Of the Emperor's attitude with respect to this act Sorel has brilliantly said: "Il étudie avec sa minutie habituelle cette prodigeuse affaire; il y prépare l'opinion; il corrige, remanie le texte de son décret sentant bien que c'est l'acte décisif, plus que le charte, le raison d'être de son Grand Empire."[5]

[4] Schlegel, *Sur le Système Continental*, p. 66.
[5] Sorel, *L'Europe et la Revolution Français*, VII, 114.

Into the story of the assiduous drafting and retouching of the decree by Talleyrand and Napoleon we can not enter here.[6] A few statements must suffice regarding its origin. Although the Berlin pronunciamento came as the immediate consequence of the rupture of peace *pour parlers* with England it was actually a belated retort to the British Order in Council of May 1806, which pretended to blockade the coast of Europe from Brest to the river Elbe. Such is the clear implication of the Berlin decree itself, confirmed by countless subsequent assertions of the French government. Moreover, it is borne out by the language of a pamphlet issued in June from the Tuileries press. This pamphlet, entitled: *Que deviendra le monde si l'Angleterre succombe dans sa lutte contre la France?* was a translation with ample notes, by one M. J. Weiler, of an article that had appeared in the January number of an important German magazine.[7] The burden of the prophet Weiler was that English commercial tyranny must be resisted by an attack upon English trade and credit. It was the same strain which since July of 1805 had appeared in the treatises prepared for Napoleon by that clever penman and arch-intriguer, Montgaillard, who, because of these memoires, is said to have incited the Emperor to proclaim his Continental System.[8] But Montgaillard as well as Weiler and his German forerunner seem to have borrowed their ideas, if not even their phrases, from an unusually able brochure entitled: *De la Preponderance Maritime de la Grande Bretagne*, published during 1805 by a certain Monbrion.[9] Yet if Monbrion furnished the prime incentive for the edict of Berlin, it was doubtless because the chief merit of his book, as his reviewers said, was its exceptional presentation of the pre-

[6] See *Cor. de Nap.*, vol. 13. As to Talleyrand, cf. *Memoirs of the Duke of Rovigo*, II. pt. 1, pp. 7-10; also note 12 below. Talleyrand himself is silent as to his share in the matter.

[7] *Europäische Annalen*, January 1806, pp. 25-41.

[8] Montgaillard, *Memoires Diplomatiques*, (edited by Clement La Croix), esp. pp. 63, 67, 71, 72, 81, 83, 166-9, 183.

[9] It is interesting to note that the copy of this brochure in the Bibliothèque Nationale seems to have come from the Emperor's own library.

vailing ideas of the period.¹⁰ The most striking demonstration of the deep roots of the Berlin decree, however, is afforded by a textual criticism of the edict itself. For one cannot fail to observe that it is the climax of a series of anathemas against England, which bear each to each a striking relationship in the nature, the sequence, and the very phrasing of their indictments.¹¹ In short, the ground broken ere the end of the monarchy, tilled by the Convention and Directory, and recultivated by the Consulate was well prepared for the Continental System.¹¹ᵃ

But if the Berlin decree was no great novelty to the world it was none the less a landmark in Napoleon's career. The very fact that it is the crystallization of long current ideas alone would give it such distinction. But it has other and stronger claims. Thus as the fruition of earlier exclusion programs, as marking a clarification of aims and the codification of previous legislation, it is noteworthy. As the point of shift in the economic campaign against England from localized strategic centers, or at best national coast lines, to a continental scope, from an eminently defensive to a pre-eminently offensive basis, it is highly significant. In fine, as the first official proclamation of a settled polity which was indeed to be a fundamental principle of the Napoleonic empire, it was a most pregnant event.

[10] Cf. Peuchet, *Bibliothèque Commerciale*, 11:236-40.

[11] Without including the strictly Revolutionary assertions of the same ideas note, for example, the striking parallelism between the ideas and expressions of (a) The message of the Executive Directory to the Council of Five Hundred, 15 nivose An VI (4 January 1798) which was written by Talleyrand, *Procès Verbal*, 2ᵐᵉCorps Legislatif, 2ᵐᵉSerie, IX, 256-62. (And see also p. 408.) [A better account is in the *Journal des Débats*, however.] (b) Instructions of Napoleon to Talleyrand, 16 frimaire An IX (7 December 1800), *Cor. de Napoléon*, 6:523. (c) Message to the Senate, Corps Legislatif and Tribunat, 24 pluviose An IX (13 February 1801), *Cor. de Nap.*, 8:19. (d) Message to the Senate, 30 floréal An XI (20 May 1803), *Cor. de Nap.*, 8:320; and cf. the arrêt of 1 messidor An XI (20 June 1803), *Cor. de Nap.*, 8:365. (e) Reports of Talleyrand, 15 and 20 Nov. 1806, *Archives Parlementaires*, 2ᵐᵉ Serie, vol. 9, pp. 439-41. (f) Berlin decree, *Cor. de Nap.*, 13:555.

[11a] Cf. Boucher de Perthes on birth of the System in 1801, *Rev. Nap.*, n. s., II: 71; III: 75.

Thus in the ultimate analysis the Berlin decree is chiefly important as the beginning rather than the end of a program. For the proclamation of a Continental System manifestly was not its consummation. Indeed, the "system" was never *un fait accompli*, it was pre-eminently a process of evolution. For until June of 1810 the system was in course of formulation, thereafter it was being transformed. The explanation of this process is found in the interplay of three vital problems, present from the very initiation of the system, namely, its *enforcement, definition and amelioration.*

The shaping of the Continental System was thus fortuitous rather than designed. It is doubtful, indeed, whether Napoleon really had been conscious of the natural course of growth by which his system of conquering the sea by the land was but the fruition of the commercial program of the Revolution. Still more doubtful is it whether, despite his previous experiences and his usual clairvoyance, the Emperor had weighed in advance or, in fact, clearly recognized even the immediate consequences of his proclamation of a holy league against the British monopolists. To be sure he must have realized that there would be an enforcement problem. He had, in fact, anticipated the need of careful arrangements for the effective inauguration of his program by premonitory directions sent to officials at strategic points and these orders actually were followed during the initiatory weeks of the system.[12] But how inadequately the imperial prevision had gauged the severity of the tests which his regulations would have to sustain, may be seen from the little zeal with which they were executed in

[12] For examples of initial instructions see *Cor. de Nap.*, 13, nos. 11267, 11276, 11282–11285 and 11308; 14, nos. 11346, 11355, 11363, 11378, 11379, 11390, etc. As to execution see *Cor. de Nap.*, vols. 14 and 15; Bertrand, *Lettres inédites de Talleyrand à Napoleon*, pp. 281, 286, 294, 298, 390, 421; *Le Moniteur Universelle, London Times, London Chronicle, London Morning Chronicle, London Sun*, etc., Nov. 1806–April 1807; *Parliamentary Papers*, nos. 339–341, etc. (These numbers are those of a special compilation of Parliamentary Papers at University of Pennsylvania.)

the spring of 1807. This complication of unforeseen difficulties was not primarily due to the greater boldness and cunning of the English traders after their first panic. Nor was it due to the veniality or carelessness of Continental officials, or even to the reputed exigencies of Napoleon, requiring him to clothe his army in English cloth and shoe them with English leather.[13] Instead the chief difficulty seems to have been the strain of that second initial problem, to wit, the need of defining the system.

[13] Marbot's anecdote of his unwilling complicity in smuggling into France some contraband goods consigned for the Empress Josephine, (*Memoires*, I, 379-82; and see a similar anecdote in Thiébault's *Memoires*, IV, 71); and Bourrienne's statement that in order to fulfill an imperative levy on the Hanse cities for shoes and overcoats he dared to allow the Hanse merchants to secretly secure part of the materials from England (*Memoires*, III, 2 and 14) have furnished the grounds for countless sweeping indictments of the Continental System, which scarcely do credit to the scrupulosity of those who have retold such gossipy tales. See, for example, J. H. Rose, *Life of Napoleon*, II, 205, *Personality of Napoleon*, p. 315, and in *Eng. Hist. Rev.*, XVIII, 722, note also his more cautious statements in *Cambridge Modern History*, IX, 378. Likewise see Sloane, "The Continental System," in *Political Science Quarterly*, XIII, 230; Mahan, *Sea Power and the French Revolution and Empire*, II, 273; Clive Day, *History of Commerce*, p. 343; Broderick and Fotheringham in *Political History of England*, XI, 56, etc., etc. Indeed it is difficult to say which is more amazing—the uncritical use of such dubious sources, the variant and expanded repetitions of the stories, or the deductions therefrom that the enforcement of the exclusion decrees was a mere farce, that Napoleon himself was from the first concerned in evading his own rules, and that, *ipso facto*, the Continental System was doomed from its inception. That there was a *basis* of truth in these anecdotes is very probable but this element of truth is far from warranting the conclusions drawn therefrom. Thus as to smuggling for the Empress, Napoleon sharply warned Gaudin, Minister of Finance: "No prohibited merchandise whatever may enter without my order, and I should be especially derelict to permit any abuse which touches my house so closely. . . . . When there are laws which press upon society, it is needful that every one set an example." Cf. *Cor. de Nap.*, 16:158. As to the Bourrienne episode, the requisitions were made prior to the Berlin decree, *Cor. de Nap.*, 13, nos. 11256—14 November, and 11269—16 November, and only at the last moment and for a brief time did Bourrienne risk the imperial displeasure by violating the blockade, (cf. Bourrienne's own statement and note *Cor. de Nap.*, 14,

12 FORMATION OF THE CONTINENTAL SYSTEM

Although today an attempt to define the Continental System seems at times the task of explaining the inexplicable, yet for Napoleon in 1806 (unless his anxiety for the proper publication and reception of his decree testifies otherwise) it would seem that any possibility of misunderstanding his program was well-nigh incomprehensible.[14] Perhaps, however, it was the very naïveté, the apparent simplicity of the *politique* of the Berlin decree which made practical interpretations of its scope and intent, its flexibility or its sincerity so imperatively necessary for others. In fact, the persistency of the need for such interpretations and evaluations has given a most uncertain character to the year after the Berlin decree.

From the standpoint of its really notable achievements it may seem surprisingly inaccurate to single out the year 1807 as "the year of uncertainty" in the evolution of the Continental System. Nevertheless, the very achievements of the year lay in the work of definition, of bringing clarity from vagueness, action from indecision, assurance from uncertainty. In this process of practical evaluations may be seen two equivalent stages separated by a brief, but significant, interlude, and marked by four focal dates: Berlin decree to the treaties of Tilsit (7-12 July), and Copenhagen attack to the decree of Milan (17 December). And from the very real testings involved in this process was resolved, in turn, any uncertainty as to (1) the *domestic*, (2) the *military*, (3) the *commercial*, and (4) the *international intent and value* of the Berlin decree.

---

nos. 11577 and 11578). The episode had no relation to the Moscow campaign or to the licence policy adopted in 1809–1810, and perhaps none to Bourrienne's later malfeasances, for which indeed he was punished by Napoleon, as were other venial officials. Cf. *Cor. de Nap.*, 21:158, 347; Lecestre, *Lettres inédites*, II, 95, 104, and Brotonne, *Lettres inédites*, 242, 250, 271, 389, 406, etc. Also Boucher de Perthes (*re* Josephine, etc.), *Rev. Nap.*, n. s., II: 113, n. 2.

[14] See *Cor. de Nap.*, 14, nos. 11276, 11285, 11289, and 11293; *Moniteur*, 13 January 1807, p. 49, etc. An interesting pamphlet issued from Berlin in defense of the Decree is found in *Arch. Nat.*, AF^{IV}1673, pièce 29. Another pamphlet "Sur le Blocus des Iles Britanniques et l'acte de Navigation d'Angleterre," signed Marec, was published at Paris, 8 Dec. 1806.

This process of testing and its significant results along the four lines indicated, with their temporary culmination in the Milan decree—*after foreshadowing the eventual navigation policy*—is the story we are now to trace.

First in point of time, and doubtless least expected by Napoleon, was a misapprehension of his system, or opposition thereto, in France itself. Despite careful preparations for the announcement of the decree to the Senate, and its publication in the *Moniteur*, it failed to elicit the hearty reception desired.[15] The explanation seems clear. Apparently the Emperor had considered the politicians and had sought to forestall legislative murmurings, hoping thereby to have a guarantee of popular support. He evidently had failed, however, to placate the commercial classes directly. Evidence to this effect is found in the protests of chambers of commerce, such as the action of Bordeaux in November and December 1806.[16] These merchants, who already were feeling the ill-effects of the Jena campaign upon the Leipzig fair, and hence upon their trade with Germany, Poland, and Russia, were apprehensive of dire results from the blockade decree. While such protests do not seem to have secured any immediate attention, the Emperor's later sensitiveness to mercantile interests would indicate that the outcry was not without effect. Moreover, the apparent neglect of such protests at the moment may be accounted for by certain elements in the general situation. These were, particularly, Napoleon's preoccupation with the Prussian situation and the campaign of Poland; also the serious industrial situation in France, of which, indeed, the uneasiness of the chambers of commerce may have been a premonition, but which required that attention to individual cries should give way to measures of general relief.

It is doubtful whether the new embargo system directly, or more than casually, affected this home crisis. Yet it doubtless

[15] *Cor. de Nap.*, 13:552, and 554.
[16] AF^{IV}1060, dossier 2, pp. 26-33.

had a depressive influence upon the morale of certain types of business that aggravated the situation. So serious were conditions that the government took measures to ease the stringency and restore confidence. Orders were given by Napoleon for Champagny, Minister of the Interior, in accordance with which a plan of relief was worked out during January and February 1807.[17] The result was a series of industrial loans made from the reserve funds under a decree of 27 March.[18] The affair required attention until autumn, although Champagny felt he could refer to the matter in his exposé of August, as a problem happily solved.[19] Yet it was still somewhat an issue in 1808; while echoes of it occur for some years thereafter.[20] Indeed, a special significance of the incident is that it created a government policy, or at least a precedent, available for subsequent economic crises during the Imperial règime.[21]

Whatever the demonstrable influence of the Berlin decree upon this crisis, evidently the British blockade of the Continent was really a factor. Apparently as early as Napoleon's own edict the pressure of earlier British measures was being felt by French business.[22] Manifestly, therefore, the situation was not improved when English mercantile interests, frightened by the Berlin decree,

[17] *Cor. de Nap.*, 14, nos. 11551, 11552.

[18] Cf. also decree of 11 May in *Bulletin des lois*, p. 242.

[19] *Arch. Parl.*, 2nd Series, IX, 491. Read, however, by Cretet.

[20] The correspondence of Napoleon affords an outline of the episode, while the papers of the Interior Ministry, etc., afford interesting particulars. See *Cor. de Nap.*, 14, nos. 12195, et seq. and *Arch. Nat.*, $AF^{IV}1060$, dossier 2, pièces 48, 54, 56, 60, 63. See L. de Lanzac de Laborie, *Paris sous Napoléon*, VI, 306-16, whose able discussion of this crisis I am able to attest from my own examinations of the documents. Also note his article in *Revue Hebdomadaire* (1910), p. 642 ff.

[21] Cf. P. Darmstädter in *Vierteljahrschrift für Social und Wirtschaftsgeschichte*, II, 559-615; III, 1-31.

[22] See footnotes 17 and 21, *supra*. Cf. also $AF^{IV}1693$, pp. 228 and 232 for effects on Prussia, and $AF^{IV}1685$ (Joseph to Napoleon, 21 March 1807) as to Naples.

goaded Grenville and his fellow-ministers into reprisals.[23] For the effect upon the pending negotiation over maritime difficulties with America was immediate and adverse.[23a] Also, on 7 January 1807 the cabinet after a fortnight's consideration adopted an Order in Council aimed against neutral participation in the port to port trade of countries embraced within the French imperial connection.[24] The Order, to be sure, was criticized as too moderate by many Englishmen and, moreover, was still further relaxed by a licence trade Order of 4 February.[25] It called forth no active neutral protests,[25a] and was apparently ignored by the French government.[26] Yet, as a precedent for future retaliation,

[23] Cf. *London Times*, 2 and 7 December 1806; *London Chronicle*, 20, 22, 27, 29 November; 4, 6, 9, 10, 13, 27 December; 2, 3, 9 and 12 January; *Morning Chronicle*, 1, 3, 5, and 9 January, etc.

[23a] This significant but futile effort to settle Anglo-American issues merits special attention. Am. *State Papers, For. Rel.*, II and III; the writings of Monroe, Pinkney, Madison, and Jefferson; *Dropmore Papers*, etc. For the inluence of reprisal agitation on the treaty of 31 December 1806 see, particularly, *Dropmore Papers*, VIII, 473,484,491; *Bowdoin-Temple Papers*, pt. II, 354-64, 375-80; *Am. State Papers, For. Rel.*, III, 151 ff.

[24] Privy Council Register (George III) 65:17; also the Malta Order p. 20. And see Privy Council "unbound papers" 5 and 7 January for preliminary drafts. See also *London Times*, 14 January 1807; *London Chronicle*, 9 and 12 January; *London Sun*, 15 and 16 January; *Morning Chronicle*, 9, 10, 12, and 16 January. Cf. *Dropmore Papers*, VIII, 468 ff. for actual origins.

[25] See Privy Council, "unbound papers," minute of 9 January and Privy Council Register, 65:144-5, and 542, (Order in Council of 4 February).

[25a] However American technical reservations of rights (in March) were followed by protests which made the Order of 7 January with the Holland-Auckland note of 31 December 1806 one ground for rejecting the treaty of the latter date. *Am. State Papers, For. Rel.*, III, 158 and 168; Courtenay, *Observations on the American Treaty.*

[26] A copy of the 7 January Order is found in *Arch. Nat.*, AF^{IV}1693 (Rel. Ext.), p. 231, but judging from Talleyrand's letter of " 11 P.M. 9 February," sent to Napoleon at Warsaw, it would appear that the imperial government had had no earlier knowledge of this important Order in Council, (Bertrand, *Lettres inédites de Talleyrand*, p. 298, no. 226). It is not noticed in the Napoleon correspondence nor in the *Moniteur*, although the *Moniteur* (p. 381 of 1807) takes account of a modifying order of 27 (sic) February.

it was an act of historic significance, while it had an immediate and sensible affect upon commerce.

Moreover, aside from its general influence upon French economic conditions, the British blockade had an important bearing upon the situation of the French colonies. At the very moment when Grenville was drafting—or redrafting—his 7 January Order, Napoleon was submitting to his Minister of Marine and Colonies a plan for using ships of war for colonial trade in order to maintain a connection between the colonies and mother-country which it had become practically impossible to keep up through ordinary channels.[27] The principal motive for the scheme was strategical— the provisioning of these last remaining outposts of old France. Yet the arrangement therein for the government's importation of colonial produce is significant. For although Decrès at once condemned the plan in plain terms and it was dropped for the time being, yet its very proposal indicates a weak point in the French exclusion policy. In fact, this colonial problem made it certain that Napoleon must fall back upon the peculiar remedy here proposed when the situation should have become more tense, and when he was at length free from his northern campaign.[28] Needless to say, the issue involved was of vital significance for the "navigation policy" of the Empire.

Yet the prime interest of 1807 for the Napoleonic commercial system lies not in these domestic difficulties with their premonitions of trouble ahead, but in the solution of other doubtful issues of great importance. For once assured that through the assistance of government loans the policy of the Berlin decree could be made acceptable to French industry it was possible for Napoleon to turn to the far larger problem of making his Continental System actually continental. Broadly this meant covering the last gaps in the coast closure system, specifically it involved the question of whether *Europe* would *assent* to the Berlin decrees. It does

[27] *Arch. Nat.*, AF^{IV}1197, IV, 3, 4 January 1807 (4 pages).
[28] Cf. plans of April and May 1808. See next chapter.

not concern us here whether this assent was but lip service; it does that assent was gained, essentially, and that doubt upon that score was resolved by the Peace of Tilsit. Steadily since the pronunciamento of 21 November, Continental assent had been won.[29] Speedily re-echoed under imperial dictation by the satellite rulers and allies, the decree of Berlin had also been accepted, nominally at least, by Denmark, Austria, the Porte (with the Barbary States), and even by Persia, until finally at Tilsit was secured the acquiescence of Prussia and the co-operation of Russia.[30] At a few points, it is true, the closure of the coasts was even yet insecure. Pressure must needs be used for Leghorn and Sardinia, the Adriatic seaboard, Portugal, Sweden, and perhaps for Denmark. And yet at the moment these breaks might well have seemed unimportant, for surely the essential goal was reached. Had not the *acceptance* of the policy by every first-rate continental state proved that it was indeed a *Continental System?* Moreover, did not British ships already "search in vain from the Strait of the Sound to the Hellespont for a port open to receive them?"[31]

When the treaties of 7 to 12 July with Russia and Prussia had been consummated Napoleon announced to his soldiers: "The peace of Tilsit puts an end to the operations of the Grande Armée. . . . It is probable that the continental blockade will not be an empty word."[32] And there is special meaning in the declaration. For, considering the secret clauses of his alliance with Alexander,[33] stipulating that England must have made peace by December or must battle with all the continent, it may well have seemed that

[29] Bertrand, *Lettres inédites de Talleyrand*, pp. 281, 324, 370, 396, 412; *Moniteur* (1807) p. 413.

[30] De Clercq, *Recueil des Traités de la France*, II, p. 222, Art. 27; p. 2, Arts. 12-13. The Russian treaty involved also the occupation of the ports of Oldenburg and Mecklenburg.

[31] *Cor. de Nap.*, 15:527.

[32] *Cor. de Nap.*, 15:415.

[33] De Clercq, *Recueil*, II, p. 213, Arts. 4 and 5; II, 223, Art. 27.

the decree of Berlin had shown its efficacy as a *military* measure and had practically achieved its end. Thus, in fine, the second uncertainty of the year touching the value of the Continental System apparently had been solved.

A new phase therefore begins from Tilsit. A new problem awaited solution. But first there must be a final strengthening of the bands stretched round the continent. Note the swiftly planned Napoleonic program.[34] Bourrienne and Bernadotte are to give an example of vigorous enforcement in the Hanse cities. Eugène must deal with Leghorn, Civita Vecchia and Ancona. Denmark must be warned. Sardinia and Sweden are provided for. Portugal in particular must have joined the System by 1 September: the attainment of that shall be the task of Junot, and of Godoy, Prince of the Peace.[35] Meanwhile England shall accept the Russian mediation, or feel the Russian threat. Thus, in sooth, "the *continental* blockade shall not be an empty word."[36]

B—*The Real Issue Disclosed*

Victory seeming now within grasp what next was to be the object of the blockade? We might infer the answer from the broad program of investigations and rewards for 1808-9, unfolded in the *Moniteur* from time to time during the late spring by the Society for the Encouragement of National Industry.[37] And we may clearly trace the new constructive tendency in a set of ministerial papers considered about the first of August. In short the military purpose is to yield to the economic. Just as it has already been forceful as a military measure so hereafter as a commercial interdict the Berlin decree is to be more than mere words. *Herein the real, ultimate aim of the Continental System is revealed.*

[34] *Cor. de Nap.*, 15:433, 449, 450, 459, 467, 468.
[35] *Cor. de Nap.*, 15:433. See other version of this letter in *Archiv für Oester. Gesch.*, vol. 93, p. 161.
[36] *Ibid.*, 15:392.
[37] See the frequent articles in the *Moniteur* from 27 March to 2 July, pp. 334-716 *passim.*

For had not the Emperor declared in Council so long since as 4 March 1806, his intention to promulgate a navigation act within forty-eight hours after peace with England?[38]

It is possible, indeed, to note this coming change of emphasis almost as soon as the victory of Friedland (15 June) has forecasted the approach of peace. Thus 20 June Napoleon writes Cambacérès to arrange for presenting the long prepared *Code du Commerce* to the coming session of the Corps Legislatif, a significant indication of a purpose to give special attention now to commercial interests.[39] The same spirit is shown two days later in his letter to Cambacérès regarding a decree just signed for the long cherished Napoleonic object of reviving the French Levant trade. Again it appears in plans for a Bourse, which with the Bank and the new commercial court should "centralize trade affairs at Paris even as they are at London."[40] Still greater importance attaches, however, to a communication dated 18 June from Champagny, for it presented a concrete commercial issue, and apparently initiated a series of significant papers.[41]

This letter from Champagny treats of new relations and trade with the Americans—of French cloths, of sugar and colonial produce—and of the exceptions to the Berlin decree desired by neutrals. Evidence is lacking that Napoleon replied. However, it was followed up, 3 July, by another letter probably like the first on Champagny's own initiative, although some request for trade statistics of which we lack evidence may have indirectly called it forth.[42] He says:

"I have had the honor of sending to your Majesty the *tableau*

---

[38] Pelet de la Lozère, *Napoleon in Council*, p. 271-2.
[39] *Cor. de Nap.*, 15:350.
[40] *Cor. de Nap.*, 15:358, 379, and 425. The *Archives Nationales* contain various interesting papers on the Levant project after 1800, such as one of 20 May 1807, AF^{IV}1318, pièce 16, cf. also *Bulletin des lois*, 1807, (3 May) p. 233.
[41] *Arch. Nat.*, AF^{IV}1060, dossier II, p. 38 (in Champagny's own hand).
[42] *Arch. Nat.*, AF^{IV}1060, I, 87.

that I have had made of our commercial relations with Portugal during a great number of years. That of our commerce with America appears to me no less important. I submit it today to your Majesty. The figures have necessitated an immense research,—I dare believe them exact. Of all the neutral powers Portugal and America are those with whom since the Revolution our commercial relations have been the most active and the most important. They are very similar in nature, both of them—Portugal, especially—furnishing us the raw material for that one of our industries which has at present most activity, cotton: both of them, likewise, but America chiefly, feeding the consumption (become almost of first necessity) of colonial produce. In the trade of both the balance is to the disadvantage of France, yet America carries away much of our brandy, the colonial goods which she furnishes us are the produce of our colonies, or reached us formerly by the English, so that England has lost what America seems to have gained with France. Besides the Americans begin to get a taste for our manufactures, especially silks,—for they export only produce: Lyons owes to them this last year the support of several of her factories. This exportation so precious for us, may increase if it is favored. The importations will diminish necessarily at the peace. This commerce merits that protecting regard from Your Majesty which I have solicited for it, in reclaiming in my letter of . . .[43] a favorable interpretation of the decree of 21 November. All the Chambers of Commerce hold the same language to me in this regard."

In view of the instructions of 19 July for Talleyrand—and Junot—to begin a coercive policy against Portugal the report of 3 July has a peculiar interest. For it should have reached Napoleon between 13 and 17 July, hence it is conceivable that its information was contributory to plans already contemplated against the realm of the Braganzas.[44] Or, indeed, it may have so impressed the

[43] Evidently the letter of 18 June (cf. p. 18 above) is referred to.
[44] Cf. *Cor. de Nap.*, 15:423, no. 12909; and 424, no. 12912. For a statement of similar designs in 1801, cf. *Arch. Parl.*, 2nd Ser., III, 54; *Cor. de Nap.*,

Emperor afresh with the strategic importance of that neutral doorway for trade with the Continent, as to hasten vigorous action to insure its closure against English colonial goods. To be sure, coercion seems contrary to the tenor of Champangy's memoir; nevertheless, the hypothesis as to its effect is plausible when we consider the singular effect of Champagny's American argument in the same memoir. For in his reply of 4 August, Napoleon overlooks entirely the appeal for his fostering protection of this significant American trade, and instead pounces upon a comparatively minor item of Champagny's statistics which seems to offer a chance for restrictions against American colonial trade in favor of France, and he thereby complicates his American relations.[45]

But there are other and stronger reasons than these why significance should attach to these reports from Champagny. Thus they seem clearly to have been influential in leading Napoleon to issue his note of 30 July, a paper of exceptional interest, for with its replies it affords the *first of a series of summarizations* invaluable for a view of the problems and the efficacy of the Continental System. Likewise, these papers are indicative of constructive, as well as destructive, elements of the System, and they thus foreshadow a new commercial or navigation policy. While, incidentally, they afford also an able presentation of the chief uncertainty of the years, the relation of neutrals to the policy of the Berlin decree.

7:49-50. See, however, the statement to Champagny on 7 September, Loyd, *New Letters*, p. 46.

[45] *Cor. de Nap.*, 15:469. He expresses approval of the careful tabulation, then comments on an item of 880, 000 fr. for Nankin cloths brought by Americans to France, and asks why their entry should not be prohibited. The result was a decree of 1 August against which the American minister protested strenuously, chiefly because of a requirement of certificates of origin from American vessels entering Hamburg, Bremen and other Hanse ports. Cf. Armstrong to Madison, 15 October, inclosures dated 10 September, 8, 10, 16 and 24 October, *Dept. of State, Desp., Fr.*, vol. 10.

Let us follow then the sequence of Champagny's significant presentation of the commercial issue. Leaving Dresden 22 July, with very brief stops en route at some of the Rhenish commercial centres, Napoleon arrived at St. Cloud by five A. M. 27 July.[46] That evening and the following day he held ministerial councils, and within three days after his return he had dictated the following instructions:

"The minister of the interior and of finance will each give me their advice on the advantages and the inconveniences of a general measure which will order that every vessel loaded with tobacco, sugar, coffee, cotton and other goods of this nature should be able to enter France under a foreign flag only under the condition of exporting at departure a value equal to its cargo, either in merchandise manufactured in France or in productions of our growth. The minister of finance will make known the quantities of the different products here designated and of other articles of the same nature, entered within the course of a year, and to give more precision to the results he will carry his researches back for several years. Both ministers will respond to the following questions. What is the diminution or the variations in the price of sugars since two years? What has been the influence of the customs on the price of sugars? What are our present commercial relations with the kingdom of Italy? Are they such as should be expected since the last measures? What can commerce desire on the part of the different princes of the Confederation of the Rhine? What measures are to be taken for introducing there the products of our manufactures? What is to be desired of Spain, of Portugal? Why do not the makers of printed cloths furnish my kingdom of Italy?"[47]

[46] *Cor. de Nap.*, 15:439, no. 12939. *Moniteur* (1807), pp. 812, 816. Cf. also Marbot, *Mémoires*.

[47] *Cor. de Nap.*, 15:455. Notice also *Cor. de Nap.*, 15:470, no. 12982, 4 August, where Napoleon asks Collin to send as soon as possible an *état* of exports and imports of France for the years X–XV, and printed customs tariffs of each article. And see likewise *Cor. de Nap.*, 15:475, no. 12991, 4 August, when he asks Eugène for similar *états* for the last three years for Italy to be sent in eight days.

As a result of these instructions we have nine or ten reports. Of these two (undated) are from Collin de Sussy, Director General of the Customs.[48] In Collin's reports the items of special interest are his remarks upon the contraband problem which was soon to call to the contest all the ingenuity and tenacity of Napoleon. For precise information upon evasions of the Berlin decree, however, the report is disappointing. Indeed it seems but another evidence of the uncertainty which had been entertained by officials as to the meaning and sincerity of the decree.[49]

The rest of the August reports, and the most significant ones, are those of Champagny, possibly because he may have anticipated this inquest, probably because he had behind him for such work Chaptal's admirably trained staff.[50] Three reports (chiefly statistical) deal with the sugar question. A fourth paper on the Italian

[48] *Arch. Nat.*, AF^{IV} 1060, I, 79 and 80. The Minister of Finance rarely ever responded personally to demands for reports on trade questions. Collin replies to four of the questions: 1st, as to the advisability of requiring foreign ships bringing colonial goods to make a countervailing export of French wares. (Related to this is his second paper—a tabulation of colonial importations for An XIV and 1806.) *Archives Nationales*, AF^{IV}1060, I, 80. 2nd, Why the drop in sugar prices in two years considering the increase in customs? A reference, of course, to the colonial goods tariff increase of 4 March 1806. Why the considerable fall in price of colonial goods, in general? Is it due, as rumored, to contraband? 3rd, As to the status of trade relations with Spain and Italy since the last measures and of what is to be desired from Spain and Portugal. (Cf. measures of 1806 (Spring) and the September action by Conseil du Adm. de l'Interieur, AF^{IV}1238. 4th, as to the improvement of trade relations with the Rhine Confederation.

[49] It may be said in passing however that this report is supplemented by another undated one, apparently later in the year, on how to prevent contraband in English goods. In this he claims he had done his best, but admits unsatisfactory results. The chief problem is some means of preventing the corruption of the customs officers; but indeed the whole customs code needs revision, being inadequate for the new and exceptional situation. Trieste and Venice are marked as places which especially need watching. *Arch. Nat.*, AF^{IV}1060, dossier I, pièce 40.

[50] *Arch. Nat.*, AF^{IV}1060, I, 78, 81-87. Except for his letter of 3 July, which is with them, all are dated 5 August.

question is a summary of complaints by French merchants. But better still as a resumé of this situation is Champagny's report on the unsatisfactory trade with Italy for French printed cloths. The decree of 10 June 1806, excluding English goods from Italy, he says, had not become operative until 31 December, and its execution is not yet satisfactory.[51] Rumor asserts the contraband at the entry of the kingdom of Italy to be still very strong, and it is certain that at least there is a sensible filtration of contraband merchandise from Italy into France by way of the *ci-devant* Piedmont, the premium of introduction into France being only 10 to 15 per cent. The advantages of Italian commerce are enjoyed by the Swiss. The French meet many obstacles, among which is the difficulty of changing old national tastes and prejudices. Regarding the German trade question he proposes liberty of transit, river transportation facilities, and full privileges of the fairs for French merchants.[52] It is advisable to aim at a revival of the overland trade from France via Germany to Poland and Russia, of which he presents an interesting historical survey.

The report on the suggested plan of a forced export to balance each importation is the most carefully argued of the reports and the most interesting.[53] Champagny opposes the plan except it be modified in five important particulars. In as much as the proposition became in time a fundamental principle of the licence trade, the able criticism by Champagny would well deserve quotation entire. Here, however, a few excerpts must suffice. He opens: "The advantages of the measure projected suppose essentially that it shall not embrace the articles which serve as first materials or ingredients for the manufactures such as cotton, dyewoods, etc. Applied to this last type of articles, the measure goes directly counter the aim proposed. Far from favoring our manufactures it would deal them a mortal blow making them

---

[51] Cf. *Arch. Nat.*, AF^{IV}1238. The Italian question had been considered also in September 1806.

[52] *Arch. Nat.*, AF^{IV}1060, I, 81.

[53] *Arch. Nat.*, AF^{IV}1060, pièce 78.

experience the double effect of the rareness of materials and their enhancement in price, when already in order to procure them, they have to fight against import duties higher than those paid by neighboring nations. The abundance of raw materials, their low price, the certainty of provision, the facility of affecting it, are the first and surest encouragement for the exportation of manufactured wares."

He balances three advantages against four inconveniences, concluding from their comparative weight that with the five modifications which he proposes the advantages of the measure would gain force, the inconveniences be enfeebled. In fact his five modifications actually become six or seven: (1) That raw materials, medicines, saltfish, fish, etc. should be admitted duty free. (2) That in the case of a cargo partly of these articles, partly of colonial produce of consumption, the former articles should be exempt. (3) That wares from French colonies—their origin legally proved—when brought by neutrals should be admitted until the peace, no other way of importation being possible. (4) That such a decree should not become effective until six months from its publication and should not be retroactive. (5) That vessels fulfilling the return cargo condition be freed from the consequences of the decree of 21 November—as a compensatory inducement to neutrals. (6) In making up the return cargo the master should not be held to a precise counter value, being allowed, instead, a choice of equal tonnage or equal value, provided the tonnage value be at least three-fourths of the value of the importation. Finally, it would be advisable to exempt generally the vessels which should satisfy these conditions from fulfilling those of certificates of origin.[54] For he says, "It can not be dissembled that the measure of certificates of origin is, at bottom, illusory and amounts only to making us pay dearer for the goods imported while augmenting the profits of foreigners; and whatever should be the origin, even, of the products imported, it could have for us only

[54] For such certificates see law of 1 messidor, An XI (20 June 1803), 14 Duvergier, *Lois, decrets*, etc., p. 335.

an advantage to receive them, while exporting their counter value in manufactured articles which suppose, in general, a very considerable benefice for the handiwork."

The significance of this ministerial discussion in affording the first formal inventory of the Continental System as a working program will be readily appreciated. That it is also indicative of a determination to have a navigation act for France is likewise evident. Its chief importance, however, is that we clearly have here not merely signs of the *purpose*, but even a fair sketch of the *plan* of such a French, or shall we even say, *Continental Navigation Act*. And as such it is, again, a significant *forecast* of the very measures which Napoleon was to adopt in 1810. The investigation, then, shows not alone a desire to check up accomplishments, but a keen hunt for weaknesses, and for supplementary measures to remedy or counteract them. While incidentally, as we have noted already, it brings out distinctly that fundamental issue of the year 1807—the question of the *neutrals*.

The strenuous interest in commercial plans at this date, of which this series of questions and reports is the most striking feature, was very evidently owing to a desire to be ready at the opening of the Corps Legislatif with projects of measures which would expand the still embryonic Continental System into a broad and effective navigation policy. This would complement the now completed *Code du Commerce,* which itself would give France a commercial system comprehensive beyond the dreams of Colbert, and effectual beyond all experience of the British monopolists.[55] The proposal of such notable commercial extensions must naturally presuppose a justification of the system as existent thus far, by means of a recital of its accomplishments. It also involved the presentation of such compensatory measures of legislation as should win for it hitherto denied popular approval. Thus he would guarantee for his grand commercial system that same continental adoption already being achieved by the *Code*

[55] See speech of Regnaud, *Archives Parlementaires*, 2nd Series, IX, 587.

Napoleon, and win for himself a monument of renown more durable than all his military glory.⁵⁶

The Corps Legislatif met 16 August. On 27 August Regnaud de St. Jean d'Angely, with Collin and Begouen presented a *projet de loi sur les douanes*.⁵⁷ This new modification of the customs legislation of the Year VIII was explained by Regnaud as a revenue measure for the government, a protection for commerce, and a weapon which would "help destroy the double commercial and political influence of those European vampires," the English. In fact, the project was, in the main, like the recent free opening of the Elbe to commerce, the establishment of new and better postal facilities for Hamburg, or the opening of new trade routes in Italy, Germany, and Poland, a broad and progressive measure.⁵⁸ As a measure of reciprocity it lowered the duties on Italian silk crepes entering France. It lifted the prohibition on the export from the Belgian and Rhenish departments of certain products needed by Holland and Germany. It gave transit privileges for wools from the realm of "our faithful" Spanish ally. It left the prohibition of English cottons, but cut in half the duty on nankins from French India.⁵⁹ Finally it granted to Ligurian fishermen all the privileges and regulations enjoyed by French subjects. It was soon followed, moreover, by another measure designed to regulate the Levant trade and to insure high standards and honesty in all goods exported there.⁶⁰ Meanwhile, book by book after 1 September the Commercial Code was presented and dis-

⁵⁶ Cf. speeches of Regnaud, Begouen and Corvetto, *Arch. Parl.*, 2nd Series, IX, 587, 590, 639, and of Bigot-Premeneau, *op. cit.*, 498.

⁵⁷ *Moniteur*, 1807, p. 934. *Arch. Parl.*, Series 2, IX, 511, 512, 630. It was in part, as explained by Regnaud, a codification of several special decrees of the year. Cf. *Bulletin des lois*, 1807, vol. I, table of contents.

⁵⁸ *Moniteur*, 1807, pp. 224, 351, 1093, 1135. Cf. also Cretet's *Exposé* in *Arch. Parl.*, 2nd Series, IX, 488-9.

⁵⁹ Evidently an outgrowth of Napoleon's 4 August reply to Champagny's American trade statistics. Cf. note 47 *supra*.

⁶⁰ *Moniteur*, 1807, p. 1053.

cussed before the Corps Legislatif by members of the Emperor's council.[61]

The other phase of the program, the defense of the Continental System, fell to the Minister of the Interior as part of his annual *Exposé of the Situation of the Empire*.[62] Aside from the inevitable denunciation of England, this address presented a fairly moderate and just rèsume of the commercial and industrial difficulties of the preceding eight months.[63] Although projected and revised under imperial dictation, the *Exposé* nevertheless reflects clearly the June, July, and first of August reports of Champagny himself.[64] This is seen in its references to brighter trade prospects with Italy, Switzerland, the Levant and the United States.[65] Thus, we are told, French commerce revives while English commerce ranges all seas searching vainly for an outlet. Indeed, "the present War is only the war of independence for commerce; Europe knows it, and the Emperor has constantly sought in the guarantee of this independence the first basis of all negotiation, as he has seen in its violation the first cause of hostilities. Each of his conquests in closing an outlet for England, has been a further conquest for the commerce of France. So this war which has suspended momentarily all its relations has been made especially for its interests, for the interest of all Europe suppressed by the monopoly of England."

Thus strikingly the Minister of the Interior "justified" and evaluated the commercial scope and purpose of the Continental System. Thus, likewise, all preparations were now made for the broader system sketched in the recent ministerial discussion. But at this point the idea was suddenly laid aside. Why, we shall

[61] *Archives Parlementaires*, 2nd Series, IX, 586-713. *Moniteur*, 1807, pp. 951, 966, 988. Cf. also Peuchet in the *Moniteur*, p. 1111.

[62] Presented by Cretet, who at this moment succeeded Champagny.

[63] *Arch. Parl.*, 2nd Series, IX, 487 ff.

[64] Compare *Cor. de Nap.*, 15:243, no. 12603 with 15:515, no. 13063.

[65] "L'Amerique," for example, "a fait à nos manufactures des commandes inattendues en retour des tabacs et des denrées coloniales qui elle nous fournit."

see directly as we turn to guage the international value of the now generally accepted Berlin decree. In so doing we shall judge first, as to the possibility of its continental execution, second, as to its extra-continental effect.

C—*The Maritime Interdict*—(*Seesperre*)

The presence of Talleyrand with Napoleon in the north during the events from the outbreak of the Prussian War until after Tilsit had devolved certain of his duties upon Champagny who was already versed in diplomacy. This, as well as certain aspects of his own Ministry of the Interior, should have made him, even as the Ministry of the Marine made Decrès, conversant with the neutral problem. His June and July reports have shown us his appreciation of the situation and his inclination to favor neutral trade, of which Napoleon was aware when transferring him to the Foreign Ministry in Talleyrand's stead.[66] The inference then seems warranted that, despite his changing policy toward Portugal and Denmark, the Emperor could not yet have entirely abandoned his vaunted championship of neutrals announced at Berlin and confirmed at Tilsit.[67] In fact, on 26 August at a session of the Council of Ministers, the Minister of Marine secured from Napoleon a secret decision favorable to the commerce of Denmark, tacitly exempting it, in large measure, from the Berlin decree.[68]

This Danish privilege may have been granted directly as a result of the protest of the Danish Minister, Dryer, on the affair

---

[66] Perhaps, indeed, in view of the surprising absence of any evidence to the contrary, Napoleon did not realize there *was* a neutral *problem* until August or September. The reasons for Talleyrand's retirement have always been a riddle. Some interesting sidelights on the episode are to be found in Armstrong's despatches dated 9 and 11 August (with enclosures)—*Dept. of State, Desp. Fr.*, vol. 10.

[67] *Cor. de Nap.*, 15:43, 459, 486, 494, and see note 77 below.

[68] *Arch. Nat.*, AF^{IV}1229-30. Procès Verbaux du Conseil des Ministres, Séance du 26 Août, 1807. St. Cloud. "Decision de S. M. Les batiments de cette nation seront reçu par mesure particuliere sans qu'il soit necessaire d'emettre un decret."

of the ship *La Liebe* touching which Decrès wrote "cela semble brouiller nos affairs avec la Danemarck."[69] It was, to be sure, in line with the interpretation of the Berlin decree given by Decrès to Gen. Armstrong, American Minister at Paris, in December previous.[70] It accorded apparently with the policy generally observed by the Ministers at home during this period of the system.[71] It can not have differed greatly in principle from the policy announced during the spring by French consuls at Hamburg and Lübeck.[72] It certainly was consonant with the program Champagny had just been urging for Portugal and America. And yet, it was at this moment that the plans against Portugal, possibly even designs against Spain,[73] were taking shape, that Hamburg and Prussia were feeling the weight of the imperial hand for stricter enforcement of his decree, and that there was beginning that long series of recriminations so fateful for the throne of Louis, King of Holland.[74] Indeed not a month earlier Denmark itself had been marked for like treatment.[75] Moreover, we should

[69] AF^{IV}1678, "Rel. Ext. Dan." Cf. another Danish concession: *Cor. de Nap.* 16, no. 13095.

[70] *Am. State Papers, Foreign Relations*, III, 242, 243-245, Armstrong to Monroe, 7 July 1807, also Armstrong to Champagny, 9 August and 12 November 1807, and Champagny to Armstrong, 21 August. Robinson, *Admiralty Reports*, VI, 471, has the French version of the letter of Decrès of 24 December 1806. See also *Moniteur*, 5 December 1810, p. 1338, for the assertions of a Federalist pamphlet translated and reprinted there.

[71] Indeed Napoleon, himself, on 2 September was ready to free certain American seamen as a *special favor* to the President of the United States. *Cor. de Nap.*, 16:5. Also Decrès to Armstrong, 3 September. *Dept. of State, Desp. Fr.*, vol. 10.

[72] For Hamburg see the item on the notice of Forbes (American Consul) in the *Moniteur*, 27 February, p. 224, also see the *Moniteur*, p. 425, for the Lübeck policy.

[73] Talleyrand, *Memoirs*, I, 246.

[74] *Cor. de Nap.*, 15:491-2, 509; 16:6, 7, 13, 20, 24, 28, 40, 57, 63, 76, 78, 83, 87, 147, 155, 160, 161, 204, 224, 226. Loyd, *New Letters of Napoleon*, pp. 46, 47.

[75] *Cor. de Nap.*, 15:459 (31 July), 467 (2 August), 486 (10 August), 504 (17 August). *Am. State Papers*, III, 243. Also *Dept. of State, Desp. Fr.*,

not forget that even in the imperial crisis of 1812 Bernadotte received no such consideration.[76] Why then this sudden favor to Denmark on 26 August 1807? Why did Napoleon even secretly allow an exemption—an official divergence from his fundamental system—and that well before the first anniversary of its enunciation? The explanation evidently lies in the fact that it was allowed on the very day in which Napoleon learned definitely of a British attack upon Copenhagen.[77]

Today few Britishers boast of how they "borrowed" a friendly nation's fleet at the cannon's mouth in order to forestall alleged plans of Napoleon to force Danish adhesion to the Berlin decree. The British government claimed to have acted upon secret information. The dusts of historical controversy still becloud the issues involved.[78] But the usual tendency to parley over the distribution of censure or palliation for this high-handed violation of neutral rights must not obscure from us its immediate far-reaching effects. The affair seemed a godsend to Napoleon for it afforded

---

vol. 10. Armstrong to Madison, 3, 9, 15, 27 August. It may be borne in mind that the "month" set at Tilsit for the offer of Russian mediation had almost elapsed.

[76] Martens, "Nouvelles causes célèbres du droit des gens." P. Coquelle, "Le Mission d'Alquier en Stockholm," *Revue d'Histoire Diplomatique*, vol. 23, p. 196 ff.

[77] Cf. *Cor. de Nap.*, 15:553, 557, 559. See in the *Moniteur* of 26 August (p. 923) Jackson's unparalleled demands and the spirited reply of the Danish crown prince. The bombardment, of course, did not take place until the first days of September although Napoleon expected otherwise. The expedition was not unexpected as the *Moniteur* had contained hints of it since 12 July (Copenhagen 29 June), hints which had become more and more definite since 20 July. Cf. *Moniteur* pp. 753, 775, 783, 789, 797—and August 6, 9, 18, 21, 23. These hints doubtless help explain the pressure upon Denmark since 31 July (see above), and certainly are reflected in, or reflect, the letters of 7 August to Clarke, 17 August to Berthier, and of 21 August to Decrès, Eugène, and Champagny. *Cor. de Nap.*, 15:480, 504 and 512-3.

[78] With respect to the reasons for the Copenhagen attack see Rose, *Napoleonic Studies*, pp. 133-166; although all conclusions therein cannot be endorsed. For other views see bibliography p. 410 below.

him needed moral aid of incalculable value.[79] Whether or not it caused Britishers to "hiss the playing of Rule Britannia," and made "Copenhagen a byword of infamy" in London gatherings it at least evoked from the anti-ministerial press and the parliamentary opposition attacks as virulent as any Dane could have wished.[80] The *Independent Whig* led in blaming upon it the immediate strict closure of all North Europe to England, as well as a chain of other misfortunes.[81] And the blame was well placed, for the Copenhagen attack spurred Napoleon to lay aside his constructive commercial projects and at once develop his still incipient program of rigor.[82] Convinced by England's action that any general peace expectations from Tilsit were illusory, and hence the alternative of united coercion a necessity, realizing therefore that there was still need to utilize the military faculties of his continental closure, he laid bold plans and moved toward their vigorous execution. Having already threatened proceedings against Dutch laxity, the presence of Louis in Paris at the moment of the definitive news of the attack on Copenhagen brought the issuance of the strenuous enforcement-decree of 28 August for Holland.[83] Following up this success by an ultimatum to Portu-

[79] For examples of European comment see: *Moniteur*, 1807, pp. 1180, 1261, 1389; *Minerva*, Sept. 1807, no. 2; *Europäische Annalen*, 1808, vol. I, p. 243. American comment was equally significant, Republican newspapers of October–December 1807, using Copenhagen as an unfailing illustration of what the United States could expect from Great Britain. See the *Aurora* (esp. 13, 23 and 28 November), *Boston Chronicle*, (esp. 7 November), *American Daily Advertiser*, etc., etc.

[80] *Moniteur*, 1807, pp. 1093, 1097, 1219, 1227, 1235, 1339. Cf. also Adams, *History of the United States*, IV, 65.

[81] *Moniteur*, 1807, p. 1044, dated London, 14 September, and p. 1155, (comment of 10 October). Cf. *Independent Whig*, 30 August; 6, 13, 20, 27 September; 4 and 11 October, etc. for strong excoriations of the Copenhagen affair.

[82] *Cor. de Nap.*, 15:553, 557, to Alexander, 26 and 28 August. Loyd, *New Letters*, pp. 45-7. Compare with *Cor. de Nap.*, 15:392 (Tilsit 6 July).

[83] F. Rocquain, *Napoleon Ier et le roi Louis*, pp. 127 ff.; *Moniteur* (1807), pp. 923, 927, 932. In fact the connection of Danish news with the Dutch

gal Napoleon has, by 7 September, brought the Prince Regent to promise a proclamation against the English.[84] Distrusting the efficiency of Dutch measures letter follows letter to Louis, even repeating the threat to send a "mobile" force and take the closure of Holland into his own hands.[85] The same day as this warning (29 September) he admonishes Eugène because of the lax enforcement of the Berlin decree in Italy.[86] He plans joint action with Russia and Denmark to compel Sweden to join the common cause.[87] Likewise he and Russia still press Austria (who already is aggrieved at the British blockade in the Adriatic) to close Trieste, and dismiss the English ambassador.[88] For he declares, "This expulsion of all English ministers from the Continent will make a great impression in London, and will especially and strongly affect their trade." Finally, he himself intends by his fleet and by a new concentration of his army at Boulogne to be ready in October for a *coup de main* against England.[89]

By October Napoleon begins to know the results of this program. Holland supplements the decree of 28 August and proves by deeds her return to the treaty of alliance.[90] The Hanse cities,

---

situation may be discerned throughout. Cf. *London Chronicle*, 23 August, and especially the *Moniteur*, 18 August, and *Cor. de Nap.*, 15:13051, (19 August). See also the *Moniteur*, 21 and 23 August, and *Cor. de Nap.*, 15, no. 13065 (24 August). The 28 August decree under caption of "The Hague, September 3," was also published in full on 14 November at Philadelphia by the *Aurora*, and the *American Daily Advertiser*.

[84] Loyd, *New Letters*, p. 46.
[85] *Cor. de Nap.*, 16:57, no. 13196.
[86] *Ibid.*, no. 13195.
[87] *Ibid.*, 15:553, 16:9, 36, 37.
[88] *Ibid.*, 15:553, 557-8 and Loyd's *New Letters of Napoleon*, p. 47. Also for the Trieste blockade friction see the *Moniteur* since March, p. 451, etc., etc.
[89] Loyd, *New Letters*, p. 46.
[90] *Cor. de Nap.*, 16:87. Rocquain, *Napoleon Ier et le roi Louis*, 127-133. *Moniteur*, pp. 1085, 1172, 1214, 1261 for decrees of 24 September, 17 October and 6 November. Also pp. 1047, 1127, 1147, 1152, 1179, 1198, 1296, 1299. See also, *Naval Chronicle*, XVIII, 225, 381, and *London Chronicle*, 1, 23, 24 September; 1 and 16 October, etc.

Italy, Tuscany, and Naples follow suit, likewise Prussia and Switzerland. Corfu and the Ionian Isles are assimilated to the System. Sardinia makes treaties and promises reparations required of her. Even Sweden grows querulous with Britain. On 21 October—a day too late—Portugal proclaims the closure of her ports to the English. Junot and Spain enforce it. Morocco, it is said, joins in isolating Gibraltar. Russia and Austria at last declare openly their hostility to the common foe. Independently Denmark wreaks her special vengeance on English ships, wares and debts. Verily the System is, in its *execution*, truly Continental. Meanwhile the unsettled Chesapeake affair brings America and England ever nearer the verge of war. Well, indeed, might the English opposition point out that they were treated like a den of pirates, isolated like men with the pestilence.[91]

Meanwhile, the strenuousness of his purpose brought Napoleon face to face with the actual problems of enforcing his System. Seeing, as he could not see during the engrossing Polish campaign, the prevalence of official uncertainty and popular evasion, he spoke his will decisively. Lavallette, Director General of Posts, who seems to have shared the misunderstanding of his ministerial colleagues as to the purpose or feasibility of the Berlin decree, was rudely disillusioned by a series of reprimands for his insufficient ardor in seizing English mail.[92] Gaudin had orders for the extension of the customs police back from the coasts even to the rivers and canals of the Rhenish departments.[93] Both measures

---

[91] *Moniteur*, p. 1299, headed London, 17 November, and p. 1257, London, 31 October. A brilliant summary of the situation is found also in a despatch of the American minister dated 22 September. See too his despatch of 15 October, *Dept. of State, Desp. Fr.*, vol. 10. Cf. also on the situation *Annual Register*, 1807, p. 227; the *European Magazine*, etc. 400-6; *Naval Chronicle*, XVIII, 351; the *Gentleman's Magazine*, 962-3, 1065-1070. For specific authorities for points in this paragraph see especially *Cor. de Nap.*, 16; the *Moniteur*, also the *London Chronicle*, Sept.–Dec. 1807.

[92] Loyd, *New Letters*, pp. 55, 57. From the English side see the account in Norway, *The Post Office Packet Service*.

[93] *Cor. de Nap.*, 16:63, 155.

came primarily from the mutual recriminations and excuses of imperial officials and the government of Holland.[94] For certain it was that the continental cordon was somehow being penetrated between Antwerp and Altona. But the imperial attention was still further focused upon this ever strategic region by the English seizure of Heligoland as an entrepôt for colonial goods and the coincident modification of the blockade of the North Sea littoral.[95] The situation demanded new restrictions on imports. Napoleon's January definition of English goods as "celles qui ont été fabriquées en Angleterre" was extended so as to exclude all colonial goods whose neutral origin was at all suspected.[96] For Baltic ports threatened by British entrepôts in Sweden a decree enumerated the permissible imports, which were Baltic products, wines and brandy.[97] For the Weser and Elbe, however, even as for Holland, a thorough reconstruction of enforcement regulations seemed imperative. The result was an imperial decree of 13 or 14 October promulgated in the Hanse ports a fortnight later, and matched by a very similar Dutch decree issued about 17 October for the district of the Dollart to the Ems.[98]

For this significant October decree in the absence of an official version we are dependent chiefly upon the preliminary directions

[94] Compare Rocquain, *op. cit. supra*; *Cor. de Nap.*, 15 and 16; and Colenbrander, *Gedenkstukken der Algemeene Geschiedenis van Nederland*, series I, vol. II.

[95] On the seizure of Heligoland see *Navy Records Society*, vol. XX, pt. 1, pp. 379-385, also *Naval Chronicle*, XVIII, 235. On the modification of the British blockade of German North Sea ports see Napoleon's letter to Gaudin, 13 October, *Cor. de Nap.*, 16, no. 13246. I am unable to identify the change referred to from my Privy Council, Board of Trade or Admiralty notes of *general* orders or instructions on blockades.

[96] *Cor. de Nap.*, 14:227, to Jerome, 23 Jan. 1807.

[97] *Moniteur*, p. 1346, 15 December 1807, dated Hamburg, 5 December. It is possible that this is a version of the 6 August decree mentioned in the 13 October decree, although it has been impossible to find such a decree of 6 August, nor any evidence of it in the correspondence of the year 1807.

[98] For the Dutch decree see The Hague news of 24 October, *Moniteur*, p. 1172. Cf. also, pp. 1085, 1261.

given Gaudin in the Emperor's letter of 13 October. But this must be supplemented by the brief synopsis of a "Banks of the Elbe" news note dated 8 December, a still briefer item in a November British magazine and by an apparently misdated, but otherwise accurate, English version of the full decree.[99] The kinship of this legislation with the Dutch edict of 28 August, which it further develops, is striking. The English version consists of nine articles which stipulate anew the nature of permissible imports, restrict the validation of certificates of origin, provide stringent precautions against the admission of suspicious goods, and particularly of any ships from England, and which reorganize and strengthen the customs police on the Elbe, the Weser, and the Holstein border.[100]

The chief significance of this Fontainebleau decree of October, however, lies not in its effort to meet the North Sea coast problem but in the fact that just forty days later (23 November), at Milan, Napoleon issued a decree for France whose five articles with very slight verbal changes are a repetition (in the order named) of articles three, four, five, two and nine of the October edict.[101] The outstanding provisions of the Hanse decree, of its Dutch counterpart, and its French replica, are those which order the confiscation of every ship with its cargo without distinction, which for any reason may have touched in England. They likewise required not only the sworn statement of the shipmaster and the delivery of all ship's papers on arrival, but also verification of the captain's declaration by the examination of every sailor and passenger on

[99] *Cor. de Nap.*, 16, no. 13246, (Gaudin was to report Wednesday, which was 14 October). Cf. *Moniteur*, 18 December, p. 1357, from *Abeille du Nord*; and *Gentleman's Magazine*, 1807, p. 1056 (with news setting 26 October as the date the decree was enforced at Hamburg). *Annual Register*, 1807 (pub. 1809), p. 777, gives the full English text, dated 13 November. See also *European Magazine*, January 1808, p. 9, for a second news item.

[100] Arts. 1 and 2 on certificates of origin extend the arrêt of 1 messidor, An XI, and are amplied further by the decree of 11 August 1808, Duvergier, *Lois*, etc., XVI, 331.

[101] For the "first Milan decree," see note 145 below.

board. Proof of false declarations entailed not only the confiscation for touching in England but heavy fines as well.

An outstanding aspect of these measures is their emphasis upon the extra-continental significance of the Continental System, for manifestly all these restrictions bore hardly upon the neutral shippers, especially the Americans. In fact, this Fontainebleau legislation was frankly confirming the disclosures of the weeks preceding that the Berlin decree, issued ostensibly as a retaliatory act in championship of neutral rights, was to be, in reality, a commercial measure for French military and economic purposes, bearing hardest of all upon the neutrals.

This new revelation of the animus of the Continental System had come partly as the result of pressure from the American government for an authoritative statement of the imperial policy. As early as 3 December 1806 when first transmitting the Berlin decree to his government General Armstrong had declared: "As this decree is susceptible of very different interpretations I shall seize the first moment that presents itself of asking the explanation which the government shall think proper to give to it."[102] The opportunity came a week later when four questions were put to the Minister of Marine which Decrès answered satisfactorily on 24 December.[103] Equally favorable interpretations of the decree were given by the Conseil des Prises on 25 March in the case of the *Hibernia*, and on 4 May by the Director General of Customs.[104] Consequently Armstrong could write on 7 July to Monroe at London that it was "admitted by both ministerial and judicial authority that this Decree did not infract the provisions of the treaty of 1800 between the United States and France."[105]

[102] *Dept. of State, Desp. Fr.*, vol. 10.

[103] *Ibid.*, Armstrong to Decrès, 10 December, and reply, 24 December. See London news of this with comments in *London Morning Chronicle*, 19 January 1807.

[104] *Ibid.*, Armstrong to Madison, 25 March and 5 May 1807.

[105] *Ibid.*, Armstrong to Madison, 12 July, with enclosure.

Unfortunately there was a rift in the lute. For Erving, the American envoy at Madrid, being unable to secure the release of vessels seized under the Spanish version of the decree, since Godoy pleaded his inability to secure a definite imperial interpretation for the guidance of Spanish courts, appealed to Armstrong. And Armstrong sought to expedite matters by appealing to Talleyrand, and then to Champagny who shunted the demand on to Decrès, and to Regnier, the Grand Judge, by whom an imperial pronouncement was sought.[106] The moment was most unpropitious for such a query, for it was the very hour when Napoleon was rousing Europe to avenge the violation of Copenhagen. Moreover "piqued by some false declarations made by neutrals entering his ports, and still more by the open disobedience with which his decree was received in the Dutch ports" the Emperor had already ordered the strict enforcement of articles 7 and 8 of the decree whereby entry in France was refused to any ship which touched in England.[107] And Collin had just issued the required circular to the customs service.[108] It was but logical therefore that the reply to Regnier's request for explicit instructions was a prohibition for the Conseil des Prises to show the consideration formerly used in cases affecting neutral vessels which might come to France after visiting England, but it is significant that with respect to vessels captured at sea for contravening the Berlin decree the Emperor withheld a statement of policy.[109]

[106] *Ibid.*, Erving to Armstrong, 27 July; Armstrong to Talleyrand, 9 August; Champagny to Armstrong, 21 August; Armstrong's circular to the consuls, 6 October; etc.

[107] Armstrong to Madison, 20 September 1807, *Dept. of State, Desp. Fr.*, vol. 10.

[108] Based solely on the items in the *Aurora* (Philadelphia) 21 November, which however are very specific and agree with the directions to Regnier.

[109] Decision of 18 September, *Arch. Nat.*, AF^{IV}1229-30. Cf. *Am. State Papers, Foreign Relations*, III, 243-45, (Armstrong to Champagny, 24 September). The issue was further complicated by the case of the *Gen. Washington.* Cf. Champagny's explanation of 7 October and Armstrong's reply as well as his comments to Madison on 9 October, *Dept. of State, Desp. Fr.*, vol. 10; and especially Lee's reports of 10-15 Oct., *Cons. letters*, Bordeaux, II.

Obviously this strict interpretation seemed to neutral governments a portentous reversal of policy.[110] Announced to Armstrong about 24 September, it was to serve indirectly—by the publication of a warning sent through Consul Bourne to American traders at Amsterdam—as the spur to the adoption of fresh retaliatory orders by England.[111] While, reported to Jefferson with Champagny's confirmation, and with the exemplification of its injustice in the case of the *Horizon*, it was to prove yet another direct cause of the American Embargo.[112]

[110] The American view of the French policy under the Berlin decree is best expressed from the standpoint of the Administration by the report of Campbell's committee, 22 November 1808, prepared by Gallatin. (Adams, *Writings of Gallatin*, I, 428 ff.) But see also Washington, *Writings of Jefferson*, V, 211, 216, 217. An influential Federalist criticism of this view is the anonymous "Analysis of the late Correspondence between our Administration and France and Great Britain," Boston (1809), which was republished in London, in 1809, and excerpts from which were translated and printed serially by the *Moniteur*, (see especially the issue of 4 December 1810, p. 1338.) The pamphlet (ascribed to Rev. L. Lowell) originally appeared in the *Columbian Centinel*, of Boston, 30 November to 31 December 1808 (inclusive). It was published thereafter as a pamphlet, and later a supplement to it was issued.

Very significant also is the British interpretation of the bearing of the Berlin decree on neutrals put forth by Sir William Scott of the High Court of Admiralty in his judgment, 18 August, touching the American ship *Sansom*, 6 Robinson's *Adm. Reports*, 412-20.

[111] *Moniteur*, 1152, 1202; *London Times* (also the *Chronicle*), 27 October; Philadelphia *Aurora*, 10 and 18 December; Bourne Papers in Library of Congress, Div. of MSS. Likewise see the item in the *Aurora*, 9 December, (from Philadelphia *Gazette*), of a similar warning from Armstrong through Consul Lee of Bordeaux, or the broader statements of the *Columbian Centinel*, Boston, 16 December. Armstrong's "private circular" to the consuls was dated 6 October. He explained to the State Department that his motives were to guard against danger to American commerce and to "alarm the interests of France," *Dept. of State, Desp. Fr.*, vol. 10. Cf. also Lee's report of 15 Oct., *Cons. Letters*, Bordeaux, II.

[112] Armstrong to Madison, 12 November, and Armstrong to Champagny, (undated copy): *Dept. of State, Desp. Fr.*, vol. 10; *Annals*, 10th Congress, 1 Sess., pp. 50, 1216-18 (18-22 December 1807). But the *Aurora* of 18 November (that is prior to Jefferson's November message to Congress) had reliable

It is probably not at all surprising that this stricter attitude toward neutrals should have come *pari passu* with the other evidences of determined rigor. English favor toward certain small flags, and the activity of Emden, that old hold of "frauds of the neutral flags," would naturally call down the Emperor's enmity upon these convenient attachés of the new English entrepôt at Heligoland.[113] Said he: "France cannot regard as neutral the flags without consideration. That of America, however, exposed though it be to the insults of England, has a sort of existence. . . That of Portugal and that of Denmark no longer exist. Those of the petty German cities whose very names are scarcely known, are submitted by the English to whatever legislation is convenient. . . It is necessary to propose a project of a decree declaring that the ships bearing these flags which shall enter, shall not be able to depart and that they should be subject to all the rigors of the blockade."[114] But the imperial animosity soon comprehended real as well as pseudo-neutrals. When Champagny again presented the case of the United States he was informed that so long as the United States should submit to search and should recognize the English blockade she could not expect consideration from France.[115]

That this resolute, comprehensive program had a very speedy and sensible effect is unquestionable. That England felt these measures—particularly the Dutch decrees, so strictly enforced—seeing in them a vital menace, is testified by London newspaper

---

information of Napoleon's reply of 23 September (sic) to Regnier. See the, Administration report of 22 November 1808, *Am. State Papers, For. Rel.*, III, 260. Also McMaster, *History of the United States*, III, 271.

[113] *Cor. de Nap.*, 16:6, 7, and 8. On Emden see *Naval Chronicle*, XXVI, 288-95, etc., XXXI, 296. Cf. *Moniteur*, 1807, 941, for English order of 19 August. See also *London Times*, 6 October.

[114] *Cor. de Nap.*, 16:20, no. 13135. For definite action see letter to Gaudin 13 November, in Loyd, *New Letters*, No. LXXVI.

[115] *Cor. de Nap.*, 16:165, and cf. *Am. State Papers, For. Rel.*, III, 247-8.

comments of September and October.¹¹⁶ This she proved by the two series of Orders in Council of 11 and 25 November.¹¹⁷ By these orders Britain made good her threat of January. In sooth, she retaliated with legislation outdoing even Napoleon's. The Emperor replied in kind from Milan, 17 December. The upper and nether millstones were set. Who could escape their action?

Thus the period of activity from Napoleon's return to Paris in the early hours of 27 July until his departure for Milan at 4 A. M., on 16 November, is one of singular interest in the story of his economic struggle against England.¹¹⁸ And not its least claim to interest is that it develops one of a series of recurrent programs with strikingly parallel features which are so typical of the Napóleonic activities. Thus, to cite but one other instance of such a recurrence, we may note the summer of 1810. For the significant program and action of that summer in all its essential characteristics—the constructive commercial schemes, the tightening of the adhesion of dependents and allies, and the wanton disregard of neutrals—strikingly repeated the tale of 1807 from Tilsit to Milan.

There is apparently no indication that the Milan decree of December was in Napoleon's original program, although it seems so consonant a completion thereof that he need not have based it upon British action. Indeed it has been asserted, at times, that the retaliatory preamble was an afterthought, not part of the decree until its publication in the *Moniteur*, the argument being that Napoleon did not know, could not have known the British action when he issued his answering decree.

---

¹¹⁶ *London Times*, 29 September, 6 October, 27 October. *Moniteur* (from various English papers, e. g., *Courier*,*Chronicle*, *Kentish Gazette*, etc.) pp. 976, 1023, 1085, 1114, 1123, 1136, 1176, 1220, 1257, etc., etc. For the *Chronicle* see issues of 1, 23, 24 September, and 16 October.

¹¹⁷ *Privy Council Register*, vol. 67, pp. *479, *482, 544-555. Cf. Adams, *United States*, IV, 83 ff. for the origin of these orders. Cf. *London Chronicle* (a ministerial organ),11, 12, 16, 19, 20, 21, 23, and 29 Nov. For Whig criticism by Auckland, author of 7 January Orders, see *Dropmore Papers*, IX, 142-56.

¹¹⁸ *Moniteur*, p. 1238. Cf. Brotonne, *Dernières Lettres inédites de Napoléon* Ier, I, 287.

It may, indeed, be true that when he issued his decree from Milan on 19 November the Emperor had not learned the precise tenor or the actual promulgation of the Orders of 11 November, for he seems to have received a copy of them only on 15 December, just prior to his second decree.[119] Moreover the November decree is traceable to other causes. And yet he certainly had had clear enough information of their framing, with forecasts of their character, from the various allusions of British newspapers, carefully excerpted by the *Moniteur* and other French papers.[120] In fact such a notice was the occasion for the writing of what was perhaps the actual stimulus for Napoleon's December edict.

On 11 November 1807—the very day during which Perceval's Orders received the king's signature—a certain Lubbert, whose suggestions, at several critical times since the return from Egypt, appear to have won consideration from the First Consul, and Emperor, sent to Napoleon a memoir entitled, *Sur le Commerce de l'Angleterre.*[121] This memoir was sent to the Emperor four days prior to the prophetic statement dictated to Champagny for General Armstrong on 15 November, just a few hours preceding the departure for Italy.[122] A passage from Lubbert will illustrate his strikingly clear estimate of the significance of the British Order. Speaking of the prohibition, probably at hand, of all products of the Indies, he says:

"This program [of prohibition] finds itself prepared and even pronounced, in great part, by the vigorous resolutions of the

[119] McMaster, *History of the United States*, III, 293 (authority not cited). The orders of 11 November, it should be noted, were not gazetted until 16 November.

[120] See the *London Times* for 29 September, 8 October, and 27 October, also the *Moniteur* of 3, 8, 12, 18, and 28 October; 1, 7, and 28 November, which gave hints or distinct predictions touching these new orders.

[121] *Arch. Nat.*, AF^{IV}1673. On Lubbert's influence, and shady career, note Pichon, *Rev. des Et. Nap.*, VII: 269n.

[122] See *Cor. de Nap.*, 16:165, also Champagny to Armstrong, 24 October, but particularly Armstrong to Madison, 15 November, 1 and 27 December 1807, *Dept. of State, Desp. Fr.*, vol. 10. In the despatch of 15 November (received 26 March 1808) Armstrong warningly writes, in part:

French Government. It will become inevitable if, as is announced already, the English Government puts, in its turn, the whole continent in a state of interdict, then it is, above all, that it will be necessary to guard against being her dupe. What would seem to be on her part only one of her ordinary acts of pride and madness, would be one of the most astute refinements of her polity, and would become one of the strongest supports of her monopoly. Besides she would employ with success the arm of *licences*, that is to say, the dispensations from blockade accorded to ships and to merchandise of her choice and she would have no longer the least competition to fear. It would become then indispensable to close to her every species of communication under no matter what form." It was for precisely such an exigency, and to provide just such a closure that Napoleon framed his Milan decrees.

On 23 November, the very day of Napoleon's arrival at his Italian capital, and a year after the decree from Berlin, he issued his first Milan decree.[123] To meet the warning of fresh British measures he had ready at hand in his North Sea regulations a

---

"The Emperor left Fontainableau yesterday, it is said, for Italy, Spain and Portugal. In each of these places great changes are predicted . . . . However, something has been decided, for which (though not officially communicated) it becomes the principal object of this letter to prepare you. We are, it seems, to be invited to make common cause against England, and to take the guarantee of the continent for a maritime peace which shall establish the principles of *free ships free goods.*"

[123] The day following the first Milan decree (24 Nov.) Champagny wrote to the American envoy a letter beginning: "L'execution des measures prises contre le commerce anglais a plusieurs fois donné lieu a vos reclamations, ..." and closing with the significant declaration: "Tous les incidens qui ont donné lieu à vos reclamations, Monsieur, seraient sans peine écartes si le Gouvernement des États-Unis, après s'être inutilement plaint des injustices et des violations de l'Angleterre, prenait avec tout le Continent, le parti de s'en garantir. L'Angleterre a introduit dans la guerre maritime l'oubli du droit des gens: ce n'est qu'en la forcant à la paix qu' il est possible de la recouvre. Sur ce point, l'interêt de toutes les nations est le même. Tout ont leur honneur et leur independance à defendre." Armstrong to Madison, 1 December 1807, *Dept. of State, Desp. Fr.*, vol. 10.

means of meeting the need of the moment. The recent Fontainebleau decree framed to counteract the latest British legislation was the most eligible precaution against the new Orders in Council, at least until they could be precisely known. Upon subsequent evidence of the adaptability of this temporary measure to the actual situation it was supplemented by yet more stringent provisions in a decree of 11 January, and thereupon published as the working basis of the extended Continental System.[124]

The fundamental measure in the new legislation, however, is the commonly known Milan decree of 17 December. It is a general pronunciamento, ranking thus with the decree of Berlin which it supplements.[125] Also like its prototype it has a preamble in justification. This assigns as the cause for new measures the English Orders of 11 November compelling ships of neutrals, friends and allies of England, not only to submit to visit by English cruisers but also to touch at a British port and pay an imposition levied upon their cargoes by British legislation. As such action infringes the sovereignty of a nation and the independence of its flag, feebleness or acquiescence would give the sanction of usage to this principle even as England had already profited by tolerance in establishing her theory that the flag does not cover the cargo, and in arbitrarily extending the right of blockade.[126] Then as an act of "just reciprocity" in five brief articles he decrees against all British lands a ban as broad and terrible, as potent— and as impotent—as ever St. Peter's Chair launched against a feudal sovereign. These measures "will cease for any nation which makes its flag respected. They will be in force until England returns to the principles of honor and international law."

Three points appear in this Milan decree enlarging the decree of Berlin: (a) denationalization, (b) neutral responsibility for

[124] See *Bulletin des lois*, 1807, vol. II, pp. 357, and 353. The November decree is bulletin 172, the January decree, bulletin 171.

[125] *Ibid.*, p. 341, bulletin 169.

[126] *Cor. de Nap.*, 16:192. Note the similarity to the ideas of the note of 15 November to Champagny for General Armstrong, *Cor. de Nap.*, 16:165.

maintaining the nationality of their flags, (c) the extension of the blockade of Britain to the *seas*—that every vessel whatsoever, to or from a port in British hands, may become thereby good prize. Napoleon's action may be explained plausibly upon the following grounds. (1) He realized that though he had closed all other apparent openings, yet surety required an outer bulwark. (2) He believed that the time had come to carry the battle of the continent on to the sea, but he realized that he must have maritime aid. (3) He comprehended that his own policy of August to November, and also the late British Orders in Council with their licence system had centered the issue upon the neutrals—and had proved neutrality impossible, a neutral status being incompatible alike with the legislation of England and France, because to both enemies, not *neutrals* but *allies* had become the prime essential. Thus by his Milan decree did Napoleon seek to define the international, that is the neutral, scope and value of the Berlin charter of his Continental System.

Profiting by the experiences of the Berlin decree, Napoleon prepared even more carefully than in the former case for the reception of his new edict. That there should be no hesitation at critical points he provided that it *must* be promulgated by Holland, Spain, Denmark, and his own commandant in Portugal.[127] It was to be published in the *Moniteur* along with certain other papers such as the Orders in Council of 11 November and the Russian declaration against England, which would fortify the impression it created.[128] By no means least, he sought this time a favorable reception by the commercial classes, for Cretet, Minister of the Interior, was to write to the chambers of com-

[127] *Cor. de Nap.*, 16:194. See the letter to Louis dated 16 December, Rocquain, p. 146.

[128] *Cor. de Nap.*, 16:192. It was not published, however, until 25 December, along with an apologetic address by Cretet, (*Moniteur*, p. 1387,) while the British Orders had appeared 14 December (p. 1341). Bathurst's explanation of 21 November had appeared on 24 December (p. 1382). Likewise the Russian proclamation had been published 11 December (p. 1331), and President Jefferson's message on 12 December (p. 1335).

merce in advance of the decree vividly painting the injuries committed by England and suggesting petitions for relief.[129] A number of favorable replies were, indeed, received, and apparently opposition thus forestalled.[130] Still another precaution was the order given to the Minister of Marine, Decrès, to prevent the clearance of allied or neutral vessels, an early step toward the notorious Bayonne and Rambouillet seizures.[131]

By the end of 1807, then, as has been seen, Napoleon had practically succeeded in bringing a sense of definiteness from what had been a year of uncertainties. For he had made it manifest that the system of the Berlin decree was not only to be assimilated to the economic organization of his empire, but that it was to be *continental* in *scope*, and likewise *continental* in *execution*; moreover that it was to be *literally interpreted* and similarly *enforced* by his officials; fourth, that even as it was intended, so actually it was going to be felt speedily by England. And co-ordinately therewith, he had shown that it was meant to be respected and supported by neutrals.[132] Whereby he had demonstrated that a neutral status with it had become untenable.[133] The two landmarks had been Tilsit which effaced land neutrals, and Milan which made maritime neutrality a mocking delusion. Nowhere has the point reached with the close of 1807 been more effectively epitomized than by Napoleon himself when, looking back two years later, he said with his own laconic keenness: "The Orders in

[129] *Cor. de Nap.*, 16:195.

[130] Cretet's letter is in *Arch. Nat.*, AF^{IV}1060, 2d dossier, pièce 66, the replies from Marseilles, 30 December 1807, are pièces 65 and 67; other replies are pièces 128 and 129.

[131] *Cor. de Nap.*, 16:196. For premonitions and effects of this embargo measure, see Consul Lee's letters of Nov. 1807–Jan. 1808, *Dept. of State, Cons. letters*, Bordeaux, vol. II.

[132] For interesting contemporary discussions see *Europäische Annalen*, 1808, I, 170, 209 and 227, and *European Magazine*, (London), 1807, 405, 495.

[133] Letter of 10 January 1810 to Cadore, *Cor. de Nap.*, 20:110. Cf. also 24 January to Cadore, Rocquain, 313-17.

Council of Great Britain necessitated my Milan decree; thenceforth there were no more neutrals."[134]

[134] Cf. *European Magazine,* Dec. 1807, p. 400: "Bonaparte declared publicly to General Armstrong . . . . that he would not admit of any neutrals in the war."

CHAPTER II
Ameliorative Experiments

The year 1808 ushered in with itself a period of imperial attempts to ameliorate the Continental System. Incredible this might seem, were facts respecters of emperors! Instead they mocked at Napoleon. He had just demonstrated his insistence upon a strict enforcement of his system without evasion or subterfuge. He had emphasized the intolerable position of neutrals, disregarding even their right to exist. But the services performed by neutrals were indispensable. Therefore the signatures to the Milan decrees were scarcely sanded before the consequences of these measures began to be apparent.[1] Even a partial enforcement of such laws—for manifestly their perfect execution was impossible—was felt ere long to be a bane to France and her allies. "From the Baltic to the Archipelago nothing but despair and misery is to be seen," reported the American consul at Bordeaux on 26 March 1808. "Grass is growing in the streets of this city. Its beautiful port is deserted except by two Marblehead fishing schooners and three or four empty vessels which still swing to the tide."[2] No wonder Napoleon was already seeking remedies for the ills of his System. An early and very significant evidence of this effort is the program of a new administrative council established by an imperial order of 11 January.[3]

The regular members of this Council of Administration for the Interior were declared to be the Minister of the Interior (Cretet), and the Minister of State Regnaud. The preliminary

[1] Note the report of Decrès (1 Jan.) on how to secure greatly needed naval stores contracted for with Russia, AF^{IV}1197, dossier 2, pièce 1; Sbornik, 89:188, 328 et seq. and *Cor. de Nap.*, 16:240.

[2] *Dept. of State, Cons. letters*, Bordeaux, vol. II. In a letter of 8 March, Consul Lee wrote: "The Literati at Paris are all engaged to find out how they can supply the want of colonial produce and English merchandize by indigenous productions."

[3] AF^{IV}1229-30, dossier 2, pièce 2.

labors outlined for the Council stipulated that the third session on 4 February should discuss industry and commerce, loans, tariffs, trade treaties, sources of raw materials, commercial statistics, chambers of commerce, etc. Out of this session came a special meeting on 14 February at which were present the Ministers of the Interior, Finance, and Marine, also the Councillors of State Regnaud and Collin. "The subject (l'objet) of this council was," according to the official minutes, "the measures to be taken for rendering the embargo the least prejudicial possible to the national commerce. The Decrees and regulations, as well as the decisions rendered by the ministers, on this matter were submitted to the Emperor."[4] He then formulated a set of questions or propositions under nine heads upon the basis of which the Ministers of the Interior and of Finance were "to present in the course of the next week a *projet* of regulations which form a complete legislation upon the matter under discussion."

These reports, if prepared, are now missing but their character may be judged from the recorded discussion of 14 February upon the questions propounded. Series 1 to 5 of the propositions deals with regulations of the coasting trade. It was the opinion of the Council that trade between port and port of France should be limited to French boats, and that small coasting craft might export all kinds of merchandise including grain. The coastwise trade from a French to a foreign port could be permitted to French and allied ships, in any goods. As for netruals this was open to discussion. Coastwise trade from a foreign to a French port, however, would depend upon the goods imported. Allied vessels might bring in products of their own countries. English goods being prohibited of course could not be considered. English colonial productions were barred, Spain had none, and Portugal only small quantities. But the whole matter of colonial produce

[4] The numerous copies of the minutes of this meeting found in the archives witness to its recognized importance. See for example AF^{IV}*169, and AF^{IV}* 1229-30, dossier 2, no. 2. It is published in *Cor. de Nap.*, 16:327.

was very important and was one of the special subjects reserved for the work of the ministers in their reports.

Sections 6 to 8 of the questionnaire deal with the *grand commerce* or ocean trade which might be open to the French, allied or neutral flags provided that no English goods were carried, and that the vessels had neither stopped in England nor been visited by the English. Allied flags were defined as the Dutch, Danish, Russian, Spanish, Italian, Neapolitan and Ottoman, and neutral flags as the Austrian and American. The question of the treatment of vessels arriving in ballast which had touched in England or had undergone search was not answered, nor was the question of legislation for Hamburg. An article of the new regulations was to establish the suppression of the flags of Kniphausen,[5] Pappenburg, Oldenburg, and Mecklenburg. Finally means of executing these various rules was to be devised, whereby no vessel might be admitted to entry as a right, but solely by decision of a council at Paris which should act upon data furnished it.

Throughout these questions and opinions there is a strong tone of peculiar significance. It is the evident effort to cling to the Blockade decrees and yet avoid their consequences, to redefine the status of neutrals, and to give a new development to the imperial navigation policy. How prophetic seems this circumstance when already within two months after the Milan decree, the imperial councils were frankly seeking to escape its effects, and when so immediately after dispensing with neutrals it was necessary to again consider them.

Although, largely because of the status of relations with the United States, the Council of 14 February was barren of the results anticipated, nevertheless it is significant as ushering in a series of experiments to ameliorate the evils of the Blockade by substituting national agencies for performing the services otherwise rendered by the ostracized neutrals. The agencies were (1) the coasting trade, (2) speculative expeditions (armements en

---

[5] Note the Dutch decree of 24 Jan. in the *Moniteur*, 2 Mar. 1808, p. 245.

aventurier), (3) marine insurance schemes, (4) government commercial-military expeditions, (5) government purchases of necessities, (6) simulations and protections, and (7) readjustments of the position of neutrals.

Because of its close connection with Napoleon's stay at Bayonne from mid-April till July this experimental phase of the evolution of his system may properly be known as the *Bayonne period.* At Bayonne, Orleans, and Bordeaux he was brought into actual contact with the maritime situation and was accessible to influences of the commercial interests.[6] This circumstance together with the American situation and the grave colonial problem largely explain the schemes tried by Napoleon at this time.

The vital importance of the coasting trade was clearly recognized in the discussion of 14 February, for not only does it receive chief attention in the questions dictated by the Emperor, but the views of the Council are most definite upon this point. As a result the Council were generally agreed as to the rights of nationals, allies, and neutrals (except Americans) in this trade, and also to a certain extent as to the kind of permissible cargoes. But this was largely theoretical. It did not guarantee a coasting trade, it rather presumed upon its existence. At Bayonne, however, Napoleon faced the actual situation. He had not been there two days when he wrote his Minister of the Marine:

"The commerce of Bayonne demand with reason that their coast trade with Portugal should be protected. If this trade were protected in the passage of the three capes it would furnish Portugal with wines and corn and would bring in return sugars and other products to Bayonne. He therefore proposes protective arrangements both for the trade of Bayonne and of Bordeaux.[8] A few days later he wrote this illuminative note on the margin of a report by Decrès, "When one sees the shores of the ocean he

[6] See his own statement to Decrès (25 May 1808), *Cor. de Nap.*, 17:197, also news in the *Moniteur* for April 1808.
[7] *Cor. de Nap.*, 17:4, to Decrès, 16 April 1808.
[8] *Ibid.*, 17:16.

groans over the abandonment in which they are. Not a gunboat, not a pinnace to protect the coasting trade, this neglect (incurie) makes it run risks, renders it difficult and that by the sole fault of the Marine. The coast trade would be as secure as in times of peace if it had the least organization and if the least precaution was taken."[9]

The traders at Bayonne, 17 April, also presented a petition regarding specified disadvantages under which their coast trade labored. Among these was the unfair discrimination in harbor dues against the French ships at St. Jean de Luz and Bilbao, as compared with Spanish ships at Bayonne. The Emperor sought a report upon this discrimination also upon the poor showing of French as compared with Dutch coasting trade in the North. The report showed that the advantage enjoyed by the Dutch was due to better economy, better knowledge of the coasts and "waters," and better ship construction. It recommended that the French ports of Normandy and Brittany adopt Dutch methods. It also proposed that the Minister of Exterior Relations take up the Bilbao grievance with Spain.[10]

Shortly after this the Mediterranean aspect of the coasting trade problem confronted Napoleon. It became necessary to station strong forces at Leghorn to protect the communications with Corsica and Elba against the corsairs,[11] and then to organize coast guards for protecting the Genoese and Piedmontese local trade against them.[12] This danger from privateers was a constant menace to the Mediterranean coasts of France and Italy. The British blockade, however, was the danger everywhere. The bearing of this blockade on the west coast is well pictured in Napoleon's letters of 11 May to Decrès. "The coast trade," he

[9] *Cor. de Nap.*, 17:45. Note also Consul Lee's reports during 1808, especially 26 March and 17 December, *Dept. of State, Cons. letters*, Bordeaux, vol. II.

[10] AF^{IV}1060, dossier 1, pièce 125, report of 27 April.

[11] *Cor. de Nap.*, 17:90.

[12] *Ibid.*, 17:174.

declared, "is the very greatest good of France, and yet we send vessels in order to be masters afar even when we do not try to be masters near by. The blockade of the coasts of France costs England only a few frigates, it is needful to organize the defense of the coasts in a manner to oblige the English to hold a number of vessels there. . . . The Garonne at Bordeaux, the Loire at Nantes are the two great arteries of France." He proposed a plan for their protection.[13] Again he pointed out the ridiculous manner of allowing the blockade of Bordeaux by which one vessel cut its communications with Spain and Portugal, another its connections with Brest.[14]

The result of Napoleon's personal experiences with the abasement of his marine was a decree of 25 May 1808 for the protection of cabotage and the fisheries. The coast was divided into eight sections with a coast-guard flotilla for each so as to protect the coast and render convoy services. In this the marine was to be seconded by the Ministry of War, a special corps being organized, apparently, for the purpose.[15] Napoleon followed this up 1 June by a project to utilize the coast trade for provisioning his army in Portugal.[16]

Evidences as to the workings of the scheme are meagre, such as the occasional references to convoys in the weekly reports of the Ministry of Marine, or infrequent items in the newspapers. Sometimes these announce a successful result, such as the safe arrival of a convoy of thirty sail at Barcelona, 7 May 1809.[17] While the Mediterranean convoys were usually more fortunate than those of the Ocean, yet even the former often had serious trouble. Indeed, the disastrous results of the loss of sea power, and the results of an effective naval blockade need no better

[13] *Ibid.*, 17:91.
[14] *Ibid.*, 17:92.
[15] *Cor. de Nap.*, 17:194-195. Apparently the scheme was first suggested by Decrès.
[16] *Cor. de Nap.*, 17:253.
[17] AF^{IV}197, dossier 4, pièce 74.

illustration than is afforded by a comparison of the routine reports of port officers and coast watchmen to the Ministry of Marine, with those of British admirals on French stations to the Admiralty during this period. One must therefore conclude that the experiment of reanimating maritime activity by encouraging the coasting trade fell entirely short of its aim, and that if France were unable to have the mastery of the home trade some other commercial remedy was inevitable.

With respect to the *grand commerce* or open-sea trade the Bayonne period saw even more extensive experiments than those in aid of cabotage. They center around the colonial hopes of Napoleon which were revived and fanned vigorously, at this moment of leisure from Northern campaigns, by dreams conjured from the occupation of Portugal and the displacement of the Bourbons in Spain. In this hour of need he encouraged the people to believe that he could create colonies and colonial products as easily as he could organize a campaign.[18] It was said he would use the Iberian strongholds in Morocco (with which state he had a quarrel) as the base for conquering and colonizing North Africa as a new source of cotton and sugar supply. Actually he drafted most ambitious schemes for exploiting the Spanish colonies—the West Indies, Mexico, Central America, but especially Buenos Ayres and the viceroyalty of La Plata. Most naturally, likewise, the remnants of the former colonial empire of France herself were objects of the Emperor's solicitude in their hour of keen distress. The chief experiment undertaken in their behalf was that of subsidized *armements en aventurier*—speculative expeditions corresponding to the merchant venturers of England and New England, or, indeed, to our modern tramp ships when armed for defense. With this scheme was closely connected a plan for government marine insurance, and another for the employment of warships for colonial sustenance and trade with France.

[18] Cf. Lee's report of 8 March 1808, *Dept. of State, Cons. letters*, Bordeaux, II. See also *Aff. Étr., Cor. Pol., États Unis*, vol. 61, fols. 13, 80, 135, etc., as well as the *Moniteur*, 1807-8, and *Cor. de Nap.*, vol. 16.

The origin of these schemes seems traceable to the arrival at Bordeaux early in April (during Napoleon's stay there), of a ship from Guadeloupe telling of dire apprehensions of want in the French West Indies owing to the American Embargo law.[19] The news created a sensation in France. Napoleon immediately consulted with Bordeaux merchants, and 15 April on his arrival at Bayonne he broached his plan to Cretet, Minister of the Interior.[20] "I desire," his letter begins, "to encourage the commerce of maritime places with the French and Spanish colonies, to give activity to our ports, to cause the arrival of colonial productions in France, and in the colonies those two objects of first necessity for them, namely, bread and wine. Note the mode I have judged most convenient for obtaining these results."

Then he unfolds a plan for the formation at Bordeaux, La Rochelle, Nantes, St. Malo, Granville and Le Havre, of stock companies capitalized at 5, 10, or 15,000 francs, using swift vessels of 150 to 300 tons, already built, or to be constructed for the purpose. These he purposes to aid by certain encouragements. 1st, He will take one-third of the shares of each expedition; 2nd, the Marine will pay the passage with each vessel of ten or twenty conscripts sent out as colonial re-enforcements, and who will also augment the fighting force of the crew and thus remove fear from corsairs; 3rd, the Marine will supply 20 or 30 tons of each outward load in either flour or artillery stores, paying the freight at departure and running the risk of loss of the ship—but this risk must not exceed the sixth of a ship's tonnage.

He hopes these subsidies will lead to numerous expeditions. The Chamber of Commerce at Bordeaux are planning for a stock

---

[19] *Dept. of State, Desp. Fr.*, vol. 11, Armstrong to Secretary of State, 15 April 1808. It was the immediate cause also of the "Bayonne decree" against American shipping, on 17 April, although the basic ideas of the Bayonne decision are discernible in a letter of 31 March, Colenbrander, X, 30, Champagny to Larochefoucauld. Cf. *Cor de Nap.*, 16:453, 17:169; and *Moniteur*, 10 and 17 April.

[20] *Cor. de Nap.*, 17:1-2.

of two millions, and the use of fifteen goelletes of 3,000 to 4,000 tons. The idea is to send to Guadeloupe, Martinique and Cayenne—preparing the expeditions during the summer and sending them during the season of long autumn nights that they may return by the end of March. La Rochelle, St. Malo, and Granville each should be able to expedite three vessels, Nantes and Havre each five. Thus he calculates upon thirty vessels and cargoes valued at four to five millions, and that by being interested in all he cannot lose his capital if but half return. He suggests men at the various ports to whom the plan should be broached with injunctions to secrecy and to take care that reliable vessels are selected. The operation may be carried to sixty vessels or 12,000 tons. He does not wish any part in the management of the expeditions. Cretet is to confer with the Minister of Marine regarding cargoes to be given at the different ports, probably wine and flour at Bordeaux, anchors and artillery at le Havre. Antwerp and Dunkirk are omitted as being apparently too immediately under the cannon of England.

Cretet replied April 22, discussing the proposition of the government's third interest in these speculative expeditions to the Leeward Islands and Cayenne, also discussing the merits of a government insurance scheme at 40% as a preferable plan, since insurance in Holland, where alone it is possible, costs 50% to 55%.[21] May 1, he sent a *precis* of first information on the expeditions being prepared.[22] May 11, he made a second report especially as to the fifteen preparing at Bordeaux.[23] To this last Napoleon replied May 27, applauding the activity of commerce in colonial expeditions, but urging that they guard against a connivance with English cruisers, by which they will receive ships from London claiming to come from Martinique.[24]

[21] AF^{IV}1060, I, 126.
[22] AF^{IV}1060, I, 124.
[23] *Ibid.*, 122.
[24] *Cor. de Nap.*, 17:215.

Meanwhile Napoleon had been considering Cretet's suggestion regarding insurance.[25] In a letter of 12 May he tells of a decree in regard to the plans of the Chamber of Commerce by which each of the fifteen ships is to put on reserve until its return one-fifteenth of the anticipated value of its return cargo. Napoleon therefore proposes the formation at Paris, at the Bank or elsewhere, of a Chamber of Assurance; 1st, by the deposit at departure of 5% of the value of all the vessels going to the colonies; 2nd, by the retention of a fifteenth of the return value of each expedition to be deposited in the Chamber. Upon the loss of a vessel by accident or capture, the undertakers would be reimbursed by the Bank in totality or pro rata out of the 5% deposit and the "one-fifteenth reserve." The reimbursement is to be on the basis of the outbound value of the expedition. This the Emperor proposes merely as a basis of discussion with men informed in such matters, but with the eventual purpose of issuing such a decree. Cretet answers 21 May that the idea is not feasible being simply a mutual guarantee and not true insurance.[26] July 3, Cretet writes again inclosing two notes. The subjects treated are the data as to expeditions fitting out and the question of insurance. On the latter point he reports that Amsterdam will insure at 50%.

On 10 July Nerac, an ex-legislator, proposed in a *memoire* a scheme for encouraging the trade of France with her colonies.[27] He spoke of the large interest aroused by the plans already initiated but urged further measures. He made two proposals. The first was a government underwriting scheme at a 50% premium. The second was a commercial operation by the Government which should send a fleet of national vessels to Martinique to purchase colonial goods to be sold in France. This *memoire* was transmitted to the Emperor together with a ministerial analysis and endorsement of Nerac's proposal. From the first proposal nothing came beyond Napoleon's original suggestions of

[25] *Cor. de Nap.*, 17:102.
[26] AF^{IV}1060, I, 121.
[27] AF^{IV}1060, dossier 1, pièces 19-21. The author evidently was that Nairac of Bordeaux who had been a member of the Council of Five Hundred.

12 May. The second proposal, however, fell in with an idea already partly anticipated by Napoleon.

Apparently the interest aroused for the *armement en aventurier* scheme tended to encourage or embolden other private expeditions.[28] Napoleon writing on 12 May to Decrès mentioned ships which have gone to Ile de France and are going to Martinique and Guadeloupe, besides the expeditions preparing at La Rochelle, St. Malo, Bordeaux, Rouen, and Le Havre. He regretted that ten or twelve recruits had not been placed on each ship, and instructed Decrès in the future to arrange in advance with shipowners regarding the recruits they are to send out with their vessels. "My intention," he added, "is to encourage all these expeditions." He also turned about the same time to Murat urging, apparently with success, that flyboats (mouches) be sent out from Spain to the Spanish colonies.[29] Indeed the ability of these flyboats to elude the British blockading cruisers so impressed Napoleon that he wrote Decrès frequently regarding them.[30] He more and more felt that they would afford a really practicable mode of getting wine, flour, and grains to Cayenne, Martinique, and the other colonies, and he also proposed that in return they should bring back colonial produce as an aid alike to the colonials and to the French manufacturers. For both in the colonies and in France the pressure of the American Embargo was being felt,[31] and during the months of May and June Cretet was sending in strong petitions and reports regarding the suffering of factories for the lack of raw-stuffs,[32] and hence soaring prices generally.[32a]

[28] *Cor. de Nap.*, 17:106.

[29] *Cor. de Nap.*, 17:170, no. 13943. Cf. Murat, *Lettres et Docs.*, VI, 80, 86, 95–100, 116-9, 122. 173-175, 179-80.

[30] *Cor. de Nap.*, 17:90, 139, 183, 198, 289, 395-7. When Decrès did not act, he bought and sent out several vessels himself: *Ibid.*, pp. 183, 185, 197.

[31] *Cor. de Nap.*, 17:169. To Murat, 20 May. Cf. Murat, *Lettres*, etc., VI, 171.

[32] AF^IV 1060, dossier 2, pièces 89-95, also see 119, 120.

[32a] Cf. Fiévée's "Note LVI," June 1808, to Napoleon. In his *Correspondance*, II:338, P.S., footnote (of 1836?), he says a commission to curb profiteering originated the licence scheme of 1809. I find no actual proofs of this.

Decrès who apparently was becoming nettled and half desperate under the continual complaints and demands of the Emperor at last protested strongly against the impossibility of the imperial requirements. Napoleon's reply of 22 May is a brilliant commentary on the situation.[33] "For a year," he declared, "when I have asked for expeditions to aid our colonies I have been answered only by prattlings (babioles). My time was employed in other things and nothing departed. You could, with some zeal, succor our colonies. See to the departure from several ports of ships loaded with flour, etc. It is not necessary to be God for that."

These letters all indicate the drift to the next step which is seen clearly in a letter of 30 May.[34] In it orders are given that the *Orestes* just arrived at San Sebastian shall be prepared to leave at the first chance for Martinique with 120 tons of flour and to bring back an equal mount of sugar, coffee, or other colonial produce for the account of colonial merchants. The premium (nolis) is to be for the marine, but declares Napoleon, "it is not for the freight that I take this measure but in order to have these products. The premium will be paid as a customs duty which you will levy so much the heavier since these colonial wares will have come on my ships."

He then names fifteen brigs and six corvettes in various ports to be used for the same object. He figures that even with the loss of one-third he will still give the colonies food for 40,000 men for 100 days. The aim is to divide the vessels between Guadeloupe, Martinique, Cayenne, and Ile de France. He will send 1200 men counting the crews and retaining enough for protection on the return trip. "The return of 60,000 quintals of sugar, coffee and spices (épiceries) is not less important for the metropolis.

[33] *Cor. de Nap.*, 17:183. Note, however, articles in the *Moniteur* for 5, 19 and 25 May, and 5 June 1808, pp. 495, 551, 574 and 584, as to the activity of warships and corsairs since the close of 1807 in keeping up trade and communications between France and the West Indies.

[34] *Cor. de Nap.*, 17:236-8.

The quintal being worth today at least 200 francs, the return will form an affair of twelve millions." The premium at 12% and the customs receipts will equal the value of the brigs themselves. He has twenty other goellettes, luggers, etc., and he is ready to devote to the purpose any frigates which can be spared from his large plans. He wishes Decrès to begin at once to give orders and to draw up a careful plan. "Bayonne, Bordeaux, La Rochelle, and Nantes can play a large rôle in this operation." If one frigate is sent it can carry 3,000 tons of flour and bring back sugar worth 1,200,000 francs. "Judge what an immense sum!" Commands may be given *carte blanche* for buying the sugars which will be put in the Emperor's warehouses for his account. He proposes also an arrangement for taking sugar on planters' accounts with equitable conditions to regulate their prices with those of his own purchases. He concludes: "In extraordinary circumstances it is necessary to do extraordinary things."

The idea grew. On 10 June he wrote Decrès regarding three such expeditions for the colonies fitting out at Nantes, L'Orient and Brest—fifty-six sail in all, with 10,600 marines, and 19,600 sailors.[35] Three days later he wrote again with further directions for provisioning Martinique and Guadeloupe for nine months.[36] He did not intend provisioning Cayenne, Senegal, San Domingo, or the Isles of France and Reunion, but he planned yet another expedition from Rochefort for Ile de France or elsewhere. He also stated regarding certain claims of Bordeaux that he was still willing to take his promised one-fifth in their *armements en aventurier*, or they could act independently if they wished. Also they were not compelled to take the conscripts whose passage money was intended as a subsidy. Summing up his program he declared: "In the last analysis I wish to prepare myself three means of victualling my colonies: 1st, the twelve separate expeditions made at my cost; 2nd, the expeditions that commerce will make; 3rd the expedition of Rochefort."

[35] *Cor. de Nap.*, 17:289.
[36] *Cor. de Nap.*, 17:302-3.

The feverish preparations during the early summer by both government and private agencies brought some friction over the drafting of workmen of the adventuring companies by the marine, until the latter was ordered to forego its privileges[37]. Then for three months the turn of affairs in France and the Erfurt interview absorbed attention, but in October correspondence from the undertakers of expeditions and various administrative questions and decisions show renewed interest in the several experiments.[38] Among the issues raised are whether the government will take a third instead of a fifth share in certain expeditions, also what to do where outfitters seek to evade paying their fifteenths to the mutual insurance scheme.[39] On 24 October, also, orders were given for the immediate sailing of the squadrons of Rochefort and L'Orient, and if necessary that of Brest, in order, with the other expeditions planned, to victual the colonies for a year or fifteen months.[40] Two thousand men were to be taken to Guadeloupe and Martinique and an effort was planned to take Les Saintes and Marie Galante.[41] Colonial goods were to be brought back.

If Napoleon had not already begun to foresee the failure of these experiments he was not long in realizing it. On 28 November he inquired anxiously whether his squadrons had sailed. "It must not be dissimulated," he wrote, "that the merchants are insufficient to provision my colonies. Only the arrival of these two squadrons will put them in the state I should desire."[42] On 31 December the Brest fleet was ordered to sail at the end of January,[43] but on Napoleon's return from Spain he found all three squadrons hope-

[37] AF^{IV}1060, dossier 2, pièces 110-115.
[38] This interest was probably increased by the return of the *Orestes*. Cf. Brotonne, *Lettres inédites*, I, 364.
[39] AF^{IV}1060, dossier 2, pièces 106-8.
[40] *Cor. de Nap.*, 18:13-15, nos. 1440-1443.
[41] They also might capture Spanish, Portuguese, American, Swedish, and Brazilian ships.
[42] *Cor. de Nap.*, 18:86, no. 14521.
[43] *Ibid.*, no. 14629.

lessly blockaded by the English.[44] He was therefore forced to rely upon the flyboats, and the rare frigate, privateer, or merchant adventurer that might succeed in running from this blockaded coast.[45] Yet even such often failed, despite the subterfuges attempted, to run the blockade that was starving the islands, or, having done so, to return to France. Indeed, it was only a matter of months until the last of the French and Dutch colonies in America were gathered in by the British navy.

In short, even before the close of 1808 the futility of these colonial expeditions could be seen. It is true that on a small scale *armements en aventurier* were kept up until the end of the imperial régime. Also as late as 1810 the question of a French national ship carrying merchandise played a critical part in Franco-American relations.[46] But these were only isolated survivors of the experiments, which had been assimilated to the new system that had meantime been adopted.

With respect to each of the 1808 colonial relief measures, as Napoleon made it clear, the object was not alone to support the colonial defense but also to maintain the French supply of indispensable colonial products. In the beginning it is true that the anxiety for French needs was a relatively minor matter, for in April 1808, it was supposed that the country had at least nine months supply of sugar and coffee, the use of which was rapidly falling off, but these calculations were soon found inaccurate and besides they had failed to take account of cotton and of quinine, for both of which articles there came pressing demands. In the case of quinine special action was at once taken to meet the demands. This action is of peculiar interest in view of a prevalent,

[44] *Ibid.*, p. 254, 7 February, p. 314, 6 March.

[45] Some of these vessels, even, were Americans using French colors, it seems, e.g., the *Swallow* (*L'Hirondelle*) a pilot-boat schooner of Baltimore, *Dept. of State, Cons. letters*, Bordeaux, II, 6 September 1808.

[46] The case of the ship *La Franchise*. Cf. *Dept. of State, Desp. Fr.*, vols. 11 and 12; *Aff. Étr., États Unis, Cor. Pol.*, vols. 63 and 64; and American newspapers of 1810.

but erroneous, supposition that it was need of quinine for his hospitals that caused Napoleon to adopt a system of exceptions in derogation of his Continental System.

So far as French records indicate the question of the quinine supply first arose in January or February of 1806 in regard to a fever epidemic in the Department of Basses Alpes when importation of bark was allowed from Spain duty free.[47] It was merely a local matter without military significance. Probably there was no special significance, either, in the raising of the sequestre on quinine seized on the American ship *L'Esperance* at Hamburg in September 1807, although the British measures to cut off the supply of Jesuit's bark and other drugs from the continent must have limited the available stock.[48] Shortly afterwards, however, the question became an actual issue.

The question seems to have been precipitated by a petition of a Mme. Rousset, a Norman merchant who asked the right to bring into France 500 to 1,000 chests of quinine which her husband had purchased and stored in England. About the same time —one suspects a connection—the dean of the School of Medicine at Paris transmitted the observations of a M. Desyeux on quinine: its virtues, the need of it in France, and its greatly increased price. On 10 Feb. 1808, Cretet referred the Rousset petition to the commercial division of his ministry with advice to examine the utility of the general measure. The report favored such action and Cretet decided to ask the Emperor to open the port of Dieppe for three months to the importation of quinine with certificates of origin. With this in view the Division of Commerce drew up for Cretet the *projet* of a decree embodying these ideas and allowing the entry of quinine even when the rest of a cargo should be condemned.

[47] See $F^{12}1966^m$, dossier marked "quinine," which is the source of statements made here, except where specially indicated.

[48] $AF^{IV}1229$-1230, Imperial decision, 3 Nov. 1808. The British policy is brought out in Hansard's *Parl. Debates*, X, 695, 1168, 1320 et seq. Note also J. Aspern's pamphlet entitled, *Public Spirit*.

Before presenting the *projet* to the Emperor, Cretet sought the opinion and support of the Director General of the Customs. Collin replied 11 April. He admitted the value and need of quinine which could enter only from the Spanish colonies, with certificates of origin, and on American vessels, the Americans being the only recognized neutrals. Regarding Cretet's desire to meet the inadequacy of this source of supply by the proposed exemption from seizure even of vessels which had put into port in England, he emphasized the need of restricting the exemption solely to quinine, or otherwise vessels would carry a small amount of the drug for a chance to evade the Continental System.

The danger of opening Dieppe to an habitual communication with England was also to be considered for he took it for granted that the quinine would come from there, since only the American vessels already in English or French ports could manage the importation within the three months limit. But having interrupted his writing to read the *Moniteur* he noted therein that England had just prohibited the exportation of cotton and quinine. The proposed source of supply was thus closed, but he believed plenty of quinine would be available at the Frankfort fair. All in all, therefore, he suggested that instead of a decree a simple decision should be made: 1st, that quinine brought in by land might be dispensed from need of a certificate of origin; 2nd, that quinine brought by neutral vessels which might have touched in England or been visited by the English should be exempted from the penalties meted out to the rest of the cargo and the vessel.

Cretet accordingly had his *projet* redrafted and submitted it at a conference with Napoleon on 20 April. He pointed out the scarcity, or at least greatly enhanced prices of quinine, due to the increased use of the drug together with the difficulty of maritime communications. While the despotism of England toward neutrals was a primary cause of the difficulty yet Napoleon's own rigorous measures had contributed thereto, and they could not supply a substitute for quinine. Prices had increased fifty per cent within a year and the chief sufferers were those least able to bear the increase. Direct communications with the country producing Peruvian bark being now almost impossible or subject to the events of major force, public interest required an exception in favor of the one irreplaceable commodity and indispensable necessity. He therefore asked a favorable decision for the two remedial measures proposed by Collin and himself.

The proposal failed, however, to secure the Emperor's sanction. He did not see the imperative need for an action so directly derogatory of his decrees. He suggested instead that Cretet first confer with Champagny as to the chance of buying quinine in Madrid and Cadiz, and of assuring its importation into France. On 10 May Cretet at Paris wrote Champagny, who was at the Spanish border, rehearsing the situation, telling of the appeal he had made at the instance of the School of Medicine, and stating the Emperor's decision to purchase quinine in Spain with government funds in order to prevent speculation. He asked Champagny's cooperation in this, or, failing in Spain, his support for the original proposal to Napoleon. Meanwhile, Cretet took measures to prevent the export of the drug from France for which he was reproved by the Emperor (27 May) who deemed it "unnecessary to give the continent the example of self-isolation," preferring that he import quinine from Portugal and Cadiz and take only the usual precautions observed as to grain at Paris.[49]

Evidently Champagny was successful as a credit of 500,000 francs on the sinking fund was authorized for this purpose,[50] and in July or August as much as 1,000,000 francs worth of quinine was sent from Vittoria to Bayonne.[51] Later in the year other large quantities were sent from Santander and Madrid. No more was heard of Cretet's "Dieppe plan," nor did subsequent conditions, at least for several years, become pressing enough to cause any marked change of policy. In July 1809 a request to introduce

[49] $F^{12}2031$.
[50] AF^{IV} 1318, pièce 23.
[51] *Cor. de Nap.*, 18:143 and 241.

quinine hid in other colonial goods was refused. Also in December 1810 an effort to exempt it from the Trianon tariff duties met with failure. It was, to be sure, included among articles which might be imported by licences, but no special interest was shown in securing it until possibly 1811 and 1812. In those years it was regularly freed from sequestre, and we find also some correspondence of Davout's in August 1811 regarding another purchase of quinine in Spain.

It should be clear, then, that the need of quinine, despite a priori reasonings of some historians, did not cause the break from the Continental System.[52] Moreover, as we shall notice presently, when the licence system was inaugurated some months later the impetus came from a very different quarter.

The attempt to use the quinine supply question as a method of undermining the Continental Closure by way of special exceptions was, however, not dissimilar to other efforts at that moment. For while Napoleon was trying to work out his remedial experiments, French commerce was seeking other forms of relief. Although these were doubtless only isolated cases, they are significant indications of the trend of the situation and of Napoleon's reluctance to countenance a system of exceptions. Most of these cases may be grouped as problems of simulations.

An awkward case of the sort came up in May at the time of greatest activity in trying to relieve the needs of the colonial planters and to appease the demands of the metropolis and home industries for colonial products. It was the problem of what policy to adopt toward vessels coming from blockaded French colonies under the French flag.[53] Cretet wrote to the Emperor 11 May regarding the action of the customs toward certain French vessels lately arrived from Martinique. In his reply, 27 May, Napoleon indicated his suspicion that there was a plan to mask

[52] As further evidence confirming this may be noted the case of "American" vessels with quinine refused admission into Holland. See *Moniteur*, 30 May 1808.

[53] F¹²2031, and specifically *Cor. de Nap.*, 17:25.

a connivance with British cruisers to break the Continental Blockade. If so, he says he is watching and will take action. If vessels actually come from the colonies it can be proved by the presence (1) of a few passengers at least, (2) of a quantity of mail for the metropolis, and (3) papers signed by the colonial prefect. "All colonial commerce is probably simulated." It really comes from London. Even the "visit" of the English "would denationalize my flag and the vessel presenting itself in a port with that stain assuredly would not be recognized, and in effect it is easy to see that this commerce would not be favored by the enemy save as illicit trade and then simply because it had subscribed to the dishonorable conditions imposed. The interest of the state is not always that of the merchant. The merchant might wish to work under the yoke of English legislation." In short the case against these colonial vessels was too strong.

Possibly a little earlier than this had come from Marseilles another effort to solve the colonial goods problem from a different angle.[54] It was the request of Magastre and Company of that port to Cretet under date of 10 May for a safe conduct to bring, in an Algerian vessel, goods they owned in Smyrna but for some time had been vainly trying to get to France. This led to a considerable correspondence between Cretet, Decrès, and Napoleon. It is not made clear just what a safe conduct was. It would seem that neither Cretet nor Napoleon was familiar with it. Decrès recognized it but apparently as a rather uncommon ship's paper. He consented reluctantly to issue such a paper, but before sending it to Cretet stated that it was a useless paper since its only object would be protection against French privateers. If the ship had not been visited by an English cruiser or paid duties contrary to the Milan decree it was safe anyway and the trouble and cost of the safe conduct might as well be spared, while if the Milan decree had been violated no paper could protect the ship against the consequences of denationalization. Cretet then put the matter before Napoleon himself, who wrote on the petition:

[54] F¹²2033.

"Si le batiment n'est pas denationalise par les Anglais point de difficulté. S'il est denationalisé et qu'il ait été conduit dans une station de forces anglaises ou qu'il ete payé quelque chose aux Anglais, Refusé.
"16 June 1808 Napoleon" [55]
Bayonne."

This decision was reported to the firm who inquired if a French vessel captured by an English ship, taken to Algiers, and there ransomed, might be granted immunity. This was referred to Decrès and on his advice to lawyers also. The decision, in which Cretet concurred, was that the collusion would be patent and could not be overlooked.[56] This was in August. It is to be presumed that the goods were not perishable, as the firm seems to have got them home long afterward under a licence.

A somewhat similar case but with new features is that of Imbert and Chataud, Marseilles merchants who wished to send provisions to Martinique and bring back colonial goods.[57] They asked permission to use an Algerian simulation and to stop at Algiers to get it.[58] They also asked a safe conduct in case of a visit from the English at sea. They wrote to both Decrès and Cretet, and these latter to Napoleon. The correspondence covered May and June 1808. The significant letter is probably Napoleon's to Cretet of 26 May. He desires a report on the matter and wishes Cretet to consult with the Minister of Finance (Gaudin) on measures to take to insure that such an Algerian vessel with colonial goods actually comes from America. He does not object to granting the request "on condition that nothing

[55] $F^{12}2033$. This striking decision seems never to have been published.

[56] See nowever the case of the *Massonda* (1807–1809), to which Magastre was a party. (Merlin, *Questions de Droit*.)

[57] $F^{12}2031$.

[58] Simulations in France had been forbidden by a decision of 30 March, but it may not have been strictly observed as we hear, 15 May 1809, of a French vessel neutralized as an American captured in August 1808 on a trip from Guernsey. $F^{12}2051$.

shall have been paid on the sea to the English; 2nd, that on arrival these vessels shall have not only the certificates of the captains general, colonial prefects, and customs officers of Martinique and Guadeloupe, but also shall have on board at least four passengers from the colonies, either soldiers or creoles coming home; and finally, that these vessels shall not have been detained either in England or Gibraltar." He closes: "I have great difficulty in believing that the English would wish to let any victuals pass into Martinique which they hold in a state of blockade and allow colonial produce to enter France exacting a tax of so much per cent on the merchandise. Write this to these merchants, informing them that if this is a pretext for fraud they will not come out of it well, (ils n'en viendront pas à bout)."

In view of the ruling of the following day regarding the admission of the Martinique vessels, and especially the contemporary refusal of a Barbary simulation for the Levant sought by Magastre, this ruling of 26 May is, indeed, a peculiar one.[59] Moreover, it has a still further and more surprising significance. It apparently bears some relation to a decision of 17 June 1808, by which Barbary vessels were "excepted from the rigors of the decrees of 23 Nov. and 17 Dec. 1807, provided they had not stopped at Malta, Sicily, or Gibraltar, that they had paid nothing to the English, and that they had on board neither colonial produce nor English merchandise."[60] As the preliminary papers in the matter are lacking, it is impossible to state positively the origin or basis of the 17 June decision, but its date and the similar features in each case would show surely some direct connection with the 26 May letter. Another like decision for Barbary vessels was made 4 March 1809. Under these decisions twelve ships were furnished with special passavants or passports sent for the purpose by the Minister of Finance to Dubois Thainville, consul general at Algiers.

[59] See p. 67 above.
[60] $F^{12}2108$.

As the Danes had been exempted in 1807 from the rigors of the Berlin decree by tolerance, so now for the Algerines the Milan decrees were moderated. Why the Danes should have been favored is evident, but why the Algerines is mysterious unless, perchance, Napoleon had special reasons to curry their favor in his efforts to overcome the British control of the Mediterranean.[61] The momentous fact regarding the issuance of these formal passports, however, is that they were the entering wedge for the license trade and became, in fact, an element in the licence system.

Not least significant among the efforts of commercial interests to remedy their situation was that of the Chamber of Commerce of Bordeaux when Napoleon stopped there (1-3 August) on his return from Bayonne to Paris. The specific question was whether American vessels in the port of Bordeaux might be allowed to depart with products of that district. "Prove to me that the products that you wish to export are not for the consumption of England," the Emperor is reported to have said, "and I shall be satisfied; but I cannot permit that my allies pay a tribute (taxe) for the products they receive from France."[62] Striking as is this declaration which Napoleon had done well to have adhered to strictly, probably the chief significance of the incident is that Champagny immediately secured from the American consul a list of the American vessels, loaded or unloaded, intimating at the same time the probability of permitting them to sail upon certain conditions. It was, in short, equivalent to a reopening of the question of the neutral carrier.

To appreciate the importance of the Bordeaux incident it is necessary to understand the actual situation of the neutral carrier, that is, at this time, the United States.[63] Directly following

[61] Cf. *Cor. de Nap.*, 17:20-21, 29, 145, 209, 229, April-May, 1808. For the Danish exemption see chapter I above.

[62] Armstrong to Madison, 7 Aug. 1808, inclosing the extract of a letter from Bordeaux, *Dept. of State.*, *Desp. Fr.*, vol. 11.

[63] Based primarily upon Armstrong's despatches, *Dept. of State*, *Desp. Fr.*, vol. 11; Armstrong's private letters to Madison, Lib. of Cong. MSS.;

the issuance of the Milan decree of 17 December 1807, there was a sequestration of neutral shipping in French ports. At first, but for only a few days, American ships escaped this. Immediately upon the inclusion of these ships in the general embargo the American minister protested strenuously, and he was destined to continue his reclamations for many weary months thereafter. At first Napoleon's reply was an effort to browbeat the United States into adhesion to the Milan decree and into war upon England, but he immediately realized his mistake and altered his tactics by seeking to bribe the United States into an alliance. This change of tactics was coincident with the discussion by the Council of Administration of the Interior regarding the amelioration of the decrees of November 1806 and December 1807 by a new navigation policy But just before the critical council of 14 February 1808, news had reached Napoleon of the American Embargo Act.[64] Therefore "though the proposition was supported by the whole weight of the council he became highly indignant and declared that these decrees should suffer no change, and that the Americans should be compelled to take the positive character either of allies or of enemies."[65]

A month's efforts through Lafayette, Marbois, Talleyrand, Fouché, Cretet, and Champagny brought a half promise of relaxation in favor of the United States from Napoleon. But this he almost immediately retracted and when, early in April, at Bordeaux, he learned of the disastrous effect of the American Embargo upon his West Indian possessions he was not slow in finding a plausible mode of retaliation.[66] The result was the so-called

---

Lee's reports, *Cons. letters*, Bordeaux, vol. II; *Aff. Étr., États Unis, Cor. Pol.*, vol. 61; and *Cor. de Nap.*, vols. 16 and 17.

[64] See *Moniteur*, 11 Feb., copied from the *Publiciste*.

[65] *Am. State Papers, For. Rel.*, III, 250, Armstrong to Madison, 22 Feb. 1808.

[66] Napoleon denied that he retaliated, but for the lasting impression made by this and later news to the same effect, see Cadore's letter of 5 August 1810, *Am. State Papers, For. Rel.*, III, 386.

Bayonne decree—a letter to Gaudin dated 17 April at Bayonne which used the Embargo as a plea for sequestring all American vessels in imperial or dependent ports on the grounds that there could be no Americans in Europe after the Embargo; therefore so-called Americans were only masked English ships. Armstrong's protests were in vain against this reasoning[67] which had sufficient basis of facts to bear the super-structure of sophistry.[68]

On 6 August the day before he learned of the Bordeaux petition Armstrong made yet another of his protests against Napoleon's attitude to Americans.[69] By happy coincidence, if not deliberate purpose, it served to reinforce the arguments of the Bordeaux merchants. In this note he recognized the right of Napoleon to favor his commerce by municipal regulations, but he pointed out the distinction between such regulations and public law. Thus France might forbid the entry of American ships from or to England, and might sequestre and confiscate vessels violating this after having due notice thereof, but she could do nothing more. He urged the restoration of good trade relations and suggested that France could guard against England's profiting from the American trade with France by requiring that American vessels should take a return cargo from France equal to the value of the imports. If such vessels went voluntarily to England with French goods it would only be to the advantage of France by turning the balance of trade against England and in favor of the United States and France. Moreover, the imports from America would make France the general entrepôt of colonial goods for

[67] Cf. Armstrong to Madison, 23 and 25 April, 16 May, 23 July, etc. Note especially, Lee to Armstrong, 18 October, *Dept. of State, Desp. Fr.*, vol. 11.

[68] Moreover there is reason to believe that Napoleon either was sincere in his interpretation of the Embargo from the first, or at least convinced himself by constant repetition of his line of argument. If in August to the Bordeaux Chamber of Commerce he indeed declared: "Since the United States have laid an embargo they have ceased to be neutrals," he speedily returned to his more convenient attitude of praising the high spirit of the American government and seizing vessels under its flag.

[69] *Am. State Papers, For. Rel.*, III, 255.

Europe. Even if England seized American vessels in this trade France could not complain for the United States could not fail to require reparation even by force. In either case, therefore, it would benefit France.

Armstrong delivered the note as a sort of hopeless, final plea for justice; then retired, sick and discouraged, to the baths at Bourbon Archambault. From there on 30 August he wrote confidentially to Madison: "We have somewhat overrated our means of coercing the two great belligerents to a course of justice;" and he suggested an armed commerce instead of the futile embargo.[70] But Armstrong could not see behind the stage and evidently underestimated both the effect of the Embargo and the consideration given his last note. Certainly he did not realize that a reconsideration of the French policy was already at hand.

Just a few days prior to Armstrong's gloomy despatch of 30 August a new element had been interjected into the situation.[71] It was the arrival of a certain Captain Haley with instructions of 22 July for Armstrong to make new representations to the French government. Having the "solemn conviction" that anything he could do at the moment would be worse than useless Armstrong declined to act and so lost his opportunity.[72] For when several days had elapsed after Haley's return to Paris without any action being taken by Armstrong, Haley was summoned by the Minister of Marine for a conference on the political situation in the United States and regarding measures that should be taken by France to win popular favor there. The interview seems to have so impressed Decrès that he sent Haley to Champagny who, after two conferences, asked him on 17 September for a written statement

---

[70] *Am. State Papers, For. Rel.*, III, 256; and Lib. of Cong. MSS. for the full letters, also Armstrong's letter of 20 October on the impression made by the 6 August note.

[71] *Am. State Papers, For. Rel.*, III, 255-256.

[72] *Dept. of State, Desp. Fr.*, vol. 11, Armstrong to Madison, 24 Nov. 1808, with inclosures. For the disavowal of Haley see Smith to Armstrong, 15 March 1809, *Dept. of State, Instructions*, vol. 7, p. 36.

of his suggestions. This, Haley was unable to send until his return from Havre a month later. Meanwhile things were transpiring in the imperial Councils.

On 11 September Collin de Sussy, Director General of the Customs, presented to Napoleon a report on the neutral, particularly the American, situation.[73] Direct evidence is lacking as to the precise circumstances which had called out this letter but its connection with the Bordeaux petition and Armstrong's note of the first days of August is obvious. Moreover, it was subsequent to the first interviews of Decrès and Champagny with Haley. In his report Collin propounded two questions which he "prejudged affirmatively." (a) "Will it be useful to hold in French ports the American vessels which arrive in ballast but load with goods useful to England?" (b) "Is it advisable to cause the arrest of all Americans who navigate in Europe?" His central argument was that the United States could not object to, and ought to welcome French aid in punishing Americans who were trading in Europe despite the Embargo.[74]

Napoleon referred Collin's report on 15 September to Decrès for his opinions upon it.[75] In his reply Decrès took issue with Collin for reasons which are an interesting development of Armstrong's views. "There is no doubt," he began, "that the Americans arrive in France only under a licence of the King of England." It was a requirement of the Orders in Council of November 1807, which could scarcely be evaded by the Americans unless the Orders were dead letter, and that they were still in force was shown by the strictness of the blockade and by the arrival on 13 September of the ship *Junon* with a British licence. "There is then a moral certitude," he continued, "that all the

[73] AF^{IV}1318, no. 25.

[74] As to fraudulent devices of American ships remaining in Europe, who were sailing under both American and French or Danish colors, with English licences, etc., see *Dept. of State, Cons. letters*, Bordeaux, vol. II, 1 Nov. and 17 Dec. 1808.

[75] AF^{IV} 1318, no. 24.

neutrals which enter our ports infringe the blockade decree of 21 November. But is it then in the interest of your Majesty to arrest them?" There is "no other means of giving an outlet to the products of our soil. This outlet is especially advantageous to the state since the vessels which are concerned in it come in ballast and the payment for the goods is made without exchange by an acquittal in specie which is the most advantageous a commercial state could desire, and has nothing preferable save an exchange of materials necessary for our manufactures. I think then that it is necessary to seem to ignore the action of England toward the neutrals who come in ballast into our ports, that it is necessary to exercise only on those who shall be convicted of violation of the decree of blockade all the penalties of that decree, but that it would be important to authorize not only the Americans, but all those who wish to export our surplus of wines, of grains, of brandy, and indeed the products of our manufactures. For the dignity of the decree of Blockade will not be violated in the least since it will be executed in all its forms and as to the effects there will result from it only the larger mass of specie in France, a small commission trade, and a benefit for the landlords and farmers, consequently for the fisc, to which they will find less difficulty in paying their contributions since the outlet for their produce will be more considerable."

Decrès also disagreed with Collin's argument "that Congress would thank Your Majesty" for the "competition" in enforcing the Embargo. "This embargo bears textually upon ships of that nation (United States) which are found in the local limits of the jurisdiction of Congress and upon no others." Moreover, no epoch having been set for the repatriation of vessels abroad there evidently was no intention to reach them. "But," he asked significantly, "is it in the interests of Your Majesty to arrest Americans on the open sea?" He thought not, and he also argued against the new rigors of blockade which would deprive the allies of the Empire of the only outlet for their products and the only source of their supplies. Yet he did hold that "just reciprocity" demanded the application of the Berlin and Milan decrees to those neutrals who went to the ports of the enemy or the enemy's allies.

Upon this last point, which he was inclined to adopt, Napoleon asked a further report which seems not to have been presented when he left for Germany on 22 September.[76] Apparently Champagny's request of 17 September for a written statement from Haley was also made after the consideration of Decrès's criticism of Collin's report. Haley's reply of 18 October stated that the United States would submit to French municipal trade regulations but would resist seizure on the high seas; also, that if the French decrees were limited to the Empire, it would disarm the Anglophiles in the United States. The letter is an interesting expression of opinions similar to those held by Armstrong and suggested likewise in his instructions from Madison. It remained, however, without reply, for as Armstrong said, "the Emperor, after his return from Erfurt did not transact any business which was not connected with that of Spain."

In truth, Armstrong's words might well have been the epitaph not only of Haley's unauthorized, and later disavowed, "diplomacy" but of the effort at a change of the imperial policy toward neutral trade in which he had played a part. Apparently the only immediate effect of the discussion was to increase the rigors of the Continental System with regard to the neutrals, as suggested by Collin and Decrès. Yet, like all the quickly abandoned experiments of the year 1808 by which Napoleon sought to ameliorate the baneful effects of the strict interpretation of his System, the freer trade policy urged by Decrès marked the certain trend of circumstances toward a system of exceptions—that is, a trade by special licences.

[76] This is indicated by notations upon these documents in AF^{IV} 1318. It is borne out by Armstrong's private letter to Madison of 20 October 1808, regarding statements made to him by Champagny that "His Majesty was disposed to remove all difficulties between the U. S. and France but that time was wanting at the moment to enter upon the business." Lib. of Cong., MSS.

CHAPTER III
Trade by Exception

By the close of 1808 unquestionably the whole drift of the Continental System was toward a trade by exceptions. Even leaving out of account the constant attrition of the English counter-blockade system with its entrepôts, convoys, licences, and smuggling accessories, or disregarding the growing political problems of the system there still remains evidence of the bald fact that Napoleon had not achieved his aims. He had failed to secure effectual co-operation in enforcing his interpretation of the system. Nor among all the expedients tried as substitutes for the neutral carrier had he obtained a satisfactory medium of maritime communication. Despite notable progress in certain respects, he was still far from having gained such economic independence for France, and the Continent, as would cause him to desire, or even permit his acquiescence in a status of isolation. Drifting was no real solution, even had drifting been possible to Napoleon. There was the chance, probably remote, and only momentarily considered, of the new toleration policy toward neutrals advised by Decrès. If Napoleon was not ready for this *volte face*, apparently the only alternative was a licence trade—a system of formal indulgences such as England had used for some years, or such, indeed, as Napoleon had inherited from the Directory and had suppressed by a decree of 16 July 1800.[1] The net result of the experiments of 1808 was to accentuate this tendency, to make the evidences plain, to provide features which could be incorporated into the new program. All the Emperor's ministers whose functions had brought them into close touch with the situation recognized the trend of conditions, especially Decrès, Cretet, and Collin, and

[1] *Moniteur*, no. 305. Pariset, in *Cambridge Modern History*, IX, 123, says Napoleon had granted licences prior to 1806, and established the system by a decree of 12 January 1806. But all evidence is to the contrary, and he evidently refers to the decree of 11 January on *diplomes de licencié* (army discharge papers.)

they had advised accordingly. Yet, however much such advice may have aided in clearing the ground, it is doubtful whether they would have proposed, or really wished, a French licence system. It is also improbable that such a policy would have been adopted by Napoleon had not pressure come at this critical moment from a most effective quarter.

Now the first article of Napoleon's economic confession was the good of agriculture.[2] Chaptal has said that the Emperor feared nothing else so much as he did the possibility of an agrarian disturbance.[3] The warning of such a possibility was at this time the decisive touch which determined the breach in the Continental System. That which the demands of allies and neutrals, of planters, traders, and manufacturers, of financiers and philanthropists had hardly been able to wring from him, that concession the farmer obtained. Where sugar and cotton, yes and quinine, had failed, there, grain succeeded. And yet we still must not forget, when we see the suddenness of the surrender, that the demand of the agriculturist had the peculiar advantage that it came hard upon all these previous assaults.

November 22, 1808, Charles Auguste Loyseau, merchant at Havre, being in Paris, wrote a letter to the Minister of the Interior enclosing a memoir of two and a half folio sheets, "On opening a means of exportation of grains from the ports of the ci-devant Basse Bretagne."[4] If the concensus of judgment be true that the Continental System was the prime policy of Napoleon and that the licence trade defeated the purpose of that policy, then this letter is surely of first importance.[4a]

The memoir grew out of an audience with Cretet the previous day regarding certain cases of vessels which being unable to sail had been forced to unload their cargoes of grain. This personal

---

[2] Las Cases, *Journal*, IV, 196-201.

[3] Chaptal, *Mes Souvenirs sur Napoleon*; see also Gourgaud's *Sainte-Hélène*, I, 561-3.

[4] F^{12}1966.^{D}

[4a] But see *supra* page 58, note 32a.

experience had led to a general investigation of the situation and had resulted in Loyseau's visit to Paris for relief.

The departments of the old Basse Bretagne being very fertile were accustomed to raise a large surplus of wheat. This once served for provisioning the fleet at Nantes, or the army, before circumstances cut off the maritime demands and removed the army to distant regions. The surplus was formerly exchanged at Bordeaux for wines but now "the coasting trade has become so difficult" that the wines have to be transported by land, a mode too expensive and slow for grains. "There has resulted a superabundance on the hands of the proprietors, they have already three harvests in their granaries without the least outlet, without power to procure the funds necessary for their daily needs and for the payment of their impositions." For their relief an imperial decree of 15 July 1806 permitted the export of grains from Nantes, a privilege extended to other ports of the province, but the ports on the Channel getting no relief, as no vessel came to take advantage of the favor accorded, an appeal to the Ministry brought a decision that dispensed with *acquits à caution* (receipts for bonds), as unnecessary, substituting instead a simple *acquit de payement*.[5] This brought many neutrals—Portuguese, Americans, and Danes— and resulted in the sale of the third crop and a doubling of prices. Then came the Danish belligerency, the Orders in Council, with the resultant Embargo by the United States,[6] and the Emperor's reprisal decree of 17 December. "The permission of exporting remained in all its extent, but the vessels retained or frightened by the measures of the two belligerent powers ceased to navigate, and the exportation ceased actually in default of vessels."

Now the same abundance as in 1805 and 1806 afflicts the region; the price is lower than in any of the markets of Europe, and "the landlords being almost all paid in kind, following the custom of the region, experience, through the impossibility of realizing on

[5] Williams, *State of France*, II, 191, gives corroborative evidence on the situation of the farmers of western France in 1806.

[6] Yet historians say the embargo was not felt in France.

their grains even at low price, the same embarrassment in providing for their daily needs and acquitting their debts to the state." Therefore, in order to bring about a new exportation, Loyseau urges the modification of the decree ordering the seizure of vessels visited at sea by the English. "The Decree of 17 Xbre has been rendered as a measure of reprisal, it is just that it subsist in all that may injure the English; but as the King of England has reserved by the same Orders in Council the faculty of making all the changes therein that circumstances shall render necessary for the good of his subjects, it would appear wise that the Decree of reprisals might equally undergo modifications in the cases where they are hurtful to us without causing the least prejudice to our enemies."

He urges that the decision of the Minister of the Interior should stand in its full extent and that also orders be given to the customs and the marine not to apply the December decree to vessels coming in ballast to export products of the soil of France. It will be equally favorable for the exportation of wines, brandies, oils, seeds, cloths, etc. The condition of coming in ballast to load a cargo of products of our soil, infers the necessity of paying the account in specie and of such operations turning entirely to the profit of the agriculture and the commerce of France."

There is no *categorical* proof that this paper caused the inception of the licence trade in France, but the indications are strongly in favor of this assumption. That is to say, we have no statement that it had such an effect, nor any specific reference to it, or to Basses Bretagne at the time of Napoleon's decision for the licence experiment. And yet other facts indicate its influence: (1) The appeals of Basses Bretagne had always received prompt attention, and from the consideration already shown Loyseau there is no reason to suppose that his representation would receive any less favorable reception than that accorded earlier appeals: (2) The manner of registration and preservation of the paper shows it was considered important. (3) The often reiterated justification for the inauguration of the licence trade was the imperative need of relief for agriculturists to enable them to pay their taxes; yet we look in vain for a concrete basis for such an assertion, except Loyseau's memoir. (4) More strikingly significant still is the fact that precisely Loyseau's arguments and proposals for relief are used by Napoleon in his initial instructions.[7]

The Loyseau memoir was received and registered 23 November 1808.[8] Napoleon was then in Spain engrossed in the task so portentous for his fortunes. If the memoir was sent him, which is improbable, he took no action upon it. He did not return to Paris until 24 January. Meanwhile, support came for Loyseau's petition from a surprising quarter. It was no less than the appeal of bitterest foe to bitterest foe for help, and the response was more surprising than the appeal.

The year 1808 closed critically for England and darker days loomed ahead. The Russian ukase of 5-17 June was cutting off the main source of her naval supplies, thus striking at her seapower. The rigorous pressure of Napoleon upon all states of Europe was closing the continent effectually as an outlet for her piled up wares. Heligoland was proving a snare, Malta and Sicily were barely "discovered." The bubble of substitute markets in South America was bursting disastrously for her deluded merchants. The American embargo had closed yet another old and reliable market, had struck at the subsistence of her West Indian colonies, had deprived her of a despised, but valuable carrier. Her dubious allies were the half-mad King of Sweden, already as good as beaten in his war with Russia, a Portuguese Regent of Brazil ungratefully wrangling over treaties, and a sandy rope of insurgent Spanish Juntas. Her credit was low, her expenses were heavy. Her capitalists were shaking, her workmen often without labor were ready for rioting. But with all this a growing scarcity of food supplies confronted her. Years of crop

[7] Licence Form 1, 11 March, Instructions of 14 April and especially 16 April, to the Prefects.

[8] "Enregistré le 23, 9bre. no. 889."

shortage had come in succession.[9] Deprived by Napoleon of her old continental resources, cut off by her own obstinate bullying from the abundant harvests of the United States,[10] she stood, as it looked, facing death and disaster.[11] And her remedy? The *Licence Trade*. Her granary? The perishing harvests of the Empire of France.

Neither the remedy, nor the source of supply was new to the British government.[12] From the inception of the licence scheme grain had headed the list of allowed articles in "import permits" for France and its "appanages." But the situation in the autumn of 1808 demanded stronger measures. The British government had therefore begun to grant a new "special licence" designed particularly to draw grains, flour, and burr-stones from France, Flanders and Holland. News of this action must already have begun to filter into France when the Breton farmers made their appeal through Loyseau. For it was the practice of the Board of Trade to send for suitable merchants on such occasions, who would present such of their correspondents as could be of service with certain of the new licences. Such, then, was the British proposal. What was the French response?

Among the archives of the imperial government touching commerce, in a bundle of papers marked "essential to the Licences,"

[9] See letters in *Gentleman's Magazine*, 1808, also the monthly grain quotations therein. Almost the entire first decade of the century had seen short crops.

[10] Cf. McMaster, vol. III, 293-4; also Pitkin, *Statistical View of the United States*. Rose says that Great Britain had imported practically no grain from the United States. If so, why then such strong statements by British pamphleteers of the time?

[11] Cf. the striking letter of Pinkney to Madison, 21 September 1808: "The Embargo and the loss of our trade are deeply felt here, and will be felt with more severity every day. *The wheat harvest is likely to be alarmingly short* and the state of the continent will augment the evils. The discontents among their manufacturers are only quieted for the moment by temporary causes." "*Suppressed Letters*," p. 22.

[12] The licence trade with France dates from September 1796. Cf. *Privy Council Register*, vol. 39 (of George III), pp. 279, 499, etc.

is found a wrapper (with enclosures), endorsed by the Imperial Secretary of State "Nouvelle Redaction Envoyée par Ordre de l' Empereur au Ministère de l' Interieur. Rambouillet, 11 Mars 1809."[13] It contains the following papers: a letter dated 21 December from a London merchant to a French correspondent replying to certain questions regarding grains and food stuffs and enclosing an Order in Council, and a grain licence granted 12 October 1808 to Richard Page, and with them the *first* and the second *draft of an Imperial licence*. That was the French response. Thus began the French Licence Trade.

As the initiation of a licence trade was an undeniable break from the Continental Blockade, so the London letter of 21 December becomes a document of special interest. It begins with a full discussion of the demands of the London market for grains and foodstuffs and then turns to a demonstration of the practicability of supplying this demand. The London merchant assures his French inquirer that neutral vessels from France to England are not confiscated, and that the simple reclamation by the owner of goods on board secures the release of a vessel when seized. This would make licences superfluous, but a licence costs less than £15 and is a good precaution. He gives rates of insurance and freight. As to the securing of vessels, he mentions that there are plenty of American and Hanse vessels there to freight because they can be assured that they can resort freely to France and will not be molested there. It is better to deal with established houses than grain factors. He suggests Greffulke Bros. as having good credit, as being well-established, and one of the best placed houses for such a business. "For business on a very large scale the house of Baring alone has the advantage over Greffulke and everyone." He continues with this very illuminative passage: "As you attach so much importance to knowing positively whether licences can be attained for vessels even under the French flag (just as I have informed you), I have required Mr. Greffulke to call personally

[13] F^{12}2051.

upon the Minister charged with this business and make this demand of him. The response is that licences would be given under the French flag to ships bringing grain here;[14] on condition that these vessels should not be French-built nor have any French men in the crew (including the captain). But all the ports of France are choked with prizes which could be freighted and even bought at a low price, and the difficulty of a crew of any other country than France (for the Dutch sailors will be readily admitted) is no greater than for the neutral ships, and the certainty of having licences for the French flag in spite of these restrictions (which will be held to strictly) is always a facility in addition, upon which you may count in your calculations." He closes with a discussion of the colonial produce situation in England, and with a depreciation of the effects of the Continental Closure, and of the American Embargo upon England.

There is, of course, no real clue as to the identity of either correspondent. The inference is strong that they were simply the channels used by the two governments for an underhand commercial deal, one of the first of a number of such negotiations induced by the anomalous situation. In other words that the correspondence was started at the instance of the Board of Trade, then the French government, following up Loyseau's memoir, learned of the original English letter and used this already opened channel to secure further authoritative information.

Thus stood the grain export question when Napoleon returned to Paris, 24 January 1809. "The affairs of Spain are finished," he had written Jerome on 16 January, as he prepared to leave Valladolid. And it seemed that he spoke truly for hot upon his track came word of the defeat and death of Sir John Moore.[15]

[14] This is borne out by action of the Privy Council on 19 and 28 January, and 22 February 1809, by which the French flag could be used except within one or two British ports and ships might have French masters but could not be French built or manned. These decisions applied to trade with France, Spain and the Baltic, (Privy Council, Unbound Papers).

[15] Napoleon left 17 January, arrived 24 January, the battle was fought 16 January, and he had the news 29 January. Cf. *Cor. de Nap.*, 18:251.

The Emperor had thus himself retrieved the reverses, and the disgrace of Baylen, met by his generals in the summer previous. He had quelled the Juntas, he had driven the English almost from the Peninsula.[16] He could look back upon an unprecedented array of victories and achievements, a record of scarcely varied success, for few and comparatively inconsequential were the checks or failures. The ultimate failures the world did not see then, surely not Napoleon. If, indeed, the results of the Continental System were yet indecisive, victory surely was far from lost. It might be—in truth, as we judge today, may have been—at hand. So lay the backward road. Just ahead he faced, even as he could foresee, another Austrian conflict. Yet what cause had he to fear a foe he had so often met, and as often signally vanquished? He was aware, apparently, of the projected Walcheren expedition.[17] Was he not able then to predict its ignominious futility? Today, we know the successes of 1809. We see also its errors. And among the latter many would reckon the licence trade.

That the licence trade or some similar readjustment must have come eventually, perhaps even soon, unless still sooner the Continental System itself were to stand victorious—this we have already seen. And the peculiar potency of the agricultural appeal—this too we have seen. Verily the impulsion was strong, and yet when the arguments are weighed and the circumstances scrutinized, that the break should have come just *when* it did, and upon the *grounds* that it did, seems neither physically necessary, nor of itself inevitable. But there are psychological exigencies stronger than physical ones, and we know that facts as they are, often are less potent than facts as they seem to be. In 1809 this was as true as it is today.

Early in February, directly upon his return from Spain, Napoleon began to receive conclusive evidence of the failure of even the

[16] *Cor. de Nap.*, 18:231. "The armies of Spain have been destroyed, that of England has been driven to the sea." (15 January 1809).

[17] *Cor. de Nap.*, 18:282, 22 Feb., to Louis; and 18:294, 1 March, to Champagny.

latest of his 1808 trade-relief expedients.[18] He also realized the strength of the pressure for a modification of the anti-commercial system which recently had been exerted by Russia, pushed on by Denmark, Prussia, and the smaller powers—"who are literally starving under the present situation"—and supported by similar demands from the United States, and even the commercial and manufacturing interests of France.[19] It was at this moment evidently that he received the various papers regarding the grain export proposition. He at once took measures to meet the situation. He offered on 16 February to release American vessels from embargo, but with later conditions which the American Minister protested were equivalent to a licence [20] Investigations were made as to the number of neutral vessels in the northern ports available for exporting grain.[21] Finally he dictated a plan to Cretet directing him to draw up a form of licence and instructions for the new project.[22]

The first effort made by Cretet to meet the Emperor's requirements having been returned by Napoleon with various alterations, a second draft was submitted.[23] Both drafts were returned in a letter of 11 March and a further report required. The response was Cretet's note of 15 March beginning: "Your Majesty has himself dictated a project of licences to be granted to foreign vessels to export from France the products of its growth. I have

[18] Cf. *Cor. de Nap.*, 18:255, 291, and 314.

[19] *Dept. of State.*, *Desp. Fr.*, vol. 11, Armstrong to Madison, 6 December 1808, et seq.

[20] *Ibid.*, Armstrong to Madison, 16 and 21 February and 25 March, and a note from Champagny of 20 February. In *Cons. letters*, Bordeaux, vol. II are copies of Armstrong's letter of 23 Feb. to Lee, also the French decree of 25 Feb. 1809, on the release of detained American ships.

[21] See Paullee to Cretet, 4 May, referring to correspondence prior to 15 March. F^{12}2051.

[22] The order itself is missing and the date is not given but a letter of some months later to Fouché indicates 14 February as the date when Napoleon decided upon licences. See *Cor. de Nap.*, 20:48.

[23] F^{12}2051.

the honor to submit this same project"—suggesting therewith four clerical provisions for effecting its execution.[24] The same day was registered in the Secrétariat Général of the Ministry of the Interior the copy of a proposition to his Majesty "for giving effectiveness to a form of licence which he had himself decreed."[25] This was the inauguration of the Napoleonic licence trade, and not, let it to be noted, the decrees of July and August 1810, as has been very commonly assumed.[26]

The onus of the adoption of the licence trade, if onus there be, is thus placed undeniably upon Napoleon. And that there was felt to be such an onus at the time is strongly suggested by the precision of the ministerial language touching its authorship. The evils of the British licence trade were already well-known, and were erelong stoutly assailed by Judge Phillimore, one of the highest legal authorities in England.[27] Within the year, in France itself, no less commercial authority than Baron Ternaux had published a "Mémoire en faveur de la liberté du Commerce contre les licences."[28] Clearly Napoleon must have been aware of the evils inherent in a licence system. The licence trade, however, was an

[24] Cf. also Cretet's notation on Montbret's letter of 10 April, "The measure of exportation by way of licences is a measure created by the Emperor *proprio motu*." F¹⁷2051.

[25] F¹² 2051.

[26] M. Chas. Schmidt of the Archives Nationales, who is an authority on the Continental System, told me that he had found no licence decree prior to February 1810. This evidently accounts for the vagueness of all writers touching licences prior to July 1810.

[27] Cf. his pamphlet: "*Reflections on the Nature and Extent of the Licence trade.*" London, 1811. Phillimore was an attorney before the High Court of Admiralty and a professor of International law at Oxford. His work was speedily translated into French and a *bound MS*. copy of it may be found among the Imperial Archives, AF^{IV}1062, dossier 2, no. 72. For a very interesting and judicial discussion of his book see the *Quarterly Review*, 1811. For earlier attacks upon the English licences see: Hansard's *Parl. Debates*, X, 185-9, 923, (January-March 1808), also pamphlets like "*Hints to Both Parties.*"

[28] Paris, 1808. Ternaux was an important member of the Chamber of Commerce. Unfortunately I can find no copy of the book.

effective instrument, as the Emperor must already have had reason to know. The English system was a keen rapier wielded with all the adroitness of a quick and practised wrist. But, even so, likewise, was the broadsword of Napoleon's closure, in his hands, a powerful weapon. Long use had taught him address with his heavier blade; his enemy's sword he did not know. How great the risk thus to change foils in such a duel! And when thereby one puts his enemy on guard even while opening one's own defense–how great, how imperative, must be the warrant for an action so foolhardy! Yet not dissimilar to this has seemed Napoleon's policy in 1809.

Thus the question becomes for the moment not so much the expediency of a licence trade, in general, as the justification of grain export licences, in particular, in the situation then existent. This has naturally evoked critical discussion. For example, that keenest of English authorities upon the Continental System, Mr. J. Holland Rose, has repeatedly emphasized the surprising tactical error of Napoleon's grain trade encouragements. "It is strange that he never sought to cut off our corn supplies," says Mr. Rose. "But that strange mental defect of clinging with ever-increasing tenacity to preconceived notions led Napoleon to allow, and even to favor, exports of corn to us in the time of our utmost need."[29] And elsewhere touching Napoleon's grain exports, Mr. Rose finds "the only explanation of this strange blindness of his in presence of the utmost favorable opportunity of his life seems to be this. He clung to the crude old mercantilist theory that imports weakened a state while exports strengthened it."[30] Miss Cunningham in her very suggestive study within the field[31] has pointed out the same critical blunder although coming rather closer to its explanation by fitting it into a consistent effort to break England's credit by draining away her gold.[32] Both scholars,

[29] Rose, *Life of Napoleon*, II, 203-6.
[30] Rose in *Cambridge Univ. Lectures*, etc., p. 75.
[31] Cunningham, *British Credit in the Last Napoleonic War*, p. 60.
[32] Cf. also, Rose in *Camb. Mod. Hist.*, IX, 372.

however, by following, here at least,[33] the common error of putting the inception of the licence trade and the grain export policy apparently in 1810, have based their explanations upon irrelevant data. This in nowise, however, impugns their judgment of the great lost opportunity, which is a conclusion based on quite other evidence. One may accept or reject this judgment; but is it not thought-provocative?

If, indeed, Napoleon thus lost the chance of his life it was not, as the evidence certainly shows, for the mere hope of breaking English credit, *per se*, and clearly not by blind clinging to an old mercantilist theory. Instead it was apparently because of the irresistible trend of events and through the choice of the only expedient offered for the pressing need of the moment.[34] Judgment then hinges upon the question "Was the situation imperative?" For if the plethora of French grains was a vital distress, if the menace to the fisc were actual and critical, if the seriousness of the English crisis could not be detected, or perhaps even if the gates intended to be opened simply for a moment, really could not again be closed, this doubtless would be an excuse for Napoleon. But if he were deluded, if he swerved from his course at the lure of his enemy, if he were frightened at a farmer's scarecrow of distress, or stumbled at a mere bogie of unpaid taxes, surely that were a clown's prank of his jester—fate. For truly it would be incomprehensible that Napoleon should deliberately have spurned a life's chance.

Napoleon himself said to Las Cases when it was all over: "The system of commercial licences was no doubt mischievous. Heaven forbid that I should have adopted it as a principle. It

[33] In one instance at least Mr. Rose refers to "analogous expedients of 1809-10" but he does not there base his interpretation on the date of 1809. Cf. *Camb. Mod. Hist.*, IX, 375. He also speaks of the licence system getting its final form in 1810, but without changing the interpretation given here.

[34] For striking contemporary judgments of the policy see the article by Wm. Cobbett in his *Political Register*, 2 June 1810, and the reply of Lewis Goldsmith in the *London Sun*, 26 June, (copied in the Philadelphia *Aurora*, 29 Sept. 1810). Note also the criticisms of Niles in his *Weekly Register*, 1:447.

was the invention of the English; with me it was only a momentary resource."[35] That was his judgment at St. Helena upon his action. He had expressed a like opinion at Elba.[36]

No recent criticism of Napoleon's action in this matter, however, is keener or more cogent than was that of Coquebert Montbret,[37] chief of the Second Division in the Ministry of the Interior, when on 10 April he reported to his chief, Cretet:

> His Majesty has just transmitted to your Excellence a licence granted by the English Government to Messrs. Cheminant and Kerkhove to favor the transport of grains even on ships going from France under the French flag.
>
> This licence is of 16 March.
>
> It shows more and more the extreme need the English are under to obtain grain from France and this need can only increase from this period, the last events in Sweden giving ground to presume that the Baltic will be more straitly closed this year to the English commerce than it could be the past year.
>
> I observe that the English admit the grains coming from France only in the King's Ports, to wit, those between Portsmouth and Falmouth on the one coast, and between Dover and Harwich on the other coast, and that they require these vessels to go there under convoy whenever the need shall be.
>
> Thus the corn which goes out of France is destined to victual the fleets, the armies, and the possessions of England.[38]
>
> Ought we to give them this facility?
>
> Should one in general, in any case when one is at war, do that which is ardently desired by the enemy?
>
> I think not.
>
> I think rather that it is advisable to require of those vessels which leave France loaded with *grain*, legal proof that they have discharged their cargoes at least elsewhere than in the British possessions.
>
> This measure might be modified by events, but I believe it a Policy, just and necessary in the present moment.

---

[35] Las Cases, *Journal*, IV, 200.

[36] *Harper's Magazine*, January 1911.

[37] One of the ablest and longest tenured officials of the Ministry.

[38] Compare: d'Ivernois, *Effects of the Continental Blockade*, p. 139. "I should not be at all astonished to find that the Victualling Office was at this moment buying up flour at Bordeaux though it were only for the sake of constituting Napoleon *principal Victualler of the British Army and Navy*."

I have believed I should tender my opinion to your Excellency, submitting always to your views (a ses lumières). I pray you to accept with your accustomed goodness, the homage of my profound respect.
Coquebert Montbret.

I add that it could happen, if the precaution which I indicated is not taken, that a ship furnished with a licence might be captured on the sea navigating under convoy, or in a port of Spain occupied by the English arms, or in fact any other place, which would decidedly conflict with the idea that should be attached to a permit given by his Majesty and delivered by his Minister.

Your Excellency has just transmitted to me at this moment a letter from the Minister of Exterior Relations which seems to me to render the delivery of licences useless in the majority of cases.

I beg Your Excellence to examine in your wisdom whether it will not suffice for the moment to deliver them to Prussian vessels of which Monsieur Champagny speaks, the inconveniences which I apprehend being no longer the same when it concerns a port like Bordeaux, of which the exportations will consist principally of wines and brandy.
Coquebert Montbret.

The comment at the head of this letter is scarcely less significant: "the measure of exportation by way of licences is a measure created by the Emperor *propria motu*. [We must] then execute it. It is known that H. M. in reserving the distribution of the licences and restricting them to a small number has arranged at the first chance to stop the operation. Cretet."

It is evident then from Cretet's statement, even as long afterward Napoleon himself admitted, that when the "British-invented" licence measure was borrowed, it was not as a principle but simply as a temporary expedient. In other words here was only another experiment such as those of a year prior. And of this the indirect evidence also affords confirmation. This is shown in three ways: 1st, by the tenor of the "form of licence" first adopted; 2nd, by the initial regulations, framed, as Cretet has explained, to control or restrict at will the scope of the affair; 3rd, through the incidents of the early stages of its evolution.

Logically the first problem in establishing the licence system was to devise a form of permit manifesting the protection granted. The licence determined upon in March 1809 illustrates well the character of the program of which it was the sign and guarantee. It typifies the great caution and the apparent reluctance that actuated the entrance upon this new experiment. In form and scope, and in principle, it differs much from the British examples which Napoleon had before him. It is not a copy, but rather a studied adaptation and modification of the model used. It also differs so essentially from its successor, the licence system of July 1810, that the two schemes are carefully distinguished in the records. The line between the *ancien système*, as it is termed, and the second program may be briefly stated as the distinction between what may be conveniently called "a *scheme* of special *exceptions*," in contrast with "a regular *system* of *exemptions*." The original licences, i.e., those of the first form or nomenclature, hedged these special "exceptions" closely round with restrictions. These were of two sorts, precautionary guarantees and limitations of scope.

One token of precaution—a visible departure from the British model[39]—appears in the mechanical form of the licence. The French passports were printed from a special "block" in diploma form with a detachable coupon portion, which would be preserved at the Ministry.[40] All required facts must be filled in before issuance. Each licence must be numbered, signed by several officials and sealed by the Secretary of State. Thus special care was taken to guard against counterfeit documents. Special provision was made by the formula of the licence to insure a *bona fide* transaction and to curtail the scope of the trade as far as the points of peculiar pressure would permit.[41]

[39] At this time the British licences were small fasciculi with no special characteristics of print or paper. They were not numbered and had no coupons. They were regularly issued in *blank* save for the grantee's name. The official signature was printed and they were countersigned and sealed merely by a Privy Council clerk.

[40] The idea was that the licences should be bound in a register but this seems not to have been done. The *talons* or stubs were cut off and are still preserved in the Archives.

[41] See for these provisions the Official Instructions of 14 April. F^{12}2051.

Cretet's report of 15 March transmitting the final draft of this first form of licence has already been noted as significant in placing the responsibility of the new measures, but it is also an interesting document typical, in its very rudimentary nature, of the transitory purpose of the licence measure. It illustrates, as well, the point put forward in Cretet's remark on the Montbret note of 10 April that the Emperor intended so to control the issuance of the licences as to end the affair immediately at will. Cretet's proposal was for the printing of a limited number of the licences, with arrangements as to the register and coupon (talon) features already noted. A certain number (say twenty) of these blank permits he thought should be signed by the Emperor, countersigned and sealed by the Secretary of State and delivered to the Minister of the Interior who should make weekly reports upon their distribution.[42]

The fundamental act of providing licences was only the first step, however, toward the execution of the experiment. Administrative organization and policy must yet be developed. This process was a gradual one for it grew out of the solution of practical problems just as they arose. It is therefore from a consideration of some of the shaping problems that the evolution of the system can best be understood.

The receipt of the first four applications on 25 March raised one of the earliest of the working problems of the licence experiment. It entailed the making of clerical arrangements to oversee the investigation of applications and to handle the resultant routine work. From the experiences of a letter on licence matters which at this stage of the affair was being shunted about among the officials of the Ministry it is evident that the new business was not

---

[42] Comments written by Cretet upon the notice sent him of the registration of the imperial decision for licences, show that by the decision reached only twenty were to be printed privately and that the "cut" was to be kept locked in the Minister's cabinet. We learn that these twenty licences were sent to the Emperor 28 March for his signature. $F^{12}2051$. They were sent by Fauchat.

welcomed. Thus Montbret had already too much on his hands, Fauchat pleaded his ignorance of the whole affair, and so they made excuses. However, we soon find the business in charge of Fauchat where it remained until the creation of the Ministry of Commerce in 1812. During this period, judging from the notable reports and innumerable papers of all types emanating from his hand, it is safe to affirm that Fauchat was probably the chief single force in shaping the foreign trade measures of the Empire.

The active inauguration of the licence measure did not wait, however, upon clerical readjustments at the Ministry. Thus on 14 April initial instructions were issued to the prefects for setting at work the new commercial experiment. Merely because of the voluminous body of correspondence which it began, and the extensive branch of administrative routine which it created the circular would be significant, but it has another interest as well. For incidentally it affords an exceptionally clear explanation of what the licence trade was intended to be. In fine both as a definition of the system, and as a program for its execution this letter is a basic document warranting our careful consideration.[43]

The circular of 14 April, probably drafted by Cretet himself, was addressed to each of the maritime prefects, the present copy being directed to the Prefect of the Gironde.[44] It runs:

> Monsieur, the Prefect, I am pleased to notify you that H. M. with the design of favoring the exportation of grains which he has permitted, and that of wines, brandies, liquors, fruits, dried or preserved, and vegetables has determined to accord some special licences to ships which may wish to take such cargoes. I am charged with the delivery of these licences signed with his own hand; but lest any might abuse this benefit His Majesty requires some conditions of which I am to give you cognizance.

---

[43] Besides the succession of circulars to the prefects and the replies and explanations which ensued, the execution of these instructions entailed much other correspondence with prefects. This is shown, for example, by the register of minutes which accompanied the expedition of all licences from the Ministry (F^{12}2050), also by the countless acknowledgments of the receipt and delivery of the licences, the admission and clearance of ships, etc. (F^{12} 2029.)

[44] F^{12} 2033.

The licences will be granted only to commercial houses, known and well reputed, who will afford surety for the captain and who will submit to answer for contraventions.

"Foreign flags will be admitted except those of England and her allies.

The requests for licences will be addressed to you to be verified by you and to be forwarded to me. They will contain the name of the ship, its flag, its tonnage, the number of men in the crew, the name of the captain.

There shall be mentioned, likewise, the name of the house under surety of which the expedition will occur, the place where it is established and the commercial title under which it is known.

Not a single one of these Passports or licences here discussed, will be delivered save on condition that it is as the result of inquests made with the greatest care. 1st, that the house which is proposed as surety has a well-established commercial existence and has never failed to meet its engagements; 2d, that the Chiefs and Directors of this house have constantly manifested their submission to the laws of the State, their attachment to the person of His Majesty, and their abstention from every criminal practice or intelligence with the enemy.

These conditions fulfilled to my entire satisfaction in a manner explicit and precise on all points, there will be delivered a passport stating that the ship described is authorized to fit out, navigate, and re-enter into the ports of the French Empire without receiving the least obstacle to its navigation or entry, the captain and the consignors fulfilling the formalities prescribed in the matter of the customs and paying the regular duties.

The passport will state, moreover, that the ship which shall be furnished therewith, shall be loaded only with wines, brandy, liquors, dried, fresh or preserved fruits, vegetables, grains and salt, nor may it when it shall come to re-enter the ports of France be allowed to introduce the least sort of colonial products, of merchandise the make or growth of England nor of any other nation except only timber, hemp, spars (*matures*) and Northern iron, quinine (*kina*) and medicines, and that if these dispositions should chance to be contravened the vessel will be confiscated, the owner subjected to damages as having transgressed the orders of His Majesty and the patent or passport declared null for him and for the commercial house which has been his guarantee.

I announce these regulations to the Maritime Prefects of the Empire because it is necessary that the traders established in the ports should be informed in order to address their petitions to me and that it should be properly arranged that no species whatever of Preference should have place in the distribution of permits among the persons qualified to receive them.

But I communicate this information to no one else and I recommend discretion in this matter to Messieurs, the Prefects, engaging them in no case to give a copy of my letter and to prevent anything contained in it from being made public, even hinted, by way of printing in the journals or otherwise. This matter, I ask you, Sir, to please observe strictly.

The measure which I communicate to you is flexible (*mobile*) in its nature, circumstances might suspend it, it is necessary to avoid presenting it as an absolute system and to preserve it in this way from the tumultous speculations to which it might give birth.

Receive, Monsieur the Prefet, etc.
(Signed) Cretet.[45]

Certain points in this circular are so striking as to merit attention, yet so clear as scarcely to need comment. Among them may be named: 1st, The temporary and secret character intended for the affair; 2nd, The reason assigned for granting the licences which is borne out by the very limited lists of permitted exports and imports, indicative evidently of the points where the situation was pressing closest; 3rd, The further proofs of the great precautions taken to render this limited concession real and beneficial to legitimate commerce, preventing all danger of treasonable acts, and, above all, any abuse in the issuance or use of the licence, such as "graft," discrimination, or speculation. This extreme solicitude on the part of Cretet, which will come out in other instances seems a really sincere effort to avoid scandal and maintain fair and impartial treatment in a transaction so extremely susceptible of all else.

If it had been possible to have secured observance of the precautions outlined in these instructions perhaps many counts would have been stricken from the arraignment of the licence system. But the British Government's experience had already shown the difficulty of maintaining equivalent precautions in such a business. For, having originated the idea with restrictions commensurate with those of Napoleon, the British had by 1809 abandoned almost all such checks.[46] The French system

---

[45] A variant version of this circular (dated 16 April) is of interest as being practically a paraphrase of the Loyseau memoir.

[46] See the *Privy Council Register*, vols. 34-84, (1794-1815), esp. the acts of 3 September and 5 October 1796, and 29 March and 28 May 1800. Unbound papers of the Privy Council show an effort in April 1809 to return to a stricter policy, but it failed.

was scarcely better calculated to resist attack. Thus in the first place not even the required secrecy could be observed, as it comes out in a protest from Fouché, 4 July 1809, that the *Journal de Paris* of 24 June had published, under "news from Rouen," a scheme of the system.[47] Nor was gossip probably incorrect in reporting much official corruption. In short the flood-gates erected to control and curtail the system at will were unable to withstand the pressure from applicants and officials. The character of this attack and the breaches made by it will appear when we come to note the actual workings of the system, or indeed, as we turn to trace the next line of administrative development, namely, the inter-ministerial relations growing out of the problem of securing proper enforcement of the licences.

Besides the communication with subordinate officials, another branch of correspondence of much significance in the licence administration, then, was inter-ministerial. There had been three initial problems in the evolution of the licence idea: (1) How to define and safeguard exportations, assuming them to be desirable; (2) how to secure applications for the protections to be granted; (3) how to utilize these protections properly, when obtainable. The solution of the first two questions was largely determined by the licence itself, by the initial instructions adopted, and by correspondence with the prefects. The solution of the third question, however, needed in addition the co-operation of other ministries, particularly those of Police, of the Direction of Customs in the Ministry of Finance, of the Marine, and of Exterior Relations.

The inter-ministerial correspondence dealt chiefly with two phases of the third problem as it has been here defined: (1) assurance of the recognition of, and respect for, the protections offered, (2) the obtaining of shipping capable of licence protection. The first phase involved Fouché, Collin, and Decrès, *ipso facto*, from the express purpose and tenor of the licences. For the licence was in the first place a protection against the ordinary

---

[47] $F^{12}2051$. Cretet replied that he was pained to hear of it.

restrictions enforced by the police, the navy, and the customs officials, but it was also conditioned in the second place, upon the performance of certain regulations from which the licence gave no exemption. Toward the solution of the second phase the Ministry of the Interior was aided by the correspondence of Decrès and Champagny.

The connection of other ministers than Cretet with the licence administration came as problems arose. Thus Fouché was formally notified of the policy on 22 May, so that the police and other local officials might no longer prevent or discourage merchants from participating.[48] Later the police had a problem maintaining secrecy regarding the trade. A news item in the *Journal de Paris* of 24 June, after some correspondence of Fouché with the Ministry of the Interior,[49] evidently resulted in edicts forbidding newspapers, without express sanction, to print anything as to government measures regarding licences.[50] Another later problem growing out of the trade was due to the desertion of neutrals, or prisoners of war who were used on the ships in order to meet English licence requirements. These desertions occuring abroad necessitated the filling of the deserters' places with seamen of dubious nationality who might be spies and hence required close watching while in French ports.[51] The Minister of Police, however, had an even more direct connection with the licence traffic than its surveillance. It was the use of this channel for secret service purposes. Little is known regarding this practice especially for the period (July-October) when both the Police and Interior administrations were under one head. But evidently, Fouché, as usual, abused his chance, for on 29 November in a sharp letter of reprimand Napoleon, after reminding him of measures taken on 14 February, said: "I have allowed you two licenced vessels,

[48] $F^{12}2050$. The prefects had written complaining of the police, *douanes*, and marine officers.
[49] $F^{12}2051$.
[50] See Fouché's letter of 11 Jan. 1810. $F^{12}2033$.
[51] $F^{12}2033$. 21 April 1810.

all others will be confiscated."⁵² Nevertheless on 23 February 1810, he asked, and two days later by imperial order obtained, four other licences, perhaps to aid in the secret negotiations about to begin with England.⁵³

Similar to the surveillance exercised by the Ministry of Police was the relation of the customs department of the Finance Ministry with respect to the licence trade. For, as part of their regular duties, the customs officers issued clearances, or admitted vessels to entry, and collected the usual tariff duties and shipping fees, after recognizing the validity of the ship's licence and verifying the exports and imports in accordance with its stipulations. Judging from the correspondence between the Director General of Customs and the Interior Ministry during the first month of the experiment, few difficulties arose except over an occasional case of a vessel entering with an expired licence, or over mooted questions of permittable goods.⁵⁴ Eventually, however, as the emphasis of the traffic shifted more and more to the fiscal side the functions of Collin de Sussy were correspondingly extended. Meantime there were immediate problems of surveillance and protection which had to be solved by the Ministry of Marine.

A not unwarranted fear of the attitude of French ships of war and corsairs toward the new passports is reflected in the recourse to marine safe conducts in 1809, as protections collateral with the licences. For the safe conducts which had been used in the experiment of 1808,⁵⁵ and earlier, were already known to the Marine.⁵⁶ They were now issued by the second division of the Ministry—"Police of Navigation"—to the Ministry of the Interior, upon application by the latter, and apparently without a special

⁵² *Cor. de Nap.*, 20:48.

⁵³ F¹²2057.

⁵⁴ Cf. F¹²2031, letters of Fouché of 12 July and 2 October 1809.

⁵⁵ See above pp. 67-70.

⁵⁶ See Peuchet, *Bibliothèque Commerciale*, VI, 340, for the use of marine passports in 1802.

fee. These safe conducts were at first written out, but a printed form soon became necessary. They repeated the essential facts and terminology of the licences, and consequently a change of the licence formula necessitated the adoption of new safe conducts.[57] They did not, however, correspond exactly in numbering.[58] They were signed by Decrès, and by Juriers *chef de la 2ᵉ Division* of the Ministry. Like the licences the safe conducts had to be returned on expiration.[59] Finally in February 1810 by imperial orders the use of safe conducts was abandoned.[60]

The securing of eligible vessels to conduct the licence trade, which has already been noted as a second phase of the problem of utilizing the passports, was a prime question. It had appeared in the first discussions leading to the licence idea, such as the Decrès report of September 1808, the Loyseau petition, and the December correspondence with London. The consent of the British Government to licence even vessels under the French flag appears not to have obtained favor in the eyes of Napoleon, perhaps because of the conditions affixed. In any case the first French licence formula, and also the circular of 14 April had stipulated the use of "any foreign flag save that of England or her allies." This was equivalent to stipulating the use of neutral vessels since the usual English licence (and English protections were a vital factor in assuring unmolested navigation) covered *foreign ships except French*. This situation permitted two courses to be pursued: (a) The selection of neutrals acceptable to both combattants, or (b) the disguising, i.e., the neutralization, of French vessels. Both courses were tried.

[57] See the correspondence of Montalivet and Decrès, 18 and 27 December 1809.

[58] Thus licence no. 3 and safe conduct 15 go together (which allows for the twelve earlier Barbary passports) but even this correspondence is soon lost.

[59] Probably two-thirds of the expired safe conducts were returned and are preserved in cartons $F^{12}2033$, $F^{12}2051$, $F^{12}2057$, $F^{12}2108$, etc. at the Archives Nationales.

[60] See $F^{12}2033$, (Decrès to Montalivet, 27 February); and $F^{12}2050$, (Montalivet's circular of 1 March 1810). They were proscribed 21 February and all blanks were burned the next day.

In the selection of mutually acceptable neutral flags three shifts of policy can be recognized during the period of inaugurating the French licence experiment. These shifts are coincident with three corresponding changes in American relations with the two belligerents.[61] This marked influence of American relations is logical, since, as the one true neutral of importance, the United States had the first right to profit by any relaxations of the anti-commercial system. This recognition of American claims had been the basis of Decrès's September 1808 report and had been the view generally held since 1806 by Napoleon's ministers. It might be inferred from the decree of 16 February, issued coincidently with the decision in favor of licences, that Napoleon had adopted the view of Decrès, for by the decree American vessels were to be freed at once from the general embargo, and apparently before those of other nations. But a few days later conditions were attached to the release which the American minister protested were not only an open discrimination against the United States but were equivalent to issuing French licences for American vessels to sail the high seas.[62] Not improbably the change of conditions for releasing American vessels was influenced by the arrival of news from the United States of the probable adoption of a non-intercourse act affecting trade with England and France.[63] Undoubtedly such news, as well as Armstrong's open objections to anything like licences for American ships, militated against allowing the use of the United States flag in the exceptional traffic contemplated. Doubtless also, Cretet and French merchants must have known that upon the score of the American

[61] See Adams, *History of the United States*, V, chapter 7.

[62] See Armstrong to Secretary of State, 21 February, 25 March, and 10 April, with enclosures including correspondence with Champagny, and with American consuls. *Dept. of State, Desp., Fr.*, vol. 11. See also note 20 above.

[63] See, the *Moniteur*, February 1809. But a private letter of 30 March from Armstrong to Madison tries to explain the change in French policy as due to suspicions aroused by statements in Parliament regarding American affairs (Lib. of Cong. MSS.).

Embargo the Board of Trade was at this moment regularly refusing licences to vessels under the American flag.[64] This was quite in line with Napoleon's own attitude toward the Embargo.[65]

The flags generally favored for English licences had for some time been those of the Hanse cities, which were peculiarly serviceable for a disreputable commerce. Consequently by special decisions of 3 February, 24 March, 10 May, and 17 August 1808 Napoleon had decreed the sequestre of ships of Pappenburg, Oldenburg, Mecklenburg, Kniphausen, Bremen, Hamburg, and Lübeck, because of their aid to the enemy in carrying on his trade.[66] Moreover, by a decree of 2 March 1808, Kniphausen had been annexed by Holland and its flag suppressed. After the release of American vessels Abel, Hanseatic minister at Paris, began a correspondence with Champagny lasting several months, reclaiming the release of Hanse vessels with permission to depart with French goods.[67] On 7 April Champagny announced that the Emperor would release these vessels on the proposed export condition.[68] Because of the general availability of these vessels they were at once accounted by both the shippers and the administration as the most eligible for use with the grain licences. In his despatch of 10 April, Armstrong told how every day strengthened his conjectures "that the creation of a spurious sort of neutrals under the name of Pappenburgers, Varelburgers, etc. is meditated the uses of which shall be commensurate with certain objects, and which shall entirely supersede the necessity of employing a flag really neutral."[69]

The almost coincident news of the passage of the Non-Intercourse Act of 19 March 1809, of the "Erskine agreement," and of the Order in Council of 26 April restricting the limits of the block-

[64] See P. R. O., B. T., 6/186 (Register of licence petitions and decisions).

[65] For Napoleon's views at this time see a letter to Champagny, 18 May 1809. *Cor. de Nap.*, 19:121.

[66] $F^{12}2033$.

[67] $AF^{IV}1318$, pièces 36 to 39.

[68] $F^{12}2050$.

[69] *Dept. of State, Desp. Fr.*, vol. 11.

ade of the Continent and contemplating the abolition of licences for blockaded ports, seemed to radically alter the commercial system.[70] It impelled Napoleon, who was involved in his war with Austria, to order negotiations between d'Hauterive, acting Minister of Foreign Relations, and Armstrong looking to a repeal of the Berlin and Milan decrees with respect to the United States.[71] This negotiation which lasted until mid–July clearly influenced the Emperor's attitude to the jeopardized French licence scheme. Cretet's report of 31 May shows that the flags selected were those of Prussia, Denmark, Hamburg, Lübeck, and Pappenburg, and that the first fifteen licences had been signed without objection. But a fresh list of licence requests was rejected on 12 June, ostensibly because of the decrees excluding the flags of Pappenburg, Oldenburg, and Kniphausen.[72] In reply to this Cretet protested that he had never been notified of the suppression of these flags and pointed out the injustice of requiring vessels already loaded and licenced to seek a new flag.[73] Maret replied 30 June that his Majesty consented that licences already delivered need not be withdrawn to change the flag.[74] The same day as the result of a long correspondence—involving the Prussian Minister and Champagny, Cretet, Montbret and Maret,—over the granting of safe conducts to Prussian vessels to export Bordelais wines, Napoleon decided " En la pavillon le plus convenable est la pavillon

[70] Adams, *History of the United States*, V chaps. 4 and 7; McMaster, *History of the People of the United States*, III, 367; *Dept. of State, Desp. Fr.*, vol. 11, (27 April–24 July), and *Cons. letters*, Bordeaux, vol. II; *Privy Council Register* and unbound papers for April 1809; the *Moniteur*, 15 and 17 May 1809, etc.

[71] The best account of this negotiation is in Adams, *History of the United States*, V, chap. 7, based upon *Dept. of State, Desp. Fr.*, vol. 11, and *Aff. Étr., Cor. Pol., États Unis*, vol. 62. But a resurvey of these sources and the use of other significant material, such as the Armstrong-Madison papers in the Library of Congress, has thrown new light on the affair.

[72] F^{12}2050, Maret to Cretet, from Schoenbrunn.

[73] AF^{IV}1242, 21 June, cf. also, Cretet's circular of 21 June to the prefects regarding flags *toujours exclus*, F^{12}2050.

[74] F^{12}2050.

Prussien puisque la Prusse n'est pas en guerre avec l' Angleterre."[75] On 13 July a further decision prescribed formalities whereby vessels of Kniphausen, Pappenburg, and Oldenburg might "participate in the measure of licences" under their "natural flags" of Holland and Prussia. The flag of Aremberg which had been called in question was also recognized.[76] Thus at the close of the second phase of the question the recognized flags for licences were those of Prussia (and apparently Denmark), and the minor flags of Hamburg, Bremen, Lübeck, and Aremberg.

The decision of 13 July was coincident with another alteration in Napoleon's view of the American situation. Having learned of the failure of the Erskine agreement and the practical nullification by England of the 26 April blockade order, the Emperor also discovered from a decree of the King of Holland that the Non-Intercourse Act discriminated against France in favor of the rest of the Continent. All this news at the very moment of his victory over Austria predisposed him against concessions to the United States. The d'Hauterive negotiations were therefore dropped, and, after considerable hesitation regarding his course, Napoleon at last offered conditions by which the United States might secure a relaxation of the Continental System. This was the famous Altenburg letter of 22 August.[77] Thereafter a few American vessels participated in the licence traffic.

The second course followed for securing eligible vessels was as already noted the use of disguised French vessels.[78] Simulations had been forbidden by the Emperor a year earlier. Probably the decree was disregarded, or was meant to forbid only one form of disguising, in any case when the prefects wrote for explications upon the question of ships permitted by the circular

[75] F^{12}2050, Maret to Cretet (*inédite*).

[76] F^{12}2050.

[77] Adams, *History of the United States*, V, 140–145; *Dept. of State, Desp. Fr.*, vol. 11, 4 and 16 September; *Aff. Étr., Cor. Pol., Holland*, vol. 613; *Cor. de Nap.*, 19:261, 374 and note.

[78] Cf. p.100, above.

of 14 April they were informed that though French ships could not be used as *such* under the licence rules, yet this restriction could be escaped by neutralizing such vessels.[79] The question came up shortly in concrete form and Cretet had to turn to Decrès for directions as to procedure in neutralization. He was informed that the initiative in cases of neutralization should come from the Minister of the Interior, who should state the name and domicile of the master, the name of the ship, the port where it was lying and the flag desired.[80] Later he was told that neutralization must follow the regulations of the *arrêt* of 13 prairial An XI (2 June 1803).[81] This act provided for neutralization of *French* vessels during the duration of a maritime war upon decision of the Minister of Marine. The master applying must give bond to the value of the ship for its return after peace to the national flag. The data touching the neutralization was registered to facilitate the enforcement of this requirement and to identify the vessel which had the right, its identity being shown, to escape any other duties than those levied on national ships during the continuance of the naval war.[82] The selection of the neutral flag was as important in this case as in that of neutrals who might benefit by licences, and the decision in the latter case applied as well to contingencies of neutralization. In other words, French vessels in the summer of 1809 might assume the flag of Prussia, the United States, Holland, Denmark, or one of the recognized Hanse cities. At the close of the year (18 Dec.) we learn that a free choice of flags (except that of the enemy) was permitted to vessels neutralized.[83] Requests for neutralization were classified according as they were for neutralization with licence, or without licence.

[79] $F^{12}2050$.

[80] $F^{12}2033$. Letter, 12 May 1809. Further directions were sent 17 June.

[81] Copy in $F^{12}2033$.

[82] Extract from the "Registers of Deliberations of the French Republic." (Transcript at University of Pennsylvania.)

[83] $F^{12}2050$. Letter of that date of Decrès to Montalivet.

With the second class the Minister of the Interior had nothing to do, such applications going directly to the Minister of Marine.[84]

Besides the correspondence with prefects, and with other ministries, the administration of licences involved some dealings immediately with persons interested in the trade. As this was usually discouraged the amount of correspondence directly with merchants or their attorneys was not great, and in many cases amounted to little more than directions to make their applications through the prefects, that is, the prescribed channel.[85] In a few cases, however, some interesting light is thrown on the actual workings of the system by petitioners upon specific points or by memorialists who relate their experiences or offer criticisms and suggestions. Some of these memoirs are well grounded and pertinent and apparently influenced ministerial policies. One of those worth especial notice is the letter of Dubois Viollette of Nantes, 14 October 1809, to Fauchat reciting his experiences with the grain licences and suggesting changes.[86]

Two of the personal petitions are of special interest as revelations of abuses which had to be fought. One of these dated 19 November 1809, from Phillibert Guillot and Co. is a complaint of the violation of a French licence.[87] The firm only succeeded in hurting themselves, however, as Montalivet was able to demonstrate from his records, as well as from an examination of the licence itself, that it was an English forgery. The other petition shows another abuse of the licence trade.[88] It was written at Paris, 11 April 1810, by a certain Mainot who was demanding justice from the minister for his having been imprisoned eight days on the denunciation of MM. Vincent and Fauchat for having

[84] $F^{12}2051$. Cf. a letter on the subject among those "Lettres aux demandeurs qui sont sollicités par des agens d'affaires." Correspondence on questions of neutralization was handled by the Division of Police of Navigation.

[85] $F^{12}2051$.

[86] $F^{12}2057$. The paper has some very interesting comments in Fauchat's hand developing those ideas advisable to utilize.

[87] $F^{12}2057$.

[88] $F^{12}2057$.

trafficed in licences. The papers in the case indicate that he probably had not been shown special consideration, but they leave little doubt that he was a rascal who had been properly denounced.

The fourth and most significant body of correspondence, in many respects, is that with the Emperor, chiefly through the medium of the Minister Secretary of State, Maret, duc de Bassano.[89] This correspondence may be classified as follows: (a) letters—usually Maret's replies to papers from the Ministry of the Interior, such as (b) weekly reports of the administration of the experiment as to its status; or (c) special queries of the Minister, etc; or (d) long general reports either at the demand of Napoleon or upon the initiative of the administration; also (e) records of licences—signed, sent, received, and delivered;[90] (f) statistics and records of sailings of licenced vessels; (g) general statistics of the trade. From this classification it is correctly inferred that the making of these frequent and sometimes elaborate reports meant the keeping of a variety of records. These records were an evolution and an experiment and thus despite their routine nature are very interesting evidences of the growth of an administrative mechanism, throughout its various stages.[91] The main interest of these reports and records, however, lies in their value as a basis for tracing the development and results of this licence scheme as a commercial experiment.

It has been purposed to show thus far in our study of the *ancien* licence system, three points: first, its origin—that is, the circumstances of its suggestion, and its adoption, with some consideration of the underlying motives and the expediency of this action; second its establishment, which has involved a definition of the

[89] These records form at least half or two-thirds of the eight large cartons, $F^{12}2050$–$F^{12}2058$, which deal particularly with the old licence system.

[90] Both offices sent check lists which gave a complete record of each licence.

[91] They are so well kept that we find records of licence distribution from the daily rough sheets to formal registers, some records being made in several copies, presumably for different officers.

project; third, the moulding of administrative policy and methods—seen through the consideration of certain elementary problems. It remains for us to consider this licence project from the special point of view with which it was undertaken—that is, as a measure of partial economic amelioration. First, how did the program work, and what modifications did it undergo? Second, what were the extent and results of the trade? Third, what were its effects, and how far did it mortgage or dictate the policy of the future?

CHAPTER IV
THE LICENCE EXPERIMENT

The developments of the 1809 policy of trade by exception were very significant for Napoleon's economic program. The evolution of this temporary, groping licence experiment into the basis for recasting the French navigation system has three phases. The first period is the administration of Cretet as Minister of the Interior, the second the *ad interim* service of Fouché, the third the first months of Montalivet's service.

The effort of Cretet in directing the new licence scheme was to inaugurate and manage the measure as closely as possible in accord with the letter and spirit of its projection under his own eye. In this his aim seems to have been as conscientious and scrupulous as his information was intimate. Unfortunately illness cut short his services about the first of July. Within the brief period of his direction the growth of interest in the licence plan was striking. It had begun with four applications on 25 March, several days before the sending of instructions to local officials.[1] Licences were first sent to Napoleon for signature on 29 March but regular weekly reports date from 3 May when 16 applications were recorded.[2] By the end of May the twenty licences originally purposed had already been signed and the pressure had begun to break down limitations. Thus the fourth *compte rendu* (7 June) reported applications for 19 ports, 48 shippers, and 156 ships, of which requests 87 had passed the required formalities. Licences had been delivered for 6 ports, 15 shippers, and 15 vessels. Already 45 blank licences were in his Majesty's hands and 60 more were enclosed. The prospects were too bright apparently for the Minister's original scruples. He argued that if 150 licences were granted two-thirds would export wine and brandy worth 4,500,000 to 6,000,000 francs, leaving but fifty ships to export

[1] $F^{12}2050$.
[2] $F^{12}2031$.

grain (150,000 quintals at 10 francs) which could cause no shade of danger. A week later with 168 applications—100 of them approved—he argued that compared with the superabundance of grain the requests to export it were limited, the season being unfavorable, because of danger of heating, and the time limit of three months being insufficient for the intended voyages to the Baltic and return. He therefore urged the speedy adoption of a more liberal policy of granting licences.[3]

Cretet's report of 21 June which discussed the difficulty raised by Napoleon on the score of certain pseudo-neutral flags is also important because it outlines a new plan of distribution intended to secure greater impartiality to all interests and sections, than by the practice of granting licences in the order of reception of applications. Thus he had made seven geographical divisions comprised in four groups on the basis of the kind of operations intended. These were (1) basin of the Scheldt and northern departments (4 ports), grains and some brandies, etc.; second group, (2) basin of the Seine (2 ports), and (3) basin of the Loire and the western coasts (4 ports), grains; third group, (4) the Charente (6 ports), and (5) the Gironde (1 port), grains and eaux-de-vie; fourth group, (6) the Adour (1 port), and (7) the Rhone (2 ports), grains, wines, and eaux-de-vie. For each river basin he had separated the completed and incompleted applications. He had acted upon two principles: 1st, to maintain the just proportion of licences granted to the total applications from each port; 2d, to distribute the licences as far as possible among the principal ports in a way to let all share in the benefits and to secure a proportional exportation of the divers products of the soil of France. Among the applicants from each port precedence was determined strictly by the date when the applications were fully and satisfactorily drawn up. This plan of distribution was destined to become a permanent feature of the French licence system. Cretet also explained that besides fifty-one applications

[3] These various weekly reports are found in AF^{IV}1342.

to use forbidden flags, there had been much pressure for licences for ships in the North Sea, regarding which required data could not be given. Such requests, therefore, he had "resolutely refused in order to give no ground for abuse, and to be assured that those passports should be given only for actual expeditions and conformably to instructions of Your Majesty."[4]

By 28 June; forty licences had been delivered, (two, however, being returned) to 36 shippers, at 14 ports. There were 215 demands from 64 shippers and 21 ports, of which 79 had met requirements, 71 were held to a change of flag, and 60 were still under investigation. On 9 July at the close of Cretet's actual service the applications totaled 222, besides 16 withdrawn or rejected. To such proportions had grown the licence measure within less than four months.

Thus Fouché on assuming his new functions found the licence plan already grown beyond its intended bounds. Occupied primarily as he must have been with the duties of his own Ministry of Police, having had neither close acquaintance nor sympathy with the original licence project, a *laissez faire* attitude was the natural course for him to pursue. Not to speak of his notorious accessibility to influences that could cross his palm, Fouché was open-minded to the needs of business and was perhaps sincerely impressed with the possibilities which the licence scheme began to reveal for relieving the chaffing economic situation. Fouché therefore frankly took the view of allowing, or even adjusting, the licence measure to meet the demands upon it.[5] This attitude may be seen in his first report (12 July) regarding the right of ships to import articles not included in their licences provided such articles were otherwise legally admittable and were accom-

[4] $AF^{IV}1342$.

[5] The exact date when Fouché assumed the *ad interim* direction of the Ministry of the Interior has not been found. Probably it was 12 July, the date when Fauchat was appointed to act in DeGerando's place as virtual assistant minister. See the *Moniteur*, 13 July. He was superseded 1 October, but he evidently acted some days longer. Cf. *Moniteur*, 15 October.

panied by certificates of origin and *acquits-à-caution*. His predecessor had so ruled, but the Minister of Finance and Director General of Customs disagreed therewith. While deferring to an imperial decision he himself thought Cretet right since the import articles in question were very necessary raw materials, while the exports were those most desirable. The report also proposed an enlarged scheme of distribution of licences. The questions involved speedily became the hardest contested points with respect to the traffic.

A week later Fouché pressed for the signature of 25 or 30 additional licences at once. He urged first that vessels bound for the North would soon find the season too late for a safe return. But his second reason was "the approach of a harvest which is announced as abundant and which is going to contribute to lower still more the price of grains which already in the Departments of the West scarcely represents the cost of cultivation and the land tax. Thus far the effect of licences on the price of wheat is still insensible."[6] This argument of the harvest he reinforced by forwarding a memoir from the Paris Chamber of Commerce the influence of which is shown in Napoleon's letter of 28 July from Schoenbrunn.[7]

"I have received a *fatras* which you have sent me on the corn trade and which is quite ridiculous" wrote the irascible Emperor. "I do not know why it does not begin by teaching me the alphabet. It is mere palaver (bavardage) of economists. Who in France is opposed to the corn trade? Who is opposed to the exportation? It is not the laws of the country; it is the English who prevent neutrals from coming into our ports and taking out our vessels (sic). The reasoning is pitiable but it has a great inconvenience; that of encouraging the commercial community to scold the government, of starting discussions and agitating the public mind. The administration is not that of economists

[6] $AF^{IV}1342$.

[7] Lecestre, *Lettres inédites de Napoléon Ier*, vol. 1, pp. 235-7, ($AF^{IV}881$).

(n'est point economiste). The principles of the grain trade are invariable. There is exportation as soon as there are outlets; there is no exportation without foreign trade. England prevents the means of commerce. I have tried to supply it by licences, if these are used they may remedy the evil. . . . .

"The Chamber of Commerce knows nothing and only chatters platitudes (preceptes). I beg you not to expose me to the annoyance of receiving such memoirs. I see that you have not the least experience with Interior business:—we have no need of any new legislation regarding commerce. France suffers greatly, I know, not from legislation, but from the blockade by England. This is due to the fact that the Danish, Russian, Prussian, etc. flags being enemies [of England] may not circulate, [and] that the Americans have laid an embargo upon themselves, and since then have passed a non-intercourse act. There is no channel for an outlet. It has been sought to supply this by patents or licences. Let me know the effect of these measures, and do not disturb the spirit of business by foolish and untimely discussion. They chatter a plenty and say nothing worth while; they have not even the first notions of the question."[8]

It was indeed a truly Napoleonic letter, and it was also typical of Napoleon that having vented his grudge against theorizers and promoters of psychological business depression he turned to a serious consideration of the issue. Three days later, therefore, he dictated a series of seven questions, touching all points of the operations and effectiveness of the licence measure, which questions strikingly recall the former questions and consequent notable inventory of the business situation in August 1807.[9]

The letter replying to the 1 August questions is dated 17 August, but the report proper was drawn up several days earlier by Fauchat or with his aid, and it underwent numerous altera-

[8] See also Loyd's *New Letters*, 140-142.
[9] F^{12}2032, Maret to Fouché, 1 August 1809. Cf. p. 22 *supra*.

tions, some of them due to the receipt at the last moment of further licences from the Emperor.[10]

As to the effectiveness of the licence experiment so far, the 17 August report held that although too few licences had yet been granted to dispose of a fiftieth part of the grain surplus, they were at least affording local or special relief. The commercial possibilities of the measure might be seen in the refitting of every possible vessel in the various ports, in the recall of vessels from the North, and the general business revival affecting the wineries, glass works, refineries, and tanneries at Bordeaux. Such meagre figures as were as yet available were given both as to the movements of licenced vessels and the goods exported or entered.[11] Thus it was estimated that fifty vessels had exported 7,000 tons of wines and 2,000 tons of grain, flour and clover seed, besides some salt. Attention was called, however, to the petitions of Bordeaux, Angoulême, Bayonne, and Rennes for enlarged schedules which would benefit manufacturing as well as agriculture and promote trade with North Germany and Russia.

As to the chance of abuse of their privileges by the shippers obtaining licences, the extreme precautions of all government officials were held to afford ample guarantees. Against English attack the ships were secure by their use of English licences in the case of vessels going to England, and evidently also in the case of those which went to the North by English sufferance. This, however, raised the issue of the status of the English licence trade at the moment, and it was pointed out that England was no longer granting licences, save those of Jersey and Guernsey for ports between Caen and Morlaix. The previous English licences available for French vessels would soon lapse, having been granted with a limit of six months dating from April. An advantageous feature of these licences had been the fact that particulars

[10] F^{12}2031. See Fauchat's report of 6 August to Fouché on the results and status of the licence traffic with special reference to news from the prefect of the Gironde.

[11] AF^{IV}1060, dossier 1, pièce 142.

as to the names of captains and vessels, the flag and the tonnage of each ship being left blank and only the name of the merchants obtaining the licences being filled in, the signature of the grantees rendered them negotiable, hence such licences could be obtained in Holland and elsewhere for from 300 to 1,000 or 1,200 francs, each. If in two or three months, after the harvest–results were known, the British government continued to refuse licences, the French licences would be valuable only for entering and leaving French ports and as protections against French corsairs, and hence only trips to the North would be possible. For communicating with England the only method then would be to use the vessels in English ports which could enter or leave without licence by paying a certain *droit d'echelle*. Several thousand such vessels in English ports were really French, though under a foreign flag, but having suffered visit or touched in England dared not enter a French port. The great obstacle to employing these ships was the difficulty in securing necessary data, and hence the long delays involving demurrage costs which soon became prohibitive. Indeed the demurrage problem had led to the repairing of most unseaworthy ships, to obviate the recourse to which rapid decisions of the Conseil des Prises and the raising of sequestres from vessels in the North were highly desirable.

Fouché's letter transmitting this first important résumé of the licence experiment summarized and supported the suggestions of Fauchat in the report proper.[12] It showed the obstacles to the success of the scheme to be: (1) the scarcity of ships and the consequent delays and expense, (2) the expiration and probable suspension of British licences, and (3) the paltry benefits of the limited trade allowed. The remedies proposed were: (1) the granting of licences in blank, (2) orders to the Conseil des Prises to expedite pending cases, (3) directions to the customs and consuls to release vessels held in the northern ports, (4) the admission of certain articles grown or made in France for a quarter or fifth

[12] AF^{IV}1060, dossier 1, pièce 140.

of the cargoes of vessels taking grain or wine, and (5) permission to import certain articles from Russia or England. And in any case he begged for commerce (whose two hundred petitions confronted him) the privilege of having *enough* licences, however restricted the terms might be.

Apparently this 17 August report received no immediate reply, nor can any speedier settlement of prize cases or the release of the sequestred vessels be noticed. This evidently explains the fact that copies of the August report were enclosed with letters of 20 September and 4 October especially urging a freer licence policy. To the same end Fouché enclosed in his 30 August report a letter from the Prefect of Gironde on the value of the licence trade, stating: "Elle fait écouler des Marchandises à l' Étranger,. elle porte la vie dans toutes classes de la Société, elle est utile au négociant, a l'ouvrier, et au trésor public." Though Fouché's efforts were slow in effecting a liberalization of terms, at least the constant plea in every report during August and September did increase the total number granted, from the forty obtained by Cretet to about two hundred by 5 October.[13]

Fouché's ceaseless efforts to let the licence traffic take its desired course evidently served to shorten his tenure of the Ministry of the Interior. Several incidents also heightened the impressions, which Napoleon had gained from the sending of the *fatras* of July, that Fouché was bungling matters. For example, the Emperor was displeased at his transmission (by Champagny's suggestion) of a request by the Grand Duchess Eliza of Tuscany for blank licences. He scolded Fouché in a characteristic letter dated 29 September.[14] Not even for his sister would he break his rule against blank licences. If the merchants of Leghorn wanted licences the Grand Duchess could get them by furnishing the necessary data. But another element in this reprimand of Fouché was the fact that he had just reported his solution of the

[13] Cf. $F^{12}2031$, and $AF^{IV}1060$, dossier 1, pièces 142-6 and 157, for reports of 23 and 30 August, 15, 20, 22 September and 3, 4 and 5 October.
[14] *Cor. de Nap.*, 19:535.

knotty problem of what to do with vessels returning with expired licences. Cretet had pointed out the difficulties incident to the limited duration of a licence and the matter had been again emphasized in the 17 August report. Now that the expiration of licences signed early in June had made the issue an immediate one, instead of delaying and risking a repetition of the neglect which his former pleas had met, Fouché decided to settle the matter himself. But Napoleon objected to the extension of licences by ministerial decision. While he wished to protect commerce, nevertheless in the event of a refusal of the customs or a French corsair to respect Fouché's ruling he would have to concur in their attitude in case of an appeal to himself. "I recognize in all your acts the same tendency," wrote the Emperor, "you have not enough legality in your mind (tête)." The remedy was to give a new licence when the old one expired. For the future, however, he admitted the advisability of making the term of licences six months instead of three.

In his reply (5 October) Fouché defended himself against the charge of endangering commerce, since the customs service had agreed to his action in advance and since the corsairs must respect the endorsements of a licence signed by his Majesty.[15] Besides he failed to see how he could give new licences when he had no new ones to give. The same day, indeed, in another letter he acknowledged the receipt of forty new ones, but at once asked for more. The great benefit was appreciated by commerce, he said, yet the demand was large, and the activity at Bordeaux remarkable.[16]

The chief interest of this letter, however, is the further light it throws upon the uncertainties and precariousness of this anomaly of an interinimical commerce. The rumors that England was commandeering licenced ships to transport troops to Walcheren had challenged a public denial from Fouché in August.[17] Now he had to allay fears, aroused by the temporary sequestration

---

[15] See for an example of such extension safe conduct no. 15, in $F^{12}2108$.
[16] $F^{12}2031$.
[17] See his letter of 30 August, $F^{12}2031$.

of a few vessels with irregular papers, that the English government had revoked its licences. Not only had these vessels been released, he said, but "the Government seems even to relax its ordinary severity against neutrals. It no longer levies the duty of six pounds sterling per ton of merchandise and since the 15 July the vessels are relieved from the unloading which before had been required for verifying the manifest of articles in the cargo and proving their origin." A letter from the Prefect of Gironde, moreover, gave him the information that many French vessels had voluntarily gone into Plymouth harbor for convoy from fear of French corsairs.

His letters of 5 October were the last reports during Fouché's regime in the Interior Ministry. When Napoleon wrote his sharp letter of 29 September he had already decided upon a change. He had suggested Cretet's resignation as nominal Minister on 10 September, and this had been obtained and forwarded by Cambacérès, reaching the imperial camp 28 September.[18] The motive stated was the hopelessness of Cretet's health,[19] and the need of having an able man at the head of interior affairs in the existing situation. As to Fouché's conduct we may draw conclusions from another letter in which Napoleon, while assuring him of his confidence and friendship and of having heard no complaints against him, stated that he desired legality in his ministers and order in the conduct of their affairs. This need not imply that there had been corruption in Fouché's handling of licence affairs. Yet the growth of the business and the change from Cretet's scrupulous methods of licence distribution[20] gave opportunity for Fouché's reputed venality, and may well have excited imperial suspicions.[21]

[18] *Cor. de Nap.*, 19:456 and 530.
[19] Cretet died 28 November.
[20] Cf. report of 12 July.
[21] For the assertations against Fouché see: Sloane, *Life of Napoleon* (ed. 1910) vol. III, p. 204. M. Charles Schmidt of the Archives Nationales informed me that a French student of the licence trade found so much evidence of this peculation that he abandoned the study as futile. My own searches, I regret to say, failed to reveal direct evidence upon this aspect of the subject.

In this connection it may be significant to notice the reprimand given both Decrès and Fouché some weeks later. The former was blamed for certain actions the marine had suffered on the part of the police, and the failure to confiscate vessels navigating without licences or imperial passports. The latter was reprimanded because news came from all sides of great abuses committed on the coasts by agents of the police who made themselves regulators of navigation. "I have allowed you two licenced vessels," the emperor reminded Fouché, "all others are to be confiscated. I have given orders to the marine that this anarchy and these pitiable abuses should cease."[22]

The new Minister of the Interior appointed 1 October was Count de Montalivet whose able services as head of the Administration of Bridges and Roads, as well as his previous experiences as prefect of the department of the Manche, had demonstrated his notable fitness for his new duties.[23] He was to hold his new portfolio until the fall of the Empire. During most of his tenure of this office the management of commerce came within his charge, and this period witnessed the rounding out of Napoleon's economic program.

The trade situation was, indeed, one of the most pressing affairs awaiting Montalivet's attention when he assumed his new office. His policy was to mold the licence project into a definite commercial system. In this by the aid of Fauchat, who furnished the link of continuity in the administration of the measure, he was enabled to bring together those elements which had stood the test of experience. This moulding of a definite policy may be considered conveniently under three phases according to the changes in the form, or nomenclature, of the licences of the *ancien système*. The first period was under the original licence formula during which time the chief question was to increase efficiency in methods and to guard against possible abuses. This policy is shown in a circular of 12 October to the Prefects requiring

[22] *Cor. de Nap.*, 20:48, nos. 16029, and 16030, (29 November).
[23] Cf. Michaud, *Biographie Universelle*, article "Montalivet."

regular reports on the licence business, and in a second circular of 20 October regarding precautions in the choice of ships to be licenced. Especial care was urged against applications for fictitious ships, or ships in the North, or in prize court, etc.[24] Montalivet's next move was to remedy the scarcity of licences. None had been signed since 22 September when on 6 November he asked for fifty or sixty fresh licences, stating as his reason the continuing demand and the lively complaints of commercial houses upon whom the lack of licences for their loaded ships was entailing heavy losses. Moreover, at Bordeaux the shortage of ships was causing exorbitant freight rates, and licences were needed to recall vessels from abroad. In the situation more licences would produce a good effect unless his Majesty were willing to go further and adopt the measures suggested in previous reports, particularly that of 17 August. These pleas proved effective. New licences were speedily sent[25] and meanwhile on 23 November, Maret wrote that his Majesty purposed enlarging the list of articles permitted for trade under the existing type of licences.[26]

It appears that after Montalivet's 6 November appeal Napoleon had referred the 17 August suggestions to the Minister of Finance for his criticisms. In his reply Gaudin commended the effects of the existing restrictions which benefited the landholders, one of the most useful classes of the Empire, and enabled them to pay their taxes. "It would be well," he felt, "to maintain these just dispositions if the shippers could continue to export advantageously only the articles named on the licences; but one may not dissemble that foreign needs for grains, wines, etc. have limits." Though first cargoes might be sold profitably the competition due to continued shipments must result eventually in losses. "In this point of view it appears expedient to extend to other merchandise the privilege of the Licence. The more latitude which shall be given to shippers, the more chances which shall

[24] F^{12}2033.
[25] AF^{IV}1342, 29 November.
[26] F^{12}2032.

be multiplied in their favor, the more will be the benefits which your Majesty extends to the territorial and industrial products of your subjects. The measure proposed will have only advantages without drawbacks *if the new Licences bear the express condition of completing three-fourths of the ship's tonnage in goods designated by the first Licences. . . . .* It will be of advantage in that the shipments will be more numerous and will procure for French factories the supply of raw materials of which they feel the need." In concluding he recommended a list of French textiles, porcelain and worked skins for exportation, and for importation tar and lignum vitae needed for the marine.[27]

The new licence form as adopted follows the proportions recommended by Gaudin, but was otherwise more liberal, in keeping with the 17 August requests. Thus a variety of other articles produced or made in France might be exported in addition to those originally permitted, provided that three-fourths of the cargo consisted of grains, wines, and the other agricultural products which had been the first object of the licence measure. The list of imports was likewise increased to embrace oils, cloths, and a variety of specified articles. The new licence also was good for six months, dating from the day of delivery to the shipper, instead of three months from the Emperor's signature.[28]

The adoption of the new type of licences marks a second phase in the licence experiment, running from 4 December 1809 to February 1810. Although Napoleon had by no means finally committed himself to the traffic his action signifies that he wished to give the experiment a full and fair test. Montalivet at once notified the prefects of the new condition and delayed the distribution of licences until those of the new nomenclature could be issued.[29] The first lot were signed 4 December, other signatures followed on 22 December, 9 January, 25 January, and 13

---

[27] $F^{12}2031$ and $F^{12}2032$.
[28] $AF^{IV}1342$.
[29] $F^{12}2050$, circulars of 27 and 30 November.

February.[30] In granting the first of the new licences the administration asked (13 December) if holders of old licences also might not be allowed the benefits of the extended traffic, but this was refused by the Emperor who wrote on the request: "Impossible. Une licence dit ce qui elle dit."[31] The prefects were then so instructed.[32]

Very soon the Emperor was disturbed by complaints of commerce and deeply impressed by demands on behalf of American commerce. He began to doubt whether the value of the traffic by licences was meeting expectations. He believed, for example, that the ships failed to export full cargoes. To meet this objection Montalivet presented a computation based upon his *compte rendu* of 3 January showing: (A) the actual value of cargoes exported, (B) the value of the cargoes which should be expected on ships of the burden stated.[33] These figures are:

20 vessels exporting	grain	(A)	708,700 fr.	(B)	624,000 fr.
63 "	" wine	(A)	3,731,600 fr.	(B)	3,628,000 fr.
7 "	" brandy	(A)	941,000 fr.	(B)	914,424 fr.

As these were French calculations the price obtained abroad would mean a fifty per cent increase. This, it was felt, should convince his Majesty "of the extreme convenience of multiplying the licences to obtain great results."

As the changed licence formula did not remedy the scarcity of ships a new concession was secured to meet the situation,[34] and 19 January it was notified to the prefects.[35] By this order the preliminary exportation of French products was dispensed with for shippers whose vessels were abroad, provided bond was given by them under certain prescribed conditions. "The aim

[30] $AF^{IV}1341^{a}$. A total of 354 licences were granted, of which 151 were of the first formula.
[31] $F^{12}2031$, (unpublished).
[32] $F^{12}2050$, Circular of 21 December.
[33] $F^{12}2031$.
[34] $F^{12}2033$.
[35] $F^{12}2050$.

chiefly proposed by the government in the delivery of special navigation licences," Montalivet explained, had been "the exportation of the products of French soil and secondarily of manufactured products." Most licences, therefore, had necessitated exportations first, but some were for importations for which exports must afterward be made. For this the ordinary bonds were not sufficient, therefore it became necessary to require a bill of sale or certificate of ownership of the goods to be exported before the licence could be delivered, and bonds were not to be returned until this exportation had taken place.[36]

This measure was followed by a decision to modify, for the second time, the licence form. In a communication of 25 January, the Secretary of State informed Montalivet of the Emperor's intention to limit to three hundred the licences then in vogue and asked for the submission of a new form which would permit the export of any French goods not otherwise prohibited and the importation of any non-prohibited wares, except cotton-wool, thread, and cloth, and which would fix the price of a licence at 1000 ecus.[37]

Montalivet in his reply of 31 January first discussed the mechanical questions involved, with the object of securing a licence which would be attractive in form and not easily counterfeited. Turning to the scope of the new permits he reported opinions he had reached in conference with Collin de Sussy. The express prohibition against cotton in any form he held to be superfluous, being already prohibited by law, hence implicitly excluded from the licences. Two dispositions of the old licences should be retained. These were (a) the requirement of a fixed exportation

[36] F¹²2033.

[37] Cf. on the initiation of this scheme Montalivet's report of 11 June 1810. F¹²2031. While it was not suggested by Montalivet, it was apparently closely connected with the status of neutral relations at the time and an outgrowth of a report of 17 January by Montalivet in favor of American commerce. It doubtless also had connection with the new tariff measures of January and February, (F¹²622).

of agricultural products (including oils from Italy and Tuscany), which he would keep at three-fourths of the whole cargo, although Collin favored one-half; (b) the inclusion not only of dyewoods, and lignum vitae, sumac and medicines, but also of dyeing drugs such as indigo and cochineal—a measure which would aid in reducing the price of French woolens (draps) and silks. As to the price, he favored a tonnage scale rather than a flat rate, and he proposed 20 francs per sea-ton with a maximum of 3000 francs. This would be fairer to small boats but would not affect the aggregate returns as the usual vessel had 150 tons displacement. Payment for these licences should be made to the Receiver General of the Department by the shipper who would present his receipt to the prefect before securing his licence. These payments would in turn be deposited in the reserve fund to be used for extraordinary expenses of the licence trade and for subsidies to industry. Instructions and administrative details could be worked out during the weeks required to prepare the licence forms.[38]

Montalivet closed: "Sir, I thank you specially in the name of commerce for a measure which, while maintaining intact the privileges of the independence of the French flag, gives nevertheless an opening for lucrative speculations, and a happy movement in our ports, procures the means of a vent for our farm and manufactured products, and finally, furnishes our workshops with indispensable materials. But I pray you to consider especially that success depends on the celerity of expediting the applications of the shippers, and the certainty they can have of obtaining, in time for use, the special acts of which they have need, and which are discussed here."[38a]

The same day news received from Bordeaux of a refusal of the English government to allow further entry of French wines threatened the success of the measure.[39] An immediate investi-

[38] $F^{12}2031$, No. 7 of 11 June.
[38a] *Cor. de Nap.*, 20:665.
[39] The findings are doubtless Montalivet's 4 February report marked "missing" from the list of important reports submitted on 11 June, $F^{12}2031$,

gation was ordered, and evidently Napoleon was satisfied with the findings, for on 14 February he issued probably his first formal licence trade decree which embodied, almost *in toto*, the recommendations of Montalivet's 31 January report.[40]

Two days later a new circular went to the prefects explaining the changes embodied in this decree. (a) Three-fourths of each cargo should be composed as before of agricultural goods, but hereafter one-half of this should be of wines and brandies. The other fourth of the cargo could embrace any permitted goods. (b) Anything lawful could be imported but this did not include cotton in wool, thread or cloth, tobacco, nor the colonial produce of both Indies—except dyewoods and drugs, lignum vitae, sumac, quinine, and medicines. (c) Attention was called to the arrangements which had been made as to payment of the licence fees which had been fixed at 20 francs per ton with a maximum of 6000 francs. (d) To secure licences hereafter a special application form was required, a model of which was enclosed.

These licence regulations were adopted coincidently with the new tariff decree of 8 February and evidently the two parts of this legislation were intended to be mutually supplementary. The new tariff was designed to meet the pressing need for raw materials felt by certain textile industries which had begun to flourish largely because of the impetus given by Chaptal's influence, the rewards given for industrial improvements, and the greater freedom from British competition then enjoyed. The spirit of the decree was in accordance with the tariff of 22 February 1806. Moreover, the principles which it involved, of doubling the duties on importa-

---

no. 3. The decree is number 2 of the MSS. of imperial decrees of 14 February. The original filing slip indexes it: "Bearers of licences may not leave hereafter unless their cargoes are composed at least one-half of wines and brandies." So far as I can discover no earlier *decree* of Napoleon on licences exists.

[40] $F^{12}2050$. See also the circulars of 10 February in $F^{12}2050$, and of 12 February in $F^{12}2033$, on other phases of the traffic.

tions of colonial goods, were to find more striking exemplification in the famous Trianon tariff of a few months later.[41]

This legislation inaugurated the culminating phase of the *ancien système* of licences. Nominally the 14 February decree was in force until July; actually none of the new licences were issued. Nevertheless the 31 January report and its resultant decree are of special interest as representing, with the possible exception of its status on the eve of the great collapse of 1814, the freest extension given to the French licence trade. Moreover, they are of real significance for the Napoleonic navigation policy, first, as introducing a period of preparation for the notable legislation of the succeeding summer, and second, because they worked out a number of features, particularly technical or administrative details, which entered into the permanent licence system.

Several reasons may be discerned for the non-issuance of licences of the third model. Before the preliminary preparations, requiring some six weeks, could be completed, the discussion of further changes arose. Vital changes had taken place in Napoleon's relations with the United States as well as with his own allies. From home and abroad came criticisms of the licence traffic. Besides Napoleon's attention was engrossed with other concerns. He therefore began to regard the entire business with distrust. In his uncertainty and lack of interest he blew hot and cold. At times he thought of ending the traffic altogether. Then again he considered reorganizing it with modifications and extensions into a fixed policy. Meantime, he refused to grant further licences. Even with the shippers there was no immediate or noticeable demand for the new licences, for the licences of the second nomenclature had met their essential requests for modifications, and their chief concern was for a sufficient supply of them. Moreover, it is probable that rumors reaching business interests of the dubious status of the whole traffic caused hesitancy and caution, hence delay in their applications.

[41] Cf. AF^{IV}1061, and *Arch. Parl.*, 2d series, vol. 10, pp. 389, 390, 452-4. For petitions of merchants, etc., see F^{12}622.

In this period of hesitancy the course of the Ministry of the Interior was: first, to continue working out details touching the decree of 14 February; secondly, to adapt the actual system as far as possible to harmonize with this decree, and lastly, to prepare for a reconstruction of the commercial policy. Circulars were sent out to the prefects 13 March and 20 March explaining and emphasizing the various new regulations as to the obligatory exports, the special bonds required, the identification of vessels to be licenced, the dating of licences, etc. Reference was also made to a plan of new licences to be granted on a grand scale which was being worked out as speedily as possible. In the meantime, it was stated, ships arriving under expired licences would be admitted, but that the new licences would have special advantages and might be obtained by holders of old licences.[42] The situation due to the cessation of the signature of licences meanwhile was met by husbanding the supply on hand. As far as possible also the new regulations were applied to the old licences. But the administration did not stop with palliative expedients, it drew up reports defending the system against current criticism.

The most significant defense of the licence trade was a report prepared by Fauchat for Montalivet, who, under date of 25 May, transmitted it with his endorsement to the Emperor. As the report was also a critical summary of the workings of the licence experiment it was a strong factor in meeting Napoleon's aversion to the traffic, and hence was directly conducive to the institution of the second or *regular* licence system. The report, therefore, is of the highest interest for our study.[43]

News from Ghent that merchants of that city, upon being informed by Maret of the discontinuance of the granting of licen-

[42] F^{12}2033. See also the letter of 24 March to Cadore who sent like instructions to the consuls. Some of the prefects replied indicating a few further changes desired, but usually complaining that the chief difficulty was the parsimony in the granting of licences. Another circular of 21 April announced the extension of the system to include the new department of the Tiber.

[43] F^{12}2031, Conseil de 11 Juin, No. 2.

ces, had ordered the holding of their goods at Paris for higher prices furnished Fauchat the occasion he desired to present his report to Montalivet.[44] Another pretext was afforded by the approaching expiration of the complementary British licences. This intensified the situation for while such licences might as yet be renewed once, nevertheless it was doubtful whether the conditions would be maintained long. Grain was now at very low price, the shipping season was favorable and would last but two months. Shippers were ready after heavy expense to export, and if disappointed now there would be small chance of reviving the traffic later. The licences had led to thirty shipments of grain, had kept up agricultural prices, had notably lowered the prices of dye-stuffs, had brought in supplies of quinine and medicines which had become scarce and dear, had reanimated navigation and had sent out two hundred and fifty boats which had been rotting in French ports. All this led to a belief "that it is important to maintain the system of licences, which temper happily the rigor of the decree of Blockade and of the actual circumstance of the maritime war." He was ready to respect secret views or political aims but if fear of abuses was the cause of the repugnance of the government to deliver new protections he felt he should report some of his investigations and notions on the subject.

He sought first to explode a current notion that the English were using the vessels with French licences for their own coasting and Northern trade.[45] This he said supposed that French licences had a market value in England, an unbelievable thing since

[44] Apparently the news was from a certain Van Aken who, after a conference during Napoleon's visit to Ghent on 18 May, became a confidential reporter to Montalivet and Fauchat regarding British licence measures. See chapter X, below. Fauchat also had the use of an eight page memoir (upon which he has written some keen comments) entitled "Notices sur les licences français par Ph. Gt. de Bordeaux," F¹²2057.

[45] Evidence of this notion is afforded by a memoir sent at this time to the French government entitled: "Convient-il à un Batiment porteur d'une Licence de se laisser employer en Cabotage anglais." F¹²2057.

English trade sailed under convoy protection; besides the restrictions of the French licences would not protect such vessels against capture by French corsairs. Moreover for the trade permitted under French licences economic self-interest would keep the vessels concerned out of the coasting or Northern trade. First, because the best and cheapest grains were to be got soonest and with least risk in France, while the distant and overstocked Baltic markets could not compete with prices on goods from England in the cross-Channel markets. And as the exportation conditions must then be fulfilled the aim of the Emperor was reached in the end. Similarly for shipments from the Baltic the London market could not compete with the additional 50%—100% profits obtainable in France. Even from the standpoint of freights alone the £5 per ton under convoy from Hamburg was offset by the £15 per ton for the voyage to France. Although certain imports had lowered 30% to 40% already in price in France, the market was still high enough to support freights of 200 to 260 francs per ton, and what coasting trade could stand such rates?

The failure of licenced vessels to return to, or come to France was not evidence of speculation in the licences. Some vessels under the first licences had been unable to return before the expiration of their short term licences. Frenchmen, who had been forced by the wars to sell their own vessels, were not blameable if foreign shipmasters with whom they had contracted failed to keep their engagements. As to the Bordeaux ships, most of them had been embargoed at London because French shippers had been unaware of the refusal of England to admit anything but grains.[46] He admitted the truth of the objection that the use of foreign vessels restricted France to a commission business, but for this there seemed no alternative. For the transactions French houses were responsible to the government. The French produce must have an outlet, and French industry required raw materials. Surely, a small profit was better than none. In short, it seemed that:

[46] See *Cor. de Nap.*, 20:165

"So long as the licences afford commercial operations with France their end will be fulfilled."

Yet another current criticism was that licences were obtained simply to get a sequestred ship away from France. Even in the rare cases where this was true the exportation at least was beneficial. If the vessels were French owned they must return at the peace or their value be paid to the government, if neutral owned they would doubtless be freed anyway in time. If neutrals could be assured that they could come in ballast unmolested there would be no lack of ships in France. And if it were solely a question of having ships in French ports then the cessation of licence grants diametrically countered that object, for many ships were waiting for licences in order to come home. At that very moment indeed M. Lubbert and Baron d'Este of Caen were awaiting the arrival of the imperial *entourage* to seek redress in person for the seizure of vessels which they had sought to bring home without the unobtainable licences, while DeClercq, deputy of Hamburg commerce, had been saved just in time from a similar attempt.

Fauchat's general conclusion then was that the traffic was mixed with little abuse, and that little not to be weighed against the advantages involved. He hoped that Montalivet would be convinced and would persuade the Emperor "of the advantages of a system already adopted, lately extended, used with a certain latitude of discretion (d'une faculté) of which the English give us multiplied examples renewed daily with respect to all nations."

Beside the Fauchat report of 25 May should be put the evidence touching the financial effects afforded by the almost daily reports which Mollien, Minister of the Treasury, began early in 1810 to render directly to the Emperor regarding the economic throbbings of the country.[47] Thus on 10 March he notes a remark-

[47] Carton AF^{IV}1088. These reports which furnish an invaluable economic register for the remaining years of the Empire have been utilized for certain limited points by M. de Lanzac de Laborie in his *Paris sous Napoleon*, vol. VI, also for his article on the Bourse in the *Revue hebdomadaire*, 1910, p. 642. From their character such reports necessarily, however, are valuable rather as suggestive glints, than as throwing a steady gleam upon the situation.

able amelioration of exchange on England. "The cause of this amelioration seems to be in the delivery of the last licences; the drafts (traités) on London find more employment because they are taken in payment for articles exported under the privilege of Licences."—When by 24 March exchange rose to 20.40 fr. per £ he sought the causes, and thus started his explanations: "The licences must have a certain part among other implicit and more concealed causes in influencing the opinion of commercial circles." A week later, noting a rise of English exchange at Hamburg 5% above the rise at Paris, he throws out the query: "Are the English ports less susceptible to our importations; are the French ports or the French custom houses on the frontiers less closed to the shipments of colonial goods since the increase in the tariff?"[48] 17 April, the London exchange continues to rise, and even more so in London than in Paris. He comments "Your Majesty is aware how the licences can influence the amelioration of the English exchange. A vessel which by virtue of a licence can import 150,000 francs of wheat into England has capacity for carrying back at least a double value of other articles, consequently it is supplied at the same time with bills on London procured at Paris and it then brings back from London in merchandise the value of the bills of exchange bought in France, in addition to the selling-price of its original cargo." After touching incidentally in a number of intervening reports upon phases of the influence of the licence system, and the general workings of the commercial situation, Mollien on 25 May delivered another direct thrust at the licence traffic. "It appears," he writes, "that on several parts of the coast, especially in Brittany, the *licences* have become the occasion, perhaps the pretext, for several hazardous operations—that it is upon their demand[49] that paper on London, which was not plentiful and yet found few buyers, has risen in price; and that the purchase of this paper made on their account has been

[48] Also like comments on 13 April.
[49] That is, of these speculators.

one of the causes which has compromised in their failures the principal houses of Paris."

Thus on the very day when Fauchat sent to Montalivet his defense of the license business, Mollien was reporting to Napoleon personally the climax of one of its evil consequences. When we compare the reports of Mollien with the defense made by Fauchat the impression is strong that the former's attack was no inconsiderable factor in the coincident repugnance of the Emperor to the licence experiment. But the reports of the opponent and the advocate have an added significance. Mollien was the strongest and most persistent exponent of the theory of breaking English power by shattering her credit. Fauchat in his sphere—which, we have seen, was significant far beyond its nominally subordinate position—was, perhaps, the steadiest and most effective representative of the effort to save, and solidify French power, by affording necessary support to French industrial life. In short the programs of the two men epitomize two principal opposing forces in the struggle of the Continental System.[50]

The valuable evidence furnished by Fauchat and Mollien, respectively, as to the administrative and financial aspects of the first licence system, is supplemented by a third test of the experiment on the basis of its commercial statistics. The need of gathering regular data on movements of trade and shipping under licence was early realized by the licence administration, and prefects were frequently reminded of their duty of furnishing this information. Similarly at frequent intervals the Minister of the Interior made reports to the Emperor. The number and character of these reports was a matter of evolution. This circum-

[50] Although Mollien on the basis of his *Memoirs* is usually cited as one of the notable opponents of the Continental System, his reports to Napoleon at the time, as pointed out by M. de Lanzac de Laborie (*Paris sous Napoleon*, VI, 56 ff.), give the lie direct to his later assertions. It is true that Chaptal was perhaps the most notable advocate of the policy which Fauchat may have learned from his former chief, but it is difficult to find proofs of Chaptal's efforts at this moment comparable with the activity of Fauchat.

stance, emphasized by the marked changes in the program as a whole, by the inadèquate provisions for forcing commercial returns by prefects and shippers, and hence the long delays and irregularity in the sending of data to the central bureau, make the statistical summaries of varying merit.

The first important summary of licence trade results is the *compte rendu* of 3 January 1810, covering 151 licences of the first type. Of these 21 had not been delivered, 39 were unreported, and 91 had reported a total export of 5,384,100 francs.[51] Passing over certain interesting reports of 7 February, and of 28 March and 4 April 1810, we may note the status of the traffic at the moment of its reorganization in June.[52] Thus the best data available shows that 354 licences had been signed, of which 351 had been delivered. Although returns were incomplete, wines, grain, and other articles valued at over 10,000,000 francs had been exported, and medicines and raw materials worth some 6,000,000 francs had been imported.[53]

An attempt to check up these statistics by the data furnished in the French Balance de Commerce and the British Customs Registers proves futile. Thus taking the figures of the 3 January 1810

[51] $F^{12}2031$. See also the 10 January report. A later report in $F^{12}2032$ on these first type licences is an interesting illustration of the scrupulosity of the licence administration. It shows that 304 were printed, of these one each, unsigned, had been sent as samples to the Minister of Marine, and Director General of Customs, while 250 had been sent to the Emperor for signature. Of 155 actually signed, 150 had been delivered and five remained at the Ministry, which with 52 others there, unsigned, and 95 returned unsigned by Maret, were formally annulled.

[52] $F^{12}2031$ on the trade of Bordeaux for October–December 1809.

[53] $F^{12}2031$, and 2032, reports of April, May and June 1810. A report of 25 May ($AF^{IV}1342$) shows the local distribution of the licences, viz: Bordeaux 123, Caen 26, Ghent 18, Dunkirk 13, Marennes 13, Antwerp 12, Nantes 11, Paris 10, Rome 10, Cognac 10, Ostend 9, LaRochelle 9, Bayonne, Charente, Quingamp each 7, LeHavre 6, St. Malo 6, Lannion 5, Ile d'Oléron 4, Vannes 4, Brest, Bruges, Cette, Marseilles, Morlaix each 3, Alost, Lyons, L'Orient, Granville, Rochefort, Saintes, and Ypres, each 2, Boulogne, Dixmude, Lille, Flushing, Les Sables, Jarnac, Marans, and Pontoise each 1, besides 4 to the Commissioner of Police at Boulogne. Cf. also $AF^{IV}1061$.

compte rendu, just cited, as the best available for the licence traffic of 1809 we may compare them with the total exports of 340,605,400 francs and total imports of 357,803,500 francs recorded in the Balance de Commerce for that year.[54] Obviously, however, the Balance de Commerce figures not only cover a longer period than the licence figures but represent also trade by both land and sea, and in the latter case include coasting and other traffic not under licence. New difficulties are also met in comparing the French and British figures. For the Balance de Commerce shows no trade with Great Britain and Sardinia and next to none with Portugal,—evidently masking this licenced trade under such "coals-to-Newcastle" records as the heavy grain shipments to Germany and other grain *shipping* ports, or of brandy to Moslem states, or under the unprecedented volume of shipments of wines to Prussia, Germany, Denmark, the United States, etc.[55] On the other hand the British Customs Registers frankly admit an importation of £737,530 12s 3d from France and exports thither of £455 5s.6d; besides a considerable importation from Flanders.[56] But here again large quantities of French wines, lawns, silks, etc. are listed as entering from Holland, Germany, etc. so that it is hard to say just how largely French goods entered England during this supposedly tight-closed year of the Continental Blockade. Yet another discrepancy is found in that the British figures are recorded not in actual but in arbitrary "official" values.

[54] F^{12}1384.

[55] Evidently the recording of breaches of the Continental System was avoided by ascribing the shipments to the country whose flag covered each transaction.

[56] Public Record Office, *Customs*, 4/5 (Imports 1809), and 10/1 (Exports 1809). The trade with France was by 189 "foreign" ships aggregating 30,760 tons, with Flanders by 31 ships of 3,745 tons. No exports went to Flanders. The imports were wheat (three-fourths of the total), cream of tartar, flax, madder, and clover-seed. France sent cereals worth £41,000, and wines and brandies worth over £496,260, of which, however, £402,826 were merely warehoused. The other imports from France (one-third of the total) were turpentine, prunes, bottles, clover-seed, olive oil, cream of tartar, lawns, and thrown silks.

Manifestly with such divergent statistics definite conclusions as to the commercial value of the licence experiment are impossible. Nevertheless, in such a comparison certain points cannot fail to strike the attention. Thus, though bearing a comparatively slight proportion to the aggregate export trade, the licence traffic is seen to be by no means negligible. Indeed French shipments to England are shown to have been much more considerable than might be inferred from French figures, or from the general situation of 1809. Moreover, English and French data agree sufficiently as to the character and even the quantity of goods to make it clear that the bulk of French goods taken to England went under French licences the terms of which would seem to have been fairly well adhered to.

These observations are equally valid when later statistics of the *ancien système* of licences are considered. For it must not be supposed that when a new licence system was decreed in July the old licences became immediately non-operative. Indeed even after 1 September, when the last licences of the old system had supposedly expired, Napoleon was irritated to find ships straggling in which had sailed under the former licences.[57] But though legally these vessels were subject to confiscation they almost invariably could be admitted by imperial decision in the Conseil du Commerce. Various efforts were made to collect complete and verified statistics for the old system which would include these belated arrivals.[58] The latest data obtainable Montalivet sum-

[57] See his letter of 5 September 1810 to Collin de Sussy, (*La Presse*, issue of 9 Mar. 1844) in which he argues that the last licences having been signed on 13 February should have expired 13 August. But he evidently forgot that licences of the second formula were dated not from their signature but from their delivery to the shippers.

[58] See AF^{IV}1340. Such an effort was made in May 1811, when most of the prefects replied that the results of many of these expeditions could not be learned. Of those for which data was available, Bordeaux reported that the majority had gone to the Baltic, especially to Riga, St. Petersburg, Danzig, Königsberg, and Carlsham; while from Charente and Nantes most ships had gone to England.

marized for his notable report of 25 November 1811.⁵⁹ This showed:

Exports:	Imports:
18,493,473 francs. Reported value.	38,859,134 francs. Reported value.
Plus 9,246,736 francs. Supposed 50% profits.⁶⁰	Less 9,714,783 francs. Supposed 25% profits.
27,740,134 francs. Estimated sale value abroad.	29,144,351 francs. Estimated cost abroad.

Thus the net result of these licences, even accepting the most favorable figures, is a difference of 1,404,217 francs on the import side—in short, a balance clearly against France.

It is doubtless but fair to suppose that the results of the first licence system have not been known hitherto. For invariable repetition has sought to make it axiomatic that Napoleon was a staunch mercantilist with whom an unfavorable trade balance was an impossibility. Hence it is commonly asserted that a cardinal principle of the Continental System, and of the licence trade, required that exports exceed imports. The truth is that such a theory has not appeared in the experiments we have hitherto traced. Certainly it did not appear in the first licence system, where above all it might be expected. Nor did it, apparently, play any real part in the formation of the Continental System as a whole. Later developments of the navigation policy in line with mercantilist doctrines came in reality from the lessons of experience. For Napoleon was an opportunist, not a theorist. He had no patience for 'the vaporings of economists.' "L'administration n'est point economiste," he declared to Fouché in 1809.⁶¹ And when in June 1816 he conversed with Las Cases

⁵⁹ AF^{IV}1342.

⁶⁰ This scheme of corrected estimates was adopted in September 1810 to maintain the impression that the balance of trade was favorable to France, or, preferably, that exports and imports balanced. See AF^{IV}1340, 29 September. The arbitrary percentages used were later found to be far from exact.

⁶¹ Lecestre, *Lettres inédites de Napoléon Ier*, 1:336.

"on trade and the principles of economists which he had introduced . . . he opposed the principles of economists in their application." For said the Emperor, "I have not fallen into the error of modern systematizers who imagine that all the wisdom of a nation is centered in themselves. Experience is the true wisdom of nations."[62]

The final figures of Montalivet's 25 November 1811 summary are confirmed by an "Etat Général des Licences de l'Ancien Système."[63] This register shows that of the 354 licences granted, 149 had returned by 9 January 1812.[64] The ships usually left for Bordeaux, Charente, Caen, Marans, LaRochelle, Dieppe, and Antwerp chiefly with grains, wheat, wines, brandies, etc., or simply "various wares." In general, the vessels returned to Antwerp, Ostend, Dunkirk, Le Havre and Bordeaux bringing, usually, drugs, quinine, Campeachy and other dyewoods. Some brought soda, "divers articles," tin, or skins, while many returned in ballast.

Particularly interesting are the names of licences recorded in this register, for among them are those of firms or individuals who for ten, a dozen, or fifteen years, yes since the first foreshadowing of a licence traffic, had been regular recipients of the special trade permits of the British government.[65] And they were to continue as active factors in the French phase of this peculiar institution for co-operation between enemies. Nor were such men singular to France, for the type was most familiar in

[62] Las Cases, *Jourñal*, 4:196-201.
[63] AF^{IV}1342.
[64] The date is a pencilled notation. The last ship whose return is reported came in on 2 November 1810 with licence no. 350.
[65] *Privy Council Register*, 1793-1815. Among them are Albrecht and Delbrück; Philippe Boissé of Hamburg; Campion; De Clercq, the deputy of Hanse commerce; Delmotte of Ostend; Delaroche, Armand, Delessert & Co. of Nantes, Garnier and Ransom of LaRochelle; Daniel C. Meyer; Lallemand & Co. of Charente; Loriol and Dagneau of Dunkirk; Serruys & Co.; Solberg & Co.; Schroeder and Schuyler; Van der Heyden; Van Aken of Ghent, and his correspondent Emmery, sometime mayor of Dunkirk.

England. These "authorized smugglers" numbered great merchants, and small ones, aristocrats, and members of government. It may be said that they represent a common human tendency, but they also especially typify the economic interests and principles which the war blockades and the Continental System were vainly trying to overcome.

It was the influence of these men that made possible such a *modus vivendi* as the licence system. They were the unseen force which maintained it, which bent and correlated the divergent purposes of the two bitter foes *knowingly* to work in concord. During this whole period they were almost the only intermediaries between England and France whose negotiations measurably succeeded. They are thus a factor by no means negligible in any explanation of that paradoxical arrangement, the licence trade. For is it not a paradox that enemies so inveterate should have co-operated to undermine and to bring to naught precisely that which they had published to the world as a fundamental principle of their conflict? Moreover, these commercial interests were a most important influence in bringing about the critical transition of July 1810 which made the licence policy the navigation policy of the Empire.

CHAPTER V
INTERNATIONAL SIGNIFICANCE OF THE LICENCE EXPERIMENT

In gauging the operations of the *ancien* licence system on the basis of its administrative and economic consequences, the viewpoint is naturally that of its significance for France, or, very incidently, for Engla d also. But neither the French nor the English could restrict to themselves the effects of their exceptional intercourse. The licence trade had, of necessity, an international reflection of wide significance. With the very initiation of the project it appeared in the question of selecting flags for the dubious benefits of covering the traffic. Nor did the matter end with the July decisions in favor of Prussia, Denmark, and certain Hanse towns. One of the more important of the German city states, Danzig, having been omitted from the special privilege, at once solicited it through the resident French consul, and Champagny.[1] Almost at the same moment the request of the Grand Duchess of Tuscany for some of her imperial brother's licences reflected the spread of interest in the opposite quarter of Europe.[2] Still the ripple of interest widened. On 31 December Champagny transmitted a request of the Russian ambassador that Lubinski, consul at Paris, be allowed to bring into a French port a cargo of sea island cotton. Though the proposition appeared contrary to regulations Cadore, being reluctant to refuse the Russian ambassador, urged for the request the most favorable consideration possible.[3] There followed directly afterward another Russian petition. In this case it was one presented by French residents of Petersburg to the consul general there, asking to be allowed to participate in the licence trade of which they had heard. Champagny on 28 February referred the consul's request to Montalivet

[1] The petition was presented by a certain Muhl. It was sent by Champagny on 10 September to Montalivet. F¹²2108.
[2] F¹²2108; and *Cor. de Nap.*, 19:535.
[3] F¹²2108.

who replied (15 March) that, since licences were designed to favor the export of French agricultural products, the only chance for Frenchmen at Petersburg to share in the trade was by arranging with some French house for them to send to France a ship which would export French goods and bring back a cargo from Russia. Such a transaction must, moreover, be in the name of the French firm.[4]

News of the French licences meantime had been brought to the attention of the Russian government. It afforded an excellent occasion for a retort to the exasperating French complaints of Russia's lax adhesion to the Continental System.[5] In reply, Napoleon on 8 February 1810 instructed Champagny to explain to the Duc de Vicence, his ambassador at Petersburg, "that I give licences for the exportation of wine and wheat, which is useful for my states, but none at all for the importation of colonial goods, . . . that England needing the wheat naturally lets the vessels enter and leave . . . and that I shall cease to give licences as soon as I learn that the English exact the payment of contributions."[6] Despite the misrepresentations of the extent of his own relaxations Napoleon's reply has a significance that has not been appreciated. For indirectly it conceded the chief Russian contention, namely, the necessity of an outlet for her raw products. Moreover at this same moment Napoleon was endeavoring to negotiate a treaty with Alexander, removing various causes of friction, particularly regarding Poland. Also he was seeking a convention with America which, had it been successful, might

[4] F¹²2108. The consul made a request also for instructions regarding the giving of certificates of origin for quinine. Montalivet stated that the admission of quinine was especially favored but that the Customs must decide whether certificates could be dispensed with for it.

[5] In August 1809 Fouché had transmitted to Napoleon a striking arraignment of Russian connivance (since the spring of 1808) at the false neutrals of the British licence system. F¹²2031. These accusations are borne out by a variety of British evidence. See also *Writings of J. Q. Adams*, III, 400.

[6] *Cor. de Nap.*, 20:193. And yet Napoleon had already decided upon the third type of licences which permitted the entry of many colonial goods.

have removed another difficulty between the two "allies."[7] Indeed, that the recent creation of an American legation at Petersburg, with a minister who could effectively present the case of American commerce, was a complicating factor in the Franco-Russian problem is borne out by the cautions sent to Caulaincourt at this time.[8]

Doubtless solicitude on account of the American factor, as well as renewed Russian complaints, influenced Napoleon's instructions of 29 June for Cadore to protest to the Duc de Vicence, "the falsity of the imputation that we carry on commerce with England; and you will say that its only foundation rests on the fact that we granted passage to a few vessels laden with corn."[9] This prescribed evasion Caulaincourt duly repeated in a personal conversation with the American Minister, who, however, promptly retorted that he had but too positive information to the contrary, as he felt sure the duke must be aware. Adams also has testified that the Muscovite Chancellory was no more readily satisfied than himself with Napoleon's transparently untrue excuses for his licence trade.[10]

At this epoch, however, the friction with Russia was as naught to the open quarrel with Holland. The British licence system which was making sorties against Russia, laid close siege to the Netherlands. A variety of special licences were created by the Privy Council especially for Holland. Licences were granted also with special secret permission from the Board of Trade to "hover off" the Dutch coast until they were met or "captured" by Dutch vessels. On his part the King of Holland winked at the

[7] See *Cor. de Nap.*, 20:148-161; Vandal, *Napoléon et Alexander*, vol. II, chaps. 5-7, etc. Of significance also are the memoirs of the moment on building up trade with Russia. Cf. F^{12}622.

[8] *Cor. de Nap.*, 20:193, etc. See also the reports of Adams in Ford, *Writings of J. Q. Adams*, vols. III & IV. Note especially Adams to Smith, 17 January 1810, *Writings*, III, 386-8.

[9] Loyd, *New Letters*, p. 188.

[10] *Memoirs of J. Q. Adams*, II, 176, 180. Cf. also *Writings*, III, 416-9, 427, 440, 444, 448, 454, 464, 468, 506, etc.

practice, or encouraged it by "most secret" instructions.[11] That British "grain-import" licence, to which Napoleon had responded in 1809 with complementary French licences, appealed particularly to Louis, since the Dutch flag and Dutch sailors would be received by England. Even Napoleon added force to the enticement by issuing his order of 22 March 1809, releasing sequestered Dutch vessels, and by making them eligible for French licences.

Communication between Holland and England was also facilitated by relaxations in favor of American commerce, notably the decree of 30 June, which, upon demand of the American consul, Louis issued in reply to the repeal of the American Embargo Act.[12] To further encourage "neutral" traders, the King decided to follow his brother's policy of giving licences for the admission of foreign vessels.[13] In a letter of 24 July 1809, Sylvanus Bourne, American consul at Amsterdam, notified a correspondent that the Dutch government "has resolved to grant licences for the free entry of all vessels of the United States *coming direct* therefrom;

[11] Privy Council *Register*, 1808, 1809, vols. 69-77, also "unbound papers," 1808, 1809. Public Record Office, B. T. 6/186, 6/187, et seq., *Licence Registers*, 1809, (esp. applications 4061, 4084, 4087, 4633, 4754, etc.). Arch. Nat., *Marine*, BB² 128, pp. 186-193, consular letters, from Hellevoet Sluys, July-September 1809. Colenbrander, V, pt. 2, pp. 34, 424, 425, 427, May-September 1808. There were secret orders for Holland relating to the importation of salt, 11 February, 18 May, 20, 28 July and 1 August 1808, in R. A. S. S. *Koninklijke Besluiten* 118, 131, 360; and to the exportation of butter, cheese, gin, etc., dated 31 March, 26 May, 22 August, and 13 December (strict embargo), in R. A. S. S. *Koninklijke Besluiten* 320, 132 (no.2), 157, and 360. For these references to the Hague Archives I am indebted to Dr. Peter Hoekstra who also discusses them in his Univ. of Pa. diss., *Thirty-seven Years of Holland–American Relations, 1803–1840*.

[12] *Bourne MSS., Library of Congress*, Bourne to Taylor, 30 June & 25 August; *Dept. of State, Cons. letters*, Amsterdam, 30 June, 1 July, 4 July, 24 and 28 August 1809.

[13] It is not certain when Louis adopted this practice but there are evidences that he was familiar with the traffic before Napoleon adopted it. See Lee to Madison, 8 March 1808, regarding a vessel under the American flag which had been trading between Holland and England under a permit of the King of Holland, *Dept. of State, Cons. letters*, Bordeaux, II.

and laden with goods permitted by the King's last decrees of March 31 and June 30, say with *tobaccos, ashes, rice, cotton, staves, medicines generally* the *product of the United States and Java, coffee* and *sugar* the property of its citizens. Should any vessels under the circumstances arrive off the coast to your direction, and you should wish to send them here, and will transmit me the name and description of the vessel, name of the master, where from in the United States and the general contents of the cargo, I will send you the necessary licences or procure them to be sent on board off the Texel."[14]

There was a speedy response to these measures but unfortunately Louis was forced to bow to imperial demands and issue a new decree of 31 July withdrawing that of a month prior in favor of American trade.[15] Thereafter his licences were no sure protection even in Dutch waters against French privateers, or the ubiquitous French agents. For a protest lodged by Bourne on 30 August indicates that even Dutch port officers dared not respect the immunity of vessels admitted by expressed permission of the King and containing cargoes "whose importance for the factories of Holland and France cannot be denied."[16] Nevertheless, Louis continued to grant licences, issuing in all more than 400 of such documents.[17]

The Dutch infractions of the Continental Closure were without question a vital injury to the imperial system. By sharp protests and by embargoes against Holland the Emperor sought incessantly to bring Louis to time. By December of 1809 the crisis was reached. To save a remnant of his kingdom Louis consented to harsh terms. Of the treaty conditions dictated 12 February

[14] Bourne MSS., Library of Congress.

[15] *Aff. Étr., Cor. Pol., Holland,* vol. 613.

[16] Bourne MSS. See also the letter of J. E. Seaman to Bourne, of 30 August, regarding the seizure of the cargo of the ship *Charles* from New York with cotton for King and Bowker, who had secured an entry licence for it.

[17] Brotonne, *Lettres inédites de Napoléon,* Ier, no. 680, 4 October 1810. To Lebrun, regarding licence no. 420.

by Napoleon the second requirement was: "To put an end to all communication with England and to permit navigation only under my licences."[18] The treaty wrung from Louis became effective 16 March. When the licence provision was taken up, the necessity for the exportation of butter and cheese was discussed, and it appears that a limited number of licences was promised, but these were not to be accorded until Louis had actually fulfilled the requirements of the treaty regarding ships of war for the French navy and the delivery of sequestered American goods to France.[19] Napoleon did consent on 24 April, however, that certain vessels with salt, alone, might enter, provided nothing had been paid to England.[20]

But the Dutch would not be constrained by the Emperor's conditions. Soon Napoleon learned that by subterfuges grain was still being sent to England, that Louis was even granting Dutch licences and had given permission to certain vessels, mainly American, to bring tea into the ports of Holland.[21] Already Napoleon was exasperated by the opposition of Louis to the French customs regulations for Holland.[22] He was also greatly incensed by the failure to hand over the promised ships and American goods, and wrathy over "insults" to his flag, his ambassador, and his subjects by the Netherlanders. Under such circumstances the knowledge of the new treaty infractions by the revival of Dutch licences was, apparently, the last straw for the

[18] *Cor. de Nap.*, 20:203, no. 16243—Article 1 of the treaty. Cf. Rocquain, pp. 319. A *projet* of the treaty is found in F[12]622. Copies of the treaty are in *Aff. Étr., Cor. Pol., Holland*, vol. 164, pièce 208; and in *Arch. Nat.*, AF[IV] 1683. On the origin of the licence clause cf. Rocquain, 249: Louis to Fouché, 5 February 1810. Cf. also *Docs. Hist. sur Hol.* I, 127; III, 155-231.

[19] AF[IV]1683: "Note de l'Ambassadeur d'Hollande"; *Cor. de Nap.*, 20:347-349.

[20] *Cor. de Nap.*, 20:306.

[21] *Cor. de Nap.*, 20:419; *Aff. Étr., Cor. Pol., Holland*, vol. 164, pièces 303, 314, 347, etc.; Colenbrander, V, pt. 2, pp. 734-5, Verhuell to Roëll, 14 May 1810.

[22] The regulations and Louis's protest of 25 May are in AF[IV]1683.

exasperated Emperor.[23] On 23 June he decided that the duc de Reggio should form a camp at Utrecht from which he could march on Amsterdam.[24] The next day he wrote his Minister of War: "Notify the duc de Reggio that the King of Holland has no right to give licences, that they should be regarded as non-effective, that he should explain it in that sense, and protest, treaty in hand, declaring that he will cause the execution with vigor of all the conditions of the treaty. If the Dutch should give licences it would be useless that I should hold customs officers there, and a corps of troops."[25] And to Champagny he wrote: "Enclosed you will find samples of the licences granted by the King of Holland. You will write to my chargé d'affaires, to demand that these licences shall be considered null and void, and suppressed, as being in contravention of the treaty made with me. At the same time he will point out the absurdity of their style, and the senselessness of speaking of emperors and kings in such a manner in any document." After touching upon another grievance, the letter closed: "Let him say clearly that I am not going to endure anything more from the Dutch: that they had better behave straightforwardly and have done with all this chicanery and deceitful behavior."[26] That same day (24 June) Napoleon ordered the duc de Reggio to march on Amsterdam.[27]

More adroitness and a happier outcome are the chief distinctions between the course of the king of Naples and that of his brother-in-law in Holland with regard to the Continental System. It was largely a case of shrewder dodging winning the treatment due to superior merits. For the poverty-ridden Neapolitan kingdom could not resist the temptations of Yankee adventurers or the

[23] *Cor. de Nap.*, 20:347-49, 427, 428; and Loyd, *New Letters*, p. 186, No. CCLXI. On the nature of these licences see *Am. Daily Adv.*, 6 August 1810, London 20 June, Holland 16 June.

[24] *Cor. de Nap.*, 20:427.

[25] Brotonne, *Dernières lettres inédites de Napoléon Ier*, 1:491, no. 1075.

[26] Loyd, *New Letters*, p. 186, No. CCLXIII.

[27] *Cor. de Nap.*, 20:428.

British smuggling agencies in Sicily and Malta, and verily even his distance from the imperial borders and from the strategic center of the Continental Blockade would hardly have saved Murat had he not been able to mask his knavery with timely evidences of subservience. This is shown in his connections with the imperial licence experiment, of which he probably first learned at the moment when American vessels, freed from the national Embargo Act, began to tempt fate in the Mediterranean. Three such vessels were captured and brought into Naples about 29 May 1809, where they were sequestered pending imperial instructions. In reporting the matter, Murat stressed the point that these vessels had come direct to Naples and carried proper certificates of origin. To drive home this hint he cited reports that Napoleon was allowing himself such trade, and this argument he followed up with pleas that, unless he might allow neutrals to export the grain and oils with which his kingdom was gorged, he could not maintain himself there, let alone supply the military contingents to the Empire.[28] When denied this resource, he merely changed his tactics and, while ostentatiously obeying imperial directions, quietly took his own course with the American ships. Indeed, he even went so far as to contract for the sale of Neapolitan oils to an English firm.[29] Thus he was able to finance a visit to Paris during December and January, from which he returned with several valuable trade concessions. Thus on 21 December he sent home an imperial decision that because of the American embargo the sequestered American ships were to be confiscated and sold, but agreeing that their cargoes might be exported from Naples. Whereupon did Murat, the robber-baron, piously comment: "God send us many ships of that nation! You will see to it that they undergo the same fate."[30] Moreover, the Emperor, who had already begun to provide a regular outlet for Neapolitan

[28] Murat, *Lettres et documents*, VII, nos. 4128, 4145, 4246, 4410, 4424, 4441; VIII, 4499, and 4507.

[29] *Ibid.*, nos. 4499, 4600, 4617, and 4651.

[30] *Ibid.*, no. 4680. See also nos. 4657, 4673, 4685, 4713, etc.

corn, now promised licences for the export of oils, silks, and other products. By dint of persistent reminders Murat actually received twenty-four of these coveted licences (26 Jan. 1810) and proceeded to interest Broadbent, the American consul in Sicily, in the affair. But Neapolitan traders refused to touch these peculiar permits, and Murat, after vainly seeking to exchange them for ordinary French licences, at last decided to complete the Broadbent contract anyway and cover the proposed oil exports with permits of his own. However, in the face of the Emperor's suspicious warnings, he had perforce to abandon and lie out of the transaction.[31] With respect to the unused imperial licences, a later statement of Napoleon mentions them as having been returned by Murat, although, strange to say, the French licence registers have no record whatever of the affair.[32]

Regarding the relation of the other Napoleonic appanages to the licence schemes of 1809, almost no information is available. Indeed, there is no record of any of these licences having been used for other than French ports of the Empire, although the Department of the Tiber was eligible for them in April 1810.[33] Joseph doubtless had too little hold on the coast of Spain to have used licences. Italy, like Naples, apparently admitted some vessels with certificates of origin under general regulations, from which abuses arose.[34] About 27 March 1810, however, special regulations were made for the expedition of grain from Rome, and from the Kingdom of Italy, to Naples, which had for some months been provisioning the Ionian Isles.[35] Apparently this was under *permis de cabotage*, since some months later Napoleon called Montalivet's attention to the large number of these granted since

[31] *Ibid.*, nos. 4819, 4822, 4828, 4835, 4843, 4853, 4875, 4894-6, 5019.

[32] Brotonne, *Dernières lettres inédites*, 1:517.

[33] $F^{12}2033$.

[34] *Cor. de Nap.*, 20:241 and 248, 269, and 372. The *Moniteur* also throws light on the Mediterranean trade of Naples. As to Tuscany see above p. 139.

[35] Brotonne, *Dernières lettres*, etc., 1:497, no. 1042, to Murat, 27 March. Murat, *Lettres et docs.*, VIII, nos. 4647, 4764, 4833, 4842, 4857, etc.

March, for Rome had sent 200,000 quintals of grain, and Tuscany 400,000 quintals by this medium.[36]

No region, unless it were Holland, felt the onslaughts of the British "entrepôt licence system" at this time as did the German North Sea coast from the smuggling center at Heligoland. Having long known the benefits of English licences the Hanseatic ports naturally took a lively interest in the French experiment. Their Minister Resident at Paris, Abel, having secured the release of sequestred Hanse vessels in time for them to share in the first favors of the traffic, took advantage of the creation of licences of the second nomenclature to make further suggestions.[37] This he did in a letter of 10 January 1810 which he accompanied with another paper showing how impossible the short time-limit of licences had been for vessels licenced for trade with the Hanse towns. To obviate the weeks lost in getting licences at Hamburg, Bremen, and Lübeck so as to send ships thence to France, he suggested that the French consuls in these cities should give passports for vessels to go to France where they would receive the licences for which they would already have applied. If, however, a licence *ab initio* were held indispensable for their journey, he asked that it might be obtained through himself as Hanse Minister in Paris, thereby saving the long delay entailed under actual regulations by the roundabout procedure through French merchants and prefects. Also, he urged, since the desired imports were chiefly northern goods, that, while maintaining the embargo generally, passports should be granted for Hanse ships to secure Baltic goods for reshipment to France, and that such passports be obtainable through the local French consul or himself at Paris. Lastly he solicited the right for Hanseatic ships to trade as before to Guadeloupe and Ile de France, stopping on the outward and return trips in France. The pertinency of

---

[36] Brotonne, *Dernières lettres*, 1:508, 21 November 1810. It was necessary to prohibit this grain export, however, about 1 October 1810. See Brotonne, *op. cit.*, 1:519, 520, 539.

[37] $F^{12}622$.

this last proposal is apparent, coming as it did so directly after the loss of the colonies to England. While there is no evidence of an immediate consideration of these suggestions, they bore fruit later in the year when the Hanseatic licences of the second Napoleonic licence system were created.

Like the neighboring Hanse ports and Prussia, Denmark shared in the advantages given to foreign ships under the first French licences. Her flag was less favored, however, as her obstinate quarrel with England since 1807 necessarily operated against her in securing the complementary English licences which made the Napoleonic passports effective. But Denmark's situation and the activity of her privateers had necessitated a special attention to the juridical character of sea papers which brought her into significant relation to the licence traffic.[38] This is shown by an incident which illustrates the actual workings of the licences outside of French waters. The case is that of the ship *La Fortuna*, Captain Wundt, sailing under the flag of Hamburg, seized by a Danish vessel early in December 1809 and sequestered at Glückstadt. The vessel was carrying wine from Bordeaux under a French licence. The Danes considered the vessel suspicious. The interrogatories put to the crew brought out the fact that the captain had gone to Plymouth and taken convoy, also that he had stopped at Dover whence he had made a trip up to London, and that when chased he had thrown papers overboard, hence he must have had and destroyed an English licence. The captain himself had declared that he had not been visited by the English.[39] Strong reclamations having been made against the Danish

[38] Denmark had just been working out, or revising, her prize court regulations. Danish interest in such questions is also reflected by J. F. Jacobsen in his *Seerecht des Friedens und des Krieges* (published 1815), pages 718-31 of which treat the licence cases of this period. It is interesting also to note from Robinson's *Admiralty Reports* how largely cases of Danish ships figured in licence trade decisions.

[39] Technically all these circumstances were incriminatory. Actually neither France nor England consistently enforced such rules. Cf. Phillimore, *Nature and Extent of the Licence Trade*; Jacobsen, *Seerecht*, etc.; Robinson,

action, Montalivet was called upon to state whether the vessel had violated its safe conduct. He replied 9 February 1810 that the bond required with each licence was adequate security against any criminal intercourse with the enemy, and that the French licence should be respected by French and allied vessels as a full protection, provided the cargo was according to licence, regardless of any use of a British licence, or of British convoy, and notwithstanding a visit to England.[40] From the legal standpoint this ruling is very important, since it affords the authoritative definition for fixing the invalidation of a French licence. Evidently, however, the identity of the ship, and the time limits of a licence, (neither of which questions were here involved) were points which must also be precisely observed.[41]

The foregoing evidence is patently incomplete. Nevertheless, it should indicate something of the geographical reach, and the varied points of contact of the licence experiment in its *direct* international effects. There is, however, another phase of the foreign aspect of the traffic which, though apparently *indirect* in its connection, is really most essential in its consequences. This is the relation of the United States to the system. This question of the relation of the United States to the *ancien système* of licenses is manifestly but the concrete statement of the query, "How was neutral trade affected?" For in 1809 and 1810 the United States was clearly the only carrier neutral in fact, and not simply by courtesy, or *par convenience*.

Admiralty Reports, (continued by Dobson and Edwards); and note the interesting case reported by Mr. H. H. Atton in vol. 2, pp. 49-57 of *His Majesty's Customs*, the papers of which case Mr. Atton kindly showed me.

[40] It is interesting to note also that when the prefect of Finisterre in a confidential letter of February 1810 reported his suspicions that French licenced ships had English licences which the customs searchers did not find, and proposed a second search, Montalivet ordered him to restrict his activities to his instructions, which neither forbade the English licences nor required search for them, F^{12}2033.

[41] *Cor. de Nap.*, 19:535, Napoleon to Fouché. In strange contrast with the numerous licence cases in the British Admiralty Courts, French records show very few such cases.

The license measure very obviously was but a fresh effort at evading the neutral problem which was such a persistent and dominating factor in the Continental System, as in every struggle of such scope and character it inevitably must be. Nominally the licences were created to win and use neutral services within prescribed channels. In reality they were a means of dispensing with neutrals by the creation of mock neutrals. Whether or not forgery and simulation were the inevitable concomitants of the inherent falsity of the licence idea, certain it is that nothing was so calculated to undermine the whole structure of the system as a frank recognition of neutral rights. It was inevitable then that, by attacking this citadel of fraud and acting as champion of the revival of legitimate trade, the United States held the pivotal position for forcing a change in the situation.

The farcical neutrality of the licence traffic had been tacitly avowed at the very outset by the practical elimination of the United States flag from participation in the partially unshackled trade. But the question of permitted flags was hardly well in hand when the whole question of American relations had demanded reconsideration in the light of the Non-Intercourse act, and the coincident shifts in the British attitude toward America. As usual, pressure had been brought to bear from both diplomatic and commercial quarters. The activity of the American Minister had been expected, but the memoir forwarded 12 July from the Paris Chamber of Commerce had evidently not been looked for, and was most exasperating to Napoleon.[42] The immediate result of the *fatras* had been the sharp letter of 28 July to Fouché, who, as imperial proxy, was to administer the rebuke to the Chamber of Commerce. But its fruition had been the 17 August inventory of the licence measure with its ultimate consequences in the altered licences of December. Meanwhile, the culmination of the discussions with Gen. Armstrong had been the Altenberg letter of 22 August, reiterating the Napoleonic doctrines of blockade and

[42] See the discussion in ch. III above.

of neutral obligations. In it, by refusing to allow his allies favors not shown himself, he struck at the non-intercourse policy by which the United States was undermining the very foundations of his imperial system. Nevertheless, Napoleon did end his letter with a declaration that if England revoked her blockading Orders, France in turn would withdraw her decrees.[43] The delivery of this Altenberg note had ended the first skirmish in the "Non-Intercourse Act Campaign" against France in support of American rights.

A tacit truce followed. For some time American ships captured were speedily released, or were not condemned by the Conseil des Prises.[44] The records also show that some Americans now secured licences. Upon such proceedings Armstrong commented bitterly in a despatch of 10 December reporting the sending of Loison to seize British goods in Spanish ports, and with him a mercantile friend apparently to buy up the goods when sold. "This," said Armstrong, "is a specimen at once of the violence and corruption which enter into the present system; and of a piece with this is the whole business of *licences*, to which (I am sorry to add) our countrymen lend themselves with great facility."[45] After mentioning a number of American ships at Marseilles, Bordeaux, and various Channel ports which were thus "openly employed in violating our laws," Armstrong stated his purpose of sending a special agent to the coast to investigate and if necessary arrest the offending Americans. The agent chosen was Leonard Jarvis of Boston whom Armstrong seems rightly to have deemed "a young man of activity, intelligence and good principles." Yet the energetic reports which Jarvis began to

[43] *Am. State Papers, For. Rel.*, III, 324-5.

[44] Armstrong to Cadore, 10 March 1810, *Am. State Papers, For. Rel.*, III, 382. But see *Cor. de Nap.*, 20:45 and 60; also the case of vessels of David Parrish, AF^{IV}1318, pièces 42-45.

[45] *Dept. of State, Desp. Fr.*, vol. 11, Armstrong to Smith. For other pertinent evidence on the trickery of American traders see the Bordeaux *Consular letters* vols. II and III, Lee to the Secretary of State, 1 Nov. 1808, 4 June 1810, and 11 Feb. 1811.

send early in March were evidently a disappointment to his principal. For Armstrong clearly had a misapprehension as to the number of his compatriots who could be caught holding French licences.[46] Perhaps he was mistaken in supposing that "delays and impediments put in the way of" the recognition of Jarvis were intended by the French government "to give an opportunity to the outcasts in question to change their mask."[47] Nevertheless, with all his pains Jarvis could find almost no delinquent Americans. Instead he "found that the whole business was carried on by vessels under the Prussian flag." Of the nature of the business he says: "This commerce is now exceedingly flourishing and from the port of Caen alone the clearances I understand amount to about thirty per month. Grain and wine are the articles of export and in eight days' time the returns are made in various raw materials that are wanted in France and, as has been insinuated, in manufactured articles of Great Britain."

Despite its meagre results the Jarvis investigation was approved by the President, for Madison wished to foster popular prejudices against the licence trade. How excellent a basis there was for such feeling in America is well stated in a despatch of the American

[46] Jarvis to Armstrong, 9, 22, 26, 29 March; 2, 7, 17, 28 April, and 18 May 1810, *Dept. of State, Desp. Fr.*, vol. 11. See on this point the French licence register, AF^{IV}1342. But note also Lee's evidence on American subterfuges (note 47 below).

[47] Report of 18 May. In this report Jarvis names but one certain offender, and this ship, the *Thomas Jefferson*, was at a port outside his jurisdiction. In his April reports, however, he gives incriminating evidence against ships of C. Coolidge & Co., of Boston, and of other New Englanders. As these were by no means all the American ships in the trade, and as there is no evidence of a change from the American flag, it is probable that Americans were advised of the Jarvis mission and avoided his district. About the same time, also, Consul Lee was writing similar complaints home regarding his countrymen, who, trading under French and English licences, were Americans in England and at sea but escaped his jurisdiction by being French in port. *Dept. of State, Cons. letters*, Bordeaux, III, 4 June 1810. These men went so far in revenge as to spread reports that Lee was himself involved, as all other American consuls in France were. *Ibid.*, 11 Feb. 1811.

consul at Amsterdam written, by an interesting coincidence, at practically the same moment as the final Jarvis report, and coincidentally with the notable 25 May reports of Mollien and Fauchat.[48] "There is," said the consul, "something so characteristically enigmatical in the conduct of both Belligerents toward our country that I am unable to solve it. It has the appearance of a combination between them to our injury, for while their measures are calculated to prevent us from trading with either, they daily are in the habit of granting licences reciprocally to trade with each other."[49] With similar but more caustic comments, also, the American press greeted the new developments in the system of interinimical amity.[50]

To combat this apparent combination against American trade, Armstrong had already begun a new manoeuvre before he determined to deploy Jarvis against the American renegadoes. He had received the "Altenberg letter" with misgivings and had reluctantly decided to delay a fresh demand for his passports.[51] Distrusting the duration of the leniency shown toward American traders during the early autumn of 1809 he prepared during the truce for the renewal of skirmishing which he foresaw must follow when the Emperor returned victorious from the peace of Vienna. His fears were fully realized when in November Napoleon began to require a strict exclusion of American shipping not only from France, Spain, Naples and Holland, but also from Denmark, and later Prussia, Russia, and Sweden.[52] This situation Armstrong met by an essay in secret diplomacy which largely because of his

[48] See the previous chapter.

[49] Bourne to Sec. of State, 20 May 1810, *Dept. of State, Cons. letters*, Amsterdam, vol. II.

[50] See for example the *American Daily Advertiser*, 30 March, 16 and 18 April, 18 and 26 June, 23 November (from New York *Evening Post*), *Aurora* 16 June, 16 July, 3 and 6 August 1810, etc.

[51] Armstrong to Sec. Smith, 16 September, *Dept. of State, Desp. Fr.*, vol. 11.

[52] See Armstrong to Smith, 18 October, 1, 10, 14, 18, 26 November; 6, 9, 10, 14 and 22 December 1809, etc., *Dept. of State, Desp. Fr.*, vol. 11; *Cor. de*

NAPOLEON'S NAVIGATION SYSTEM   155

own perverseness apparently just failed to result in a brilliant diplomatic victory. Several unsigned letters criticizing the Continental System and the licences, which he wrote under the personation of a Frenchman, were presented with the connivance of certain imperial councillors. In this way and with the strong support of the Paris Chamber of Commerce, the influential cotton industry, and other powerful commercial interests he pressed for an immediate change in the commercial attitude toward the United States.[53]

Napoleon was brought face to face with the demand by a report of Montalivet at a council of ministers on 20 December. He at once began to parley, but yielded only after several weeks of heated discussion during which important reports were made by various ministers, including Montalivet, Gaudin, and Pétry on behalf of the Minister of Exterior Relations.[54] The culmination was a famous note of 10 January transmitting to Cadore the reports *on the grand object of our actual relations with America*, wherein Napoleon reviewed the growth and motives of his Continental System, and announced his purpose, on certain conditions, to

---

Nap., 20:45, 60, and 78; Murat, *Lettres et docs.*, VIII, especially nos. 4670-73, and 4680; the *Moniteur*, November 1809–August 1810; *Journal de l'Empire*, November–December 1809, etc.

[53] See his private despatches of 18, 25 October, etc., to Smith; his personal letters of 20 Aug., 18-19 Sept., et seq., to Madison (Lib. of Cong. MSS.); and the confirmatory French documents in F^{12}622. These documents as well as Armstrong's November-December despatches would indicate that he was also quietly supported by the Dutch, Danish and Russian envoys. Cf. also *Writings of J. Q. Adams*, III, 372 ff. He was aided by Fouché, Montalivet, d'Hauterive and perhaps other ministers. Indeed the idea grew out of a request by Fouché for a note "on the impolicy of the Imperial policy with regard to neutral commerce" which could be used to open up the question, but the scheme had to be modified when Fouché lost the portfolio of the Interior. Cf. Armstrong to Madison, 19 September, Lib. of Cong. MSS.

[54] See *Cor. de Nap.*, 20:77, 81; the very important carton F^{12} 622 at the Archives; *Aff. Étr., Cor. Pol., États Unis*, vols. 63 and 64; and Armstrong's MS. despatches of December 1809, and January 1810, *Dept. of State, Desp. Fr.*, vol. 11.

immediately change his system with respect to the United States.⁵⁵ By a striking coincidence, on the very day of this momentous decision the American minister received urgent instructions from Washington, dated 1 December. They were in reply to the Altenberg letter of 22 August, and he was ordered to open negotiations with France, upon almost the precise lines which Napoleon was dictating to Cadore.⁵⁶

Then Armstrong adopted a policy by which he cast to the winds the laurels which providence and his own clever efforts had brought within reach of his hands. On this same 10 January, despite the accurate confidential forecasts of the imperial action which had been given him but a day or so earlier, and disregarding the important instructions just received from Washington, he sent to Cadore a sharp query protesting against the reported seizures of American shipping in certain countries under French influence.⁵⁷ Upon this subject of spoliations Armstrong continued to harp for months with ample justification, but unhappily with the worst of results. Nor did he attempt to obey his instructions of 1 December until 25 January, when he did so, apparently, in reply to Cadore's

⁵⁵ *Cor. de Nap.*, 20:109-111. The importance of the American question is indicated by the great secrecy and utmost haste urged upon Cadore. Historians have long recognized this letter as a classical exposition of the Continental System, but have failed to recognize its momentous significance in Napoleon's foreign policy. The character of the letter is misinterpreted by Henry Adams in his *History of the United States*, vol. V, page 227, in noting merely such portion as harmonizes with an evidently untenable thesis as to Napoleon's policy.

⁵⁶ *Am. State Papers, For. Rel.*, III, 326. This was considered so important that copies were sent to other American ministers in Europe. See *Writings of J. Q. Adams*, III, 406.

⁵⁷ Armstrong to Smith, 6 and 10 January, *Dept. of State, Desp. Fr.*, vol. 11. Armstrong, indeed, tries to imply that his protest was several days earlier, but the note itself (*Aff. Étr., Cor. Pol., États Unis*, vol. 64) is dated 10 January. Even granting the strong reasons he had for protesting, Armstrong's note, by his own confession, was not calculated to secure redress, and was clearly inadvisable at the moment.

complaints of the neglect of the Altenberg letter by the United States.[58]

In marked contrast wtth the inaction of Armstrong is Napoleon's attitude at this moment. For despite the common consent among historians to decry the Emperor's dealings with the United States, despite even the undeniable instances of his aggressions both before this and afterward, it is difficult with fairmindedness to deny his earnest desire for an arrangement with the United States in January 1810. In keeping with this attitude of Napoleon, Montalivet on 17 January presented a report summing up the previous weeks of discussion and advocating a modification of the Continental System for the United States. The next day Cadore, through his aide Pétry, opened negotiations with Armstrong for a new commercial treaty, which he pressed assiduously for several weeks. During this time also he prepared the report demanded by Napoleon on 10 January, which, after some modifications and delay because of the attitude adopted by Armstrong, was embodied in a note to the United States bearing date of 14 February.[59] At the same time, by modifications of the tariff laws, and by the adoption of the liberal third-type licences, the Emperor brought his commercial regulations into line with the proposed new policy.[60]

The Emperor's enthusiasm for his new policy, however, soon waned. The suspicion and apparent reluctance, the reticence and querulousness with which Armstrong seemed to meet Cadore's advances piqued Napoleon from the start and his prejudice only increased with the progress of the discussions. Such a mutual feeling of distrust naturally made mutual understanding and concessions impossible. But above all by his continued emphasis

[58] Armstrong to Smith, 28 January, *Dept. of State, Desp. Fr.*, vol. 11.

[59] Armstrong to Smith, 20, 28 January, 2, 17 and 18 February, *Dept. of State, Desp. Fr.*, vol. 11; *Am. State Papers, For. Rel.*, III, 141, 381; *Cor. de Nap.*, 20:132, 141, 237; Loyd, *New Letters*, 170; *Moniteur*, 8 and 22 February 1810; etc.

[60] See p. 125 *supra.*

upon the spoliation issues Armstrong threw Cadore upon the defensive. In seeking to justify the imperial policy on the score of the Non-Intercourse measures, Cadore discovered that the law of 1 March 1809 not only discriminated between the Empire and its dependent allied states, but provided for a confiscation of French vessels in American ports.[61] Napoleon was immediately impressed with this discovery, and the idea of retaliation grew upon him as the probable outcome not only of his *pour parlers* with Armstrong but also of his negotiations with Holland, and the coincident secret mission of Labouchére to England became apparent.[62] When, therefore, Armstrong intimated that a preliminary settlement of spoliation claims would be a *sine qua non* to any treaty which he should negotiate, the *pour parlers* were quietly dropped with the view of shifting the negotiations to Washington.[63] This decision was reached at Rambouillet between 18 and 25 February and at approximately the same moment Napoleon returned to his program of confiscating American shipping, justifying his course on the plea of retaliation for the confiscation proviso of the Non-Intercourse law. To legalize this course there subsequently was published (14 May) an edict dated 23 March 1810, infamous as the Rambouillet decree.[64]

[61] *Cor. de Nap.*, 20:141.

[62] *Cor. de Nap.*, 20:229, 235, etc. Important papers on these famous negotiations are in AF^{IV}1683, and AF^{IV}1673.

[63] *Cor. de Nap.*, 20:237, 241, etc.; *Moniteur*, 22 February 1810; *Aff. Étr., Cor. Pol., États Unis*, vol. 64 (cf. Adams, *History of United States*, V, 230, ff.); also the important *unused* material in the Archives Nationales, AF^{IV} 1681, *Relations Exterieures, États Unis* (An VIII-1813). For the American side see Armstrong to Smith, 2, 17, 18, 21 and 25 February, *Dept. of State, Desp. Fr.*, vol. 11 and Smith to Armstrong, *Dept. of State, Instructions*, vol. 7, which are in part published in *Am. State Papers, For. Rel.*, III, 380 ff. The account of the negotiation by Henry Adams (*History of the United States*, vol. V, ch. 11), upon which historical opinion has been founded, despite its brilliancy, is based unfortunately upon an incomplete and evidently biased presentation of the sources used.

[64] Careful criticism would indicate that this decree was drafted at Rambouillet in February as a mere *sequestration* measure, that it was revised as a

Such was the outcome of Armstrong's conscientious maladroitness. How slight seemed the chance of a peaceful outcome of Franco-American relations! Nor did the failure of Armstrong's negotiation affect America alone. There was an immediate and fateful stiffening of the harsh conditions to which the unhappy King of Holland was forced to set his hand in the treaty of 16 March. Simultaneously, also, the liberal third-formula licences were dropped, carrying down the hopes of the business interests of Europe for a more liberal commercial order. Gloomy indeed was the prospect. Yet in the period of uncertainty and indecison which followed there was to come a transformation of the status of all these factors—of American relations, Dutch relations, and French economic forces—which should radically affect the navigation policy of the French empire.

---

confiscation law and signed in March in revenge for Armstrong's famous 10 March protest, and was finally published in May in order to legalize the seizures for financial and other reasons. What seems evidently the first draft of this decree is document 60 of *Arch. Nat.*, AF^{IV} 1318. Cf., also, Picard et Tuetey, *Cor. de Nap.* I, 3:482, 5 March 1810.

CHAPTER VI
THE ABANDONMENT OF EXCLUSION

The spring of 1810 held events of high personal interest in the life of Napoleon which largely account for his negligent indecisive attitude at the time toward questions of commercial policy. In the first days of April occurred the ceremonies of his marriage with Marie Louise, daughter of Austria's ancient imperial line. Preparation for this event had engrossed attention during much of the preceding month. Also directly following the ceremonies at Paris the imperial couple had set out for the Chateau of Compiègne where for several weeks Napoleon's chief interest was to play the devoted husband to Josephine's successor. Moreover from Compiègne on 27 April the imperial party set out upon a journey through the northern departments of the Empire—the former Austrian Netherlands. Designed at first to last only until mid-May, this journey proved a triumphal progress not ending until 1 June, when St. Cloud at last was reached.

This whole preliminary period is well characterized by a statement made by Champagny when replying, early in April, to several importunate notes on the topic of seizures of American property.[1] He explained, says Armstrong's report, that "for some days past nothing in the nature of business and unconnected with the marriage of the Emperor could be transacted; and that for some days to come, the same cause of delay would continue to operate, that my letters were still before the Emperor, and that he would seize the first moment to get some decision in relation to them." Upon which Armstrong aptly commented: "Thus you see everything is yet in the air." In truth it was not until 10 July that he could at length write to the Secretary of State: "Since June 1 the vacillation which had for some time marked the Emperor's policy in commercial matters has given place to great activity."[2]

[1] *Am. State Papers, For. Rel.*, III, 383, Armstrong to Smith, 4 April.
[2] *Dept. of State, Desp. Fr.*, vol. 11, Armstrong to Smith.

Yet in reporting this sudden "great activity" little did the American minister guess its real significance for the imperial policy in commercial matters. Indeed, perhaps not even Napoleon himself nor his advisors then realized that the change which came after 1 June portended an essential transformation of the Continental System. Aside from the fact that the Emperor once more was ready to give his chief attention to general public affairs, this end of vacillation may be accounted for by the alteration which, while he was otherwise concerned, had been taking place in the three factors that for some time past had so largely determined his commercial policy. First, in the affairs of the allied kingdom of Holland the final crisis had begun; (2) at home economic pressure had found a new opportunity of making itself felt, and (3) American relations were taking a new turn which must speedily force the imperial hand.

From a perusal of Napoleon's correspondence during the spring of 1810 one might well assume that his relations with Holland were at least one matter of general concern which received his consistent attention.[3] Relentlessly he had forced the making of the treaty of 16 March which had left Louis the mere name of an independent kingdom. With equal insistence after the exchange of ratifications (31 March) he pressed, in letter after letter, for an exact fulfillment of its terms, refusing all relief by his promised grant of licences until Louis should have first met his engagements. Moreover the ostensible reason for prolonging his visit in the north was the Emperor's desire to inspect the newly ceded Dutch districts and to have a personal conference with Louis. Surely then it would seem that Napoleon had shown no negligence touching Holland. And yet at Antwerp during the first week of May mere chance gave him the clue to a secret intrigue which had quite escaped his vigilance. This was Fouché's attempt to carry on an indirect negotiation for peace with England, such as Napoleon himself had attempted in February with the fate of Holland as a

[3] *Cor. de Nap.*, vol. 20; Colenbrander, Duboscq, etc.

pawn, but which he had soon abandoned as futile. Proofs of Fouché's intrigue were quickly secured and a few hours after his return to St. Cloud the Emperor began to vent his wrath upon the offending minister and certain of his accomplices.

The effects of the audacious negotiation, however, were not felt solely by the intriguers. One result was to make the idea of a secret diplomatic arrangement with England henceforth an impossibility for Napoleon. Thus, apparently, it lessened the chance of peace *pour parlers* developing from the negotiations begun at Morlaix for an exchange of prisoners with England. Likewise the innocent share of Dutchmen in such unauthorized negotiations regarding their country certainly did not soften the suspicions nor sooth the exasperation which embittered all Napoleon's dealings with Holland. Under the circumstances he was pitiless. He seemed, to keen observers, to be goading the Dutch to beg him to end their independence as a merciful relief from an unendurable situation.[4] When thus every slightest incident fed the heat of the imperial resentment the result was rapid. On 1 July by an act of abdication Louis barely anticipated the inevitable brushing aside of his shadow throne. And Napoleon answered on 9 July by the annexation of Holland.

But if the imperial wedding journey was thus memorable because of its incidental connection with the affairs of Holland how incalculably more important was it from the standpoint of his commercial policy. Like the sojourn at Bordeaux and Bayonne two years earlier, it was one of those far too rare occasions when the Emperor came into actual contact with the economic interests of his subjects, and so acquired first-hand knowledge of their views regarding the problems of the Continental System.

How ample this opportunity was to see the varied aspects of the workings of the System is shown by the imperial itinerary,[5]

[4] See *American Daily Advertiser*, 30 June 1810.

[5] For the information regarding this tour see especially *Cor. de Nap.*, vol. 20; IV *Bulletin des lois*, vol. 36; the *Moniteur*, April–June 1810; the *Journal de l'Empire*, April-June 1810; The *London Courier*, May-June 1810;

which included stops at such industrial and commercial centers as St. Quentin, Cambrai, Brussels, Ghent, Bruges, Lille, Rouen, and Louviers, and at commercial and strategic ports like Antwerp, Middelburg and Flushing, Ostend, Dunkirk, Boulogne, Calais, Dieppe and Havre. And when throughout the accounts of triumphal arches and illuminations, of guards of honor, banquets and balls, processions, launchings of ships, reviews and inspections which mark a royal progress, we note that Paris had almost daily news of leading citizens who had had audiences with, or been accorded honors by the Emperor, that London was on the *qui vive* with rumors from the over-Channel ports of impending changes of system, and that even American newspapers had comments upon the significance of the imperial visit to "the principal places of manufacture in Brabant and Flanders," we can rest assured that the economic interests of these northern departments had not failed to impress upon the Emperor and his advisors a realization of their importance and of their vital needs.

Apparently, moreover, Napoleon was as anxious to obtain information as these leading Netherlanders and Normans were eager to give it. For if Rouen paraded her workmen, Napoleon and his Empress devoted hours to inspecting the factories of Louviers. If the manufacturers of St. Quentin and Lille showed the imperative need of raw materials in order to continue industries rivaling those of England, if wholesalers of Ghent by a threat to corner the market in colonial goods roused defenders of the licence trade, and if fishermen of Boulogne and St. Valéry demanded the right to fish by night in the Channel, let it be noted also, that Napoleon, on his part, investigated the need of new canals, examined the advantages of Terveere and Dunkirk as smuggling ports of export to supplement the licence trade, that he called his Director of Customs in haste from Paris to Antwerp for consultation and

The *New York Commercial Advertiser*, the *Aurora*, the *American Daily Advertiser* (Phila.) etc., etc., June, July, August, 1810. Schuerman, *Itinéraire générale de Napoléon Ier* is very handy but not altogether adequate nor dependable.

kept his other ministers engaged securing information for future decrees. And on the other hand, if Napoleon made early morning visits to the quays interrogating masters of newly arrived licenced ships upon the possibilities of an understanding with England for future regulation of the trade, it was in fact the merchant Van Aken of Ghent who effectively served as Montalivet's medium in actually securing from the Board of Trade such a mutual adjustment of the opposing licence systems.[6]

Thus the Emperor came back from his tour not only persuaded of the devotion of his people but impressed with the importance of adopting immediate measures for their advantage. And just at this critical juncture came a turn in his American relations vitally affecting his future policies.

In no respect is Napoleon's shifty course from February to June 1810 more clearly illustrated than in his dealings with the United States. Nominally negotiations for reviving the Convention of 1800 were not broken off, although Pétry never returned, after 25 February 1810, with the promised counter-proposals of his government.[7] Moreover plans were pushed forward for sending a special negotiator to Washington until suddenly, to the manifest relief of Armstrong, Moustier was deputed on another mission.[8] All the while, however, fresh evidence of "the daily and practical outrage on the part of France" was goading Armstrong to repeated, but futile, remonstrances.[9] To be sure the renewed demand for his *congé* with which, on 10 March, Armstrong accompanied the ablest of his protests, gave some uneasiness to the imperial government.[10] But for this Napoleon had full revenge when Cadore ascertained that Armstrong's request for passports

[6] See below, pp. 263 ff., for a discussion of this negotiation.
[7] Armstrong to Smith, 25 February, *Dept. of State, Desp. Fr.*, vol. 11.
[8] *Ibid.*, 17 March, 24 March; also Armstrong to Madison, 18 March, Lib. of Cong. MSS. Cf. also *Cor. de Nap.*, 20:297. About 20 April Moustier was sent to negotiate at Morlaix for an exchange of British prisoners.
[9] Armstrong to Cadore, 10 March, *Am. State Papers, For. Rel.*, III, 381.
[10] Armstrong to Smith, 24 March, *Dept. of State, Desp. Fr.*, vol. 11; and see Brotonne, *Lettres inédites de Napoléon Ier*, no. 567.

reflected no probable variation from the truly American policy of multiplying vain protests. For the Emperor not only frankly persisted in his retaliations for the Non-Intercourse Act, but gave stronger expression to this policy by the Rambouillet decree, which, after quietly enforcing it for some weeks, he openly avowed by its publication on 14 May, during his stay in Belgium. Meanwhile Armstrong was held at Paris chafing under the Emperor's failure to provide the promised passports and ship for his return to America.[11] Nor was his situation helped by the lack of instructions, for months previous, from his own government. Hence as he waited, he could only continue filing his "morose" protests at the Quai d'Orsay, writing candid advices for the directors of America's foreign policy and clutching at the vague hints of a chance "to bring to a conclusion of some kind our long protracted business here."[12]

Such, *apparently*, was the status of American affairs at Paris on Napoleon's return there the first of June, 1810. Yet on 1 May a new factor had entered into the situation. For, after months of hopeless indecision and debate, Congress had passed the so-called "Macon Bill No. 2," repealing the Non-Intercourse law, upon a very important condition.[13] This proviso was that if within three months after the repeal by either France or England of its obnoxious legislation with respect to the United States the other belligerent had failed to take like action "non-intercourse" should be revived against that power which still offended. It was a direct challenge which had peculiar potency with Napoleon, coming, as it did, as the culmination of all the experiences and forces which had been working for the reconstruction of his commercial system. It made the critical breach in the Continental System, which must either be abandoned or transformed into the Navigation program which had long been the Emperor's aim.

[11] Armstrong to Smith, 7 April, *Dept. of State, Desp. Fr.*, vol. 11.
[12] *Ibid.*, 24 March.
[13] On the passage of this law see Adams, *History of the United States*, V, 194-8.

News of the American challenge reached France, moreover, at a most psychologic moment.[14] Already a fortnight earlier, directly after returning from his notable northern tour, Napoleon had begun a reconsideration of his economic policies. Preliminary to this he had created as a medium for his purposes a new adjunct of the Ministry of the Interior, the *Conseil du Commerce et des Manufactures*. It was a most significant measure. For if one may safely draw conclusions from a comparison of their existing minutes and papers it would seem that of all the special ministerial councils of the imperial régime no other was so important from the standpoint of regularity of sessions or the scope of business transacted, while none typifies better than this Conseil du Commerce the organizing and administrative genius of Napoleon.

The creation of the Conseil du Commerce seems to have been a sudden resolution on the part of Napoleon. At least the usual evidences of premeditation, such as suggestive *memoirs* or preliminary *projets* for its organization, are lacking. It has points of similarity to the *nominal* composition and functions of the contemporary Privy Council Committee, known in England as the Board of Trade, which suggest, as in the case of the licence trade, and other notable features of the Napoleonic navigation policy, the influence of the British prototype. But if Napoleon borrowed ideas he did not blindly copy institutions, instead he adapted them, through the medium of French organizing genius, to the needs of French experience. Hence the Conseil du Commerce fitted at once and properly into the imperial administrative system.

The character of the new institution is best seen from the imperial order of 6 June which called it into being and provided its working constitution.[15] This minute affords at once so charac-

[14] "It came at a moment of extreme vacillation between the old system of exclusion and the new one of licences." Armstrong to Secretary Smith, 10 July 1810, *Dept. of State, Desp. Fr.*, vol. 11.

[15] AF^{IV}1241. A copy of this and of the decree of 6 June was secured by Armstrong and enclosed in his despatch of 10 July. *Dept. of State, Desp. Fr.*, vol. 11. It reads as follows:—

teristic an example of Napoleon's methods, and so excellent a forecast of his program, that it deserves quotation entire. It states:

"There shall be held Monday of each week beginning next Monday a Council of Commerce and Manufactures to which will be called the Ministers of the Interior, of Exterior Relations, of Finance and of the Marine, the Ministers of State Defermon and Regnaud, the Councillor of State, Count de Sussy, Director General of the Customs, and Senator Chaptal.

"The Minister of the Interior will bring before this council memoirs, information and opinions of merchants upon matters which will be discussed in the Council of Commerce and which will be determined upon thereafter. The Minister of Exterior Relations will bring the papers relating to the United States of America and to the complaints which the system of licences has caused on the part of different powers. The Minister of Marine will bring the lists (états) of French or foreign vessels which have cleared from or entered our ports, as well as the orders for the

"Extract of the Minutes of the Secrétariat of State.
Decree of St. Cloud, 6 June, 1810:
On the report of our Minister of the Interior our Council of State assenting, we have decreed and do decree as follows:

Art. 1st.
There shall be held Monday of each week in our presence a council of administration of commerce and of manufactures. There shall be drawn up minutes of each session of this council.

Art. 2d.
The members which we have designated to participate in this council are to present us their views on the measures to be taken for favoring our commerce and manufactures to the detriment of our rivals.

Art. 3d.
Our Minister of the Interior will submit to us in this council all the affairs relative to commerce and to manufactures.

Art. 4th.
All measures relative to the customs can be submitted to us hereafter by our Minister of Finance only in this council.

(Signed) Napoleon
Bassano."

diminution of crews. The Minister of Finance will bring up all the regulations touching the Blockade.

"The subjects to be considered in the next council will be: 1st. Licences. Is it advisable to give new ones? 2d. Exportations and Importations: What are the products the exportation and importation of which should be permitted and under what flag should these exportations and importations be carried on? 3d. Contraband Trade. Ought the contraband trade to be authorized in any manner? Under what form? With what precautions? etc. etc. etc. 4th. Fishing. Should it be permitted to fish by night as well as by day, and to fish everywhere?

"After examining these topics the Manufacturing interests will be considered.

"1st. What are the obstacles which our manufactures meet in Italy, in Spain, in the North, and in Germany? What should be done to remove these obstacles and to favor the sale of goods made in France?

"2d. What duties should be laid on the cottons of Naples, Macedonia, etc.?

"3d. What encouragement should be given to the manufacture of stuffs of thread (fil) and silk, or of cotton stuffs to replace them?

"There will be considered also what encouragements are to be given with the view of supplying sugar and coffee, or at least maintaining these products at the present price and of offering the people the facility of replacing them at a fair price.

"Finally there shall be presented drafts of measures intended to give a new organization to the navigation of the Scheldt, Meuse, and Rhine such as shall turn to our profit the advantage drawn therefrom by foreigners and check (nuire) the commerce and manufactures of Switzerland.

"To each council the Ministers will bring the reports of business, the information they will have gathered and whatever may lead to adopting modifications in the commercial legislation."

The preliminary plans thus outlined at its creation indicate well the breadth, thoroughness, and, in general, the fairness to French interests which were to characterize the deliberations of the Conseil du Commerce during the three years, and more, of its existence. In the accomplishment of this program, however, it is evident that the share of a council with a personnel composed of cabinet councillors was pre-eminently that of the final shaping of legislation and the ultimate oversight of its administrative problems. The main tasks of preparing and executing the measures deliberated upon by the Conseil du Commerce devolved, consequently, upon the several ministerial staffs or upon supplementary organizations, adapted or specially created for such purposes.

The provision of the necessary administrative machinery was indeed an important phase of the program of commercial reconstruction before the Conseil. Consequently, although a proper view of this aspect of the problem requires a previous knowledge of the full development of the Napoleonic Navigation System, we may, at least, by way of anticipation, indicate at this point the new organs of administration formed to supplement the activities of the Conseil du Commerce. There should be mentioned, then, two semi-official adjuncts of the Ministry of the Interior, organized during the summer of 1810, the *Conseil General de Commerce*, and the *Conseil General* (or *Consultatif*) *des Arts et Manufactures*, which were designed to associate the leading business interests of the Empire directly with the government's program, winning their co-operation and obtaining a constant expression of of their needs. Likewise the various local chambers of commerce or of industrial arts were multiplied and linked more closely with the Interior Ministry. In August a special commerce court (*Conseil de Contentieux*) was created to aid the Ministry of Finance in dealing with the new problems, while in October further aid was afforded by the erection of a system of customs courts to adjudicate exceptional fiscal cases. Most important, however, was the reorganization and development (in July and August, 1810) of the commercial and industrial divisions of the

Ministry of the Interior, for from this reorganization was soon to grow a special new Ministry of Manufacturers and Commerce.

The deliberations of the Conseil du Commerce began on 11 June when Montalivet presented a long and able report in which he discussed, in their order, each of the questions propounded by Napoleon when outlining the business for that session of the Conseil.[16] Thus this report, together with the imperial minute of 6 June, affords at the very outset a fair preliminary sketch of the notable program of reconstruction which was to engross Napoleon's attention during the several succeeding months, and was to give a new character thereafter to the imperial policy. The features of this program were a reconstitution of the system of France—and the Continent—with respect to neutral relations, navigation regulations, fiscal measures, and commercial institutions, concurrently with a new adjustment and development of Continental connections, of non-maritime trade, the supplying of colonial produce and the fostering of home industries.

How much of this comprehensive program the Emperor and his Councillors actually intended or wished to carry out when Montalivet made his 11 June report it is hard to conjecture. For in the few measures adopted before the third session of the Conseil, whatever the momentary sensation they caused, one would scarcely find the initiation of any broad or radical plans. Particularly is this true respecting the determinating question of neutral relations. For, despite the specific provision in the minute of 6 June,[17] any consideration of American relations prior to 25 June seems to have been merely incidental to such issues as the enforcement of the treaty of 16 March regarding the handing over of American property confiscated in Holland, or the disposal of similar property long under sequestration at Antwerp. These were merely administrative questions incident to the Rambouillet

---

[16] F^{12}2031.

[17] "The Minister of Exterior Relations will bring the papers relating to the United States of America."

policy and discussed from the viewpoint of the fisc.[18] The same is true of a comprehensive report by the Minister of Finance intended to suggest the speediest and most profitable mode of disposing of American property seized under the several decrees of the Continental System.[19] It was in this report, that Gaudin recommended, in accordance with the provisions of the Rambouillet decree, that American cargoes condemned by the Conseil des Prises be sold at government auction. The first of such sales he thought should be held on 1 August and the proceeds be put in the treasury.

Gaudin's report was accepted on 25 June, but the Conseil du Commerce of that day found itself face to face with another and far more important aspect of the American question.[20] This was the informal confirmation, just made by the American minister, of the challenging repeal of the Non-Intercourse Act. The Emperor summed up the situation in a typical statement of his opinions.[21] The Americans, he explained, had raised the embargo on their vessels, although it was unlikely that any would utilize the permission to sail to France until assured of the reception awaiting them there. For himself two courses were open: "Either to declare that the decrees of Berlin and Milan are revoked, and re-establish commerce as it formerly was; or to announce that these decrees will be revoked on the 1st of September, if the English have then revoked their orders in Council. Or the English will revoke their orders in Council and then it will have to be considered whether the situation which ensues will be advantageous for us. This situation will have no influence whatever on the customs legislation which will regulate at will the duties and prohibitions." Thus when the Americans would come with their colonial produce it could no longer be captured by French corsairs, "because the flag covers the merchandise," but at least

[18] AF^{IV}1241. Cf. also Napoleon to Collin de Sussy, 5 July, *Cor. de Nap.*, 20:444 and Adams, *Writings of Gallatin*, II, 193, et seq.
[19] AF^{IV}1241, annex 25.
[20] AF^{IV}1241, annex 26.
[21] *Cor. de Nap.*, 20:431.

the customs could prohibit the entry of their cargoes. On the other hand the productions which France actually needed, such as Brazil sugar, Georgia cotton, staves, and fish-oil could be admitted, and also, indeed, even the productions of Martinique, Guadeloupe, San Domingo, Cayenne, and Ile de France, if it could be assured that English goods would not be included.

There would be ample time yet, however, to plan for theoretical contingencies. Meantime it was necessary to decide as to the advisability of granting licences called *permits* (so as to avoid the inevitable objections of the United States) allowing a score of ships to import Georgia cotton. The Emperor thereupon proceeded to sketch the chief features of a very restricted licence, which should embody the lessons of the previous licence experiments, and should also obviate the manifest difficulties peculiar to the American trade. Not only were these permits to be few in number and for a single American product, but they were to be limited to trade from one stipulated American port to one or another of designated French ports, from which must be exported in return wines, brandies, silks and other French goods to the value of the cargo imported. Special precautions against the introduction of English goods would be provided by requiring certificates of origin and cipher letters for the Minister of Exterior Relations, to be furnished solely by a specified French consul in America. The only derogation from the restrictions of previous French licences would be that the consul delivering the licence, instead of the central authority at Paris, would fill in the names of vessels and masters. This was a concession to the repeated arguments of Fauchat, but was admitted only because of the special necessities of the American trade.

The unique licence scheme, thus outlined, bears striking resemblance to a long project of a decree for American permits found among the papers of the Ministry of the Interior.[22] It bears dates of 29 and 30 May, coinciding with the return of Montalivet to Paris after accompanying Napoleon on his northern

[22] $F^{12}2031$.

tour. Its direct basis, moreover, is to be found in a certain undated and unsigned minute, of approximately this moment, written by Montalivet and entitled: "Observations sur les licences pour l'Amerique."[23] If its dating is not a clerical slip for 29 and 30 *June*—for no order for preparing the earlier project is found—this draft decree has special significance as anticipating a more favorable attitude toward the United States even before news of the "non-intercourse" repeal. In such case it would have an especially interesting connection with Fauchat's familiar 25 May report, as it certainly has with the pressure at Antwerp, Ghent and Rouen for American raw products.

Whether the *projet* of "29 and 30 May" inspired, or was inspired by, Napoleon's opinions of 25 June it in any case has significance as a step toward the adoption of the first measure of the new navigation system. It opens with the declarations: "There will be granted forty permits (1st) to favor the importation into France of cottons, potash, fish-oil, salt-fish and cod, hides and peltries coming from the United States of America and by American ships, (2nd) to favor the exportation from France of wines, brandies, silks, cloths (toiles), stuffs (draperies), jewelry, modes, and all other articles manufactured in France, by the return of the said American ships." Such trade was to be permitted between New York or Charleston, and either Bordeaux, or Nantes. To insure the legality of the trade elaborate precautions were outlined very like those suggested by Napoleon on 25 June, although even more irksome in certain particulars, for, in addition to a full page cipher letter there was required a cipher *visé* of the "permit" by the French consul general at Philadelphia. These permits were to be granted "to forty different commercial houses chosen among those merchants most distinguished by their probity, by their credit, and by their attachment to our person."

The broader scope and in general the rather more liberal terms of this project, as compared with the ideas dictated by Napoleon

[23] $F^{12}2164$.

on 25 June, are very evident. A further comparison with the ultimate decree, moreover, shows very significantly that it is modelled upon this draft of "29 and 30 May." The full reasons for these broader provisions—whether they represent the return to a previous plan, or merely the practical elaboration of the Emperor's brief sketch—we do not know. It is known, however, by the statement of Montalivet, that after consultations with merchants, and others, he deemed it necessary to modify the imperial instructions. Particularly interesting is it to find that among those sounded regarding the plan was the American minister.[24] Although Armstrong does not name the official who approached him, and although the scheme was communicated only in a vague and casual way to him, he seems at once to have guessed what was projected and to have expressed his frank disapproval. He declared clearly that not only was his government unalterably opposed to the participation of its citizens in a foreign licence trade, but that a scheme which attempted to restrict an American commerce to a few prescribed articles between a single port of the United States and a stipulated French port, and which was hedged about with technicalities, and the use of such exceptional documents would never be accepted by American merchants.

As some time passed without his hearing more of the scheme, Armstrong concluded that the idea had been dropped and so reported on 8 July only to be immediately disabused by information that the decree was already signed.[25] In fact on 2 July, at the session of the Conseil du Commerce next following the dictation of the Emperor's instructions on the subject, Montalivet had presented a draft decree, and an extended report discussing the objects and features of the proposed American permits.[26] After full consideration by the Conseil the decree in final form had been signed on 5 July by the Emperor who added in his own hand

[24] Armstrong to Smith, 18 July, *Dept. of State, Desp. Fr.*, vol. 11.
[25] Armstrong to Smith, 8-13 July, *Dept. of State, Desp. Fr.*, vol. 11.
[26] $AF^{IV}1241$, annex 32; and $AF^{IV}1061$, pièce 29.

qui restera secret.[27] Hence it was only after the next session of the Conseil at which a form of "permit" had been approved and it had been decided to inaugurate the plan by letters to selected merchants, that some information of it became public.

The secrecy of the decree, naturally gave rise to quite divergent versions of its provisions. Armstrong at once sent home a very brief synopsis of its chief points, and after his return to America furnished another statement which was officially, but incorrectly, published as the decree.[28] The first news of the scheme reached London on 22 July and from thence came to America about 9 September.[29] It was meagre and distorted as were subsequent reports by the same channel. Yet another version from an American at Bayonne appeared in the *United States Gazette* of 14 September.[30] Although it differs much from the decree itself this version was probably the best information of the permit scheme known in the United States, except to those concerned in the traffic.

The actual decree of 5 July consisted of ten articles. It authorized thirty permits, although a month later Napoleon states his readiness to grant one or even two hundred of them.[31] The lists of permitted articles differ from those in the May *projet* by the substitution of dyewoods for potash, from America, and of furniture for modes, in the French exports. Although these articles were named in the permits themselves, the secrecy of the decree facilitated later changes in the conditions. Thus, while the decree itself is vague as to the condition of balancing imports by French exports, Napoleon later required this:—the exports to consist half of wine, half of cloths, etc. These permits were to be of three series—Bordeaux, Nantes, and Marseilles—and were to be granted to responsible shippers of these ports who were

[27] AF^{IV}463, dossier 3503, no. 3.
[28] *Am. State Papers, For. Rel.*, III, 400.
[29] *Am. Daily Advertiser*, 10 September.
[30] Cf. the *Aurora*, 22 September.
[31] *Cor. de Nap.*, 21, no. 16778, 10 August.

associated with manufacturers of Paris, Rouen, Ghent and other important industrial centers of the Empire. The trade, indeed, was swaddled with precautions. Ships could come only from Charleston or New York and must bring with them a local newspaper of the date of their sailing. Captains must have their permits viséed by the French consul, from whom also they must bring a certificate of origin, bearing a cipher sentence as well as a cipher letter to the Minister of Exterior Relations. They must enter one of the three designated French ports unless compelled by major force to enter elsewhere. Immediately upon arrival all letters and papers must be delivered to French customs officers, non-admissible goods must be stored in government warehouses, and no ships might depart until all precautions had been met and new permits taken out.

The peculiarities of the decree are best understood, however, when interpreted by the light of Montalivet's significant 2 July report.[32] In drafting the decree Montalivet says he has considered the Emperor's primary motive to be a desire "to facilitate by the intermediary of the Americans, and by means of special permits, the arrival in our ports of certain raw materials needed by our manufacturers, and the exportation of products and manufactures the outlet for which it is essential to augment." The natural products and objects of trade of America could thus be specially admitted, and also the Americans could be utilized to furnish such colonial goods as could be proven not of English origin. A free exchange with the Americans, he felt, would be a benefit for agriculture, commerce and industry but, the Emperor's intention being not to tolerate any English productions, the trade must be limited strictly to American products, for merchants assured him that the distinctions between kinds of sugar, coffee and indigo could be too easily masked. Only when there were Spanish colonies free from English influence so that French consuls might be placed there to give certificates of origin could Americans serve as French factors for such trade. Something of the sort might be expected at Caracas and Buenos Ayres.

[32] AF^{IV}1061, no. 29.

The trade required special precautions and definiteness. It must thus be limited to certain ports. Of the five eligible American ports Charleston and Boston were the export centers of the raw materials needed, but Boston, like Philadelphia and Baltimore, was closed by ice in winter. Hence shippers had urged New York as first choice, Charleston second, and Boston a possible third. Strict insistence on entry into but one or two ports of France was unwise, but a vessel might be required for precautionary and administrative purposes to clear from either Bordeaux or Nantes.

Montalivet admitted that in this American commerce the balance had been always against France, due almost solely to the imports of sugar, coffee and tobacco, amounting to 40 million francs in an ordinary year. But this would be changed by excluding tobacco, the French crop being adequate for the current needs, while sugar and coffee would be excluded because their neutral origin could not be assured. "One ought therefore to expect that the pecuniary advantages would be about equal for both countries; were there, however, an apparent difference against us, the fact should never be lost sight of that the raw materials which the Americans will furnish we will draw from somewhere else at a higher cost, while by our exports which they will take there is actually an increased output." In accompanying tables he entered more precisely into estimates of imports and exports and painted a glowing picture of the trade to be expected under forty permits, involving 80 voyages and equal imports and exports aggregating 40,000,000 francs yearly.

Doubtless these figures duly impressed the Conseil and the Emperor, but the leading merchants whom Montalivet advised to apply at once for these valuable permits—to be got apparently without money and without price—evidently made their own calculations and so straightway began to make excuses. For when on 16 July Napoleon wrote Montalivet to send him some of the permits the next day for signature he received instead a letter of excuse, explaining that the permits were still in the hands of the printer, but that it was needless to hurry them as he had not yet received replies from Bordeaux or Nantes.[33] The answers from Marseilles were even slower, and judging from the few yet preserved were not encouraging for they are chiefly excuses for not applying, or else applications conditioned upon liberal modifications of the scheme.[34]

The difficulties found in inaugurating the scheme led Montalivet, before presenting the first applications, to seek a supplementary decree modifying that of 5 July.[35] But this Napoleon refused. On 10 August he wrote: "My decree of 5 July says all that is necessary for American permits, consequently I have not deemed it advisable to issue another."[36] At the same time he returned a model of these permits, modified to meet certain of the difficulties, with the impatient injunction: "As soon as the permits have been printed and you have filled in the names of the firms who have sought them, send them to me; I will sign ten for each series. There is not a moment to lose." The next day, consequently, the granting of the permits began. By the first of September some sixty had been signed, and one hundred and nine within the first year.

In short, whatever their objectionable features French industry could not dispense with these permits, and Americans to whom they were sent, whether from financial need, or greed, did not stickle to submit "to the humiliating system." Indeed some of the chief commercial houses of the United States used either English or French licences and, when the lieutenant governor of Massachusetts[37] and even some American consuls engaged in the traffic, there would seem to have been grounds for the assertion made to Napoleon that Americans were like the Dutch shipmaster

[33] Lloyd, *New Letters of Napoleon*, p. 192, and F^{12}2031.

[34] F^{12}2058.

[35] Cf. F^{12}2031 (5 August) and AF^{IV}1318, pièce 85 (8 August).

[36] *Cor. de Nap.*, 21, no. 16778.

[37] AF^{IV}1342, (Wm. Gray). But the *Columbian Centinel* of 11 July 1810 indicates that Gray's experiences with Bonaparte's "freedom of the seize" privateers provided an excuse for using licences.

who when brought before William the Silent for trading with the Spanish forces replied: "Your Highness, if there were profit to be had I would traffic with hell, though I burned my sails in the voyage."³⁸

With the United States government, however, the "American permits" found no favor. Anticipating this, Armstrong decided to "present a note on this new system" before leaving Paris. "As it now stands," he wrote to Madison, "it is quite rediculous (sic) and none but madmen will meddle with it." He had heard of only one American "mean enough to take one of these licences."³⁹ On 8 September, therefore, he intimated to Cadore in a series of questions his apprehensions lest it was intended to limit all American trade with France to that under licences which assumed "to prescribe regulations to be observed by the holders of them within the jurisdiction of the United States, which confined the permitted intercourse to two ports only of the said States, and which enjoined that all shipments be made on French account exclusively."³⁹ᵃ Cadore in replying denied, despite a secret imperial decision of 5 August, that all American trade was restricted to that under licences. He admitted, however, that "the Emperor has given licences to American vessels. It is the only flag which has obtained them. In this his Majesty has intended to give a proof of the respect which he loves to show to the Americans."⁴⁰ But such proofs of imperial respect were not welcomed at Washington for, when Armstrong's report arrived, not only were fresh protests ordered at Paris, but the matter was taken up at once with Gen. Turreau, especially touching the certificates and the evident purpose to exclude sugar, tobacco and

³⁸ Lubbert's memoir, AF^IV 1673.
³⁹ Armstrong to Madison, "private," undated, about 1 Sept. 1810, (Lib. of Cong. MSS.).
³⁹ᵃ *Am. State Papers, For. Rel.*, III, 388. For a later protest by Russell, cf. AF^IV 1241, *Conseil* of 29 October; cf., also, Napoleon to Cadore, 7 October, Brotonne, *Dernières lettres inédites*, 1:523.
⁴⁰ *Am. State Papers, For. Rel.*, III, 388, Cadore to Armstrong, 12 September.

other American staples from France.⁴¹ The president threatened to revoke the exequaturs of any consuls who abused American sovereign rights by performing, in the United States, the exceptional duties required of them by the licences.⁴² Congress also was urged to pass stringent measures to prevent Americans using such licences and to forbid the entry of any vessels from abroad which were restricted to trade with designated ports only.

Moreover, as reflected in the newspapers, the general American opinion concurred in the President's attitude toward the licences. To be sure the first vague rumors of an accommodation with Napoleon were hopefully received, but fuller news evoked suspicion and criticism from journals which had long been decrying the immorality and tyranny of British licences. Besides, one of the first specific reports of the new permits (from Bayonne, 1 August) carried the warning: "No confidence, however, should be put in these licences and as the aspect of affairs is daily changing it is very possible that they will fall through, as nobody can rely upon their being executed."⁴³

Suspicion and uncertainty regarding Napoleon's action were natural under the circumstances. Indignation over the Rambouillet decree was still fresh. Nor was the giving of a few licences a *quid pro quo* for the repeal of "non-intercourse." Even the first report of an accomodation had been greeted with the statement: "If General Armstrong has made an arrangement with France it must include more than the opening of French ports. That is not the real cause of complaint. He must get the repeals of the unjust decrees violating neutral rights and the restoration of sequestred property."

Very much stronger still were the long instructions sent to Armstrong on 4 and 22 May, 5 and 22 June and 5 July as to the terms of the arrangement expected by the United States as a

---

⁴¹ *Am. State Papers, For. Rel.*, III, 400-1.

⁴² *Dept. of State, Instructions*, vol. 7, pp. 127-8, Smith to Armstrong, 8 November 1810.

⁴³ *Am. Daily Advertiser*, 21 September 1810; also *Aurora*, 22 September.

result of the repeal of the Non-Intercourse law.[44] But from causes unknown these directions never reached Paris or else arrived too late for their purpose. Left thus since early January without instructions, dependent upon a chance newspaper item for his sole information of the latest move of his government, realizing the almost unvaried futility of his efforts to obtain satisfaction from the imperial government, Armstrong could see only the weakness and not the potential strength of his position. To him the latest act of Congress seemed only the "Ne plus ultra" of "government by negotiation" to which he apprehended unanswerable French objections. Having therefore with the "utmost frankness" expressed his dislike of the permit decree where word would reach the Emperor, he could only "state his fears" in a despatch of 10 July, and "resort to patience the only remedy for incurable cases."

The inactivity of the American minister in this critical moment for an aggressive diplomacy was incomprehensible to Napoleon who was too astute to delude himself with the idea that he had laid the ghost of his American difficulties. The decree of 5 July was, as Armstrong interpreted it, an evidence of the abandonment of "the old system of *exclusion*" for "that of *liconcos*," and hence was an integral part of Napoleon's new policy. But from another standpoint, which Armstrong did not appreciate, the American permit scheme was essentially a *modus vivendi* and had been so originated by the Emperor, who realized that further concessions to the proposition of the "Commercial Intercourse" act were inevitable.[46] It was an awkward situation for the Emperor, who both to save his face and to backstep as little as

[44] *Dept. of State, Instructions*, vol. 7, pp. 90-114. Cf. *Am. State Papers, For. Rel.*, III, 383-386.

[45] *Dept. of State, Desp. Fr.*, vol. 11, Armstrong to Smith, 10 July.

[46] The editor of the *London Times* (10 September) however declared regarding American permits: "We consider this a greater departure from Buonaparte's system than his conditional revocation of the Berlin and Milan decrees."

possible, was anxious to discover the extent of the American demands, and the prospective policy of Great Britain with respect to the conditions of the repeal of non-intercourse. Under such circumstances it is not surprising that he so lost patience with Armstrong's course that he desired a protest sent to Washington through the American minister at Petersburg.[47]

Napoleon's first intention, as stated on 25 June, had been to play a waiting game but too much was involved and after several weeks without further information he began to find time pressing and determined to act for himself. A step forward was taken on 17 July when Montalivet presented to the Conseil du Commerce a report "on American ships" and the "means of insuring that they have no dealings with the English" to which he added information on the movements of American shipping since the raising of the embargo on 1 May.[48] Thereupon Napoleon instructed him to submit copies of "the London orders in Council, the Berlin and Milan decrees and the last act of the United States." Along with these Montalivet was to present a report which should "remark that this act (of the United States) is by no means authentic, but which should propose to decree that the decrees of Berlin and Milan will be recalled (rapportés) at a certain epoch if at the same epoch the English have revoked their orders in Council."[49] This report was duly prepared for the next session of the Conseil du Commerce (23 July.)[50] After a brief resumé of the measures of France, England, and the United States since the Berlin decree it gave a somewhat unfavorable interpretation of the Macon act, and recommended merely a reiteration of the declaration of the Milan decree that it would be revoked for any nation which made its flag respected by England.

[47] See *Cor. de Nap.*, 20:505 to Cadore (instructions for Caulaincourt), 18 July. Cf., also, *Writings of J Q. Adams*, IV, 48, Adams to Secretary of State, 13 April 1811.
[48] AF^{IV}1241, pièce 75.
[49] AF^{IV}1241, pièce 63.
[50] AF^{IV}1241, pièce 78.

Possibly the Emperor was inclined to go further than Montalivet, but he was still hesitating when his hand was forced in a surprising manner. For with dramatic fitness at this critical instant a rumor reached Paris about 25 July that Congress had been called to declare war in retaliation for the Rambouillet decree. Messengers were sent in haste to Armstrong who argued for the credibility of the rumor. Once more, therefore, Napoleon took counsel with his ministers, and himself. Then he decided upon one of the most famous expedients of his tortuous diplomacy.[51] On 31 July when he announced to Champagny his new American policy the world's greatest belligerent bowed to the force of neutral coercion. This candid document is for historians his real reply to the "Commercial Intercourse" act. "After having reflected much on the American business," he explained, "I have thought that to revoke my Berlin and Milan decrees would be without any effect." It seemed better simply to reply to Armstrong's informal notice of the Non-Intercourse repeal saying that he could "count that my decrees will have no more effect, dating from the 1st November and that he should consider them as revoked in consequence of the said act of the American Congress, on condition that, if the British Council does not revoke its orders of 1807, the Congress of the United States will fulfill the engagement that it has taken of reviving its prohibitions upon the commerce of England. This seems to me more convenient than a decree which will cause a sensation (secousse) and not fulfill my aim. This method seems to me more conformable to my dignity and to the seriousness of the affair."[52]

[51] Note Cadore's report on reprisals, 30 July 1810, *Aff. Étr., Cor. Pol., États Unis*, vol. 64, no. 66. See, also, the allusion in Montalivet's tariff report of 30 July: "Si Votre Majesté rapporte ses decrets de Milan et de Berlin, à l'égard des Américains" . . . (F¹²2031). Yet the same report states that only "Your Majesty knows whether we are to be at war with the United States or not." However the point of this is made clear by the Armstrong to Madison letter of 5 August 1810, (Lib. of Cong. MSS. The neglect of these letters by historians is surprising.)

[52] *Cor. de Nap.*, 20:554.

As further evidence of the seriousness of his action Napoleon himself drafted, and corrected with his own hand, the note for the American minister.[53] This note went to Cadore 2 August and three days later, after some retouching of phraseology, it was ready for Armstrong. Before he could announce his unexpected, if not unearned, diplomatic triumph, there arrived belated instructions from his government. So far as it was still possible, therefore, he sought to execute these instructions with the view of getting the most liberal and definite interpretation of the new imperial policy toward America.[54]

Cadore's letter, besides a very diplomatic assertion of the prospective revocation of the Blockade decrees, consisted of a review of Franco-American relations during the Continental System.[55] Its character is too well known to need discussion here. Suffice it to say that a formal decree could scarcely have caused a greater sensation or have influenced history more deeply than did this letter of 5 August 1810.[55a] Through its immediate despatch by Armstrong to Pinkney at London, and its official publication in the *Moniteur* of 9 August, it reached the United States by 23 September.[56] There followed a thorough public

[53] *Cor. de Nap.*, 21:1, no. 16743. Also see Brotonne, *Lettres inédites de Napoléon I*[er], p. 263, on the special clause justifying the Rambouillet reprisals. The original drafts are in *Arch. Nat.*, AF[IV]469, cahier 3563, nos. 15-19, and in *Aff. Étr., Cor. Pol., États Unis*, vol. 64, nos. 27-28.

[54] Armstrong to Smith, 5-24 August, 10-12 September, etc. *Dept. of State, Desp. Fr.*, vol. 11, and cf. *Arch. Nat.*, AF[IV]1681. Yet Adams, *History of the United States*, V, 259-61 says Armstrong did nothing.

[55] *Am. State Papers, For. Rel.*, III, 386. For special discussions see Adams, *History of the United States*, ch. 12, or McMaster, *History of the People of the United States*, III, 364-69.

[55a] The sensation was enhanced by Napoleon's remarks to the Americans at his "birthday *cercle*" (15 August) that American cannon ought to talk if England did not follow his example and repeal her Orders in Council. Armstrong to Madison, Lib. of Cong. MSS. Cf. also Czernischeff to Alexander, 20 August 1810, Sbornik 121: 84.

[56] It was first published in the *New York Commercial Advertiser* of 24 September.

discussion and official consideration of its trustworthiness and probable consequences, after which it was accepted on 2 November in the manner prescribed by the Commercial Intercourse law of 1 May.[57] This action has commonly been deemed a prime cause of the War of 1812. Also it has been asserted that Madison was hoodwinked into his fateful decision through ignorance of Napoleonic duplicity as shown in a secret decree by which Napoleon on the very day of Cadore's revocation letter confirmed beyond recovery the confiscations made under his Rambouillet decree.[58] This assertion involves such misconceptions that it should not go unchallenged. For not only is the character of the said secret decree dubious, but the measures involved had been practically determined by Gaudin's report of 18-25 June, and were being carried out before 5 August.[59] Moreover it was frankly avowed to Armstrong, and well known in the United States before 2 November, that although the Rambouillet decree had been inoperative since June, previous confiscations were final under the law of retaliation.[60]

There were, however, other measures of 5 August which had direct bearing upon Napoleon's new American policy. One was the famous Trianon tariff laying new duties on colonial goods nominally prohibited under the Continental System. Another was a decision that no American ship might enter a French port prior to November except under a French licence. These famous measures of 5 August thus bore signal testimony to the influence of the American factor in finally determining Napoleon to abandon

[57] For Madison's proclamation see Richardson, *Messages*, I, 481.

[58] Cf. Adams, *History of the United States*, V, 259; E. Channing, *Jeffersonian System*, 249; Woodrow Wilson, *History of the American People*, III, 208, etc.

[59] See Adams, *Writings of Gallatin*, II, 196, 198, 205, 209-11, 221, 225. Cf. p. 171 above. The pertinent documents for the 5 August decision are to be found in *Arch. Nat.*, AF^{IV}469, cahier 3563, nos. 9-13.

[60] *Dept. of State, Desp. Fr.*, vol. 11, Armstrong to Smith, 7 August, 10 September, etc., 1810, and Armstrong to Madison (private) 5 August, 1 September, Lib. of Cong. MSS. Cf. also *Arch. Nat.*, AF^{IV}1681. Note, too, the

"the old system of exclusion" for "the new one of licences." Thus the Continental System became the new "Navigation System."

---

editorials of the *Columbian Centinel*, 26 Sept., et seq. Regarding Madison's own views on this score the most important expression is to be found in his private letter of 29 October 1810 to Armstrong, Lib. of Cong. MSS.

[61] For these and other measures, particulars may be found in *Arch. Nat.*, AF^{IV}467, cahier 3563; *Aff. Étr., Cor. Pol., États Unis*, vol. 64; *Dept. of State, Desp. Fr.*, vol. 11; and the Armstrong–Madison letters, Lib. of Cong. MSS.

CHAPTER VII
THE NEW ACTS OF NAVIGATION

Aside from the readjustment of the imperial commercial system with respect to neutrals which had been necessitated by American relations, most of the first measures taken by the Conseil du Commerce seem to have been the direct outcome of the Emperor's tour of observation in the North. Such measures were the legislation: (1) restricting the export of grain from the Empire, (2) regulating the fisheries, (3) creating a government-supervised smuggling scheme, and (4) reconstructing the licence trade policy.

The curtailment or stoppage of those grain shipments from France to England which had been the object of his first licences seems to have been contemplated by Napoleon before the creation of the Conseil du Commerce. That it was made the first important measure to be considered was, however, largely because of the fears aroused by the representations of Councillor of State Maret.[1] According to Maret forty millions of grain had been exported to England since the previous August, and it was estimated that by the end of the year all grain of the harvests of 1808 and 1809 would be gone. Apprehensive lest the reserve supplies for the army, the hospitals, etc., should prove inadequate, Napoleon at the opening session of the Conseil raised the question of laying a complete embargo on all grain shipments.[2] A definite decision was deferred until further information could be secured but meanwhile several restrictive decrees were issued on 12 and 15 June. These decrees forbade the export of grain to Holland (whence it went to England), along the land frontier, or from ports between Schoewen and L'Orient. The export of rye, which had become very dear, was also provisionally forbidden for the whole empire, and a double export duty was laid upon corn (blé). Also the distribution of new licences, which had been expected since 12

[1] *Cor. de Nap.*, 20:414.
[2] AF^{IV}1241, 11 June 1810.

March, was held up for another six weeks awaiting the results of the harvest. Finally a decree of 22 June prohibited all exports of corn, oats, or flour after midday of 1 July.³

On 2 July, at the fourth session of the Conseil, a preliminary report on crop conditions was presented, however, which raised the question whether the embargo on grain exports need be absolute or could be limited to points beyond Marans.⁴ The concensus of opinion in the Conseil evidently was reflected in a decree of the same day which reaffirmed the embargo for the Schoewen—L'Orient line even for vessels having licences, and which restricted the shipments in the L'Orient—Bordeaux district to French ships for which half of every cargo must be wine and brandy.⁵ The matter continued under discussion, moreover, during several succeeding sessions, at which new reports on the harvests and on the status of reserve supplies of grain were made. In the end a decree of 10 August, effective from 25 August, made the prohibition absolute for the exportation of corn and flour on all the land frontier, the Alps and the Mediterranean.⁶

Apparently these restrictions were dictated by mixed motives. Undoubtedly the uncertainty as to crop conditions and uneasiness as to the maintenance of sufficient food reserves for French needs was an actual factor which determined Napoleon's attitude, for his fears were soon confirmed. Nevertheless it is impossible not to observe the relation of the precautionary measures taken to the radical commercial changes then under consideration For even if intended merely as temporary expedients the grain trade regulations clearly had their influence upon the new licence legislation, and served meantime to accustom the French to the coming

---

³ For these measures see especially: AF^{IV}1243, annexes 208 and 213; *Journal de l'Empire*, 28 and 29 June; *Aurora*, 21 August; also Armstrong to Smith, 8 July, *Dept. of State, Desp. Fr.*, vol. 11.

⁴ AF^{IV}1241, annex 32.

⁵ Cf. the *Aurora*, 6 September 1810.

⁶ AF^{IV}1243, annex 231, but annex 233 (17 August) allowed the export of grain from neighboring ports into Holland.

changes.⁷ Also they were effective beyond France. For whether or not they were intended as warnings, and at the same time feelers to try the temper of the British government with the view of reaching some mutual basis for the reconstructed licence system, certain it is that the public reception of the measures fits such an interpretation.⁸

News of the curtailment of the corn trade and rumors of its early prohibition evoked wide comment in England. The precarious state of the food supply there—despite the reported arrival of eight hundred corn ships from the continent before 1 June—may be inferred by the zeal with which the newspapers sought to offset alarmist letters regarding the French embargo with news of the arrival at Harwich or Plymouth of several ships *"with those necessary articles of life,* corn and flour." It also led to pressure upon the Board of Trade to reach some understanding with France by which those necessities might still be obtained.

The grain trade decrees and orders of June, in fact were a significant part of the labors of the Conseil du Commerce. For granting that from the standpoint of the imperial administration they were, in themselves, merely experimental measures, they were at least convenient steps toward the policy soon adopted by which a limited export of cereals should, as of yore, be governed strictly by crop conditions and prices at home and also should be possible only under special grain licences, dependent upon reciprocal concessions from England. In short, the June regulations were fundamental to the new navigation system. For while striking at the very cause and basis of the original French licence policy they made it clear that Napoleon was no longer deliberately feeding his enemy, and that if a licenced trade were to be continued he intended it to be upon terms of reciprocity, satisfactory to himself.

⁷ See F¹²2031—Minutes of the *Conseil* of 16 July, where Napoleon states that as soon as he is sure of the harvest he will begin to sign new export licences.

⁸ The negotiation which was at this moment being conducted toward such an end through Van Aken of Ghent is discussed in chapter X below.

In somewhat the same category with the grain trade decrees is the action taken at the initial session of the Conseil du Commerce with regard to allowing night fishing along the northwest coast.⁹ This limited concession to demands made upon the Emperor during his recent visit to the Channel ports was largely a measure of police supervision and of military precaution. Hence we need merely mention that it embodied provisions to prevent illegal intercourse with the enemy. Yet the decree on night fishing may properly be counted a feature of the new navigation laws. It was supplemented speedily by special licence provisions touching other local problems of the fisheries, and some months later, by a general measure regulating this whole branch of national navigation.¹⁰

In striking contrast with restrictions of the night-fishing decree was another of the first measures taken up by the Conseil. This was the plan to deliberately foster a smuggling trade with England under official supervision. While on his visit to the northern ports two reports regarding such a trade had been presented to Napoleon. These were at once forwarded to Gaudin with a note asking their consideration by himself and by Count Collin, preliminary to a council which would be held as soon as the imperial party reached Paris.¹¹ In this note Napoleon stated his inclination to favor Dunkirk and Ostend and perhaps Flushing. "My aim," he said, "is to favor the exportation of products of France and the importation of foreign specie."

The question as put before the Conseil du Commerce a fortnight later, however, was very guarded. It was merely whether "to stop or restrain as much as possible" the *commerce interlope* of Dunkirk.¹² This would seem to indicate a change of attitude on the part of the Emperor, but Montalivet in his reply considered

⁹ AF^{IV}1241, annex 2; and AF^{IV}1243, annex 212.

¹⁰ Cf. AF^{IV}1198, dossier 3, pièces 39 and 41; AF^{IV}1199, dossier 2, pièce 214; *Cor. de Nap.*, 23:385, etc.

¹¹ *Cor. de Nap.*, 20:380. Cf. Rocquain, p. 276, (22 May).

¹² F^{12}2031.

the matter as already favorably settled, and indeed the decree of 15 June throughout its three sections and thirteen articles is dominated by the motive of the note of 29 May to Gaudin. Its tone is indicated by the astonishing declaration of its first article that "the boats known under the name of smugglers will be admitted into the port of Dunkirk without being subjected to the measures and dispositions relative to the Continental blockade."[13]

The explanation of this surprising decree is that Napoleon had decided to bend to his own purposes an evil which could with difficulty be suppressed, it having for many years been a firmly established and important institution of Dunkirk and the Channel coasts. It was therefore decreed that under most rigid marine, police, and customs supervision these little boats should export the brandy and manufactures of France, and the gin of Holland. In return they could bring nothing but ingots of gold, guineas, piastres, or commercial paper. They could carry no passengers, but might carry letters and papers, subject to police censorship. They were to be restricted to a certain section of the prescribed port where they were to be under constant surveillance, and the least contravention of regulations would be sternly punished.

It is easily seen how important an adjunct this institution might be to the licence trade of France in evading the strenuous efforts of the English government to prevent the introduction of certain products which Napoleon was obstinately determined to force upon his enemy, and at the same time to secure a return for such goods in specie, the exportation of which England most rigorously forbade. So quickly was the value of this experiment demonstrated that within a few weeks Schiedam asked to be assimilated to the port of Dunkirk for this trade, while subsequently Terveere in Zealand and Wimereux near Boulogne were also made smuggling centers.[14] Later still, when for military reasons most

[13] AF^{IV}1243, pièce 209. A copy was also sent by Gen. Armstrong to Sec. Smith on 10 July, *Dept. of State, Desp. Fr.*, vol. 11. Yet he did not know that this trade was to be carried on under the American flag.

[14] Decrees of 6 February and 3 May 1811. See also 1810-12 letters of Boucher de Perthes.

of these centers had to be given up, the business was transferred to Gravelines where it continued until the fall of Napoleon.[15] The most important function of the Wimereux-Gravelines trade was its use as a channel of financial communication for the Continent with England. In short this tiny hole in the wall of exclusion was the clearing house of Europe. The dramatic story of how Napoleon developed this function of his scheme as a weapon for destroying English credit and of how in the end it was made to work the undoing of the great Emperor himself, is one of the strangest untold chapters of Napoleon's career. Despite its intrinsic connection with the imperial program of 1810, however, we must omit its consideration here in order that we may turn to certain broader and less clandestine features of the new commercial system.

It will be recalled that in outlining the labors of his new Conseil du Commerce Napoleon had indicated as the first question to be treated "the utility of licences and the advisability of giving them."[16] We have seen how this question had been forced upon the imperial attention not only by the arguments of officials in the Ministry of the Interior,[17] but likewise by the constant demands of those economic interests with which Napoleon came in touch during his tour of the North. Yet it is not certain how far by the date of the first meeting of the Conseil du Commerce this pressure had already succeeded. Had it, in particular, overcome that instability of purpose, or even the decided repugnance to the licence trade, which had largely contributed to the non-execution of the decree creating licences of the third type? Apparently the first thought was merely to rehabilitate these yet untried licences with certain modifications and additional precautions.

[15] Decisions of 30 November 1811, 29 January, 22 February, 15 March, 1812.

[16] $F^{12}2031$.

[17] See Fauchat's memoir of 25 May, ($F^{12}2031$); also an unsigned "Rapport à l'Empereur pendant les voyages du Nord-Belgique 1810. 2d Division. Renseignements sur navigation avec et sans neutres. 31 May 1810." ($F^{12}2115$, dossier 3, No. 1).

Such, at least, seems to be the central idea of Montalivet's report of 11 June, and with this interpretation other evidence agrees.

For the continuance of a licence policy Montalivet's report argued favorably but in general terms.[18] "So long as the English system shall force Your Majesty to maintain that of the Blockade," he declared, "certain principal products of the soil, certain raw materials necessary for our manufactures can be exported or imported only through fraud or by means of exceptions, tolerated or specially authorized." Importations might still be possible from prizes made by French corsairs, but measures were needed to facilitate the export of grains, wines and oils lest surplus harvests should become a curse to the land. Exportations might occur under great hardships, indeed, without licences, but if the destination were other than England the chances of capture were too great, while shipments to England would violate the laws of the Blockade. "Besides a formal authorization is preferable to a connivance of which subalterns would become the arbiters." Licences also were needed to supply the demands of manufactures. And while such imports might "seem to turn the balance of commerce against us, yet if we consider that they provide us raw materials which we, in part, re-export after giving them by manufacture a much enhanced value, we find therein a real benefit." He admitted, it is true, that the system of licences was unquestionably "very bad as an ordinary regulation, but here," he urged, "the concern is a measure of exception."

While thus advocating more licences Montalivet took occasion to advise the imitation of the English method of granting licences for special imports rather than under a general nomenclature. For this he believed would better distribute the imports and curb speculation. Regarding the commodities permissible for the licenced trade he proposed a continuance of the lists adopted for the previous licences, subject, however, like the customs tariff to constant revision and adaptation to changing circumstances.

[18] F^{12}2031. Report with annexes.

With respect to the Emperor's further question: "Under what flag should these exportations and importations be carried on?" Montalivet explained that neutral flags were being used and neutral captains employed in this licence trade, although the ships were largely owned and manned by non-French speaking subjects of the Empire, also that the captains carried double papers— simulations upon which the English closed their eyes. His opinion was, therefore, that it was not desirable to exclude neutrals from the French licence trade, but specific instructions might enjoin the exclusion of true neutrals wherever French ships and crews were obtainable. As a further means of controlling the trade for the fullest benefits to France importation ought rarely to be allowed before exportation.

Such general ideas, however, were quickly changed to the purpose of working out a definite new licence scheme, a change of purpose to which Montalivet's arguments, the reports of his confidential agents as to the English attitude, and the discussions regarding the corn trade all contributed. Nevertheless the evidence would indicate that Napoleon did not determine upon a radical reconstruction of his system until his hand had been forced by that unexpected turn in the American phase of his policy which led immediately to the creation of "permits" for American ships, and then to the conditional repeal of the Berlin and Milan decrees.

Evidently the repeal of the American Non-Intercourse law was known to the Conseil du Commerce by 18 June. It was certainly an engrossing topic for consideration during the next two or three weeks thereafter, in which interval it is difficult to ascertain precisely what was being done regarding the general licence policy. It would seem, however, that after Montalivet's report of 11 June the Conseil agreed to discuss "the form of the new licences on the 16th instant."[19] It is known also that for the session of 18 June Montalivet prepared a "*projet* of regulations for navigation and licences" which was "given to His Majesty,"

[19] *Aurora*, 21 August 1810, (news dated Paris, 13 June.)

and is now missing.[20] No action upon the "*projet* is recorded, but it was understood that the crop situation would make it inadvisable to grant new licences for another six weeks.[21] Montalivet therefore turned to consider a proposed tariff revision upon which he prepared a report for the next meeting of the Conseil. Then the decision of 25 June regarding American permits changed the situation, since such a measure seemed to require a preliminary recasting of the general navigation policy.[22] Such action was taken, therefore, on 2 July, presumably upon the lines already sketched by Montalivet.

Although the disappearance of the *projet* of 18 June prevents our knowing the scope of the regulations proposed, surely the combination of navigation and licence regulations in the same *projet*, as indicated by its title, is most suggestive. This significance is enhanced, moreover, when we find among the documents which seem to have accompanied Montalivet's report such papers as: a tabulation of the navigation acts of the Revolution (1791-1793), a minute carefully defining the use of the terms *navigation* and *cabotage*, a copy of the law on the neutralization of French vessels (13 prairial An XI), and two drafts for an imperial decree on "licences of navigation."[23]

The special emphasis thus laid upon the navigation act idea is the more striking when we note the absence thereof in Montalivet's earlier reports.[24] Yet such emphasis can scarcely be deemed fortuitous, for its influence at this critical moment is unmistakable. Since neither Montalivet's reports nor other papers of the Conseil du Commerce afford clues as to the reasons or

[20] $F^{12}2033$.
[21] Armstrong to Smith, 10 July, *Dept. of State, Desp. Fr.*, vol. 11.
[22] Also an important action on 25 June was a decision for the use of English licences. Cf. Rovigo to Montalivet, 30 June, ($F^{12}2033$).
[23] See $F^{12}2031$, where these papers are placed by error with reports of 17 and 30 July, instead of 13 and 30 June as is shown by $F^{12}2033$.
[24] There is, however, a report of 31 May: "Renseignements sur navigation avec et sans neutres." ($F^{12}2115$, dossier 3, no. 11), which must be taken into account.

responsibility for the introduction of the navigation idea it may be pertinent to note the possible bearing upon the problem of an unindentified document, apparently of about this critical moment, which is preserved in a carton of most important commercial documents of the imperial régime.[25]

The memoir—or report—in question starts off with the assertion that "The measure of licences places the commerce and policy not only of France but of all Europe in an entirely new situation." It indeed opens a small door for the partial disposal of French goods, but it allows a far greater advantage in return to English trade, "and another consideration not less important is that the admission of licences is a tacit recognition of the sign and of the form given by the English to that absolute empire which they exercise on all seas and upon all mariners." And again: "the régime of licences which we imitate from England is on the part of that power the most audacious and tyrannical act which she had yet imagined, for she says the sea belongs to me and you shall not traverse it unless you pay me tribute." Such a régime the writer urged should be overturned, but "without renouncing meanwhile the continental blockade with the most absolute Prohibition of English merchandise."

The first means he proposed was "the admission of all neutral nations upon conditions determined solemnly, and invariably pronounced," and if it be urged that France did not repel the neu trals but merely refused to recognize as such, those who allowed themselves to be visited and taxed by the English, he would reply "that it would not appear just to punish the victims of the Tyranny because they were not able to resist it."

Particularly he proposed to change the situation "by an act of navigation," which he declared was "worthy of the power of the Emperor" and "in the interests of France to promulgate." He conceived this act, he said, under very simple forms and principles. Since a commerce of exchange was most advantageous

[25] AF^{IV}1318, no. 15.

to France he suggested free admission of allies and neutrals, but with the first condition that they bring only their own goods and receive French products in return—and he mentioned in this connection especially the United States and the Spanish colonies which were becoming independent. Second, he would control prices and quantities of goods admitted by a carefully adjusted tariff. Lastly he would resolutely exclude English goods, confiscating the ship which brought them and punishing the master, but not punishing such ships as had unwillingly submitted to the visits and impositions of English cruisers. Such an act he insisted would, without involving embarrassing explanations for the past, free France from the vicious circle in which she was involved, and while maintaining the Continental System would so throw the blame upon England as to enlist the cordial support of all against the English monopoly.

Despite the simplicity and naïveté of the proposed navigation plan it undoubtedly suggested a not impracticable solution of the problem before Napoleon. That he ever read this anonymous paper there is no evidence, yet there is a striking analogy between the points proposed and the great project of July 1810. Indeed the analogy even extends to arguments and almost to the phraseology used by Napoleon at this time. Particularly significant is it also that Napoleon actually reached the sudden determination to transform his Continental Blockade into a new navigation system. It is equally significant, however, that the Napoleonic navigation act instead of abrogating the régime of licences, founded itself directly upon that trade.

The new and fundamental licence decree bears the date of 3 July. Shortly afterwards Maret, duc de Bassano, the Secretary of State, who says he drew up this *"very long decree of his Majesty which has organized our System of Commercial Navigation and which has established the Licences,"* wrote Montalivet asking for a certain minute of the decree which he wished to use for a report to Napoleon. If he refers to an outline of the law dictated by the Emperor himself the minutes of the Conseil du Commerce fail to indicate such a dictation. What is clearly such a minute, however, exists among the papers from the Ministry of the Interior.[26] Evidently written in great haste it is scarcely legible. It is undated but must have been taken down not later than 2 July, nor earlier than 11 June, and probably on the latter of these two dates.

This minute lays down in the Napoleonic manner the basic principles of the proposed decree and indicates certain of its strikingly new details and then devotes itself to an exposition and defense of the motives underlying the new action.

The features of the new plan thus indicated were (a) the restriction of the licence trade to a few stipulated ports, perhaps only Ostend, Dunkirk, Le Havre, St. Malo, Morlaix, La Rochelle, Nantes, Bordeaux; (b) the permission of the export of all articles not prohibited, but the conditions of exportation and importation to vary according to the port; (c) the creation of a separate series of licences for each permitted port and the adaptation of administrative arrangements to meet such changes; (d) the responsibility of the merchant applying for the licence for any transactions under it; (e) restriction of the licence trade to French ships and subjects; and (f) the relation of the French to the British licence trade.

The inconsistency from the standpoint of the Continental System of a navigation system based on a recognition of the British measures, as well as the injustice to neutrals involved therein was patent. Napoleon attempted to defend it, however, by sophistry flimsier even than were the usual palliations of his policies. He frankly admitted that "all these boats are able to navigate only with English licenses," and that "the French license should be granted them only so as to go from a French port to some port of England." The holder of a French licence therefore must certify to his British licence declaring what it had cost him, such declarations to be used in verifying the transaction. He also suggested that it would be well to see from an examination of the stipulations of the licences whether it would not be possible

[26] AF^{IV}1342.

to recede in some respects from the Berlin and Milan decrees (revenir sous quelques rapports sur les decrets de Berlin et de Milan).

On the other hand he maintained that to limit this licence trade to French ships, and to permit them to handle the colonial trade from which the Americans had been excluded by the Continental System, would not affect "the principal part of the System of the Berlin and Milan decrees and would change nothing." The decrees were designed in fact not against the French but to prevent the neutrals becoming the factors of England. The light patent tax paid the English for the licence was of no moment so long as nothing else was paid. It could have little effect on the price of the goods, and "the English have a right to require this payment since one has no right to pass through a superior force."

The arrangement could scarcely fail to secure English protection since it was to their interests, but it would be much more to the interests of France whose commerce would be enriched and whose navigation would be ameliorated. To prevent too large an advantage to the British the outlet afforded for their colonial goods could be regulated at will especially by a very high import duty on sugar and coffee which would lessen their consumption. Also he could declare that only goods from Guadeloupe and Martinique (which he claimed were still French colonies) would be received and French officials could always see to it that they were not tricked on that score.

In short, here was a scheme which would "procure for France the sailors of which she has need, the prosperity of her agriculture and her commerce and in fine the products the consumption of which is necessary for her." And, all this gain would be without violating the Continental System since "the decrees against the decrees of the British Council have chiefly as their aim to prevent the English spreading their flag over the universe and levying an *octroi* upon the consumption of the Continent."

Thus did great Napoleon save his face, prove that the fundamental policy of his Empire was undefeated and unchanged, and clear himself of any infraction of his great system. It was doubtless quite as well, however, in view of the actual *volte-face* which he was about to execute that this little "ease to conscience" remained in the bosoms of his official family and was not destined to the consumption of the continent.

The imperial navigation decree of St. Cloud of 3 July 1810 consists of eight chapters and thirty-seven articles.[27] Chapter one (article 1) defines under three headings what are French ships. It shows distinctly the influence of article two of Barère's revolutionary Navigation Act of 21 September 1793, although the phraseology has been recast and the provisions extended and adapted to the altered situation of France. Chapter two (article 2) permits vessels meeting the conditions of chapter one which have been neutralized to become again French ships. Chapter three (articles 3-6) provides for the use of simulations by such ships to avoid capture, prescribing the formulas for obtaining and using legal permission for this purpose. Such simulations might extend not only to a change of the flag and the name of the vessel but even to changing the names of the crew.

Chapter four (article 7) on the coasting trade (cabotage des côtes) represents nominally an important modification of French navigation laws, as it permitted such trade to foreign vessels if they held an imperial permit, while the law of 21 September, 1793 (article 4) forbade alien ships to carry French goods from port to port of France. The next chapter (articles 8-10) headed "Foreign Ships" embodies a fundamental principle of the British navigation acts and corresponds with, but is simpler than, article 3 of the Navigation Act of the Convention (21 September 1793). It states succinctly that "the cargo of any ship will not be admitted into the ports of France if it is not of the production of the country to which the ship belongs." In cases of contravention instead the penalties of confiscation, fine, and imprisonment of the revolutionary act, it stipulates merely that the non-admissible portion of the cargo shall be re-exported or placed in bonded warehouses at the option of the master or supercargo of the vessel. An impor-

[27] AF^{IV}463, dossier 3502, no. 19.

tant new provision is that restricting to French vessels the exportation of "grain, vegetables, oysters, etc., and other articles of first and indispensable necessity."

These distinctly navigation articles, however, merely form the basis for navigation legislation of which the sixth chapter of the decree is the corner stone. It is headed "of the Blockade" and article 11 declares that the preceding articles in no way derogate from the Berlin decree, the Milan decrees, and the Tuileries decree of 11 January 1808, while article 12 adds that no ship can be exempt from the provisions of the said decrees except by an imperial licence.

Upon such a foundation was erected the imperial system of licenced navigation. Chapter seven outlines this system, the first principle of which (article 13) is that such licences will be granted only to French ships. Thus the licence system becomes assimilated to the navigation acts of France and indeed the chief working principle of the new navigation system. The scheme which is elaborated in twelve articles is an extension of the ideas sketched by Napoleon as reported in the undated minute already noted. In other words, hereafter licences are to be limited to specified ports, two hundred for each port, forming a separate series, with a varying nomenclature for the different series, although with the general regulations common to the system as a whole. The decree names twenty licence ports for the western coast from Antwerp to Bayonne, and nine for the Mediterranean from Agde to Ostia. Finally it is stipulated that the exemption given by the licences extends only to the blockade decrees and not to tariff and customs or grain trade regulations.

Chapter eight assimilates to the coasting trade regulations the navigation of the Rhine, Scheldt and Meuse and, indirectly, even their tributaries. It particularly stipulates that cargoes destined for points beyond the French border must be transferred at Nimwegen, Wesel and other entreports to French boats and pay a transit duty in order to reach their destinations. Whatever may have been the motive for these particular regulations, its effect could hardly be other than to make the commerce of West Central Europe tributary to France, and to simplify, perhaps, the enforcement of the Continental Closure along the North Sea Coast.

The final article (37) seems to have been recast by Napoleon. It declares that "the present decree shall not be printed but shall be sent in duplicate to our Minister of the Interior, of Finance and of Marine and a copy transmitted by our Minister of Finance to our Director General of the Customs. Our said Ministers are charged with the execution of the present decree. They will carry into execution its provisions by circulars without citing it and without any other person than themselves having knowledge of it."[28]

The enactment of the navigation decree of 3 July was followed at once (5 July) by the signature of the complementary decree creating a scheme of American trade permits or licences.[29] In reality this second decree had been adopted on 25 June but its formal enactment had been deferred until the general measure, the immediate adoption of which it made inevitable, could be perfected.

The principles of the new licenced Navigation System having been laid down by these two decrees the Conseil turned immediately to provide the necessary administrative or special supplementary measures for carrying the program into execution. On 9 July, Montalivet brought in first drafts of the new licences and permits, and also made a special report on the basis of information from his confidential agents as to the actual status of communications with England. In the discussion Napoleon took occasion to stress briefly certain aspects of the situation, which, as developed more at length a week later in a letter to Montalivet, afford the classic statement of the commercial program then in the emperor's mind.

[28] Accordingly duplicates were furnished on 4 July to the three ministers specified, and on 19 December 1811 the Minister of Exterior Relations received a copy.

[29] AF^{IV}463, dossier 3503, no. 3.

"I have regulated the system of Commerce with the Americans," began this letter of 16 July.[30] If there are difficulties modifications can be made but meanwhile prepare the thirty permits at once. "By this means my manufactures will be abundantly provided with cotton."

"The grain trade of France is forbidden as a measure of public security. As soon as I shall be reassured as to the harvest, I will reopen my ports, and I shall permit the exportation along the whole frontier." Meanwhile enforce the embargo, but prepare permits for the non-embargoed Atlantic ports, also for the Mediterranean in order that the Levant and Barbary trade may grow.

"Having thus provided for the most indispensable needs of the export trade of the empire it is needful to provide for the exportation of the allied countries." A licence scheme for Hamburg and Bremen somewhat upon the lines of the American permit plan would seem advisable. "I will follow the same plan for Dantzic which will benefit Poland. . . ." "Hamburg and Bremen are the outlets of the Elbe and the Weser as Dantzic is for the Vistula. I can thus lay a considerable import tax upon these ports, provision my marine with the timber of the North, and achieve very advantageous results. As to Italy I shall give licences for Venice, and for Ancona," on certain conditions as to exports and imports.

In fine: "You see that this vast system will tend to feed my ports, to make of this commerce a commerce of exception and to bring me a considerable revenue. This is an advantageous system from every point of view. It is responding to the English maritime tax (contribution) by a continental tax, it is rendering injustice for injustice, arbitrariness for arbitrariness. I am not undertaking therefore a piece of folly."

"Your Majesty," replied Montalivet, "seems to have conceived for the glory of his Empire and for the conquest of peace,

[30] Lecestre, *Lettres inédites de Napoléon I*er, II, 52-54, no. 652. See also Loyd, *New Letters of Napoleon*, p. 192-194.

one of those vast projects the consequences of which astonish at first, and then appear not only probable but, in a manner, certain. The system of vigorous exclusion of all the products of the English soil or commerce has without doubt greatly injured our enemies, but progress is slow, we ourselves suffer from it. Your Majesty has seen a means of diminishing for us these inconveniences and of succeeding, promptly, in creating the formidable forces with which your Majesty will be able to give to the world the Liberty of the Seas."[31]

With such words Montalivet began a significant report of 30 July; meantime he had been busy endeavoring to do his part in the completion of the vast project. Thus in accordance with the imperial instructions of 16 July Montalivet presented at the Conseil of the following day a draft decree for Hanseatic licences, accompanied by a report upon the advantages and inconveniences of the plan.[32] Among the disadvantages he listed the chances of forging licences, of trafficking in licences, of cheating their object by unauthorized trips, the danger of renewing commercial ties with England and the fear of rivalry with French licence holders. Above all, however, he pointed out the infeasibility of the proposed exports of grain and naval supplies. When there was superabundance of grain in France and no special lack in England it was good policy to relieve agriculture and facilitate tax payments by this trade. Now, however, that the situation was changed and it was not a case of ordinary commerce but of feeding the enemy in his direst need, surely the reasonable policy would be for France to induce her allies to adopt a legitimate reprisal and visit upon England her own policy toward the Continent. Besides how would it be possible to restrict the trade of the Baltic to Lübeck and Danzig? As to naval stores, it was impossible to believe that England would suffer a vessel to leave her ports for France with such supplies. Hence, the only way the plan could be managed would be for the vessel to alter the course

[31] AF[IV]1061, pièce 50.
[32] AF[IV]1241, annexes 73 and 74.

prescribed by her English licence and pretend to be captured by a French corsair and to be released on condition of carrying wine to England. In other words, Montalivet proposed just such trickery in the licence trade as the English Board of Trade was working upon its own part.

Although the searching criticism of the absurdities of the imperial proposals was not able to turn Napoleon from his purpose, nevertheless the result was that the Hanse licence decree as signed 23 July was greatly altered and contained the most elaborate safeguards of any licence scheme.

This decree was followed immediately by measures to assimilate to the licenced navigation system the remnant of French colonial trade, the commerce of Italy and Naples and that of Holland which latter had, since the decree of 3 July, been formally annexed to the French Empire.[33] Another of the immediate changes in the system was the decision to make the licences contribute to the imperial budget. Accordingly on 22 July a decree was signed subjecting all licences to a retribution of 1000 francs to be turned into the treasury as customs receipts.[34]

Meanwhile the discovery of evasions of the embargo on grain shipments brought out the need of more stringent prohibitions, and of a decree categorically restricting such trade to licenced vessels.[35] By imperial request therefore Montalivet on 17 July proposed such a decree.[36] It seemed on consideration, however, that it would be preferable to combine this and others of the supplements of the 3 July decree into a single amendatory decree, and such a decree was signed on 25 July at St. Cloud.

The minute of this decree, as proposed by Montalivet with his report of 23 July, consists of some thirteen articles, but in the

[33] $AF^{IV}1241$.

[34] $AF^{IV}1243$, annex 218.

[35] $F^{12}2033$. See Rovigo to Montalivet, 14 July, and Montalivet's reply of 20 July.

[36] Napoleon's letter of 16 July above, and Montalivet's reply of 17 July ($F^{12}2031$).

decree as signed these are reduced to five.[37] Article one forbids *any* vessel to leave the ports of France for a foreign port after 1 August, without a licence. Article two requires every vessel going from one French port to another to obtain an *acquit à caution* which receipt must be returned with a certificate of arrival in a French port before the guarantees of the said bond or "caution" will be cancelled. Article three places the Mediterranean trade with Naples under the category of coasting trade although with the difference that the French consuls instead of the imperial customs are to carry out the formalities. Article four provides similarly for trade with the Ile de France, the prefect issuing the certificates of arrival there. The last article entrusts its execution to the Ministers of the Interior, Marine, and Finance.

This decree of 25 July and the decrees of the 3d and 5th of the same month may be termed the constituent acts for the reconstruction of the French navigation system upon the licence trade basis. Thus the first decree had blocked out the general plan and had worked out the importation features except as to neutral countries supplying their own goods. The decree on American permits had remedied this omission both as to imports and exports from neutrals, and the decree of 25 July had filled out the scheme by bringing all French export trade under analogous regulations.

But the framing of the constituent acts must not imply the completion of the new licence scheme, and certainly not of the new navigation code. Indeed some of the supplementary licence decrees were from the practical standpoint scarcely less important than the three chief decrees of July. Most of such additional acts can best be considered later, as modifications of the July legislation, but the significant measures of the beginning of August properly require consideration here.

Coincidently with the measures taken to remedy the oversights in the decree of 3 July Napoleon was considering certain very im-

[37] Cf. $F^{12}2031$, no. 6, and $F^{12}2113$.

portant changes in his commercial system not mentioned in the "grand project" of the letter of 16 July. After the decisive opening declaration of that letter: "I have settled the system of commerce with the Americans" one finds with astonishment that on the very next day the Conseil du Commerce suddenly began to debate the question of changing it all by repealing the Berlin and Milan decrees with respect to the United States.[38] After considerable discussion, therefore, to which Montalivet, Cadore, and perhaps other ministers contributed reports, the decision was reached to make a conditional and prospective repeal of the offensive decrees. This, as we have already seen, was formally announced on 5 August to the American Minister.

This discussion afforded Montalivet an opportunity to argue, in season and out, for a liberalization of trade regulations. One of the strongest of such pleas was by way of introduction to a report on tariff revision made about 30 July.[39] In this connection he frankly criticized the licence system for which he stood as sponsor. He reasserted his belief in the licences as affording at least "a useful means to diminish the evils of the present system, but they are an insufficient remedy always badly distributed; they are a privilege at best hazardous and not at best wise." He, therefore, scrutinized the advisability of the restricted licences in the new system which was supposedly intended to multiply the arrival of needed goods at reasonable prices. "The licences," he declared, "will always be a constraint (gêne), they will be delivered only with formalities with some sort of precautions; they will render the freight of the vessel which obtains them dearer, and hence also the price of products which will be able to come only upon these vessels; they will prevent prompt and secret shipments, they will curb competition. "But," he admitted "they will preserve the system of the blockade at least as a principle, since it would require a special exception to derogate from it. Their inconvenience will be diminished by multiplying them

[38] AF^{IV}1241, annex 67.
[39] F^{12}2031.

indefinitely and by giving them with great promptness and facility. This would be no more than a species of passport or recognizance which would be obtained like the other papers of a ship." If the licences were to be continued he advocated revising and liberalizing them upon lines which he indicated. But he did not fail to suggest also that, "if Your Majesty rescinds his decree of Milan and Berlin with regard to the Americans *the permits* would apparently become useless." But, as he hinted, only Napoleon knew whether he would retract those decrees. In short the matter came to this: "To tolerate the entry and sailing of ships without a licence would be, without doubt, the simplest measure, and better from the commercial standpoint; but would one dare to profit by it if Your Majesty did not formally and in a general manner rescind the Milan and Berlin decrees. Is it advisable to rescind them?"

Within a week after this report, Napoleon had announced the conditional retraction of his decrees, with regard to the Americans. To be sure this did not, according to Montalivet's argument, warrant the abolition of regular licences, but it did seem to nullify the permit scheme and the watchful minister seized the opening to urge in a letter of 8 August that the new licence system was vitally affected and that a comprehensive revision of the recent legislation was necessary. He thus hoped to remedy the difficulties he was encountering in his effort to put the new scheme into operation. He, therefore, proposed three *projets* of decrees; one to modify the decree of 5 July, another covering Mediterranean permits, and a third and most important one to supersede chapter VII (on licences) of the decree of 3 July.[40]

The draft of this substitute plan of licence trade organization, Montalivet formulated in four chapters and twenty-seven articles. This expansion of the twelve articles, which for chapter VII of the 3 July decree was an attempt to incorporate with the main legislation the various supplementary measures which had fixed

[40] AF^{IV}1318, pièces 85-86.

the price of licences, worked out their detailed provisions, and extended the system to Holland and the Mediterranean. It likewise involved many more or less important changes of the principles as well as the forms of the system.

Thus Montalivet urged the *nominal* removal of the strict limitation of licences to French ships, arguing that this limitation having been published, and made known in England, and the Board of Trade being determined not to permit the use of known French ships, the trade was in jeopardy. If, as seems possible, his argument was based on word from a secret agent who had just gone to England to negotiate indirectly a working agreement with the Board of Trade, clearly he had grounds for apprehension. Also he had excellent grounds, on the arguments presented by French shippers, to urge a relaxation of the requirements as to the proportion of Frenchmen in a ship's crew and as to the absolutely fixed export requirements. Yet their practical difficulties seem to have blinded him to the fact that to have embodied his proposed relaxations in the form of a general law would have been a vital blow at the central idea of the new commercial system, for it was tantamount to abandoning the conception that the licence trade was the French navigation act put into practice.

Other changes suggested by Montalivet were the creation of another series of licences (the thirtieth) under the name of Amsterdam, with six sub-series for all of Holland; that the thirty licence series be divided into three groups, that of the North (Amsterdam to L'Orient), that of the Ocean (Nantes to Bayonne), and that of the Mediterranean; and also that three types of licences should be created, viz., *licences simples, licences diverses* or *speciales,* and *licences pour sucre.* It is to the development of details for these three types of licences that the last three chapters of the draft decree are devoted.

Napoleon replied 10 August returning the three proposed decrees to Montalivet, unsigned.[41] He stated that he could not

[41] *Cor. de Nap.,* 21, no. 16778.

see the necessity nor desirability of such a general revision at the moment, that most of the purposes in view could be attained more directly by instructions, or by decisions on the merits of special cases, by modifications in the formulas of the licences, or even by the granting of special licences. Besides the fact that all of his secret decrees became known on the spot made him averse to the issuance of others. He also cogently pointed out that Montalivet's desire to settle and codify the whole system at the outset, only tended to delay its inauguration and to clog the general plan with administrative details which would hamper its operations. On the other hand Napoleon did accept many of the suggestions, either embodying them as immediate decisions, or reserving them for future elaboration. Among the reserved measures may be mentioned the Dutch licences, sugar licences, and the *licences diverses*, as well as new Mediterranean and American measures.

In fact the Emperor had in hand other features of his grand scheme of reorganization which could not well wait on a perfection of the licence system. His chief interest at the moment may be seen from the closing words of a letter which he had written a few days earlier to Collin de Sussy. "It is not a question of licences," he declared, "nor of extraordinary laws, but it is needful before all to regulate the customs legislation as to these things, then I will give licences for the merchandise to come."[42]

[42] *La Presse*, 9 March 1844.

CHAPTER VIII
THE CONTINENTAL ZOLLVEREIN

"My Son, I am occupied with a great plan relative to navigation and commerce," wrote Napoleon to Eugène on 6 August. "I pray you to send me the customs tariff of the kingdom of Italy as it is today in force. I desire hereafter that no change be made except by a decree from myself. . . . . You will receive a decree which I am just adopting in order to regulate the import duties on various kinds of colonial products. . . . . You will receive likewise the general decree which I have enacted for navigation. These two decrees are binding upon the kingdom of Italy." Whereupon follows an explanation of how the licenced navigation system and the neutral permit scheme are to work with his new tariff.[1] To Jerome, likewise, he wrote two days afterward regarding the adoption of his new customs reforms for Westphalia.[2] Clearly then this new tariff had an important place in the great scheme. But what was this tariff and why had it been adopted?

The idea of linking a complementing tariff measure with navigation acts was not a Napoleonic invention. So vital was the connection between navigation acts and customs laws in the English commercial system that distinctions were not always made; and the abolition of the one practically doomed the other. In France, moreover, when the Convention passed its famous act of 21 September 1793, its fifth article specifically promised that "the tariff of national customs will be reformed and combined with the act of navigation."[3] This act was destined with certain modifications to remain throughout the revolutionary régime and to be inherited by Napoleon as an effective weapon in the attack upon England. Likewise it will be recalled that the anonymous proposal made about June 1810, to replace the licence trade by a

---

[1] *Cor. de Nap.*, 21:24, no. 16767. For the reply see *Mem. et Cor. de Eugène de Beauharnais*, VI, 360-63, (14 Aug.), 365, etc.
[2] *Cor. de Nap.*, 21:28, no. 16774.
[3] Duvergier, *Lois*, VI, 222.

simple navigation act suggested, as a chief feature in such a scheme, a specially adjusted tariff to control the importation of certain goods.[4] Indeed Napoleon himself apparently had had an analogous tariff readjustment in view in connection with his quickly abandoned commercial reorganization project of 1807, while as recently as February 1810, a tariff readjustment had accompanied the adoption of new licence terms.[5]

Judging from the questions outlined by the Emperor when he created his Conseil du Commerce et des Manufactures on 6 June further tariff revision was already contemplated, either as a corrective for the high prices of colonial goods and raw materials, or as a protection for French industry, with, of course, an incidental revenue purpose.[6] The first definite step toward such an end, however, seems to have been the instruction to Montalivet on 18 June to prepare a report on the tariff and to present certain trade statistics.[7] These instructions were complied with at the next session. The immediate action taken is not clear but there followed during the next four or five weeks a thorough discussion of the tariff problems. It is impossible to enter into the details of this discussion or enumerate all changes made in the existing tariff legislation. There may be noted, however, the action intended to exclude foreign soda and soap, and particularly several measures taken to restrict the export of raw silk from Italy to France alone, thus cutting off the supply to England via Germany.[8] Larger measures were the readjustment of regulations for the Franco-German and Franco-Spanish customs.[9] At last on 31 July a decree was signed modifying in many particulars the tariff on exports from France.[10]

[4] Cf. *supra* pp. 195-7.
[5] Cf. *supra*, chapter I, for the 1807 project.
[6] AF^{IV}1241.
[7] AF^{IV}1241, annex 22.
[8] AF^{IV}1241, annexes 23 and 51; also AF^{IV}1243, annexes 210, and 224-226
[9] AF^{IV}1241, annexes 32 and 63; also AF^{IV}1243, annex 215.
[10] AF^{IV}1243, annexes 220 and 221, modifying the tariff of 4 nivose An V. See also IV *Bulletin des lois*, 13:104.

Although this decree of 31 July was one of the most extensive tariff revisions made under Napoleon it is by no means so important as is a short decree of three articles enacted five days later with respect to import duties on colonial goods. Regarding the idea of this tariff of 5 August so many speculations have been expressed that it seems *apropos* to trace its origin carefully. For so largely does it reflect principles laid down in the preliminary reports by Montalivet, and so close is its relation to other measures of the moment, that no better commentary can be made upon its purposes than is afforded by the review of its making.

The Trianon tariff was a logical consequence of the navigation acts of July, which Napoleon was impatient to put into effect. The preparations to inaugurate the new licence system immediately brought into special prominence the question of the probable effect of the large arrivals of raw materials, which were to be anticipated from America and England, in depressing market prices.[11] Equally important was the relation of such importations to the imperial budget, for revenue questions also were receiving the Emperor's special consideration at this moment.[12]

The problem was made the subject of a very significant ministerial report for the Conseil du Commerce. This report was a frank avowal of the impotence of the Continental System.[13] It affirmed the justice of the Berlin and Milan decrees as measures of reprisal against England calculated, if strictly enforced, to bury the enemy beneath sterile wealth, but declared that because of "a great number of modifications which have diminished the success of the system" France, and not England, was actually the chief loser. The English trade in colonial goods had, indeed, been cut in half but increased profits and especially those on freights

[11] AF^{IV}1241, annex 63, Napoleon's remarks upon news from America, 17 July 1810.

[12] *Cor. de Nap.*, 20:444 (5 July). For decrees, see AF^{IV}467. For the connection with American issues see Adams, *Gallatin*, II, 211.

[13] F^{12}2031. I identify this as the report made by Montalivet on 17 July. Cf. AF^{IV}1241.

and insurance kept the net returns little below the former level, while France for indispensable raw materials must pay not only the enhanced English prices, but also the high costs of indirect land importation, smuggler's risks and speculator's profits.

The writer of the report therefore reasons that "it is to the interest of the Government: 1st, to maintain the colonial products of simple consumption at a cost high enough to diminish their usage; 2d, to maintain those of the products which may be considered as first materials at a tax high enough that their culture should be encouraged with us or that our indigenous raw materials should sustain the competition with the least disadvantage possible. But it is not less to its advantage, as is well understood, to get into the coffers of the state all the benefit which can result from this increase of price . . . in place of inviting to [the enjoyment] of these profits the English, the foreigners and various speculators."

He confesses that he sees no other way to accomplish these ends, while maintaining the principle of the blockade, than by giving licences which is an objectionable policy uncertain in its workings and tending to foster adventurers and speculators. Consequently he urges the most liberal possible licence policy, not limited simply to French ships, and he even suggests the free admission of Americans. For only thus, he contends, can the increase in the tariff bring into the treasury an increased consumption tax, and not prove, instead the final burden for French consumers.

In line with the arguments of the foregoing report Napoleon at the session of 17 July put forth a series of propositions upon which he desired a further report.[14] These propositions were made with the object of ascertaining (1) the differences in the returns from the consumption *octroi* on colonial goods since the tripling of prices, (2) the quantities of such goods ordinarily required, (3) the rate of import duties which might restore a balance in prices, and (4) what this would produce for the benefit of the marine.

[14] AF^{IV}1241, annex 67.

A report upon these questions was made about 30 July by Montalivet.[15] In his preliminary remarks he referred to Napoleon's assertion of his willingness to receive the colonial goods of French colonies, of neutrals, and allies, stressed the former importance of the colonial trade to France, and urged a recovery through the encouragement of arrivals of such goods, and the allowance of reasonable profits to the traders. He, therefore, raised the question of the advisability of retaining the licence policy, or of revoking the Berlin and Milan decrees. Then before turning to the question of tariff rates he indicated certain guiding considerations which he thought should not be lost sight of in the research. These were: (a) that the tariff should be for the widest possible extent of country in order to prevent fraud, to shut out foreign goods, and to give the advantage to France in competition with other countries; (b) that preferential duties should be levied in French ports; (c) that drawbacks should be allowed to French manufactures upon the export of goods the raw materials for which had paid the Continental *octroi*; (d) that the official value or basis of the duty should not be the exorbitant French prices but those obtaining in neighboring states, which better reflected the actual effect of fraudulent importations; and finally, he advised that the duty should be made as popular as possible.

Having thus stated what he considered should be the underlying principles of the new tariff he took up specifically the question of rates, illustrating his discussion by careful tabulations of the market prices and import and consumption duties for the chief commodities, under the tariffs of 30 April 1806, and February 1810. These results he also compared with such similar data as he found available for neighboring states. Thereupon he recommended that the official standard for the new rates should be based upon the market prices of 1807 raised by a duty to a mean between the current Basel and Amsterdam rates. Such a duty he roughly estimated would yield 100,000,000 francs for the Empire, even after exempting cotton from Naples and Spain. To

---

[15] $F^{12}2031$. The report is undated but corresponds with the report which he gave on 30 July. Cf. $AF^{IV}1241$, annex 89.

this he would add fifty millions from the subservient states, and after deducting ten millions for drawbacks to manufacturers he estimated a net result of 140,000,000 francs for the imperial fisc.

These estimates were evidently over-sanguine, however, for on 5 August, Montalivet presented another report with revised conclusions based upon fuller data.[16] He now noted a decline of customs receipts from 76,000,000 in 1807 to 36,000,000 for the latest available period and stated that the element of fraud was so great that a reliable estimate for the consumption duty was impossible. He also pointed out that due allowance must be made for adequate returns to the merchants. Hence he urged the advisability of temporarily, at least, lowering the duties and allowing prices to find a new level, thereby making legitimate commerce more profitable than fraud and encouraging a commercial readjustment. Particularly did he urge the public announcement of a broad licence policy, of the granting of drawbacks to manufacturers, and of preferential duties, in favor of the French and Dutch colonies.

The new report was too late, however, to influence the imperial decision. The tariff decree was already prepared and was signed at noon of 5 August at the Trianon. The day before Napoleon had sent a draft copy of the decree to Collin de Sussy, Director General of the Customs, together with an illuminative comment upon it.[17] "I have followed for the tariff," he wrote, "your report to the Minister of the Interior. My intention is to diminish the duties rather than augment them, yet to maintain the colonial products at the price at which they are in France so that the goods of our production may come to enter into competition with them." Then he added: "It is not a question of licences nor of extraordinary laws, but it is needful before all to regulate the customs legislation as to these points; then I will give licences for the merchandise to come."

[16] $F^{12}2031$.
[17] *La Presse,* vol. 16, 9 March 1844.

The schedule of the Trianon tariff is a brief one of but twenty-four items, and fewer articles, affecting only cottons, sugars, teas, coffee, indigo, cocoa, cochineal, pepper, cinnamon, cloves, nutmegs, mahogany and a few dyewoods.[18] Despite Napoleon's statement to Count de Sussy a comparison with even the doubled rates of the February revision fails to show where he carried out his "intention to diminish the duties." On the whole, the schedule shows a revision upward to the level of 40%-50% ad valorem which had just been adopted as the basis upon which colonial goods in Holland or confiscated American cargoes elsewhere might enter into the commerce of the Empire.[19]

In the effort to cling to the blockade decrees and yet to meet the demands of the manufacturers for raw materials, especially cotton, the device was adopted of varying the rate according to the source of the material. Thus on cotton from Brazil and the Guianas, and on Georgia long staple, which cottons could scarcely be imported unless through British channels, the duty was 800 francs per metric quintal, on Levant cotton by sea, and hence perhaps via Malta, 400 francs per quintal, or 200 francs on the same cotton arriving by land through Cologne, Coblentz, Mainz and Strassburg, while cotton from any other sources (except Naples which was favored) paid 600 francs per metric quintal (i.e., 1,000 kilograms). The effort to help the manufacturer did not go to the extent, however, of allowing him the drawbacks urged by Montalivet with respect to exports of goods made from raw materials which had paid the Trianon duties. Neither did the distinctions made as to the origin of certain products discriminate, as Montalivet had advocated, in favor of goods from French and Dutch colonies. Yet these omissions which, indeed, were not essential to the decree, are readily understandable in the light of further developments of Napoleon's policy.

[18] Duvergier 17 *Lois*, 148, or *Bulletin des lois*, 4th series, vol. 13, p. 93. The original decree with complementary papers can be found in *Arch. Nat.*, AF[IV]469, cahier 3563, nos. 4, 5, etc.

[19] Cf. AF[IV]1243, annexes 212, 219, 222 and 223, decrees of 21 June, 9 and 31 July.

Despite its rather dramatic importance in Napoleon's Continental program, it should be particularly borne in mind that the Trianon decree was in many respects only a partial and incomplete measure. As a tariff act it has already been shown that it was only one phase of a broad schedule-by-schedule revision. Even from the standpoint of its primary object, to wit, the supplementing of the new navigation acts, it was far from covering the case. It was of necessity so hastily drawn up that the solution of the more difficult aspects of the problem had to be deferred for fuller consideration and subsequent enactment. Such aspects were the omitted provisions in favor of French manufacturers and French colonies, just noted above, although even more urgent was the problem of goods coming from the United States.

This problem of American goods was a three-fold one. There was the problem of sequestred goods already in France; second, the question of goods arriving during the interval between the repeal of the Non-Intercourse act (1 May) and the proposed withdrawal of the Berlin and Milan decrees (1 November), and lastly, the matter of regulations as to goods coming under the "permit" decree of 5 July.

The question of sequestred goods had been practically decided by permitting their entry after private redemption or public auction provided they paid an entry duty of 40% or 50% ad valorem.[20] As future arrivals were only partially covered by the decrees of 5 July and 5 August further action was necessary. General Armstrong's note of 20 August regarding the admission of American ships, answered by Cadore on 7 September, brought the question to an issue.[21] If American vessels were to be admitted the tariff must be readjusted. On 10 September, therefore, Cadore presented to the Conseil du Commerce a draft decree, "supple-

[20] Cf. AF^{IV}1243, annexes 211, 219, 223, etc.

[21] *Dept. of State, Desp. Fr.*, vol. 11. The original drafts dictated and altered by Napoleon himself are in *Aff. Étr., Cor. Pol., États Unis*, vol. 64, fols. 192-194. In the meantime several cases were handled on their individual merits. Cf. AF^{IV}1241.

menting that of 5 August last."[22] Two days later at St. Cloud it received the imperial signature, and the same day fresh assurances were given Armstrong that American vessels with American products would be received in France.[23]

At the moment of the adoption of the St. Cloud decree it also happened that the attention of the Conseil du Commerce was focused on another aspect of the remote commerce of France, namely the maintenance of a direct colonial trade. Nominally the meagre remnants of the French colonial empire had, by the decree of 25 July, been brought under the new navigation acts, although the details of the application of these acts had not been worked out for the colonies. Moreover, the 25 July decree did not embrace the colonial possessions of newly annexed Holland, and it was particularly the problem of maintaining connections with Java which brought before the Conseil on 3 September the problem of working out the colonial trade policy.[24]

The investigation which followed lasted for some weeks and embraced even such questions as the practicability of establishing relations with, and supporting, the negro empire of San Domingo and the revolutionary republics which were being set up in Spanish America.[25] The only definite results of the discussion, however, aside from the marine program of keeping up regular communication with Batavia seem to have been the establishment of a form of colonial licences for vessels sailing "in adventure," and the adoption of a colonial customs act.[26]

The decree regulating the colonial customs is dated 1 November, and follows the principles urged by Montalivet in his reports

[22] AF^{IV}1241, annex 157.

[23] *Dept. of State, Desp. Fr.*, vol. 11. First drafts are in *Aff. Étr., Cor. Pol., États Unis*, vol. 64, fols. 201-202, and 307.

[24] AF^{IV}1241, annexes 136, 144, and 145. The issue was brought up because of demands of chambers of commerce.

[25] AF^{IV}1241, annexes 157, 163, etc.

[26] *Arch. Nat.*, Imp. Decrees, 14 November, no. 27 (decision); and AF^{IV} 1243, annex 271, decree of 1 November.

of 30 July and 5 August.[27] It provides: (1) that colonial goods comprised in the tariff of 5 August whem coming from Ile de France, Batavia and other colonies under French rule in the East and West Indies should be exempt from customs duties if they came directly on French or Dutch ships, or (2) should pay one-fourth the tariff of 5 August if they arrived on American ships; (3) all ship's papers must be submitted to the Conseil du Commerce for validation before the admission of the ship; and (4) the decree was declared retroactive, to date from 5 August.

Besides the St. Cloud and colonial tariff decrees numerous other measures were soon adopted to modify or supplement the Trianon decree, which we cannot stop to discuss. Some of these modified the schedule of duties, raising or lowering rates or increasing the list of enumerated articles. Thus, for example, tobaccos, hides and ashes were assimilated to the new tariff policy, while on the other hand drugs and medicines were exempted.[28] Of the articles in the original list cotton being the most important from the industrial point was the subject of frequent modifying decrees or decisions, particularly with respect to the Levant, Neapolitan and Spanish product. Levant goods, moreover, were the occasion for various administrative decrees, complementary to the decree of Trianon. Yet important and interesting as are these measures regulating entrepôts, and transit routes and dues, their significance is pre-eminently for the land trade, and hence their relation to the navigation problem is primarily an indirect one.[29]

For analogous reasons, also, the various compensatory and protective measures for the aid of French manufactures while intimately related to the workings of the Trianon tariff are so much more distinctly industrial and financial than they are commercial aspects of the Continental System, that their discussion

[27] Duvergier, 17 *Lois* 233.

[28] AF^{IV}1243, annexes 270, 275, and 282.

[29] On the transit scheme see: AF^{IV}1241, 10 and 24 September, 8 and 15 October, 5 and 12 November, and especially the report of 24 September. AF^{IV} 1061, pièces 67 and 68.

must perforce be excluded from a study of the Napoleonic Navigation policy. We may turn therefore to the problems of the execution of the decree of 5 August.[30]

The significance of the Trianon decree was recognized immediately upon its publication.[31] In his daily reports to Napoleon on 7 and 8 August Mollien refers to the presentiments of commerce over the new customs measures, and thereafter for some weeks reports the speculations which followed on the Bourse.[32] The news of the decree created a great sensation at Frankfort where it was totally unexpected by the great dealers there in colonial goods, and word was sent at once by couriers to Berlin, Leipzig, and Vienna, where it was predicted that it would create a revolution in the markets.[33]

The sensation in England was scarcely less marked although London merchants had had some premonitions of the change. Sugar rose 10% at once and other colonial goods in proportion because of large purchases made for Continental houses.[34] The newspapers declared that the decree had been extorted from Bonaparte, that it was a tacit acknowledgment of the failure of the plans to ruin England.[35] Taken in connection with the new licences and news of Cadore's letter of 5 August to Armstrong regarding the withdrawal of the Berlin and Milan decrees, it was generally heralded as equivalent to the abandonment of the Continental System. So influential, moreover, was this inter-

[30] These problems moreover have been admirably treated by Darmstädter Tarlé, and Lanzac de Laborie. (See Bibliography, p. 406.)
[31] IV *Bulletin deslois*, no. 5778.
[32] AF^{IV}1088.
[33] *Journal de l'Empire*, 27 August, (Frankfort news of 22 August). See also the Dutch and Turkish protests inColenbrander, VI, pt. 1, pp. 51, 53, 62, and 63.
[34] *London Chronicle*, 17, 18-20 August. This paper says the decree was published 7 August. Cf. also *American Daily Advertiser*, 27 September.
[35] See excerpts from London papers in the *Moniteur*, 27 and 28 August, and in the *Journal de l'Empire*, 29 August. Cf. also *London Courier*, 10 September; *Bell's Weekly Messenger*, 19 August, etc.

pretation that Napoleon found it necessary for Cadore to assure the Danish minister "that my decrees of Berlin and Milan are not repealed, that all the reasonings of the English journals . . . thereupon are false."[36]

In America the new tariff aroused much discussion but it was received dubiously for it was generally considered that the high duties nullified Cadore's offer to Armstrong and many felt that it simply transferred the exclusion of American goods to another basis.[37] Perhaps American journals would have expressed even stronger views regarding the resuscitation of the Continental System in its new guise if the editors had had the reading of the despatches from the American ministers in Europe during the autumn of 1810. Thus as early as 10 September, Armstrong in writing to the Secretary of State regarding the promised repeal of the Berlin and Milan decrees says: "By the way the system of which these decrees make a part is fast recovering the ground it had lost; and I should not be astonished, were it soon to become as great a favorite as formerly. The secret of all this is the belief, that the late failures in England are monitory of the approaching failure of the nation, etc.[38] What perhaps may give to this belief new life and currency is (sub rosa) the assistance it lends to the march of French views and French influence on the Baltic "[39] About the same moment from the Baltic itself another American plenipotentiary was ringing changes upon this same theme.[40]

[36] *Cor. de Nap.*, 21:82, no. 16856.

[37] Cf. *American Daily Advertiser*, 25 and 27 September 1810. Yet Armstrong in his private letter of 5 August to Madison (Lib. of Cong., MSS.) hoped that the United States might turn this bad law to good account, and predicted that the high tariff must defeat itself. After the actual publication of the decree he commented further upon its unfairness.

[38] Mollien on 4 September wrote in just this strain to Napoleon. $F^{12}2033$.

[39] *Dept. of State, Desp. Fr.*, vol. 11. It may be needless to say that this was suppressed when Armstrong's despatch went to Congress. This paragraph should come between the two paragraphs published in *American State Papers, For. Rel.*, III, 387.

[40] *Writings of J. Q. Adams*, III, 482 et seq., especially pp. 542 and 543.

Contradictory as these British, Napoleonic, and American interpretations of the new French measures may seem, yet in a sense all three views are not far from right. For the Trianon tariff of 5 August was actually a public evidence that the old Continental System of rigid exclusion, of a commercial crusade against England, had failed, and while nominally it had not been abandoned, really it had given place to a new system of regulation, to navigation acts, and to a continental protective tariff system directed against English and colonial wares.

When the Trianon tariff was adopted recent annexations had so increased the coast lines of the French Empire that the new decree was at once law from the Ems to the Pyrenees, and around the northern Mediterranean from Catalonia to the Tiber's mouth. It is clear, judging from his proposals put forth on 17 July, that Napoleon intended probably from the first to extend the operations of his new tariff over Italy and other indirectly governed regions.[41] Indeed the like purpose is indicated some days earlier in the regulation, direct from Paris, of the Italian silk trade and of the Leghorn customs.[42] It is not surprising therefore that the ink was barely dry on the decree of the Trianon when a copy of it, of the silk trade measures, and of the new navigation acts were sent to Eugène for execution, with the information that henceforth the commercial regulations of Italy would come only from the Emperor.[43] Meanwhile the Conseil du Commerce had begun investigations and discussions which were to bring the Italian customs into line with those of the Empire both as to policy and organization.[44] The work was done with thoroughness and occupied much of the attention of the Conseil particularly during August and September. During this time one or more Italian representatives participated in the deliberations of the Conseil, while the Italian government

[41] F¹²2031. Fourth proposition.
[42] AF^{IV}1241.
[43] *Cor. de Nap.*, 21:24; *Mem. et Cor. de Eugéne*, VI, 360-65 et seq.
[44] *Cor. de Nap.*, 21:60, no. 16824, (22 August), also *ibid.*, 21:65, no. 16829, (26 August).

contributed reports to the discussion.⁴⁵ Consequently, while French interests were usually given first consideration, Italian rights and interests were not ignored and in some cases were given preference over those of France. In other words, in principle at least, the revision was on a basis of reciprocity.

Coincidently with the harmonizing of the Italian and imperial customs, Marmont under the direction of the Conseil was reorganizing the customs of the Illyrian provinces as Lebrun was those of Holland, while analogous measures were being taken for the Hanseatic cities.⁴⁶

Aside from the definite object of securing a more effective fight against smuggling these measures were designed to protect and foster French industries at the expense of all rivals. These purposes had been fully indicated by Napoleon's questions of 6 June and Montalivet's reports of a week later. But nowhere are they more succinctly and bluntly expressed than in a letter of 23 August replying to Eugène's protests against the changes in Italy, in which letter warning was given that if Eugène followed the example of Louis, Italy would meet the fate of Holland.⁴⁷

"My motto," Napoleon wrote significantly, "is *France before all*. You should never lose from view that if the English triumph on the sea, it is because the English are strongest there; it is proper then since France is the strongest on land, that she also should make her commerce triumph there." And after pointing out the advantages of obedience as against the consequences of failure to execute his measures in Italy he warningly added: "Take, then as your device also, *France above all*."

In the spirit of this letter, moreover, Napoleon already had formed the design of securing for his reconstructed Continental System the same general adoption that he had secured for his

⁴⁵ Cf. AF^IV 1241, Sessions of July to November. See also *Cor. de Nap.*, vol. 21; and *Mem. et Cor. de Eugène*, vol. VI.

⁴⁶ *Ibid.*, cf. also (for Illyria) AF^IV 1243, annexes 287, 279, 296, etc., and *Memoirs of the Duke of Ragusa*.

⁴⁷ *Cor. de Nap.*, 21:60, no. 16824.

continental closure decrees, and had planned in 1807 to obtain for his commercial-maritime code.[48] He therefore, first, brought pressure to bear upon all continental nations under his influence to adopt the same or analogous customs and consumption duties on colonial goods, and likewise to adopt similar measures for the prevention of smuggling and fraud, in short to form a *Continental zollverein*. Second, by means of his new navigation act with its licence trade and its *cabotage* regulations for rivers as well as coasts, and by his guinea-smuggling decree he planned to establish the commercial and financial hegemony of France on the Continent. Meanwhile, third, by multifarious modes of encouragement he wished to secure an industrial leadership as well. Fourth, he sought to secure the general recognition of such an economic leadership by the negotiation of new commercial treaties with the Continent and America. Finally, to facilitate the workings of this French-centered commercial system, he planned to supplement his navigation acts by further development of rivers, roads and canals, and above all by the revival of overland routes of trade. In short it was a design so truly Napoleonic that few even of *his* imperial dreams surpassed it in boldness of conception. But if it was Napoleonic in its possibilities, it was Napoleonic in its elements of failure, which is but saying, in other words, that it was a project full of prophesies and mighty in its influence upon the century that has followed.

The Trianon tariff was recognized at once as the rallying point of the renewed Continental System. It struck at the smuggler, the grafter, the speculator and their clientele. With dramatic directness it showed the focal point in the fresh attack against English economic power.

Realizing the potentialities of this new instrument of attack and convinced from the beginning that its effectiveness would be proportionate to the extent of its adoption, Napoleon had kept

[48] Indeed at this very moment he was having the Code Napoleon and commercial code adopted for the Grand Duchy of Warsaw, *Moniteur*, 12 July 1810.

it simple and broad in language and adaptable to all countries by eliminating all such provisions as would have restricted its application to the French Empire. Then when his expectations had been fulfilled by the sensation caused by its announcement, he took immediate steps to insure its general execution.

On 29 August, therefore, Cadore was instructed to send the new tariff to Cassel insisting upon its adoption for the customs of Westphalia.[49] The same course was to be taken as to Saxony, the Prince Primate, and in fact all princes of the Rhine Confederation. Like insinuations, moreover, were to be made in Prussia and in Russia. "I would desire," he explained, "that the same day each prince should *tariff* the colonial merchandise in his States. This would be a great advantage to us and the loss would fall partly on the English commerce and partly on the contrabanders."

On 5 September fresh instructions and a project for a circular to accompany the transmission of the new tariff were sent to Cadore.[50] The tariff and circular were to be sent to the various powers, especially Russia, Prussia, Saxony, Westphalia, Mecklenburg, Denmark, Switzerland, Naples, Bavaria, Würtemburg, and all the other princes of Germany. Austria, Sweden and the Grand Duchy of Warsaw, although not mentioned here, were evidently also notified. It was explained that more or less of modifications of the tariff might be agreed to according to the country concerned. Thus for Prussia he would demand "that the tariff should be adopted at least for the sugars, coffees, and cottons of America, and for dyewoods. By this means Prussia will get considerable resources; the products will be maintained at a high price, and this will establish an equality of system upon the continent."

[49] *Cor. de Nap.*, 21:75, no. 16843, and see his own earlier letter to Jerome, *Cor. de Nap.*, 21, no. 16774.
[50] *Cor. de Nap.*, 21:38, no. 16865. A possible motive for this new demand may be found in Mollien's 4 September report on the English situation as reflected on the Bourse, $F^{12}2033$.

The instructions sent by Cadore to the French diplomatic agents probably stipulated about 1 October as the common date for the adoption of the Trianon tariff by the States of the Continent. Thus Napoleon himself dated his decrees for Berg, Mecklenburg, Lauenburg, and the Hanse cities on 2 October.[51] This same day the Saxon decree was issued while a day previous Austria had inaugurated her independent colonial goods tariff upon which she had been working for months previous. Darmstadt adopted the Trianon decree on 4 October, Frankfort, and Nassau on the 8th, and Baden, Würtemburg, Westphalia aud Prussia had done so by the 10th or 11th, while on 25 October the *Moniteur* announced that all the members of the Rhine Confederation had accepted the tariff.[52] By 1 November Naples, the Duchy of Warsaw, Switzerland, Bavaria and Denmark could have been included in the list. In fact it was on this very date that the American Minister at Petersburg wrote to a friend: "The new tariff spreads like a leprosy and renders the Berlin and Milan decrees altogether useless. It strikes more effectually both at English and neutral trade than the decrees and makes all discrimination of flags unnecessary."[53]

The initial success thus scored with respect to the adoption of the tariff of 5 August was immediately followed up by Napoleon with the demand for its application to goods already arrived in the various states, and by insistence upon the adoption of most stringent administrative measures to prevent smuggling under it.[54] The response was, perforce, the same as for the first demand. In fact in some states both requirements were met by a single decree, while in the Swiss cantons the second demand was complied with before the adoption of the tariff itself.[55]

[51] *Cor. de Nap.*, vol. 21, no. 16983.
[52] *Moniteur*, October and November 1810, *passim*.
[53] *Writings of J. Q. Adams*, III, 553-4; and note also 534 footnote, (letter of 6 November to Sec. Smith).
[54] *Cor. de Nap.*, vol. 21, nos. 17011, 17012, 16983, and 17053.
[55] *Moniteur*, November 1810.

Meanwhile Napoleon himself was grappling strenuously with the problem of evasions of the Continental embargo. Not content with providing by his licence and tariff measures a chance for the competition of legitimate commerce with the smuggler he engaged in a direct attack upon the contraband trade.[56] He reformed the customs administration, he shifted and increased his lines of *douaniers*, he occupied, and then annexed the districts between Holland and the Danish frontiers. He abolished certificates of origin and for a time he imperatively insisted that Denmark, Prussia, Sweden, Russia, and all other Baltic states should strictly exclude colonial imports and shut out all "American" and Portuguese vessels, while Naples and the Mediterranean states were to seize Ottoman ships as well.[57] All this was calculated to reduce the trade of the Continent to vassalage to France or assimilation to the French system. Such had been the program of the spring and summer of 1810, and the policy preliminary to the general adoption of the Trianon tariff.

Rigorous as was this program, Napoleon had ample reason, still, to be dissatisfied with results. Therefore profiting from the lessons afforded by his efforts he set about organizing a uniform plan of campaign for continental resistance against the guerrillas of evasion. On 1 October the question came before the Conseil du Commerce.[58] The result was the infamous decree of Fontainebleau for the enforcement of the reorganized Continental System.

This Fontainebleau decree, dated 18 October 1810, perfected the machinery for crushing contraband and for insuring the effectiveness of the legislation of July, as well as of the Berlin and Milan

[56] *Cor. de Nap.*, vol. 21, *passim*; AF^{IV}1241; *Moniteur*, 1810, pt. 2, etc.

[57] See *Cor. de Nap.*, 21, nos. 16768, 16788, 16827-9, 16838, 16844, 16857, etc., 16883, 16885. Cf. *Am. Daily Adv.*, 13, 14 August and 20 September; the *Moniteur* (2 August) gives the Prussian decree excluding American ships. See also *Writings of J. Q. Adams*, III, 460-80, 495, etc., despatches to the Secretary of State, containing the Prussian, Danish, etc. decrees

[58] AF^{IV}1241, annex 201

decrees.⁵⁹ It consisted of six chapters and some thirty articles. Chapter I established seven *cours prevôtales*, and thirty-four *tribunaux ordinaires* of the customs; chapter II prescribed their procedure; chapter III stated the penalties to be enforced; chapter IV regulated seizures and rewards. By chapter V it was ordered that no transactions should be allowed to stop a suit against defrauders of the customs, while the final chapter provided for the disposition of merchandise seized in cases of fraud. Thus goods whose introduction was prohibited were to be burned, or otherwise destroyed, while other goods were to be sold at auction and forced to pay the tariff duties.

When the news of the Fontainebleau decree crossed the channel there was such a panic of righteous indignation as if London had been bombarded from the very air. The honest British trader (whose smuggling warehouses in Heligoland, and elsewhere, were menaced with ruin) hastened to his ever-ready confidante the *London Times* to vent his horror of this "*tremendous act of oppression,*" this "*monstrous novelty of commercial policy.*"⁶⁰ To all which the French retorted, as Britain's opponents ever do, that the shocking weapon had been filched from that very handy arsenal of precedents the past history of England.⁶¹

It was, in sooth, a strong measure which Napoleon had forged, though surely not so unjust as is usually supposed. But it was a fatal mistake for it was sure to recoil upon its maker. When Count Romanzoff on 30 November 1810 in a private interview with the American envoy to Russia asked his opinion regarding the late French measures, he received the prophetic reply: "That

---

⁵⁹ AF^{IV}1243, annex 262, also see the decree of 15 November 1810, annex 280. Also 17 Duvergier, *Lois*, 205-9, 234, 258, 305, 312, 352, 434, 460, etc., etc. Lepec, *Bulletin annoté*, XII, 121-5 gives valuable notes with the decree which cite judicial decisions and also trace the growth of legislation on contraband from 1793 to 1815. Cf. also Lepec, II, 341, IX, 384, 493, and X, 24 (notes).

⁶⁰ See the *Times* for 5, 7 November etc., etc.

⁶¹ AF^{IV}1242, annexes 198, 199, 3 December 1810. Later published in the *Moniteur*.

with regard to the burning decree, it would distress and perhaps ruin great numbers of merchants upon the continent, to whom a large proportion of the merchandise thus consumed will unquestionably belong, and will shock, as it has shocked, the moral feelings of mankind. . . . . They will naturally say, seize and confiscate the property of your enemy if you will, but destruction is the policy of a Vandal."[62]

This "burning decree" Napoleon proceeded to force upon the Continent as he had done with his Berlin and Milan decrees, and was doing with the Trianon tariff. Once more the *Moniteur* furnished announcements of the submission of the various governments, followed directly by account upon account of auto-de-fés of English goods, and auctions of colonial products, also of consternation and disaster in England.[63] This it followed at once by publishing, day after day for weeks, the laudatory addresses praising the success of the Continental System furnished, to be sure, upon command, by French commercial bodies.

But the *Moniteur* did not tell of the protests and wails that poured in upon the government from all sides, did not know perhaps that the bonfires were more straw than English cloth,[64] did not give the lists of French bankrupts that came suddenly like the casualty lists of another Eylau and did not publish the bold addresses from the commercial bodies of Frankfort, Paris and the other great centers[65] which afford the explanation of certain decrees allowing payment of duties in goods instead of coin, exempting goods from seizure, and making great government loans to failing banks and industries.[66] And what the *Moniteur*

[62] *Writings of J. Q. Adams*, III, 545-7. The whole despatch is significant. Cf. testimony of Boucher, inspector of such "*brulis.*"

[63] *Moniteur*, November-December 1810, January-March 1811.

[64] The ablest and most candid statement I have seen of actual conditions was the memoir of Vital Roux to Napoleon, 7 May 1811, "On the Situation of Commerce and the means of Re-establishing confidence and credit." AF^{IV} 1060, pièces 11 and 12.

[65] AF^{IV}1060, AF^{IV}1241, etc.

[66] Decree of 8 November, AF^{IV}1243, annex 276. Cf. Lanzac de Laborie, *Paris sous Napoleon*, VI, 48 ff. and 306 ff.

did not tell, the other journals were wise if they did not know, for Napoleon read the newspapers as some of them learned to their sorrow.[67]

To Napoleon, alarmed by the portent of the great economic crisis of the winter of 1810, the response to his demands for the adoption of his measures elsewhere, brought but cold comfort. The very preambles by which the princes sought to justify to their people the obnoxious Trianon tariff and supplementary enforcing measures were significant.[68] Few were the monarchs who like Jerome lauded the new means of making the great Continental System a complete success, or like the king of Bavaria assumed to inaugurate a propaganda against colonial goods and for the protection of home industries. Instead the majority shielded themselves behind the plea that every one else was doing it, or frankly stated that the imperial demands could not be resisted. Yet it was not the replies which the *Moniteur* printed, so much as the failures to respond, which brought a clear warning to Napoleon.

A report prepared by Cadore showing replies to his several demands received up to 3 November,[69] gives little cause for satisfaction since, of the important states, Prussia had enacted an inadequate ordinance, and Denmark a doubtful tariff, Sweden had given no reply, the action of Austria was rather dubious, and Russia had definitely refused to adopt the measures proposed.[70] In short the response was so far from satisfactory that it is not surprising that the Emperor saw the need of reinforcing his demands with other tactics in order to secure the all-important continental co-operation in his *zollverein* schemes.

[67] On 8 March 1811, for example, Napoleon wrote: "The Journal du Commerce is not to speak of vessels which arrive from England. This paper does more harm than good. Prevent it speaking of all the bankrupts." Brotonne, *Lettres inédites de Napoléon Ier*, p. 312, no. 771.

[68] *Moniteur*, October, November 1810.

[69] AF^{IV}1318, pièces 100-105.

[70] *Writings of J. Q. Adams*, III, 557, to Secretary R. Smith, 5/17 December 1810, says Austria as well as Russia refused.

In order therefore to avoid open discredit before the world it was sought by arguments, cajolery, and secret concessions to win over the recalcitrant. Prussia was led to vigorous action by a convention accepting confiscated colonial goods in lieu of the unpaid war indemnity of 1806. Denmark was mollified by a grant of French licences and by a secret limited admission into Hamburg of colonial goods, heaped up in Holstein.[71] An outlet for Polish grains and other products was allowed by French licences, a measure subsequently extended to Prussia as well. Austria as well as Bavaria and other states of the Rhine Confederation benefited by the overland transit scheme for Levant goods and they were further held by commercial conventions.[72] The Swiss were held partly by force, partly by limited trade concessions.[73] An alliance strengthened the hold upon Austria and a similar bond was sought with Sweden to overcome her stubborn inactivity. With Russia all methods were used to induce Alexander to maintain the Tilsit bond, and to adopt all the features of the reorganized Continental System including licences and preferential treaties. But other and stronger influences were at work against the French demands, and the licence trade, in favor of American trade and the economic independence of Russia.[74] It is not surprising therefore that when Alexander issued his reformed tariff ukase it struck more distinctly at French than at English or colonial goods. And disclaim it as he might, Alexander could not conceal the real animus of his decree.

[71] *Cor. de Nap.*, 21:168, also see pp. 244-6 below. Regarding the arrangement with Prussia note the report of Czernischeff, 16 Jan., 1812 (Sbornik, *Imperatorskago*, 121:116).

[72] On Bavaria consult Paul Darmstädter, *Studien zur bayerischen, Wirtschaftspolitik in der Rheinbundszeit*, and see the *Denkwürdigkeiten* of Montgelas.

[73] On Switzerland, Cerenville or Chapuisat may be consulted.

[73a] On Sweden see Martens, *Nouvelles causes célèbres*, II, ch. 7, and P. Coquelle in *Revue d'Histoire Diplomatique*, 23:196-239.

[74] *Writings of J. Q. Adams*, III, 540-8, 550-52; IV, 3-5, 14-16, 20, 38-41.

Such circumstances indeed were ominous and each monarch treasured up his grievances against a day of reckoning. On the last eve of that fateful day, Napoleon declared to his soldiers: "At the end of 1810, Russia changed her political system; the English spirit recovered its influence; the ukase on commerce was the first act."[75] On the other hand conspicuous among the grievances cited against Napoleon at the same moment by Sweden and Russia, as reported by Austria's secret agent, was the attempted encroachment upon their commercial independence by the Trianon tariff and allied measures.[76]

In short, in so far as the Trianon tariff was dependent upon continental adoption for its results, in so far as it was the new Continental System, it was doomed to failure and of this Napoleon had ample premonitions before the close of 1810. To be sure the tariff continued to be levied, judgments of the prevôtal customs courts to be rendered, and auto-de-fés of forbidden goods lighted till the end of the game, but despite it all, despite his angry harangues, his impatient demands, and his vaunting proclamations, Napoleon knew in his heart that he had played his card, and lost.

Nevertheless in so far as the Trianon tariff was but the adjunct of a comprehensive navigation scheme it seems to have had virility, to have contributed greatly to the imperial treasury, and to have left an enduring influence wherever it was enforced. In Germany it inspired the *zollvereins* which forecast ultimate unification.[77]

[75] First Bulletin to the Grand Army, Gumbinnen, 25 June 1812, (*Moniteur*, 8 July 1812). Compare this with Napoleon to Alexander, 28 February 1810, (*Cor. de Nap.*, 21:424-6) and Napoleon to Cadore, 3 March 1811, (Loyd, *New Letters of Napoleon*, p. 227). Note also the long and momentous farewell interview with Czernischeff, 28 Feb. 1812, wherein Napoleon rang the changes upon this grievance, Sbornik, 121:162-7.

[76] *Rev. des Études Nap.*, 1914, Lebzeltern to Metternich, 29 May 1812. See also the *Writings of J. Q. Adams*, III, 554-5, IV, 3-5, 28, etc., and note the words of Caulaincourt in his *Napoleon and his Times* (Phila. 1838), vol. 1, 236-7. On Central Europe in 1811 cf. reports of Boucher's secret mission, *Sous dix rois*, vol. II.

[77] Cf. Hoeniger, *Die Kontinentalsperre und ihre Einwirkungen auf Deutschland*.

Elsewhere it influenced tariff policies for years. In France, and elsewhere on the Continent, it fostered the rise of industries which are still flourishing. The very manufacturers, who groaned under the burdening costs which it maintained, testified that the financial crisis of the winter of 1810-11 was not comparable with the industrial catastrophes which attended the sudden and decided reduction of duties by the restored Bourbons.[78] Indeed even during the spring of 1811 men of affairs and economists who presented to Napoleon the frankest criticisms of his fiscal decrees urged great caution as to changes in the tariff.[79] Moreover, of the attack upon the use of colonial goods which the Trianon decree represented, no less a critic of the Continental System than Chaptal declared "that if the fall of Napoleon had been delayed two years France would have been freed forever from the tribute which she pays the new world for sugar and indigo."[80] Such a judgment accords well with the words of Napoleon when discussing the matter at St. Helena: "What might I not have done," he exclaimed, "under more favorable circumstances."[81]

[78] A pertinent commentary is the pamphlet *De l'influence du Système maritime de l'Angleterre sur le repos de l'Europe* . . . *Par G* . . Paris, 15 April 1815. See also the *Memoir of Richard-Lenoir* 387-9. The revised tariff of 23 April 1814, is in V *Bulletin des lois*, I, 50-51. Its revolutionary character may be judged from the reduction on sugar from 300–400 fr. to 40-60 fr. per kilo. See also 19 Duvergier 20, also 340-347, 351, and cf. the *Moniteur*, 1814, April, September and November.

[79] Vital Roux one of the compilers of the *code du commerce* is an excellent example. His memoir of 7 May 1811 has been cited above, p. 230, note 64. For Napoleon's purpose not to make new changes, see AF^{IV}1061, dossier 1, nos. 33, 34; and AF^{IV}1242, 1 April 1811.

[80] Chaptal, *Mes Souvenirs sur Napoleòn*, p. 289.

[81] Las Cases, *Memorial of St. Helena*, IV, 196-200.

CHAPTER IX
LICENCED NAVIGATION

The Nouveau Système

Despite the undeniable importance of the Trianon, St. Cloud, and Fontainebleau decrees, they should not be over-stressed. The popular tendency, prevalent from the very first, to identify the reorganized Continental System solely or primarily with such fiscal legislation, is a clear misconception. Actually the Napoleonic navigation policy as formulated in 1810 was based not upon its striking fiscal measures, but upon its very effective industrial and commercial programs.

The industrial program was comprehensive, embracing the agricultural as well as the manufacturing pursuits. Being based upon a compensatory idea it had four functions, namely, the protection, creation, regulation, and distribution of industrial activities and materials. For the Conseil du Commerce, and the Ministry of the Interior, with its adjuncts, sought not merely to sustain the industries of the Empire against the shocks of the exclusion system, but to give them an undisputed leadership in Europe. These ends were sought by means of tariff and prohibitory laws, by commercial treaties, by loans and subsidies. They were promoted by fixing standards and introducing improved machinery and processes, by the industrialization of chemistry, by social and sanitary regulations, by aiding the provision of raw materials, if not by importation at least through the naturalization of such products as cotton, or else by the creation of substitutes such as beet and grape sugars, pastel, madder and artificial soda. And finally their attainment was aided by the improvement of internal communications, and even the effort to revive the overland trade routes of the Middle Ages. In short it was a Colbertian program upon a continental scale.

This industrial program, though always a Napoleonic policy, becomes especially notable with the reorganization of 1810 because of the greater breadth and effectiveness given it at that time. It was necessarily an important complement of the new Navigation System whose occasion and result, alike, were the problem of fostering French industry. This navigation legislation was surely the most significant feature of the commercial program of 1810. Most nearly, also, did it come to being of itself the reconstituted Continental System, for the ultimate aims and principles of both the Navigation and Continental Systems were not identical.

Moreover, in as much as the navigation acts of July were pre-eminently licence trade decrees, it results that the working Continental System was primarily the licenced trade system.[1] Such, essentially, is the interpretation given to Lebrun on 20 August in reply to his urgent request for an official explanation of the decree of 25 July which he had been ordered to execute in Holland.[2] No neutral trade was desired—only French. "Foreign ships may not trade with our ports nor clear from them because there are no neutrals, and as to French vessels either they leave for a port of France and then they take the *acquit-à-caution* stipulated by article 2 of the decree, or they leave for foreign ports, and then they take licences since it is evident that they go to England, or at least that they get the authorization of the English. The system is clear."

In line with this explanation also is a concrete decision made two days later, in consequence of arguments of Cadore and Montalivet that foreign vessels entered previous to 2 July under licences might freely depart without the new licences which could be given now only to French ships. This request had been first made on 30 July at the instance of the Danish chargé but being unanswered

---

[1] Napoleon's strict insistence upon the decree of 25 July, viz., no navigation but by licence is strikingly shown in *Cor. de Nap.*, 21, nos. 16777, 16794 and 16992. And yet there has been a supposition that the Trianon decree did away with licences. Cf. Smart, *Economic Annals*, p. 220.

[2] *Cor. de Nap.*, 20:53, no. 16810. Lebrun's query of 12 August is given in Colenbrander, VI (1810-13), pt. 1, p. 55. Cf. notes 52 and 78, below.

was renewed on 20 August only to receive the typically Napoleonic endorsement: "Ce seroit les donner à l'Angleterre. Refusé."[3]

The system of licenced navigation having been established by the decrees of 3 and 5 July and confirmed by the decree of 25 July, immediate steps were taken to put the scheme into operation. A licence form was adopted, and two hundred of the licences were struck off and sent to the Emperor for his signature by 19 July.[4] Meanwhile leading merchants were notified of the plan and advised to apply for licences. Instructions were sent to local officials for the execution of the decree and at the same time steps were taken to insure the proper working of the British end of the traffic.

Since by article 37 of the decree of 2 July that act itself was to be kept absolutely secret and executed solely by administrative instructions,[5] such instructions necessarily furnish the best idea obtainable of the system as it was executed. The first of such instructions was sent about 20 July to the various maritime prefects in the guise of modifications of instructions of 13 March.[6] This circular of 20 July stated that licences were to be granted only to a few fixed ports of each prefecture within each of the three divisions into which the maritime prefectures had been grouped, although other places could obtain licences for the permitted ports.[7] No variations from these limitations would be possible, since not only would they be expressly stated on every licence, but each licence would bear, also, distinct numbers indicating the division and the port, the sequence of the licence in the special

[3] $F^{12}2031$. Some Danish ships soon received licences, however, cf. p. 245 below.

[4] $F^{12}2032$. Of these, 55 were signed on 18 July, but changes in the licence form before their distribution nullified them.

[5] $AF^{IV}463$, dossier 3502, no. 19.

[6] $F^{12}2050$.

[7] These restrictions were made on the basis of the experience and practice of the previous system. The three divisions were informally established by Cretet. The ports were selected largely on the test of those which had been found best situated or most interested. The restrictions therefore were for administrative as well as precautionary reasons.

series of the port, and its sequence in the imperial system as a whole. Licences were to be granted free and would be valid for six months but at the end of each trip must be turned in together with a record of the trip, in order that they might be viséed by the central administration at Paris.

The export and import conditions for these ordinary or so-called *simple licences* varied with the three divisions. For the first division (Antwerp to L'Orient) one-sixth of the exports must be wines, the rest composed at will of wines, brandies, seeds (except grass) and non-prohibited produce and merchandise of France. The imports could be building timber, flax, spars, etc., quinine and medicine, fish-roe, wax, Russian tallow, fish-oil, pitch, tar, sulphur, potash, sumach, lignum-vitae, dyewoods, staves, mats and sailcloth of Russia, Spanish piastres, lead, tin, litharge, arsenic and hides.

For the second division (La Rochelle to Bayonne) the permitted imports were the same as for the first division. The exports also were the same for both divisions,—except that Charente Inferieur (La Rochelle, Marans and Charente) could export grains, wheat and cereals. Moreover the conditions for this division required that one-half the export cargo be of wines and brandies.

The third division (Agde to Ostia) could export French wines, vinegar and brandy, grains, fruits (not yielding oil), oils (except those for manufacturing) and agricultural products of France whose exportation was not contrary to law or custom. Grains and cereals could be exported only subject to local port regulations. The ships of this division could go to Algiers, Tunis, Smyrna, the Levant ports, Constantinople, Malta, Sicily, Sardinia and Spain, and bring back any produce and merchandise of the Levant and Spain not prohibited by law.

A second circular (22 July) instructed the prefects, acting ostensibly upon their own responsibility, to refuse licencès to any but French built or nationalized vessels, except that such vessels might bear a fictitious neutral character.[8] In a letter of 15 August

---

[8] F¹²2050.

to Collin de Sussy, regarding instructions to be given the customs service, the requirement was emphasized that exports must equal imports in order that no cash be paid out by French commerce.[9] Three days later this point was reported in a circular to the prefects.[10] Merchandise brought *to* France was to be rated at the market price of the place where it was purchased, while exports *from* France were to be reckoned at the price of the place where they were sold. Simple licences, as those of the 2 July scheme were now known, were to cost forty napoleons instead of being granted free. Other modifications of the instructions of 20 July were made, due to a change in the new licence formula. Thus the condition of a fixed proportion of the export cargo to be of French wines could be estimated either on the tonnage or the value of the cargo at the option of the master. For the first and second divisions indigo, dyeing-drugs, pepper, cinnamon, cloves and nutmeg were added to the permitted imports. For the third division Spain was eliminated from the list of destinations, but all Levant goods, such as coffee, cottons, etc., might enter with certificates of origin.

Theoretically the navigation system of 1810 after the first of August embraced, besides the simple licences, two other types intended strictly for French shipping, in addition to the adjunct licence schemes designed for foreign or subsidiary shipping which could not be incorporated into the imperial system. The additional types of licences for the French system proper were the *licences diverses* and sugar licences. The *licences diverses* were intended to be special exemptions differing so distinctly from the regular licences that it was deemed preferable to write out a licence to meet the particular case rather than to make special modifications of the printed licence forms. Such special licences were of course rare and were granted only at an enhanced charge. Later, however, the term *licences diverses* was applied to the general group of special licence types for French commerce even

[9] $F^{12}2033$.
[10] *Ibid.*

when they were granted in quantities and a printed form used. The *licences to import sugar* were adopted in principle at the adoption of the new system.[11] A formula was worked out, and licences were printed and sent to the Emperor for signature by the first of September (1810), and here the matter slept. No formal decree seems to have created the series, and no sugar licences were granted, although at the end of 1811 an extension of the idea became one of the series of *licences diverses*. Meanwhile, however, other supplementary licences for limited purposes, such as oyster licences, eel licences, etc., had been engrafted upon the central scheme for French shipping.

Almost, if not quite, as important as the central scheme of navigation licences were the subsidiary licence schemes. They were of two general sorts, the one, "permits" for the shipping of strictly independent and neutral states, such as the United States; the other, "licences" for the dependent but nominally separate governments under imperial control, such as Italy, Naples or the colonies. The creation of these separate series was due partly to the experiences of the previous licence experiments, partly to apparent necessity, and partly to a policy of giving the system a continental extension. Nevertheless it is manifest that to a large extent these distinctions, the segregations of parts of a general imperial licence program, were more theoretical and artificial than real. Practically, for example, *licence simples* and *permis amèricains* were alike imperial licences granted for trade to or from France.

Next to the *simple licences* the *American permits* were most important. Originally they were of a single type but in the course of time it was found advisable to create American permits for French citizens employing the French flag, and also American permits to import grain and rice. The original American permits as created by the decree of 5 July followed the restrictive principles of the decree of 3 July. Commerce was limited to Bordeaux,

[11] F^{12}2031. On 13 August a "proof" sugar-licence was submitted. A bundle of papers in this carton shows the development of the idea.

Nantes, and Marseilles, each of which constituted a "series," while shipments from America were restricted to Charleston and New York. Cottons, fish-oil, dyewoods, salted fish and cod, hides and peltries could be imported, and the return cargo must consist of wines, brandies, silks, *toiles*, *draps*, jewelry, furnishings and other manufactured products. As distinguished from regular licences these permits were hedged about with special precautions the execution of which was given to French consuls at the foreign ports of export, such as countersigning the permits and writing a cipher phrase on them, sending cipher letters, etc. Parts of the cargo which were not admittable were to be put in bonded warehouses. These permits were good for a single voyage but were renewable if the conditions of the previous voyage had been properly met.

The letter of instructions sent to the duc de Cadore, as the basis of instructions to be given to the French consuls, adds some interesting details regarding these permits.[12] They were to be given to French houses who might themselves employ them for exporting by American ships or might send them to their correspondents in America, who would first send a cargo to France. These permits could be used only for American ships although these need not be necessarily American built or manned with strictly American crews, provided no Portuguese, Spanish, Danish, Swedish or other ships masked themselves under the American flag. The article of sugar need not be strictly American provided it was loaded in America. It was chiefly important that the ships should not take any part of their cargoes in England. The consul therefore was to indicate in cipher the quality and quantity of the goods carried to prevent changes being made at London.[13] While ships were supposed to enter either Nantes, Bordeaux or Marseilles they might for valid reasons go elsewhere.

[12] $F^{12}2033$.

[13] The provisions as to ciphers seem not to have been well enforced during 1811. Cf. Bassano to Montalivet, 18 September 1811, $F^{12}2108$; and Napoleon to Sussy, March 1812, $AF^{IV}1343$.

The customs were instructed to see that the exports equaled the imports and that they did not include grains, cereals, oysters, cheese, butter and other articles for England which would compete with the trade under French simple licences.[14] In order to protect French industry, muslins and tobacco were not to be imported but later some tobacco was admitted by special permission. Another later change, also, was the inclusion of Baltimore and Boston among the ports whence such ships might come.[15]

The American permit scheme was ostensibly the model for the *Hanse licence scheme* which was adopted directly afterward, although in reality the Hanseatic scheme has many features of its own. Originally suggested by the Hanse minister resident at Paris during the previous winter, the idea was revived by R. De Clercq, commercial deputy from Hamburg, in memoirs of 14 and 25 June which on 30 June Fauchat indorsed over to Montalivet. The actual plan, however, had been sketched by Napoleon on 16 July, formulated with modifications by Montalivet and the Conseil du Commerce on 17 July, and decreed six days later.

The decree consists of some dozen articles providing for four series and two types of Hanseatic licences to be obtained from the military governors of Hamburg, Bremen, Lübeck, or Danzig.[16] The first type of these licences permitted the holder to leave from one of the four named ports (according to its series) for either Dunkirk, Nantes, or Bordeaux. The vessel might stop *en route* in England and unload part or all of its cargo, but must then proceed to the stipulated French port in ballast or with a cargo of timber, hemp, tar, masts, iron, or other products of the North suitable for the French navy, or with other permitted goods not included in licences granted to firms in France.[17] It could enter

[14] F^{12}2033.

[15] *Ibid.* Instructions of 25 March 1811.

[16] AF^{IV}1243, no. 13. Cf. also *London Times,* 31 August, for instructions sent to General Molitor.

[17] Eudel, director of the customs at Hamburg, posted a notice about 26 August allowing the export of German linen and hemp yarn, steel, brass,

its French port and unload at once but could not clear again until its papers had been viséed, its licence surrendered and an *acquit-à-caution* taken out for the original port of clearance. A return cargo of wines, brandies, and any other exportable French goods (except grain) was allowed. In fact after 27 August the principle of equalized import and export cargoes was applied to these licences.[18] While in December a condition of exporting one-third silks and one-third wines, etc., was imposed.[19] The price of such licences was at the rate of sixty francs per ton of the ship's capacity. Although limited to the single trip, the strict fulfilment of conditions gave a right to claim a second licence.

The other type of Hanse licences was obtainable without charge by vessels which would go directly from one of the four stipulated ports to a port of France or Holland with naval stores.[20] Naturally, however, most elaborate precautions were prescribed to prevent fraud in the use of either of these forms of licences. Thus every ship must have its manifest viséed by the local director of customs who sent a copy to the Director General of Customs at Paris. Its papers must be viséed by the local French consul who wrote upon them a cipher phrase, as in the case of the American permits, and reported it to the Minister of Exterior Relations. Every fortnight the military governor who delivered such licences must report all clearances of licenced ships (with their licence numbers, etc.) to the Minister of War. The latter then reported to the Minister of the Interior from whom he had secured the blank licences, and who must in turn keep the final record.[21] Besides this the Marine had to see that a strict embargo was maintained against the departure of any but licenced ships from the

---

bronze, laten-wire, sickles, hog's bristles, Northern skins, white lead, and Saxon smelts, besides wheat, flour and naval stores. *London Times*, 17 September 1810.
 [18] AF^{IV}1241, annex 120.
 [19] AF^{IV}1243, annex 289.
 [20] AF^{IV}1243, no. 13.
 [21] For examples of such correspondence see F^{12}2033, liasse 3.

Hanse ports. All this was preliminary to the precautions as to entrance at the French port in which the customs, local officials, and finally the Conseil du Commerce, or in some cases even the Conseil des Prises shared.

The inauguration of this elaborately guarded system entailed much supplementary regulation, especially since a French customs system had to be set up at Danzig, a consul sent to Lübeck, a better coast guard system devised, and efforts. made to secure Prussian co-operation.[22] Even then it did not work well. For without sincere Prussian co-operation it was impossible to so watch the Baltic shore with its numberless coves and creeks as to prevent evasions by non-licenced craft. Besides few even of the licenced vessels could complete their voyage to France on account of embargoes in English ports or other causes.[23]

The difficulties thus encountered in operating the system, the demand for Baltic grain in Holland, pressure from Denmark and Sweden, and petitions from the Hanseatic ports led eventually to the working out of a modification of the system.[24] At every session of the Conseil du Commerce for a month following 25 March 1811, Collin de Sussy or Montalivet made a report on the subject. Then on 24 June and 1 July, Montalivet proposed and discussed a new Hanse licence decree.[25] This Napoleon declared unnecessary but he decided that the export duty should be reduced one-half, with special reductions for Danzig and the region beyond the Oder, and that Prussia should be required to levy an export duty equivalent to the grain licence charges, and to allow no ships to clear without carrying evidence of having paid this.[26] A special

[22] *Cor. de Nap.*, 21:136, no. 16933, 20 September to Cadore. See also no. 16966, 29 Sept. to Gen. Clarke, on French consular abuses. Prussia was asked to impose a 60 fr. per ton tax on grain exports from Memel, Stettin, Königsberg and Kolberg. See also F^{12}2033, *passim*.

[23] Such an embargo was laid, for instance, in January and February 1811. Cf. *Moniteur* 28 February and 1 March 1811.

[24] AF^{IV}1242, annex 378; AF^{IV}1061, dossier 2, pièce 61; etc., etc.

[25] AF^{IV}1242, and F^{12}2031.

[26] F^{12}2031, 5 July 1811.

licence scheme proposed for Danzig were also refused at this time.[27] Yet further changes for Danzig were afterwards made, and in 1812 and 1813 two special types of licences for Danzig were offered to meet the military exigencies of France and Denmark.[28]

Perhaps the chief significance of the Hanseatic licences, however, is that they were pre-eminently the medium by which *Napoleon sought to make the French navigation licences a Continental System*. How far this *continentalizing* objective was consistently present from the inception of the licence plans of 1810 it is difficult to say. Certainly, however, the Danzig licences were created specifically for the needs of the Grand Duchy of Warsaw, and were at once so recognized by the King of Saxony both for the Duchy and for Saxony.[29] The regulations urged on Prussia were equivalent to creating a Prussian licence policy. But besides this, Danzig and Lübeck licences, or "special" licences, were given upon request, to the Prussian government. These were chiefly for the export of grain and Silesian cloths, returns to be in silver, or at all events not in colonial goods.[30] A similar policy was adopted almost from the first with respect to Denmark and later Norway, and to some extent Sweden also, by means of the Lübeck and Bremen licences.[31]

The connection of Denmark with the system began about September 1810, that is soon after the efforts in July and August to sail without licences.[32] The first of such licences recorded, however, are seven granted 27 November "by request."[33] A *special* Prussian licence is noted as being granted in January 1811, although evidently earlier ones had been given.[34] Licences

[27] *Ibid*.
[28] Napoleon to Sussy in March 1812, Lecestre, *Letters inédites*, II, 197.
[29] *Moniteur*, 1810, p. 1151 (20 October); p. 1335 (4 December).
[30] *Cor. de Nap.*, 22:363, no. 17974, 1 August 1811.
[31] AF^{IV}1241 and 1242, *passim*.
[32] See p. 236 above, and *Cor. de Nap.*, 31:82, 1 September.
[33] Decision no. 5, of 25 November on request of Mr. de Waltentorf. See also AF^{IV}1242, 7 January 1811.
[34] Decision no. 14, of 15 January for the ship *Triton*.

for vessels of Norway and Sweden are not mentioned until a few months later—e. g., June, July, and November 1811.[35] Also in July 1811 special Hanse licences were allowed for Mecklenburg and Swedish Pomerania.[36] Swedish interest in the Napoleonic licences apparently was short-lived, ending with the French seizure of Pomerania at the beginning of 1812. Danish interest, however, continued to the breakdown of the system.[37] In some cases, Napoleon refused such licences, as in the case of trade solely between Denmark and Sweden, but wherever French ports and vessels were engaged no difficulty was raised.[38] Perhaps the last of such licences were given in 1813 to take naval stores from Danzig for the Danish fleet.

A tendency to extend still farther the mission of the Hanse licences is seen in a request of Lübeck in April 1811 for a protection for a ship to Russia.[39] The result is not known. Nor is it known how much pressure was brought to bear directly upon Russia to adopt the licence system.[40] It is known, however, that the idea of Russian licences patterned on the French system was suggested by French diplomats to the Russian government and urged upon it by Russian merchants. According to the American Minister at Petersburg, who consistently threw his influence against the idea, Alexander flatly refused to countenance such a scheme.[41] If it be inferred from this that Russia never issued any of the all prevalent trade permits then surely she was the only maritime power of Northern Europe not in the traffic. The British licence

[35] AF^{IV}1242 and 1243, also 1342.

[36] AF^{IV}1342, Montalivet to Daru, 20 July 1811. Ten were granted for Mecklenburg, and three each for Sweden and Prussia.

[37] Cf. F^{12}2108, 31 March 1812 and 10 April 1812, also 21 January 1812, when seven Mediterranean licences were given for Danish ships at Cagliari. Note Czernischeff's report of 21 February 1812, Sbornik, 121:158.

[38] AF^{IV}1345.

[39] AF^{IV}1242, annex 430, 22 April.

[40] See *Writings of J. Q. Adams*, III, 445 and 506.

[41] *Memoirs of J. Q. Adams*, II, 176, 180, 360-5, etc.; *Writings of J. Q. Adams*, IV, 41, 3 April 1811. But see the *Annual Register*, 1812, p. 169.

system infected the Baltic like an epidemic. Scarcely a vessel entered or left those waters without a permit from London, while local trade was done under British admiralty protections.⁴² At the same time Sweden granted her own licences as well as using English ones.⁴³ Prussia did something of the sort, and there is reason to believe that Denmark did likewise for Norway and perhaps also for Holstein.⁴⁴ In fact the situation was such that even the American vessels entering the Baltic were given protection papers popularly called "Joy's licences," since they were issued unofficially by George Joy, the American agent at Copenhagen.⁴⁵ That the situation in the Baltic was not an exceptional phenomenon of the trade policy of the period is shown by the fact that even a non-maritime country like Austria issued licences for the importation of coffee.⁴⁶ Even the Spanish Juntas issued licences not only for Europe but also for Spanish America.⁴⁷ Moreover the revolted Spanish colonies were on their own part issuing licences for trade with the hostile West Indies.⁴⁸

What the Hanseatic licence scheme did for the Baltic and North Sea, the *Italian licences* were expected in a measure, at least, to accomplish *for the Mediterranean* in connection with the ordinary licences of the third division. Although there were precedents

⁴² See the Board of Trade records and any contemporary journals.

⁴³ Ad. 2/1074; and B. T. 5/23, 76-81 (10 December 1813), an historical review of the Swedish situation. Cf. also *Moniteur*, 8 September 1810, from the *Morning Chronicle*.

⁴⁴ Nominally Prussia issued no licences after 1809. Cf. Speyer's letters, *Dept. of State, Desp. Fr.*, vol. 11. Regarding Denmark see B. T. 5/20, 21 November 1811; B. T. 1/55, E² 31 (14 March 1811), etc.; cf. also *London Times*, 5 February 1811 (*Moniteur*, 5 March 1811); and Ad. 1/3845 letter of J. Mitchel, 20 July 1813.

⁴⁵ On Joy's licences see *Writings of J. Q. Adams*, III, 480, 31 August 1810, and 506-7, 20 September. The British refused to respect Mr. Joy's papers, however, and their life was thus cut short.

⁴⁶ Cf. *Am. Daily Adv.*, 23 July 1813.

⁴⁷ Notice of Spanish consuls in all American newspapers, June 1810. See also P. R. O., Ad. 1/144, June–October 1810.

⁴⁸ *Moniteur*, 10 March 1812.

for such licences in the earlier system, the formal scheme of Italian licences grew out of a letter of 23 June 1810 by Champagny to the French consuls in Italy asking about the use of English licences there. The consul at Venice gave important information and suggestions in his reply of 4 July which seems to have influenced Napoleon's plan of 16 July.[49] Cadore also gave this consular information to Montalivet who apparently used it in drafting his report of 23 July.

The draft decree legalizing the Italian licences is a long one of some thirteen articles allowing licences for native firms, or for French firms, in the ports of Venice, Ancona, Trieste and Naples, or for firms in other ports provided their vessels cleared from one of the ports named.[50] These licences were to cover the navigation of Italy, Naples and the Illyrian Provinces with each other, or with French Mediterranean ports, either by means of native or neutral ships as *such*, or under Ottoman simulation. Italian vessels bound for France could stop at Trieste, Naples, Malta, Tripoli, Tunis and England. Trieste vessels had similar privileges, and vessels from Naples could stop at Sicily, but the ultimate destination must be Nantes for vessels going to England, or else Cette, Marseilles, Toulon or Genoa for the strictly Mediterranean trade.

Under these licences native products and wares could be exported but goods suspected of being of Levant origin must have certificates. These were especially required for cotton from Naples, though not for sulphur. Vessels of Ancona and Venice could also break cargo at Naples going and returning. Vessels from England to France must be in ballast or with permitted goods, except colonial produce or articles allowed for regular French licences. Return cargoes must be three-fourths of French products other than grain. Besides certificates of origin, consular ciphers, etc., were required as in the case of American permits.

[49] $F^{12}2031$. Cadore on 21 July answers Montalivet's of 19 July. Cf. $F^{12}2108$, and $F^{12}2033$, liasse 3.

[50] $F^{12}2031$. Cf. Napoleon's very frank explanation of his system to Eugene, 19 September 1810, *Cor. de Nap.*, 21, no. 16930.

In its application to the trade of Naples this decree was interpreted to have created four types of licences, (1) for French ports, (2) for Italian ports, (3) for Illyria, and (4) for Barbary and the Levant.[51] The direct coast-wise trade from Naples to French Mediterranean ports was at first regulated under the *cabotage* decree of 25 July by the simple requirement of *acquits-à-caution*. Another decree of 28 August also regulated this and even the similar trade with Spain.

The general Mediterranean licence decree was at once supplemented by various special measures such as licences for tuna fishing in Sardinian waters, grain coasting trade permits, and Barbary and Ottoman permits, to which were added subsequently several forms of licences for trade with Sicily, Corsica, Sardinia, Albania, etc.[52]

The Ottoman permits were devised early in September 1810, partly as a means of settling the problem of disposing of the numerous Ottoman vessels recently sequestered in French and Italian ports, and largely as a means of securing Levant products needed by French industry.[53] In fact the problem being similar to the American problem a similar solution was adopted.[54] Since the American and Ottoman or Barbary flags were the only flags of great nations "which obliged England to respect their flag or at least tricked her and obliged her *à des ménagements*" these two

[51] $F^{12}2031$, 28 May 1811. However it was declared that no vessels from Naples could enter a French, Italian, etc. port without a licence or suffering confiscation ($F^{12}2108$). But see 29 April, Sussy's report, $AF^{IV}1242$. Note also *Cor. de Nap.*, 21:272, 13 November 1810, to Jerome.

[52] $AF^{IV}1198$, no. 41; $AF^{IV}1242$, nos. 294, 433; and $AF^{IV}1243$, annex 260, 20 September 1810. Cf. also $F^{12}2108$ for licences to Danish ships at Cagliari and see 1342 for licences to the Mayor of Caprara in 1810-11 to trade with Sardinia.

[53] See the *Moniteur*, 30 August 1810, p. 951, etc.; also *Cor. de Nap.*, vols. 20 and 21 (see index); likewise Picard et Tuetey, *Cor. de Nap.* I., vol. III, pp. 743, 783, and 793.

[54] *Cor. de Nap.*, 21:89.

flags alone were to be admitted, by special *permits*, into French controlled ports.⁵⁵

The American permits served as the model for the Ottoman-Barbary permits, although the latter were somewhat less stringently guarded since, as Montalivet expressed it, the French *sentiment d'amour propre national* was less directly concerned.⁵⁶ Three series of such permits were created, viz., for Leghorn, Marseilles, and Genoa. They were supposedly granted to French firms to bring goods from Algiers, Tunis, Smyrna, or elsewhere in the Levant upon Barbary, Greek or Ottoman vessels.⁵⁷ These vessels could stop at Malta but they could bring to the French ports only Levant cottons, Moka coffee, or other strictly native products, accompanied by certificates of origin of French consuls in the ports whence they came.⁵⁸ They were expected to carry back French manufactures, especially silks and Carcassone cloths, and such agricultural products as could legally be exported by foreign ships.⁵⁹ Such permits cost 50 napoleons each.

Coincidently with the adoption of the Ottoman permit scheme the Conseil du Commerce was working upon a project for *colonial trade licences*. This idea, urged first by Montalivet early in August 1810 as a measure supplementary to the 25 July decree, was soon forced again upon the Emperor's attention by various commercial interests.⁶⁰ Important Chambers of Commerce protested against the bearing of the new licence and tariff measures upon the expeditions pending under the *armament en aventurier* scheme of 1808.⁶¹ At the same time came proposals of certain merchants to use

⁵⁵ F^{12}2031, Montalivet's reports of 6 September.

⁵⁶ F^{12}2031, Report of 10 September.

⁵⁷ AF^{IV}1241. In the summer of 1811 special permits were revived for Barbary vessels. Cf. Montalivet's report of 12 August 1811, F^{12}2018.

⁵⁸ Cotton would be admitted only at Leghorn and Genoa, and sugar and indigo were supposed to be admitted only by special orders.

⁵⁹ F^{12}2108.

⁶⁰ See his note of 5 August, chapter VIII, page 216 above. Cf. *Cor. de Nap.*, 21:18, no. 16760.

⁶¹ AF^{IV}1241, no. 163.

confiscated American ships for new adventuring expeditions to the colonies.[62] Besides there came pressure from Dutch merchants and from the governor of Batavia.[63] After promising a settlement of past engagements on a basis of accounts between employer and clerks, Napoleon on 3 September outlined the future status of such expeditions under the new Navigation System.[64] Thus colonial trade was to be considered as a sort of coasting trade, or *grand cabotage*, and to encourage such communication with the French and Dutch colonies special reductions from the Trianon tariff were to be granted, but, to insure that no English or other foreign products benefited by these concessions, the trade must be under special licences with precautions like those of the American permits. After several reports by Montalivet, who was instructed to investigate the practicability of the scheme, the measure was decreed on 1 November.[65] On 14 November a special decision stated that licences would be taken out by thirty ships departing for Batavia.[66] Later requests and grants of licences for Ile de France and Guadeloupe as well as for Java are recorded. In reality, however, very few were ever used. Equally futile, apparently, was another form of the scheme considered in November 1811.[67] Effectively, therefore, the colonial licence was merely an additional ship's paper nominally required in order to preserve the integrity of the navigation act.[68]

Another measure urged strenuously from the first by Dutch merchants and supported by Lebrun, Montalivet and de Sussy was the inclusion of Holland in the general licence system.[69]

[62] AF^{IV}1241, no. 136.
[63] AF^{IV}1061, no. 123. Cf. *Cor. de Nap.*, 21: 93, 142.
[64] AF^{IV}1241, no. 136, and see no. 157 (10 September).
[65] AF^{IV}1241, especially nos. 144, 145, and 163; also Duvergier.
[66] AF^{IV}1342; AF^{IV}1241-1243, etc.; also *Cor. de Nap.*, 21:227, 244-6, 258-60, etc.
[67] AF^{IV}1199, pièce 220.
[68] It is interesting to note, however, that the *grand cabotage* idea was subsequently made the principle governing the trade between France and Algeria.
[69] AF^{IV}1241, and Colenbrander, vols. V and VI, *passim*.

Napoleon promised this in July 1810, not to speak of his earlier engagements by the treaty of March.[70] Therefore, on 21 August, 17 September, 14 October and 12 November, Montalivet presented draft decrees for such licences but was always informed that the question would have to wait until the complete customs system for Holland was ready.[71] Dutch pleas for an outlet for their butter and cheese brought some concessions, and a few exceptional licences to export eels to England seem to have been allowed.[72] But it was not until 18 March 1811, after several weeks of renewed solicitation, that the Emperor actually redeemed his promise.

The decree of 18 March 1811 differs little from the scheme proposed the previous summer.[73] It created two additional simple licence series (numbers 30 and 31) for Amsterdam and Rotterdam. Fifty of each series were to be available by 1 April that the vessels might sail by 1 May. Vessels must be French (including Dutch) and must fulfill the conditions of the decree of 3 July 1810. They could sail only to England, but special licences would be granted for the Baltic. No passengers could be carried, and all letters and papers brought back must be given at once to the commissary of police, while unauthorized imports must be warehoused under government control.

With respect to the articles of trade permitted by these Dutch licences there are striking differences from the nomenclature of the original simple licences which reveal the influence of events since the previous July, as well as the economic differences between North France and Holland.[74] Thus one-third of the exports were now required to be of French silks, the remainder being composed, at the option of the shipper, of butter, cheese, clover seed, flower seeds and bulbs, mustard and garden seeds, wines, cement,

[70] *Cor. de Nap.*, 21:526, no. 16701, 22 July; Colenbrander, VI, 13.
[71] AF^{IV}1241, annexes 106, 284-7, 354.
[72] AF^{IV}1241, nos. 128, 129, 157, 164, 170-173; 1242, annexes 327, 341, 350; and *London Times*, 16 October 1810.
[73] AF^{IV}1243, annex 309.
[74] AF^{IV}1342.

bricks, tiles, fish, eels, linens of Holland and Harlem, camelots or polemites, silks, Holland paper, knives for cutting sugar cane, and all other Dutch or French exportable goods. In return it was expected that the imports should be of building and ship timber, hemp, cordage, pitch, tar, quinine and medicines, sulphur, hides from Buenos Ayres, flaxseed, Spanish piastres and gold or silver coins or bullion.[75]

The tardy adoption of the two series of licences for Holland thus at last completed the general basic scheme of licences of the *nouveau système*, as it was called in contradistinction to the licences of the experimental or *ancien système* of 1809-July 1810, which were declared to be superseded and void after 1 September 1810. The actual operation of the "new" licences began in August of 1810 and continued nominally until the overthrow of the Empire. But while the general system of licenced navigation continued until the end, it must not be supposed for a moment that the form or even the bases of the licences remained unaltered throughout. Instead economic and political pressure, with the omnipresent influence of international relations, were still effecting constant modifications, amounting in several instances to very marked changes in fundamental principles. These special occasions thus divide the story of the system, as we shall follow it, into the periods from July 1810 until December 1911, from January 1812 until the beginning of 1813, and from then until the end of the imperial règime.

Throughout this whole story runs one central principle. It is the same dominant idea which we have seen embodied from the first in all phases of the *nouveau système*, in the *licences simples* and *licences diverses*, the American, Ottoman and Barbary permits, the Hanseatic, the Italian and Mediterranean, the colonial and the Dutch licences alike—namely, the idea of a Continental Navigation System. Moreover, like the Trianon tariff policy,

[75] One article which the Dutch sought to import was tea. After a year's efforts this was allowed in December 1811. Cf. AF^{IV}1242; AF^{IV}1243; and AF^{IV}1721; also Colenbrander, VI, pt. I, 195, 208, etc.

it demonstrates conspicuously that pervading spirit of Napoleon's refurbished commercial system, epitomized in the Emperor's declared motto: *La France avant tout*. Such a policy could have but one result: to rouse the jealousy and distrust of all who felt the pressure of its harsh selfishness. Indeed so early as 20 September 1810 the American Minister to Russia strikingly expressed this attitude in an official despatch.[76] Said he: "The repeal of the Berlin and Milan decrees is upon conditions which render it apparently of little effect. . . . Possibly the change of system has not really been great. But the substitution of enormous duties for total prohibition will not so well suit the professed purpose of annihilating all commerce between Great Britain and the continent of Europe, and the sale of licences by the Emperor Napoleon for all sorts of vessels at a tonnage duty of sixty francs by the last, is neither disguised nor concealed. While he allows trade by special licences it is not easy to see how he can deny to his neighbors and allies the benefit of granting licences also; and although there may be a great part of Europe to whom he is rather in the habit of signifying his will than of urging persuasion there are others who still consider his example as authority quite as good as his precept. I have long considered the Continental System as little more than extortion wearing the mask of prohibition. The system is now at least so far changed that the mask is laid aside and extortion shows her natural face. . . ."[77]

[76] Ford, *Writings of J. Q. Adams*, III, 506-7. This may well be compared with Napoleon's own statements to Lebrun and to Eugene;—cf. notes 2 and 52 above.

[77] For a similar contemporary French criticism of the licence trade see Lafitte to Rovigo, in *Memoires of Savary*, III, 373-4. Cf. also Pasquier, *Memoires*, 315; Bourrienne, *Memoires*, II, 401-404; Marmont, *Memoires*, III, 364-367; Mollien, *Memoires*, III, 196, 290-91, etc. Of the English criticisms cf. Phillimore, *Reflections on the Nature and Extent of the Licence Trade*, (1815) and his *Letter to a Member of the House of Commons*, (1812); the anonymous *Inquiry into the State of our Commercial Relations with the Northern Powers*, (1811); "The Licence System," (article in the *Quarterly Review*, May 1811), etc.

To the justice of this arraignment we might well demur, but that it accurately anticipates popular opinion, the legends of vast sums of specie stored in the Tuileries vault as Napoleon's personal returns from the licence traffic interestingly bear witness. Indeed until our own day the licence system has been stigmatized as the very embodiment of injustice and corruption—a program of unmasked extortion. Nevertheless not by mere opinion but by the searching test of its actual operations, as we shall see, must the system of licenced navigation be judged.

CHAPTER X
THE "NOUVEAU SYSTÈME" IN OPERATION

When President Madison by his proclamations of 2 November 1810 and 2 February 1811 met the conditions of Cadore's 5 August letter, by which Napoleon had accepted the challenging repeal of the Non-Intercourse law, the outcome was a pretty problem for diplomatic haggling. Over it England and America and France parleyed for many months, juggling words and gambling with time. England declared that the Berlin and Milan decrees were not, had not been repealed. France and the United States insisted that they had been *recalled*—as to what that implied they could not agree. It surely meant, insisted the ever theoretical Americans, that the decrees were *revoked*. Yes, argued Napoleon, thinking dramatically, as usual, that is to say they have been *encored*. In American diplomacy it was a period of small honor, and much watchful waiting. It was a situation which invited the bullying of Wellesley, and the double-dealing of Napoleon.

"The United States have not declared war upon England," explained the Emperor to his Conseil du Commerce on 29 April 1811, after weeks of procrastination, "but they have recognized the decrees of Berlin and Milan since they have allowed their citizens to trade with France and forbidden all relations with England." Unfortunately for this specimen of Napoleonic reasoning and bad faith, he had to admit that the Americans were irrevocably opposed to even the latest expression of his Continental System. "For example the permits or licences shock the United States." Strange to say they obstinately refused to consider these marks of his imperial favor save as "a restriction upon the liberty of commerce."[1] For notwithstanding his concessions in allowing a few non-licenced vessels to be admitted, and despite the fact

---

[1] *Cor. de Nap.*, 22:122-4. Other notorious expressions of the imperial attitude were reported by Russell on 13 Feb. and 15 April 1811, *Dept. of State, Desp. Fr.*, vol. 12. See also the Russian agent's report in Sbornik, 121:121.

that on 25 March he had allowed Boston and Baltimore to share in the licenced trade—the "impertinent" American *chargé*, Jonathan Russell, was still protesting.[2]

Under the circumstances a reconsideration of the American problem seemed advisable to Napoleon and he called for ministerial reports upon a policy which would interpret the American non-intercourse with England as an embargo, violations of which would subject a vessel to confiscation in America. Then by the same theory he would seize in his ports all American vessels which went to England. Other American vessels would be admitted if they brought only American produce and as substitutes for licences carried consular passports. If this system should seem illogical then the best plan was to be obscure and play for time until the United States should become involved in war with England over Spanish America.[3]

His ministers, however, assured him that this notion of a revamped Bayonne decree was untenable, seeing that the American measure against England was simply one of non-importation, and that besides he was morally bound by his recall of the Berlin and Milan decrees.[4] Whereupon he fell back upon his policy of playing for time, retained the permit scheme while pretending to abandon it and, as a blind, allowed a few non-licenced American ships to enter. And meanwhile he did all things possible to encourage American interest in Latin America.[5] This program had

[2] See Russell to R. Smith, 15, 26 March and 4 April 1811, *Dept. of State, Desp. Fr.*, vol. 12.

[3] *Cor de Nap.*, 22:134. Cf. also Russell to Secretary Monroe, 13 July 1811: "It is my conviction . . . . that the great object of the actual policy is to entangle us in a war with England . . . . and I have frankly told the Duke of Bassano that we are not sufficiently dull to be deceived by this kind of management." *Dept. of State, Desp. Fr.*, vol. 12.

[4] AF^{IV}1242, Report of Montalivet 6 May 1811; and *Aff. Étr., Cor. Pol., États Unis*, vol. 64, Maret's report of 6 May.

[5] *Cor. de Nap.*, 22:477; also, *Aff. Étr., Cor. Pol., État Unis*, vols. 64, 66. and 68 on the Spanish-American issues.

to be reconsidered, it is true, by the end of 1811, but in the meantime other forms of American permits had been created.[6]

The new forms of American permits show to some extent the influence of protests against the regular American permits; but they are chiefly significant as being indicative of a striking economic change in France. Two years earlier the licence system had been forced upon Napoleon by the demands of farmers for an outlet for unsaleable harvests, and even in the reconstruction of June-July 1810, the agricultural interest—at least the winegrowers—had been chiefly considered in the enumeration of exports under the new system. Two causes, however, had speedily led to a change of emphasis. The first was poor harvests, the second industrial demands.

The fears of crop shortage, which had led even in June to an embargo upon grain exports, while perhaps not well-founded for the northern departments of the Empire, proved only too true for the southern and eastern departments. In August of 1810 an absolute embargo was laid upon the export of grain from the Mediterranean ports.[7] Active measures were taken, also, to provision Paris. Coincidently "coast-wise trade permits" for grain shipments were issued to supply the needs of western Italy.[8] In September measures were taken to secure grain from Sardinia through Genoa and Leghorn.[9] As Corsica in particular was suffering from dearth, licences were granted, on 10 October (a) for Marseilles, Genoa, and Leghorn allowing holders to import grain into the island from wherever they could secure it, also (b) for Ajaccio, Bastia and Bonifacio, to import grain from Sar-

---

[6] Compare *Cor. de Nap.*, 22:432, 448, Napoleon to Bassano, 23, 28 August 1811, with Barlow to Monroe, 29 September 1811, *Dept. of State, Desp. Fr.*, vol. 13. See also Decrès to Napoleon, 27 November 1811, AF^{IV}1199, no. 220.

[7] AF^{IV}1243, annex 231, 10 August.

[8] Brotonne, *Dernières lettres de Napoléon Ier*, I, 519, 520, 531, and 538; also *Cor. de Nap.*, 21:275, no. 17135.

[9] AF^{IV}1241, 24 September.

dinia.[10] As the need continued throughout 1811, in June of that year yet another type of Sardinian licence was issued which included meat, lard, and other food stuffs, as well as grain.[11]

Various other expedients for securing foreign grain were tried, besides the effort—which because of prohibitive charges was largely vain—to send grain from northern to southern France by inland transportation. In February 1811 it was decided to grant licences for ports of the North and Holland, on condition that the vessels bring back grain.[12] By the mobilization of the army against Russia the provisioning problem was further aggravated. Hence during the summer of 1811 licences were offered upon liberal conditions even to Ottoman ships, to bring grain for the commissariat from Sicily, Sardinia, Greece, North Africa, and as far as the Black Sea.[13] Moreover, at this time, even a number of licences *in blank* were sent to the French consul at Algiers.[14] Eventually another special licence series was needed—the Illyrian licences, granted to Albanian vessels, especially for provisioning Corfu.[15] These sources of supply proving inadequate the French government turned to the last visible source. By giving special American permits to French citizens for French ships, and, in the fall of 1811, by creating American permits with special concessions for those bringing rice, flour, corn, etc., to Nantes and Bordeaux it was hoped to draw upon the cheap grain of the United States.[16] Verily great was the change, within three years, from the day when abundant harvests were the curse of France.

[10] Cf. original card-index entries of decrees of Napoleon in the Archives Nationales.

[11] $AF^{IV}1242$, 24 June 1811; also $AF^{IV}1243$, 14 August.

[12] On these operations interesting light is shed by a letter of 31 October 1811, from Heligoland. P. R. O., B. T. 1/61, L^2 no. 15.

[13] $AF^{IV}1243$, annex 57, 6 August 1811; $AF^{IV}1342$, 28-30 August 1811; and $F^{12}2108$, 12 August.

[14] $F^{12}2108$, 12 August 1811.

[15] $AF^{IV}1342$, August 1811. Also report of Montalivet 25 November 1811.

[16] $AF^{IV}1342$, 28-30 August 1811. See also Montalivet's report of 29 July 1811.

Offsetting the change in agricultural conditions, however, was the increasingly serious industrial problem. This problem which had chiefly demanded the retention of the licence system and its reconstruction upon the basis of supplying raw materials to manufacturers was aggravated, quite as much as it was helped, by the Trianon and St. Cloud taiiffs, and the Fontainebleau decree, which precipitated the financial crisis of 1810-11. Among the measures of relief tried were modifications of the licence system. Some of these changes were primarily administrative, such as allowing the payment of duties with a portion of the produce imported, or the requirement of special guarantees for full exportations. But besides these features special licences were granted to export particular articles like laces, books, etc., while with the standard types of licences a *requirement* was made to export certain important lines of manufactured goods.

The industry which seems to have felt the economic depression most severely was that of silk. In fact conditions in the silk trade must have been unsettled before the panic, judging from the legislation of the summer and autumn of 1810 for checking competition and facilitating the securing of raw silk from Italy. The crisis brought appeals for aid from Avignon, Tours, and, above all, Lyons.[17] News of the Russian ukase directed largely against French silks increased the distress.[18] It was therefore debated by the Conseil du Commerce whether a silk export requirement should not be substituted for that of wines and brandies in licences where such conditions were stated, and a similar requirement be inserted in all other licences. On 31 December Montalivet advocated a partial modification of this sort.[19] His report was adopted.

[17] AF^{IV}1062, nos. 19, 21 and 26; AF^{IV}1061, dossier 2, pièces 11 and 12.

[18] Cf. Caulaincourt's reports, December 1810-January 1811, AF^{IV}1699; Loyd, *New Letters*, p. 27, 3 March 1811; and Ford, *Writings of J. Q. Adams*, IV, 2-5 and 13-16.

[19] F^{12}2031, and AF^{IV}1061, pièce 123. The licence trade remedy was, of course, but one of the means adopted to aid Lyons. Another resource was to order new silk furnishings for the imperial palaces. A kindred scheme was to

By this decision of 31 December American permits and Hanse licences required that *one-third* the export cargo be of silks, and another third of wines and brandies.[20] Illyrian, Ottoman and Neapolitan licences, however, required that *half* the cargo be of silk, wines being omitted because of the Neapolitan wine growers, and especially because of protests from the ports against attempting to force Moslem vessels to export wine.[21] A similar condition was inserted, also, in "simple" licences of the third division (Mediterranean), and despite Montalivet's opposition it was extended to all "simple" licences and to all American ships entering without permits, and was even intended to be imposed upon vessels already loading under licences previously secured.[22] Later the silk export requirement was even made of those getting licences to export oysters. On the other hand, due probably to strong protests from the Chambers of Commerce of Bruges, Ostend, Marseilles, etc.,[23] the proportion of silk to be exported was reduced to one-third in the two new series of licences created for Holland.[24] The encouragement thus afforded through the licence trade to the silk industry was, during 1811-1813, extended on a smaller scale to other industries. The stipulation of a *fixed* exportation of such goods was not made, it is true, but special licences were granted for exporting lace, batistes and porcelains of France or the Netherlands, and even (in 1812) for a quantity of Swiss muslins and watches.[25] Other concessions were made from time to time for

---

require the wearing of silk clothing at court functions. The consternation caused at the Russian embassy thereby is more than amusing in view of the Russian ukaze against the use of French silks (Sbornik, 121:117).

[20] $AF^{IV}1243$, annex 289.

[21] $F^{12}2105$, Protest from Genoa, 15 November 1810 and reply, 6 December 1810.

[22] $F^{12}2031$, 14 January Conseil du Commerce; also 28 January, $AF^{IV}1061$, dossier 1, nos. 33 and 34. Even Van Aken in July 1811 was refused a licence which did not include silk, $AF^{IV}1342$.

[23] $F^{12}2105$, February 1811.

[24] $AF^{IV}1242$, also $AF^{IV}1342$.

[25] The Swiss muslins, however, had to pay a 50% export duty. Cf. Napoleon to Sussy, 2 March 1812, (*La Presse*, 9 March 1844).

securing raw materials not embraced in the original plans of July 1810, notably hides and cotton from Spain and England. The aid given by the licence trade was cited as a principal cause for the marked revival of the industries of Lyons and Rouen and other manufacturing centers whose flourishing condition from the close of 1811 stood out in marked contrast to the lamentable stagnation in British industry.[26] Consequently after an investigation of the relation of the licences to industrial progress Napoleon determined at the close of 1812 to distribute to industry generally the favors which before had been shown chiefly to the silk trade.[27]

Not only agriculture and manufacturing thus sought support, however, but also fishing and mining. Besides the original tunny-fishery licences (which underwent modifications), special licences, as previously noted, were granted for the shipment of eels, oysters and cured fish.[28] The mining industry most favored was that of Istria and Dalmatia. On 30 April 1811 it was decided to offer licences for exporting quicksilver and mercurial products from Trieste to America, and a variety of such products as well as other minerals were listed for export by the Albanian licences.[29]

With respect to all these ameliorative measures, however, a most vital question was whether they would work, or, indeed, be allowed to work. That is above all whether the other party in the proposed transactions—the English—would consent to the conditions. To be sure the English had long shown a general readiness for a co-operating licence trade and in 1808-9 had aided in the initiation of the French experiment. But then the trade had been distinctly to their own advantage, and when Napoleon had tested their attitude under altered conditions by requiring

---

[26] AF^{IV}1089^B, Mollien to Napoleon, November—December 1811. At Lyons the silk workers employed had risen from 3000 to 7000. At Rouen business had doubled in six months. On Lyons also see E. Pariset, *Histoire de la fabrique lyonnaise*, p. 294.

[27] AF^{IV}*171, p. 224-5.

[28] AF^{IV}1242, annexes 294 and 433.

[29] Imperial Decrees, decision 21 of 30 April 1811; and AF^{IV}1342.

that a fixed proportion of wines should be exported with each shipment of corn, the results of the measure were so unsatisfactory as to constitute a strong motive for discontinuing the traffic.[30] The seriousness of the situation was realized by those economic forces on both sides of the Channel which at this critical moment were requiring larger relief through the medium of the licences. It was evident if the British continued to get French corn, or were to furnish the raw materials demanded by French industry, that Napoleon must be assured in advance of British concessions, and that the commerce should be arranged under mutual guarantees.

Various feelers were put out, therefore, to discover what sort of engagements the British commercial authorities might be ready to subscribe to, and what special conditions would be offered or accepted. For example on 19 May 1810 British East India merchants, who were as anxious to sell as Continental merchants were to buy, petitioned the Privy Council for permission to export cotton to France and Holland.[31] Other pressure regarding trade with France came at about the same time from Jersey and Guernsey.[32] Also throughout June and July the Council was beseiged by various interests urging new grain import licences, or at least, the extension of those about to expire.[33] These efforts may have been solely upon British initiative but there was a significant co-operation at this critical moment between London merchants and their over-Channel correspondents. This is strikingly shown in the case of one Van Aken, a councillor of the prefecture and an influential merchant of Ghent.

Van Aken, who if not especially coached for his part by his London connection at least had unusually reliable channels of information regarding the British trade policy, had a conversa-

[30] See the *Moniteur*, 30 August 1810; also *Am. Daily Adv.*, 3 August, from Harwich, 6 June.

[31] *Privy Council Register*, 80:37, 38. Cf. *Am. Daily Adv.*, 16 April and 23 July 1810.

[32] *Privy Council Register*, pp. 278. Cf. B. T. 5/20, 105, 106.

[33] *Privy Council Register*, pp. 459, 462, 505, etc.

tion with Montalivet, or Napoleon himself, about 18 May during the imperial stop at Ghent.[34] To this conversation is traceable the suggestion of reaching an informal trade arrangement with the British ministry. The idea must have especially impressed the Emperor for a few days later during his visit to the neighboring seaports he instituted further inquiries. Indeed it was widely reported that on Sunday, 20 May, at Ostend, chancing to be at the docks when a licenced ship arrived from England he closely questioned the master as to the attitude of the British government. "After this, according to the report of the captain, Napoleon formally announced to the Chamber of Commerce of Ostend, his determination to sign no more licences for imports unless England would consent to receive French wines and brandies; in which case he was willing to grant licences to enable vessels to proceed directly to an English port and thus to secure to both governments the reciprocal advantages of circumscribed trade."[35]

True or false, this story and other information arriving from Ostend, Dunkirk and Boulogne, where Napoleon made further inquiries, created some sensation in London. Meanwhile Van Aken was receiving fresh information from London which he communicated to Montalivet. And Montalivet on his part, in consequence of the investigations at Ostend and Dunkirk, referred to Van Aken further inquiries upon which Napoleon desired better information.[36] To these inquiries Van Aken replied on 28 May explaining the British policy regarding vessels with wine and the evasions practiced by French vessels.[37] Vessels which did not leave their wine in Holland or empty it into the sea, he stated, ran the risk of capture by an English cruiser, which entailed confiscation of the wine and the ship, or if it eluded the coast guards it could enter harbor safely but must warehouse its wine for re-expor-

[34] $F^{12}2051$.
[35] *Am. Daily Adv.*, 23 July; and *Aurora*, 24 July, from London 29 May.
[36] Van Aken to Montalivet, 20 and 21 May, and Montalivet to Van Aken, 24 May (Lille), 25 May (Boulogne), $F^{12}2051$.
[37] $F^{12}2051$.

tation. On the other hand Van Aken asserted that not only was there no prohibition against wine in British import licences but that it was permitted in licences for Spain, and in the Channel Island licences, and he pointed out that the high prices which wines were then fetching in England would likely force a freer admission of the French product.

Encouraged by the information furnished by Van Aken, confirmed as it was by further information from various persons in the Channel ports, including the commissary of police for the coast of the Manche and Pas de Calais, Napoleon proceeded with his purpose of forcing the English to terms.[38] Having frightened them by rumors of his plans and by a temporary embargo upon their corn supplies, he adopted his new licence conditions and then sounded them definitely as to an adjustment.

Regarding the very peculiar but effective negotiation which ensued the French and British records are officially oblivious, although indirectly they afford confirmation of our other sources of information, such as the clearly inspired press accounts and diplomatic "gossip."[39] According to the London newspapers British merchants were kept informed of Napoleon's plans by news from the prefect at Ostend, and on the basis of this news had for some time been negotiating with the Board of Trade for a modification of the licence policy in favor of French wines.[40] These pleas had been well received and the merchants encouraged

[38] Cf. Fauchat's report of 31 May, $F^{12}2105$, dossier 3; Fauchat to Montalivet, 1 June, $F^{12}2051$; and Van Aken to Montalivet, with reply, $F^{12}2051$. See also the letter of DeVilliers du Terrage, Boulogne, 31 May, $F^{12}2051$.

[39] See the *London Times*, 8, 9, 10, 11 August; the *London Courier*, 9 August, (cf. *Am. Daily Adv.*, 21 and 22 September); *London Chronicle*, 10 August; and also the *Moniteur*, 17 August; all being official, or administration newspapers. At a later stage of this secret negotiation semi-official news seems to have been given to General Armstrong. See his letter of 1 Sept. to Madison, (Lib. of Cong. MSS). See also note 47 below.

[40] For indirect confirmation and particulars of this earlier negotiation see *Privy Council Register*, vols. 80 and 81, May-July 1810; also Montalivet to Napoleon, 2 July 1810, $F^{12}2031$.

to expect results from a continuation of their efforts.[41] Accordingly on 7 August, three days before the final date set by Privy Council for the expiration of all outstanding licences for trade with France,[42] the merchants again waited upon Lord Bathurst and his Board. They reported that a gentleman who enjoyed the confidence of Napoleon's Council of Commerce had just arrived from France authorized to communicate with the Board of Trade regarding "a commercial intercourse by means of neutral flags upon principles of reciprocity." The Board expressed their readiness for this if it should be advantageous to England. They were willing to admit French wines and other goods but on condition that British manufactures and colonial goods should enter France. This was the *sine qua non* of the arrangement. It was also expressly stated that the conduct of the negotiation on the part of each country was to be wholly in the hands of merchants.[43]

Such is the English side of the incident. The French side is equally curious. On 11 August, Montalivet wrote a hurried autograph note to Napoleon giving news from London which he had just received from his Ghent correspondent.[44] He enclosed an unsigned French letter received from Van Aken.[45] Under date of 7 August, at London, this letter reported that the Board of Trade would admit cargoes composed for one-third of French wines (but not brandies), the rest of grains, flour and burr-stones,

[41] The newspapers refer especially to a conference early in July, and it is significant that the Privy Council on 12 July recorded its willingness to grant licences for Bordeaux to Nantes as well as the usual Boulogne–Nantes licences for grain. *Privy Council Register*, 81:140.

[42] The date of 10 August had been decided on at the council of 27 June. *Privy Council Register*, 80:505.

[43] "Modern Commercial Treaty" is the caption of a crisp editorial on the affair in the *Columbian Centinel*, (Boston), 20 Oct. 1810.

[44] AF^{IV}1061, pièces 46 and 47. See also pièce 49, a letter of Montalivet dated 13 August, commenting on an English licence which the day previous Napoleon had sent him for examination.

[45] Van Aken's letter enclosing the London letter is dated 10 August and was sent by special courier to Paris, F^{12}2058.

provided the ships had first exported cargoes from England composed one-third of English manufactures and East India goods, or sugar or coffee, and the remainder of non-prohibited goods. There was reason to believe, moreover, that the English could be induced to make further concessions.

Meanwhile reports of the affair had gotten out, perhaps prematurely, in London. The stir which the news created there can be judged by the industry with which the papers for some days denied, repeated, modified, or explained the story of the negotiation.[46] But possibly the most significant reflection of the importance attached to the arrangement is that before a month had passed the Russian Chancellor, Romanzoff, had heard of it and discussed the matter with the American Minister who, in turn, lost no time in informing his government.[47]

The significance which attached to the London version of the arrangement, moreover, was naturally enhanced by the publication at this juncture of the Trianon tariff decree.[48] This seemed at its first appearance to meet the conditions of the Board of Trade and hence to ratify the understanding. But more definite information regarding the requirement for a French permit led the merchants interested once more to hold a long consultation with Lord Bathurst (on 21 August) regarding further concessions.[49] Practically nothing was gained but the right to import seeds and olive oil, while brandy was definitely excluded. The merchants were also informed that licences were already being prepared, and accordingly some were granted within the week.[50] Among other

[46] See the *London Times, Courier, Chronicle*, etc., of 8-11 August, as cited above.

[47] Adams to Secretary Smith, 5 September 1810, *Writings of J. Q. Adams*, III, 494.

[48] *Moniteur*, 9 August.

[49] *Times*, 22, 24, 27 August; and *Aurora*, 2 October (London, 22 August).

[50] *Privy Council Register*, 81, p. 549, although the Order in Council is of 1 October, *Privy Council Register*, 82:10, *Times*, 27 August, House of Lords, *Sess. Papers*, 1812, no. 5, p. 50-52. One granted to I. Horstman is in AF^{IV}1061, no. 64, dated 28 August. It cost £1 10s for stamp duty alone.

conditions prescribed by these licences were the insistence that the vessel should not be French built or manned and that it must take convoy at Falmouth or Plymouth.

Montalivet was informed of these new developments, on 25 August by Guérin de Fencés (or Foncia) on behalf of Van Aken and Son of Ghent and of Joseph Serruy of Antwerp and Ostend, for whom French licences were asked and obtained.[51] Also Van Aken himself wrote three days later sending a copy of one of the new English licences which had been granted him.[52] Continuing the negotiation, Van Aken was able to announce on 18 September that the British had been induced to add French linons and batistes to the imports permitted by licence and that his British co-workers were insisting on the addition, likewise, of brandy and other articles of French growth or make.[53]

Yet it was not merely with regard to the direct trade between France and England that an effort for mutual adjustment of their licence trade was made by the two countries. News of the Hanseatic licence plan aroused interest in England—whither a copy of instructions given to General Molitor for the operation of the system was sent late in August.[54] It was followed directly by the adoption of a new British licence for the North applicable to the district between the Island of Juist and the Eyder. When after some months it was found that all advantages of this arrangement accrued to England, Napoleon undertook a readjustment of his Hanse licences to meet the situation. This change was adopted in July 1812.[55] Also similar readjustments of the British licences for Malta and Gibraltar were made directly upon

[51] $F^{12}2058$.

[52] $F^{12}2058$, and $AF^{IV}1061$, nos. 123-4.

[53] $F^{12}2058$. Cf. also an undated London letter received on 6 October, forwarded to Montalivet by Guérin de Fences and Co.

[54] See *London Times*, 31 August, 4, 17 September.

[55] Napoleon to Collin de Sussy, 2 March 1812, published in *La Presse*, 9 March 1844.

the adoption of Napoleon's various Mediterranean licences.[56] Whether these additional instances of the "dove-tailing" of the two supposedly hostile commercial systems were due to the same mercantile mediators who were at that moment securing modifications of the direct trade is not known, but it is to be noted that Van Aken was one of the first to notify Montalivet of the Juist-Eyder licences of August 1810.

Partly as a reward and partly to facilitate his activities, Van Aken was granted special trade licences, and he was named as Ghent representative of the honorary Conseil General de Commerce which was created early in August.[57] Meanwhile his activities were being extended in still other directions. Napoleon having determined at the Conseil of 3 September to open up fresh relations by licences with the colonies and with Spanish America, it was necessary to investigate the feasibility of these projects.[58] Besides reports by the Minister of Exterior Relations, and of the Marine, Montalivet shared in this inquiry. Once more he turned to Van Aken for information.[59] The first letter asking him to sound the British government Montalivet rejected after signing because it seemed too formal. It was then decided that Fauchat, who was directly in charge of the licence business and was also known to Van Aken, should conduct the correspondence under Montalivet's direction. This was done and Van Aken replied promising the utmost discretion on his part.[60]

The first question put to Van Aken was in a letter of 7 September regarding the possibility of opening a direct line of trade for sugar, coffee, etc., between Martinique and Guadeloupe and

[56] Order in Council, 29 August 1810, *Privy Council Register*, George III, 81:562.
[57] F^{12}2058, Requests of Van Aken and his agents, 13 and 25 August. Montalivet in submitting the licences for signature mentions that Napoleon understands the reasons.
[58] AF^{IV}1241, annex 136.
[59] F^{12}2058 contains the draft letters and notes of Montalivet and Fauchat of 5 and 6 September.
[60] F^{12}2058, 10 September 1810.

France.[61] Van Aken showed in reply (10 September) that the produce of these islands was not sold but merely warehoused in England, and hence prices were so low that France could get such produce cheaper in London than from her former colonies. He doubted whether England would so far depart from her system as to permit such a trade without touching in England, although such an exception had lately been made in connection with the provisioning of Portugal. However, he would make cautious inquiries as instructed. Unfortunately the continuation of this correspondence is missing, but that its object was eventually achieved is shown by the decision of the Board of Trade on 24 June 1811 to grant licences for Martinique and Guadeloupe, ostensibly because of their distressed condition for lack of a market, to export sugar and coffee direct to France and even upon French vessels.[62] The situation of the islands, said the Board, was not the fault of England but of France.

A second letter of 7 September asked Van Aken to find out from England whether it was possible to establish commercial relations with the independent states of South America and what facilities England would grant for such trade.[63] It was also hinted that he get in touch with Miranda. Van Aken replied four days later that the matter was so entirely new to him that he could offer no information himself but that he had connections with a prominent firm trading chiefly with South America, of whom he would make inquiries, and that he would investigate the influence of Miranda. The reply is missing but evidently the prospects were unfavorable, for the idea was dropped by Napoleon

---

[61] $F^{12}2058$, dated 6 September here.

[62] P. R. O., B. T. 5/20, 442; and a letter of Greffulke Bros., London, 11 July, to Hottinguer & Co., Paris, *Arch. Nat.*, $F^{7}3643^{12}$, annex 69. On 9 August similar measures were asked for Mauritius, and Bourbon, B. T. 5/20, 487.

[63] $F^{12}2058$, (draft dated 6 September). The reasons for this move are shown in the minutes of the Conseil du Commerce of 3-10 September, AF^{IV} 1241, nos. 136 and 157.

during almost a year until somewhat similar negotiations were opened with the United States.[64]

Van Aken must have been impressed during his negotiations by the difficulties of carrying on intercourse between France and England because of the lack of proper means of communications. On 17 September through his Paris representative he proposed to establish a line of packets from Ostend to England, if special concessions (including the right to import oysters) were granted him.[65] This Montalivet declined on 22 September, perhaps because he had meanwhile received and recommended to the Minister of Police a more favorable proposal from a Joseph Chamoulard of Dunkirk who had been somewhat active already with suggestions for the licence system.[66] His proposal was to run a single packet under the surveillance of the police, paying the government two francs per letter carried, besides taking passengers for the government without charge other than twelve francs for their board. He asked in return merely a protective licence which did not require an export of wine.

The immediate occasion for these proposals evidently was the adoption of new and stringent measures to prevent the carrying of mail and passengers by licenced ships.[67] As to the workings of these regulations most interesting evidence is afforded by a member of the Virginia house of Ellis and Allan who was in France

---

[64] It is suggestive that between November 1810 and March 1811 British merchants tried to get a new law passed for a freer trade to South America but failed. See B. T. 5/20 pp. 155, 269. The proposal to Barlow is told in his letter of 29 September 1811 to Secretary Monroe, *Dept. of State, Desp. Fr.*, vol. 13.

[65] $F^{12}2058$.

[66] See $F^{12}2057$, 28 July 1810, and $F^{12}2033$, 19 September 1810. But a letter of the Commissary of Police at Boulogne, dated 11 January 1811, shows that Chamoulard's reputation was such that his proposal was rejected by the police. And yet in May 1811 he was granted a special passport to London on commercial business, F^7 3643.[11]

[67] See a police order of 2 July, $F^7 3643$.

in the early summer of 1810.⁶⁸ Desiring to return through England in order to attend to shipping business of his firm, he was informed that he must wait until the new navigation measures, upon which Napoleon was engaged, could be worked out. After resorting vainly to a variety of other devices for assisting him, General Armstrong was able to get Ellis out of France early in August as a diplomatic messenger. But getting out of France was no harder than getting in. According to news carried to England about 25 July by a vessel which managed to slip out of Ostend, a decree had just been rendered strictly forbidding licenced vessels bringing any but their crews from England to any point on the French coasts.⁶⁹ The news of the decree was apparently premature but on 28 August licenced vessels were, indeed, strictly forbidden to carry passengers either to, or from England.⁷⁰ Despite this decree, however, on 13 September Napoleon signed "passports for passengers to England on board vessels carrying licences."⁷¹ Moreover in May 1811 at the urgent request of the Minister of Police Montalivet promised to get some new licences signed so that persons having passports for England might find passage thither.⁷²

It is also certain that mail communication was not entirely cut off. Indeed from the letters of Savary (duc de Rovigo) and Montalivet regarding the disposition of English licences inter-

⁶⁸ The letters of Charles Ellis to Mr. Allan, foster father of the poet Poe, are in the *Ellis-Allan MSS.* of the Library of Congress.

⁶⁹ *Moniteur*, 11 August, from the *Morning Chronicle* of 27 July. This item aroused Napoleon's wrath and led to greater strictness. Cf. *Cor. de Nap.*, no. 16777 (9 August). Also see Brotonne, *Lettres inédites de Napoléon*, p. 267, no. 647, 14 August, regarding passengers on a police boat from Dunkirk.

⁷⁰ For the decree see $AF^{IV}1243$, annex 234. For the sensation which it caused in England see the *London Times*, September 1810. The issue of 20 September for instance has an account of the seizure of a ship at Boulogne with passengers on board. This, however, was probably a smuggler.

⁷¹ Brotonne, *Lettres inédites*, p. 274, no. 665, to Rovigo.

⁷² Rovigo to Montalivet, and reply, 7 May 1811, $F^{12}2033$.

cepted by the police, which were usually forwarded to their French address, it is evident that both these ministers were, at least until September 1810, personally assisting French participants in the licence trade.[73] Moreover in its issue of 13 September the *Moniteur* copies London news of a negotiation being undertaken to establish a regular postal service between the opposite shores of the Straits of Dover.[74] Perhaps, however, the wish was but father to the fact, and not improbably both Van Aken and Chamoulard were acting in behalf of their English correspondents as well as of their own compatriots in offering their proposals.

The solution adopted, though not precisely identical with either of the rejected plans, which had been proposed by Montalivet's correspondents, was at least somewhat similar to both. Thus on 9 October, the Duke of Rovigo took occasion to return expired licences granted to his predecessor, Fouché, and to ask for others.[75] The same day Montalivet sent him four new ones of the series of Dunkirk, which seem to have been used for private vessels to maintain intercourse with England under police protection.[76]

It is evident, however, that communications were not actually restricted to the channel of police licences. Indeed ordinary licenced vessels must have continued for some time to carry mail, judging from imperial orders of 10 February, and 4 August 1811, requiring Rovigo to intercept and examine all letters coming on licenced vessels from England, and insisting that no letters should go thither except through Morlaix, and only after passing the police censorship.[77] Apparently, moreover, even this restriction did not affect such mail as could be carried by the Dunkirk guinea-smugglers, for we find the Minister of Commerce in February

---

[73] F¹²2033.

[74] *Moniteur*, 1810, p. 1007, from the *Morning Chronicle*.

[75] F¹²2033.

[76] *Ibid.*, nos. 26 to 29, Dunkirk series, or nos. 193 to 196 of the general distribution.

[77] Loyd, *New Letters of Napoleon*, nos. 227 and 366.

1813 asking the extension of such rights as they enjoyed to licensed ships also.[78]

Of these methods of communicating with England that under police licences was probably the worst. Few such licences were granted, but being given in blank and without obligation to balance imports by exports they led to great abuses. On 6 April 1811, Kenny, Mayor of Dunkirk, complained to both Montalivet and Rovigo that they were defeating the purposes both of the smuggling system and the regular licence trade.[79] The service at Dunkirk was in the hands of Loriol and Dagneau, the latter of whom had begun as a smuggler. They were able to obtain English licences as they wished,[80] and by means of the failure of the police licences to stipulate the vessel protected thereby, or its tonnage, they could make unrestricted voyages. Moreover they had monopolized the smuggling trade and bent it to their own ends. Similar conditions he said were the case at Ostend, Boulogne, etc. Rovigo in reply declared that Kenny had exaggerated the abuses, which had already been checked, and accused Kenny of negligence in his own duties.[81] After further mutual recriminations, however, the matter seemed to blow over.[82]

In July Rovigo asked for three additional police licences and the request was transmitted to Napoleon who required an accounting for the seven which had already been granted. Rovigo therefore made a report on 24 July of results at Dunkirk, Ostend, Hamburg, Boulogne, etc., which apparently satisfied the Emperor as three days later two additional licences were given.[83] But when in the autumn Napoleon made another journey to the

[78] $F^{12}2033$, Collin de Sussy to Rovigo. They had been warned in 1812, however, not to carry any letters at all, $F^{12}3643^{11}$.

[79] $F^{12}2033$; $AF^{IV}1061$, dossier 2, pièces 66-68, 6 April.

[80] Cf. B. T. 6/190, et seq., (*Licence Registers*).

[81] $AF^{IV}1061$, dossier 2, pièce 69, 9 April.

[82] *Ibid.*, pièces 70-72, 15 April. Kenny submitted statistics and papers, but they were somewhat dubious in character as proofs, $AF^{IV}1061$, dossier 2, pièces 81-86.

[83] $F^{12}2058$, nos. 82 and 83, and 88.

northern ports the Mayor of Dunkirk had his inning. The evidence presented convinced Napoleon that at Ostend and Boulogne as well as Dunkirk there had been great abuses and that Rovigo had been taken in by his agents who had imported four or five millions of goods without an equivalent export. He therefore censured both Rovigo and Collin de Sussy and ordered the suppression of police licenses.[84]

If the Minister of Police and the Director General of Customs could be so imposed upon in connection with licences used for the public service, the watchfulness required to prevent abuses in the ordinary trade can be imagined. One of the most troublesome problems was that of the "equivalent export" requirement. Especially was this so when vessels were allowed to begin operations by importation, or when having begun by exportation they brought back an excess cargo. In the former case the difficulty was met by a decree of 5 December 1810 requiring that 20% of the cargo imported should be warehoused with the government as a guarantee until exportation conditions had been satisfied.[85] The other difficulty was met by allowing the transactions under one licence to be balanced by that of another licence, provided this was done within the life of the first licence and at the same port.[86] This was the basis for the so-called balancing or equation licences. The plan was supplemented by a retro-active decision of 7 April 1812 which regulated the evaluation of licenced cargoes.[87] Another troublesome administrative question was the collection of the price of licences, which function was entrusted as early as September 1810 to the customs service.[88] Much difficulty was also found in suppressing old licences of the series of 1809.[89]

[84] *Cor. de Nap.*, 22:498, no. 18148, to Savary, 24 September 1811; Lecestre, *Lettres inédites de Napoléon Ier*, II, 162, no. 874, to Sussy, 23 September; and *ibid.*, II, no. 6, 30 September, to Savary. Also *Cor. de Nap.*, 23:28, no. 18277, 20 Nov. 1811, to Sussy.
[85] AF^{IV}1243, annex 287; AF^{IV}1061, no. 121; and F^{12}2115.
[86] F^{12}2115.
[87] F^{12}2034-37. The basis was the market values at London and Havre.
[88] AF^{IV}1243, annex 238.
[89] Decree of 5 September, copy in F^{12}2031.

The matter of the certificates of origin required in connection with many of the licences was a most nettlesome question. The illegal granting of these protections by French consuls for destinations other than France and the wholesale counterfeiting of these papers, in England, Malta and the Levant, in order to cover the transactions of false neutrals in the Baltic and Adriatic, became a crying abuse in the summer of 1810.[90] To Denmark, Prussia and Russia, Napoleon denied the validity of all such documents declaring that his consuls did not grant them.[91] This statement, however, was so palpably false, that the United States and other neutrals, his allies, and apparently even some of his own agents, who felt themselves unjustly compromised, protested vigorously.[92] On 13 August therefore Napoleon had the Conseil du Commerce investigate the matter.[93] As a result a fortnight later he gave most stringent instructions that French commercial agents must under no pretext whatsoever deliver certificates of origin for any sort of goods except for vessels destined for France.[94] The report of this which reached England was hailed as an abandonment of these documents and as a body blow to the Continental System. But the English once more were deceived by their wishes, although in October and again in December fresh instances of the abuses of the certificates did lead to further restrictions and the consideration of abandoning them entirely.[95]

On 31 December, Montalivet in accordance with imperial orders presented an interesting report tracing the history and dis-

[90] *Cor. de Nap.*, 21:65, 26 August, and 21:76, 29 August. Also *Dept. of State, Desp., Fr.*, vol. 11, correspondence of Armstrong, Forbes, etc. Cf. also, *Writings of J. Q. Adams*, vol. III, 371, 523-5, etc.

[91] *Writings of J. Q. Adams*, III, 495; IV, 9-10, 17-18, 48-9. Brotonne, *Dernières lettres inédites de Napoléon*, I, 494, no. 1082.

[92] *Am. State Papers, For. Rel.*, III, 400-3, November-December 1810.

[93] AF^{IV}1241, annex 96.

[94] *Cor. de Nap.*, 21:68, no. 16838, to Cadore, 28 August. Cf. also, *ibid.*, p. 76, no. 16844, 29 August.

[95] AF^{IV}1241, Conseil du Commerce, 10 September, 1 October, 29 October, 24 December 1810.

cussing the value of certificates of origin.[96] Originally created by a law of 1 March 1793 as proof that goods did not arrive from an enemy country, they had been required by a law of 10 brumaire An V (31 October 1796) for all goods not expressly prohibited by that law. It especially required that all India goods should be accompanied by such certificates from the Dutch and Danish East India Companies viséed by the French consuls. A Consular order of 1 messidor An XI (20 June 1803) had extended their requirement to all goods brought by neutrals to French ports in order to prevent the entry of produce or wares of England and her possessions. And the Continental System had attempted to extend the workings of this regulation to all the continent. Despite the frauds to which they had given rise, and the fact that in many cases they were superfluous documents, Montalivet felt that certificates of origin were an additional precaution which it would be inadvisable at present to discontinue, although under ordinary conditions they should be suppressed. As a result of this report no further action was taken to abandon their usage.

The forging of ship's papers, however, was but one of the numerous fraudulent practices which had to be dealt with. The difficulty of fulfilling the licence requirements, for example, led to manifold evasions. Some of these, such as varying the prescribed sailing course, entering the wrong harbor, entering with an expired licence, or changing the crew while in a foreign harbor were usually condoned, or led to little worse than the inconvenience and expense of a temporary sequestration.[97] Greater difficulties and more serious subterfuges, however, grew out of the efforts of both belligerents to utilize the licence trade to force prohibited goods upon the other. Smuggling, of course, was rampant particularly in the English Channel and it was by no means monopolised by

[96] AF^{IV}1061, piece 124. Cf. Brotonne, *Dernières lettres inédites, de Napolèon* I, 554. But see Chuquet, *Inédites Napoléoniens*, nos. 637, 640 and 766.

[97] Cf. AF^{IV}1241-1243, *passim*; also F^{12}2033.

those smugglers of the Pas de Calais who were fostered and watched by imperial officials.[98] It also flourished against the imperial will.

Unauthorized contraband was especially strong between the Channel Islands and the neighboring French coast. Here small boats carried poultry, eggs, and other French goods, including particularly brandy, silks, velvets, etc., and took back sugar and coffee, until both England and France fearing that the disadvantages exceeded the benefits resorted to restrictive measures.[99] Thus England, in particular, felt compelled to suppress Jersey—Guernsey licences because of the quantities of brandy which were got from thence into Britain itself despite the strictest prohibitions.[100]

This constant prohibition of brandy, and, except for the brief period between August and November 1810, the almost equally strict exclusion of all French wines rendered trade very precarious for all who held French licences requiring the exportation of these very products. Indeed so serious did the matter look on the eve of the temporary British relaxation that Montalivet demonstrated mathematically to Napoleon that the loss on wines exported would ruin all who undertook the trade.[101] Occasionally the wine could be saved by arrangements with English fishermen who introduced it as salvage from the sea, or with English privateers who entered it as prize goods. In fact so strong was the English demand for these liquors that the English wine merchants would themselves provide a privateer at a stipulated point to complete the transaction, although they sometimes found that even after getting such "booty" safely past admiralty judges the obdurate customs would

[98] Cf. decree of 15 June 1810.

[99] P. R. O., Adm. 1/225, 22 April 1810, d'Auvergne reports on abuses at Guernsey. *London Times*, 23 August 1810. Cf. also, French police reports in F^73643^9, especially 9 June, 24 July 1810, etc.

[100] Cf. the *Board of Trade Journals* and *Privy Council Register*, 1810-13, for the changing Jersey regulations.

[101] Report of 8 August 1810, $AF^{IV}1318$. Yet by 20 August 4,595 pipes and 204 hogsheads of French wine had been entered in the King's warehouses, *London Times*, 25 August 1810.

merely warehouse it for exportation.[102] Under conditions such as these it can be seen that almost invariably the wine had to be emptied out during the passage and to minimize the financial loss only the cheapest wines and vinegars were exported or even nothing but colored water, while to meet the English requirement cheap earthenware was purchased and thrown overboard before reaching the French coasts.[103]

The substitution of a silk export requirement for that of wines only led to new evasions. French manufacturers indeed managed to dispose of some old and worthless surplus stocks, and they also in time manufactured a very cheap fabric which could be passed off with the customs as superior goods but withal the loss was so great that many who had applied for licences refused to take them out, and in order to overcome so serious a situation the licence administration lent itself to encouraging smuggling schemes to force the silk into England. Some of these devices Montalivet explained, with apologies, to Napoleon.[104] Since the publicity given the matter by the imperial decrees, he said the English government had become very strict and smuggling was the only possibility. He asked for the granting of eighteen licences and showed how the vessels from the Manche and Pas de Calais would first go out with cargoes composed one-third of silks and arrange to meet English contrabanders at sea who for a payment of 25% would get the goods into England. Vessels from distant ports, as those of the Gironde, Finisterre, or Charente Inferieure would start for England but hang off the coast under various pretexts so as to meet English smugglers and give them the silk by night. Certain captains also would go to the Channel Islands where, despite reports of a rigorous customs service, ways were also found to get the goods past the local tidewaiters and then to

[102] *London Times*, 21 October 1811

[103] Cf. Rovigo to Montalivet, 29 January 1811, F^{12}2033; also the case of *La Marie* of Ostend; *Moniteur*, 30 August 1810. Cf. also the letter of Capt. Dangibau, April 1810, P. R. O., B. T. 1/59, I², 5.

[104] AF^{IV}1342, Reports of Montalivet, 6 May and 25 November 1811.

England. Thus bales, barrels and chests were mislabelled as to their contents, and yet no inspection made. Silks were put into bolts of cloth or hidden in shipments of clover seed, of which England was importing quantities, and so got through safely.

The Dunkirk smuggling system also supplemented the licence trade in these transactions.[105] Here the smugglers usually required that the silks be wrapped in waterproofed canvas with sinkers attached and these bundles were left by prearrangement where English fishermen would cast their nets and deliver the goods at Deal, Folkestone or elsewhere in accordance with previous orders.[106] Yet even with such precautions the risk and loss was great, for the goods often floated to land and in France, as well as England, became the property of the marine as flotsam and jetsam. Thus although the various devices were effective enough to call forth English newspaper condemnation of the unpatriotic fashions of dressing in smuggled French goods, the actual losses of the French shippers at length compelled the substitution of a countervailing surtax in place of the export of the silk.[107]

Manifestly where so many subterfuges had to be resorted to in order to avoid ruinous operations there was little hesitancy about swearing to falsely evaluated invoices of imports and exports, although this was minimized by the creation of special boards of appraisal and by other precautions.[108] Another subterfuge was the exportation of fine laces, paintings, jewelry or other small objects of exceptional value which if not entered in England could at least be concealed and smuggled back into France to figure in future exportations.[109] Even special regulations for inspection, with rewards for detection of fraud and heaviest penalties for the defrauders proved vain.[110] It was necessary therefore to forbid

[105] See $F^{12}2034$-37, and $F^{7}3643^{11}$.
[106] See $F^{12}2007$, Letter of Richard Faber to Burton l'aîné, of Brussels.
[107] Note the letter in the *London Times*, 26 November 1811.
[108] See $F^{12}2034$-37.
[109] $AF^{IV}1061$, pièces 78 and 79, 20 October, 1810.
[110] Decree of 25 November 1810, 17 Duvergier 255.

the counting of articles of fanciful value when appraising the required export cargo.[111] The regulation evidently had its bearing upon the troubles of Las Cases regarding the licence-trade edition of his atlas from which he expected rich returns.[112] Also it affords an explanation for the long case of the gilt bird cage which finally required a ministerial decision to determine whether it was jewelry or machinery.

It was, of course, part of the game that those who held licences and sought to evade their terms must expect to be checkmated in their trickery, but all of the regulations to which they might suddenly be forced to conform were not of this just character.[113] Thus on Napoleon's part the requirement in January 1811 that all licenced vessels export silks was a manifest injustice in case of shippers who had previously obtained licences under the conditions of which they had made up their cargoes.[114]

But Napoleon was by no means the chief aggressor in the matter of unexpected changes of the licence system. Thus at the end of October 1810, the Board of Trade suddenly declared its determination to grant no more licences for trade with France.[115] It was even expected that an embargo would be laid and word was at once sent across by the English merchants to Van Aken and others who warned the French licence administration. Steps were at once taken for a protective counter-embargo in French

[111] AF^{IV}1243, annex 303, Decree of 15 March 1811, reported by Sussy, 4 March 1811, F^{12}2031. A decree of 24 September 1811, also forbade the entry of any article not in the licences.

[112] *Journal of Las Cases* (Phila. 1823) III, 210-4. He assigns the incident to 1813, but the official records indicate 1812. Cf. F^{12}2034-37.

[113] An example is the case of eighty Danish vessels detained in French ports which after long negotiations with Napoleon, and even the securing of English licences, dared not sail because of the silk export requirement. Sbornik, 121:158, 21 Feb. 1812.

[114] There is some reason to believe, however, that this was modified in February (cf. AF^{IV}1061, dossier 1, pièces 33 and 34).

[115] AF^{IV}1061, nos. 80, and 86; F^{12}2031 and F^{12}2033. See also *Am. Daily Adv.*, 10 and 25 December 1810, (London news), *Moniteur*, 8 November, and *London Statesman*, 30 October.

ports.[116] But within a few days fresh news came. It was first, that ships already loaded might sail; and then, that after the first of November nothing could be imported but corn and flour, the export of which from France was practically prohibited.[117] This was soon followed by another flurry when late in January the receipt of news that the British had sequestred licenced ships in their harbors led Napoleon to decree an embargo on shipping in French ports which, indeed, continued in force for some weeks after the Board of Trade had made another juggler's change.[118]

Perhaps the October action of the Board had been the consequence of news of the Fontainebleau decree, even as the sequestration of Hanse vessels in January 1811 is supposed to have been a belated retort to French annexations of the German North Sea coast.[119] But both episodes are typical of methods of Lord Bathurst and his committee (or the Privy Council itself) which are often inexplicable from any available evidence. In fact the mysterious instability of the licence system was openly assailed at the time as a proof of its immorality. Already in January of 1810, at the risk of a libel suit, the *London Morning Cronicle* had voiced accusations that Lord Bathurst was acting in the interest of licence speculators, and thus had aided a parliamentary attack upon the traffic.[120] But the labor was in vain. Equally futile were the re-echoed accusations of pamphleteers, and even such determined Parliamentary attacks upon the system as were led by Brougham and Baring during the spring of 1812. For still in January 1813 the *Moniteur* was repeating London newspaper complaints against the shiftiness of the Board of Trade's latest licence rulings.[121] In short the licence trade continued with

[116] Decree of 27 November, AF^{IV}1243, annex 286.

[117] Order in Council, 6 November 1810, *Privy Council Register*, 82:271.

[118] AF^{IV}1061, dossier 1, pièce 97, dossier 2, pièce 14.   See also, AF^{IV}1199, dossier 1, pièce 23; F^{12}2115; AF^{IV}1061, no. 41; and F^{12}2105.

[119] See *Privy Council Register*, 83:329.

[120] See the *Morning Chronicle*, 29 and 31 January and 13 February 1810.

[121] *Moniteur*, 1 January, quoting the *Courier* of 12 December 1812.

impunity in the old way, while the British and the French governments like desperate gamblers continued manoeuvring their respective systems in the effort to force concessions from each other.

CHAPTER XI
THE GRAND SYSTEM

In November 1811, a singular conjunction of factors, which for some time had been quietly preparing, led Napoleon to another sudden but searching reconsideration of his commercial policy. Among these compelling influences was a new version of the still unsettled American problem, a fresh realization of the economic needs of his Empire, and a surprising alteration in the British policy. There was, besides, indirect pressure from the ominous situation of Russian relations, with all its forebodings of disaster for the Continental System.

One element of the Russian problem, the closure of the North to colonial goods had vital relation to the American problem. Wholesale confiscations were made of American vessels in the Baltic on the score of their entering those waters under British convoy. Several such cases came before the Conseil du Commerce of 9 September.[1] To legalize these seizures Napoleon attempted another of his specious definitions of neutral rights and risks. This new interpretation of the treaty of Utrecht was to be the keynote of notable declarations of his policy in the following months. A few hours before this action—surely an unpropitious moment—there arrived in France, Joel Barlow, a new minister from the United States, primed with positive instructions for obtaining from the imperial government the redress of all standing grievances, with guarantees for the future.[2]

In keeping with his program of dodging the American issue as long as evasion was possible, it happened that on the day of Barlow's arrival at Paris (19 September) Napoleon set out from Compiégne for a visit to the Belgian coast, Holland and the Rhine. The Minister of Exterior Relations, however, remained long

[1] AF^{IV}1243, annex 185. See also *Cor. de Nap.*, 22:477.
[2] *Am. State Papers, For. Rel.*, III, 509. He landed at Cherbourg, 8 September 1811.

enough to receive from Barlow a preliminary explanation of his mission, and in reply to assure him of their "being able on the return of the minister to remove all obstacles to a most perfect harmony between the two countries."[3] At the same time he endeavored by certain proposals to encourage American rivalry with England in Latin America, and by complicating the issue relieve France from the insistence of American demands.[4]

A prolonged wait followed since the imperial journey was extended far beyond original plans. It gave Barlow a fair augury of the experiences before him, for like his predecessors he was to labor in vexation for the ashen fruits of Napoleonic diplomacy. At last on 9 November the duc de Bassano returned to Paris and the following day Barlow left at the Ministry of Exterior Relations a note presenting the demands of the United States.[5] This note was the American contribution to the situation of November 1811. As Barlow waited impatiently for a reply he learned that they were "discussing in the Emperor's councils of commerce and of state, the principal points of my note."[6] Then he was made to believe that Napoleon was "really changing his system relative to our trade." In both respects Barlow's information was not incorrect. Unfortunately, however, he seems not to have seen that his interests were closely involved with other weighty influences which must first play their part in changing the imperial system.[7]

When the Conseil du Commerce met on 18 November it faced a heavy program. Besides the American note, it must deal with pressing petitions from several important Chambers of Commerce, with other business accumulated because of the suspension of

[3] *Dept. of State, Desp. Fr.*, vol. 13, Barlow to Monroe, 29 September.

[3] *Ibid.* This was in line with suggestions by Roux in a note of 26 August to Napoleon, *Aff. Étr., États Unis*, sup. vol. 8, fol. 254.

[5] *Am. State Papers, For. Rel.*, III, 513.

[6] *Am. State Papers, For. Rel.*, III, 513, 515, Barlow to the Secretary of State, 21 November and 19 December.

[7] For the culmination of this story and with it the triumph of American demands in June 1812, see pp. 314-9 below.

its sessions during the Emperor's tour in the North, and by no means least, with the influences of the two months' journey.

As compared with the tour of May 1810, this second northern trip was much less significant in its results. Yet the impression made by Napoleon's observations is clearly evidenced by a note written directly after his return to St. Cloud. In it he announced to Montalivet his purpose of holding a council of the Interior each week until March to treat in turn all activities of that Ministry, beginning with commerce and manufactures.[8]

The chief commercial influence of his tour of observation—aside from the discovery of certain abuses of the licence trade in Flanders—had been brought to bear upon Napoleon during his stay in Holland. Moreover it was from Belgium and Holland that most of the significant petitions for commercial relief had lately come. The effect is seen in the new measures considered by the Conseil du Commerce, including proposals to allow importations from the Dutch plantations in the West Indies, to permit the entry of tea into Holland from Antwerp, Hamburg, and Gottenburg, for the entry of a ship load of American tobacco, to accept colonial goods in payment of debts owed by Brazil, to make Emden a licence port, and to export butter and cheese to England in return for cash.[9] Of these proposals some were ultimately granted, others refused, and some played their part in a general commercial reconstruction.

Several of these measures for the benefit of Dutch trade received consideration by the Conseil du Commerce at its session of 18 November. On the basis of news from the North coast, likewise, certain propositions were favorably discussed for the exporting of silks, silk laces and certain other French products from ports of the English Channel. This, however, presented the question which Napoleon wished first to consider, whether "there are any

[8] *Cor. de Nap.*, 23:23, no. 18270, 20 November 1811.

[9] $AF^{IV}1243$, September-December 1811; and $AF^{IV}1061$, dossier 2, pièces 104, 105, 131, and 135.

products of which we have need, and of which it would be necessary to permit the importation from England which would facilitate in return the exchange of our goods."[10] Significant also at this session was the endorsement of the project for importing cotton motril from Malaga, and of the policy of granting American trade permits for use by French ships. This latter policy, however, raised important issues regarding American and Levant permits, and the problems of provisioning France with foodstuffs and raw materials. For these various reasons, therefore, and because of the demand for new licences it was felt necessary that Montalivet should at once present a general summary of the licence trade.[11]

The report which Montalivet, in accordance with his instructions, presented at the following session of the Conseil (25 November) is a notable paper.[12] In many ways it is *the* most important summary of the French licence traffic covering as it does the *ancien systéme* and the initial stage of the *nouveau systéme*. Moreover it is one of the ablest and most important commercial reports of the Napoleonic period, ranking thus with Chaptal's famous reports of 1801-1802, the reports and *exposés* of July-August 1807, and those of June-July 1810, and even with Montalivet's great *exposé* of February 1813.[13] So thorough and clear-cut is its presentation of statistics, its explanations of conditions and its suggestions for the future, that it seems incredible that but a week was allowed for its drafting. Indeed one must believe that, anticipating this call, Fauchat—whose work it was—had already prepared for just such a report. It was accompanied (1st) by a general chart presenting all the final statistics, (2d) by detailed sheets for each of sections into which the general *résumé* was

[10] AF^{IV}1061, dossier 2, pièce 134.

[11] AF^{IV}1243, annexes 107-13.

[12] AF^{IV}1342, (bottom of the carton).

[13] Cf. Montalivet, *Exposé de la situation de l'Empire*, 25 February 1813. See, for Chaptal, d'Ivernois, *Exposé de l'Exposé*. . . . For 1807 and 1810 see earlier chapters of the present study.

divided, and (3d) with papers giving full data for all licences mentioned. It is, indeed, a striking illustration of the high efficiency which had been attained by the licence administration at Paris.[14]

The statistics showed that since the establishment, in August 1810, of licences of the "new system," 1153 had been signed, of which 494 had been delivered, 466 had expired unused (having been sent back or never delivered), while 193 unexpired licences remained to be delivered, being the larger part of the 349 which were yet valid.[15] From these licences the treasury had received 828,430 francs and 90,520 francs were still due. Exportations by licences used were appraised at 45,053,753 francs, imports at 26,705,198 or a balance apparently of 18,348,555 in favor of France, although it was expected that further imports would reduce this excess.[16] Besides the excess was partially to be explained by the method of evaluation used, by which 50% was added to the invoiced value of French exports to get the foreign selling price, while 25% was deducted from import appraisals in order to estimate the foreign purchase price.[17]

The great bulk of the trade was with England. Of 397 ordinary simple licences signed for this trade 210 had not been used at all, 186 had been given out and 1 remained to give, of these all but 12 had expired. Under this type of licence 28,496,021 francs of wines, brandies, silks, bees, clover seed, paintings, etc., had been exported and 22,014,092 of colonial goods brought in. By special licences 1,684,805 francs of goods had been exported, with imports

[14] See chapter XIII, pp. 358 ff. below.

[15] As to the rate of granting licences other reports show 136 for August 1810, 292 by 5 November, 479 by 24 June 1811. Cf. AF^{IV}1342 and 1061.

[16] By the report of 24 June 1811 exports were called 30,611,996 francs (really 20,681,741) and imports were called 11,276,857 francs, AF^{IV}1061, dossier 2.

[17] In the report of 24 June 25% additional is said to be nearer the truth for the export valuations. Unfortunately the English report on real values of exports and imports combines France and the North, so that checking up the French statistics is impossible. See House of Commons, *Journals*, 67:766 ap. 11.

of 76,655 francs in goods, the rest in money. Of such licences 81 had been signed, 26 taken out and 2 returned, the other 53 would probably be employed. Of 171 Hanseatic licences 40 had been taken out and exportations of 6,196,430 francs had been made but no imports.

The main reasons for the expiration of so many licences unused had been in many cases the insufficiency of time to make the necessary arrangements, but more often the silk and wine export requirements or the obligation with most of the special "diverse" licences to bring back only money. The best remedy for the situation seemed to be a policy of special licences for the special exportable commodities of various localities, such as the cheese of Holland, the oysters of Granville, the laces of Caen, elsewhere the raw silks of Italy or the stuffs of Lyons, the clocks of Geneva, and so for all the exportable products of the Empire. Such licences in special cases had already shown their effectiveness because of the direct interest of the producers in the exportations, which were rarely undertaken without previous arrangements for the success of the enterprise. To a certain extent the idea already had the imperial sanction. But the present temper of the British showed that a vessel attempting to return in ballast would be sequestred or even confiscated. This would directly defeat the Emperor's purpose for "the extraction of specie, the exportation of our products and the increase of the number of vessels now in our ports." It was advisable to adopt a "mixed system" by which a certain proportion of the returns for an export cargo could be in products from England.

The products needed in France which could well be received from England Montalivet said, in reply to the question raised a week before by Napoleon, were pig lead (except from Granville to Nantes), skins in the hair, raw copper, tin, timber for the marine, dyewoods, iron, tar, hemp, building timber, potash, linseed, medicines, fish oil, mother of pearl, ivory, etc., the needs for which were not yet urgent but the supply of which should be maintained. Indigo, spices and some drugs should, he thought, be excluded.

For American ships 101 permits had been signed only two of which had been returned although the absence of any time limit rendered results uncertain. The income from such licences had been 59,400 francs, exports were for 3,608,181 francs and imports 2,955,704. Four special American licences for French ships had been signed but only one had been taken and no results were reported. However the continuance of such permits was favored. Ten permits to import "Carolina rice," flour, and grain had been granted for Nantes and ten for Bordeaux. All had been delivered but it was feared that to obtain results it would be necessary to apply to them the principle of mixed licences, allowing part of the cargo to be in the colonial goods authorized by the regular permits. In fact he demonstrated that for an American vessel of 150 tons to bring only a cargo of rice would entail a probable loss of 16,000 francs on the voyage.

In similar manner he discussed the effectiveness of the two types of northern licences—for Norway and the Baltic; the eight types of Mediterranean licences—French simple, French diverse, grain licences for southern France, Corsica-Sardinia grain, Corsica-Sardinia *comestibles*, Ottoman permits, Ottoman grain permits, and tunny-fishing licences; and lastly the colonial or "tramp ship" licences.

In summing up his report Montalivet recommended for the future, (1) the system of "mixed" and special licences for England, so that returns could be both in goods and in cash but retaining the principle of silk export requirements with suspension thereof in certain cases; (2) licences for Dutch vessels at London to bring home cargoes of grain, etc., from the Elbe and Weser. For the North he suggested the retention (1) of Norway licences, with similar licences for ships already in Norway and Denmark to come to France, and (2) the granting of Baltic licences for Lübeck, to trade with Denmark, Sweden and Russia. For the Mediterranean, he advocated, in general, mixed licences, and the granting of certificates of origin at Tunis simply as to the character of the goods. He also repeated his proposal of 16 September for Corfu licences. Finally he proposed the mixed licence scheme for America, with greater freedom of importation and requiring exportation for but a part of the value of the cargo imported.

Although the recommendations of Montalivet's report were based distinctly upon the preservation of the navigation principles of the licence trade they at least indicate the tendency to a simpler and more practicable system. Moreover taken in connection with the discussion at the Conseil of 18 November it seems significant of a readiness to liberalize trade conditions. By a striking coincidence at this most auspicious moment there came from the British government a surprising offer of a *rapprochement* of systems.

On 15 November 1811, London papers made the following momentous announcement: "The British Government has agreed to permit merchants to trade with France on a system of reciprocity; and a circular letter was sent round to the merchants yesterday making the proposal, of which the following is a copy:—

'Mr. —— is requested by the Board of Trade to inform those interested in the trade with France, that licences will be granted permitting the importation of wine from France in return for certain articles to be exported from this kingdom, the conditions of such exports may be learned at the council office.'

The conditions alluded to are: For every ton of wine imported the merchant must be obliged to export either 1 hogshead of sugar of 12 cwt., 10 cwt. of coffee, 1 ton of copper, or £100 value of British cloths, woolens, or linens. The wine on importation to pay the duties for home consumption. Other licences are said to be in contemplation for the importation of corn."[18]

This inconspicuous news item without preliminary forecast or subsequent comment would probably pass as an unnoticed incident in that commercial anomaly, the licence trade, did we not recall in marked contrast the part of the British Ministry in the last abortive effort for reaching a trade agreement with France.

[18] *London Times*, 15 November 1811.

In November 1810 the Board of Trade had suddenly cancelled the favorable arrangement which it had dictated in response to mercantile solicitation. Barely a year had passed and behold the Board was itself soliciting Napoleon to accept an arrangement more favorable, if possible, to his own needs than the conditions to which he had readily acceded in August 1810. For the Ministry, which had haughtily launched the Orders in Council of October 1807 and which was still obstinately quibbling with the United States over any concession whatever on account of the partial revocation of the Berlin and Milan decrees, to make such a proposal looked suspiciously like the donning of sackcloth and ashes.

It is safe to say that nothing but the approach of economic disaster could have brought the Perceval Ministry to humble themselves thus before Napoleon. In truth such a crisis as that of 1811 the British people have rarely known. Consols fell to 63, that is, at Paris exchange rates, less than 47.[19] "The almost simultaneous explosion of forty-four new failures in England"—"defiance and alarm increasing daily among the commercial classes of England"—such were typical news items of that winter in Mollien's daily reports to Napoleon.[20] Despite parliamentary aid for months previous, industries were closing down more regularly and completely than before. Already among the suffering artisans were heard mutterings of the Luddite madness which for months thereafter was to frighten British manufacturers. Again, as for several years previous, poor harvests threatened dearth in the land. And with all this warehouses were crammed with the sterile wealth in which Napoleon hoped to smother his rival. Verily even the Board of Trade realized that they must parley for terms or be drowned in their "butt of Malmsey."[21]

While we are left largely to surmises as to the preliminary discussions and mercantile negotiations which led to the circular letter of 14 November, yet it is clear that it was not a precipitate

---

[19] *London Times*, 28 November; and AF^{IV}1039^{B}, 14 December.
[20] AF^{IV}1089^{B}, 2 and 30 December.
[21] *Writings of J. Q. Adams*, III, 400.

surrender on the part of the Board of Trade. In fact during several months previous it had been yielding at discretion, and these earlier capitulations to beleaguring circumstances themselves emphasize the abasement of which the November action is conspicuous evidence.

As early as 24 June, yielding to pressure from the West Indies interests, to which the Perceval Ministry was ever particularly responsive, the Board of Trade agreed to grant licences to export the sugar and coffee of Martinique and Guadeloupe to France even under the French flag.[22] When this brought no response from France Greffulke Brothers, financial agents for the British government, on 22 July wrote to Hottinguer, the chief Parisian merchant and a member of the Council of Commerce, calling attention to this concession and inquiring "by request" whether a still further relaxation could be arranged with the French government.[23] He intimated that matters were getting critical for colonial merchants. Apparently no response was given by Napoleon although to encourage the holders of colonial goods London newspapers published rumors that *two* French licences for importing Guadeloupe and Martinique produce had been granted.[24]

Meantime other efforts were being made to relieve the desperate economic situation. In April 1811, while obstinately refusing to allow the importation of French silks required by Napoleon's licences, the Board of Trade consented to grant licences for the importation from the Baltic of raw, organized and thrown silk.[25] Within a few months this entering wedge had brought similar British licences for the Dutch ports and then for French ports on the English Channel. The French records fail to indicate that this was the result of any negotiations sponsored by Mon-

[22] P. R. O., B. T. 5/20, 442.

[23] F^{7}3643^{12}, annex 69. It was intercepted by the French police.

[24] *London Times*, 3 October 1811, publishes French denials, of 22 September, of these rumors. There is no record of the granting, or discussion about granting, such licences by France at this time.

[25] P. R. O., B. T. 6/199, 15 April, no. 31848.

talivet or other French officials, or that Napoleon was aware of the British action until fall. However, the minutes of the Conseil du Commerce do show that dating from July or August strong pressure was being exerted by Italian and French silk raisers to be allowed precisely corresponding export licences.[26] The idea seems to have impressed Napoleon at once and he had the matter carefully gone into. Already before his departure for the North he had practically determined to licence such exports from Havre or Dunkirk, and the definite information which he received during his trip regarding the English silk licences for the Channel ports led him to take further measures for the adoption of such a plan immediately upon his return to Paris.

In the discussions of 18 November, Havre was definitely selected as the port.[27] It was also thought possible to combine with the scheme a plan for exporting laces from Caen. Apparently the two schemes were separated, however, as special lace licences were granted for Caen, and Rouen was associated with Havre in the silk export business. Six were granted on 5 December to export 25,000 kg. of silk. Only naval stores or cash could be brought back.[28] It was decided to levy an export duty of 15 francs per kilo or 30% on worked silks, and 50 francs per kilo on organdies and Italian silks.[29] In order to allow the Italian silk producers favorable conditions for sharing in the trade modifications were made in the Italian tariff laws. Yet the conditions still worked to the prejudice of the Italians, chiefly because of the greed of Havre merchants and the inconvenience of meeting customs regulations at both the Italian frontier and Havre. However, on 20 January the protest of Count Aldini, Italian represen-

[26] AF^{IV}1243.

[27] AF^{IV}1243.

[28] *Moniteur*, 3 February 1812.

[29] An interesting aspect of the working out of this plan is the part taken by French prisoners of war who wished to share in the profits. The English government, however, became frightened, thinking a plan to aid in the escape of prisoners was involved. Cf. Ad. 1/4357, nos. 9, 11, 12, December 1811.

tative in the Conseil du Commerce, was at once met by the granting of special silk licences to Italian merchants who were permitted to discharge all customs obligations at Havre alone.[30]

Meanwhile, conditions were forcing the British to still further relaxations. An instance of this pressure exerted from all quarters upon the Board of Trade is a petition of the Glasgow Chamber of Commerce "that measures be taken to give effect to the system of reciprocal intercourse with hostile nations."[31] With the idea of concessions in mind, therefore, the Board investigated the question of recent exports to France and Holland.[32] A few weeks later (15 October) it was inquiring as to the foreign brandies, especially French, warehoused in Great Britain, or exported therefrom—surely a surprising question considering how straitly such brandies had been excluded, and that so late as July 1811 the Board had curtly refused to reconsider its exclusion of *all* French wines.[33] After this inquiry it needed but a few weeks for the Board to retract its July declaration by its reciprocity letter of 14 November

The proposition of the Board of Trade to receive wines against sugars reached the French government through Van Aken of Ghent, and various Paris merchants, about 23 November. "This disposition of the British government caused a great sensation among the commercial class both at London and in France."[34] Napoleon was scarcely less astonished. Coming as it did on the very eve of the important 25 November session of the Conseil du Commerce at which Montalivet was to present his important memoir on the status of the imperial licence system, naturally the

[30] AF^{IV}1243, annex 181; AF^{IV}*171, p. 184.

[31] B. T. 5/20, 485, 14 August 1811.

[32] B. T. 5/20, 514, 20 September.

[33] B. T. 6/200, no. 33335.

[34] AF^{IV}1061, dossier 2, pièces 123-124. An interesting indirect attack on the action of the Board is the letter in the *London Times* of 26 November: "To the Drinkers of Champagne and Claret."

English news became the paramount topic of the session. Napoleon at once sketched the lines upon which he was ready to consider the proposed exchange.[35] Against an importation of 120,000 cwt. of sugar he would have exported 10,000 tuns of wine, with silks to one-third the value of the wine, and other permissible goods at the option of the merchants, the whole transaction to be divided into tenths, each comprising five or six licences. Regarding the feasibility of this plan, and the chance of fraud on the part of wine exporters, the Minister of the Interior was instructed to report at the next session of the Conseil.

Other reports were required from Montalivet at the ensuing session upon two new licence schemes, outlined by Napoleon, both of which had been already under discussion.[36] The one was for the importation of cottons motril from Malaga and Valencia to an entrepôt at Bayonne, on condition of exporting an equivalent amount of silks. The other was for the importation, by licences to be given to Amsterdam, Rotterdam, Ostend and Havre, of needed English goods such as wools, leathers, potashes, medicines, quinine and raw copper. In this scheme one-third to one-half of the exports were to be of wines, brandies and manufactured goods not desired by England, the remainder in articles needed there, such as cheese, clover seed, etc. For both these schemes Napoleon desired preliminary estimates of the total imports to be allowed, and their division into tenths, and even calculations for each shipload for which a licence would have to be given.

In his report of 2 December on the "wine-sugar exchange" project Montalivet showed that the wine exportation was feasible and would be so profitable for the merchants as to offer no temptation to fraud.[37] Also there would be a great advantage to the fisc of both England and France. But he pointed out strong objections to the Emperor's scheme. The annual consumption of sugar was but half the proposed 120,000 cwt., therefore he called

[35] *Cor. e Nap.*, 23:37, no. 18290.
[36] *Ibid.*
[37] AF^{IV}1343, no. 6.

attention to other exports which England offered to exchange for wine. Second, physical problems of shipping showed that the proposed number of licences would not suffice. As to the silk requirement it would almost certainly defeat the plan. The loss of the silk would ruin those merchants who did not resort to fraud in France and smuggling in England, while the Bordeaux merchants capable of so great a transaction would not sully their reputations thereby. Hence he had prepared two licence projects, one with, the other without the silk condition. Above all, however, he opposed the whole transaction with the enemy because it would be fatal to the flourishing trade in wines, silks and manufactured goods, which was just being established at Bordeaux with the United States, and would also make it impossible to get the much needed grain and rice from America. Moreover, the effect would also be harmful to good relations between the two countries at this delicate moment.

Dissatisfied with this report and resolved to insist upon the scheme he had outlined, including the silk export condition, Napoleon required further investigation and a new report for the succeeding session.[38] Montalivet was also instructed to write to the merchants of Bordeaux regarding the project. He was likewise to make inquiries in Holland regarding an interchange there of silks against sugar and coffee. In other words having forced England so far as he had, Napoleon wished to compel the acceptance of this other essential condition (silk), and was determined to leave no avenue untried to attain this end.

The scheme of allowing a restricted importation from England of various needed colonial goods, upon which Montalivet also reported, was primarily designed for the same object.[39] In making his report on this project Montalivet estimated that France would need 13,850,000 kilos of the colonial products yielding for the customs 5,084,000 francs including the *decime*. Discussion of the question led to the understanding that the importation

[38] AF^{IV}1243, annex 128.
[39] AF^{IV}1343.

was to be about 14,000,000 francs, to be balanced by exports. A total of one hundred licences would be given, one-third of them at once. As to the articles of trade it was determined to eliminate copper, quinine and potash from the permitted imports, and to make the addition of garance, brandy, and books to the export list of laces, horlogerie, butter, cheese, and clover seed. These changes necessitated a new report upon the matter from Montalivet.

In his revised report of 9 December on the importation of needed products from Great Britain, Montalivet by the elimination of copper, quinine and potash reduced the proposed transaction to 10,300,000 kilograms (10,300 metric tons) valued at 10,393,190 francs in England and producing 3,796,089 francs for the imperial customs.[40] He also reduced his first estimate of licences required from 100 to 66 for 150-ton vessels, and he proposed the immediate signature of 22 of these licences, each being for the value of 196,060 francs. Regarding the regulations for exports he adhered to the list as already decided upon but urged that the proportion of silks required should be only one-sixth or at most one-quarter of the value of the total exportation, and that the wine and brandies be one-sixth the tonnage. He explained his attitude on the silk requirement more fully, however, in a second report of the same day.

In accordance with the new suggestions of his report of 25 November, Montalivet had presented a number of special reports upon a quantity of new licences for which he asked the imperial signature. It would seem that most of these schemes had already been endorsed by Napoleon but he deferred signing the licences until a report could be made upon a plan which he outlined for reducing the licence system to a simpler classification.[41] It was upon this that Montalivet made his second report of 9 December.

[40] AF^{IV}1061, dossier 2, pièce 141.
[41] Cf. AF^{IV}1342, bordereau of 11 December 1811.

The bases proposed by Napoleon for the simplification of the licence system were three.[42] The first class which was to comprise all licences for the importation of cereals, would be granted without any export requirement. The second group—licences to export butter, cheese, oysters, clover-seeds, and swan skins—would be given under condition of importing the counter value in specie. The third group, or licences for the exportation of silk and wines, would be accorded with the faculty of importing an equal value of indigo, dyewoods, hides from Buenos Ayres, medicines, and other like goods. With these ideas Montalivet disagreed. For while admitting the desirability of thus simplifying the details of licence administration and reducing the number of special decisions on commercial matters he did not believe the plan proposed would stand the test of every-day experience. The terms of licences of the first class were not sufficiently liberal to bring results. Licences of the second class must prove abortive also, since it would be highly dangerous, if not impossible, for ships to attempt to leave London with returns only in cash. Hence he again urged the idea of "mixed" licences. As to the third proposition he recommended the elimination of indigo from the imports and above all the reduction of the silk export requirement to one-sixth the value of the cargo, except in American and Levant permits. He emphatically declared that the persistence in the effort to force such quantities of manufactured silks on England would be practically equivalent to the absolute prohibition of communication with the enemy and would defeat the very ends which the Emperor sought to attain.

Apparently Montalivet won his point so far as to secure the granting of the special licences and the mixed licences which he had advocated in his report of 25 November. At least the signature of a quantity of such licences took place on 11 December.[43] These were all licences which would naturally fall within the first two groups of the proposed new classification. Of licences of the

[42] AF^{IV}1061, dossier 2, pièce 140.
[43] AF^{IV}1342, bordereau of 11 December.

third group, those for the importation of English goods needed in France were granted after the final adoption of the plan on 30 December.[44]

In his second report on the wine-sugar deal proposed by England Montalivet stated that it was now agreed, in consequence of fresh information, that by hogshead the English government meant a barrique and not a tun of wine.[45] Consequently it would be advisable to restrict the exportation to fine wines for shipment to British India. Upon this basis he made his new calculations of 2,500 tuns of wine for the 120,000 cwt. of sugar which he believed was all that it would be advisable to import. To carry out such a transaction, he said, would require several trips, involving several French ports. In order to insure the accuracy of his calculations, Montalivet had written to Bordeaux for opinions of merchants. Their replies were analyzed and reported to the Conseil on 23 December.[46] These replies somewhat modified Montalivet's estimates, but supported the feasibility of his proposals. Especially they showed the proportion of silks they were willing to try to export, and showed that to insure the success of the plan simultaneous exports should be made from London and Bordeaux.

Napoleon, however, was averse to consenting to the change in the British terms, which would be equivalent to forcing his acceptance of 48 instead of 12 cwt. of sugar per tun of wine.[47] By a decision of 17 December, he had gone so far as to except sugar, coffee and indigo from earlier import licences, and here the matter hung fire until the Board of Trade were ready to compromise on a middle term of two barriques per hogshead. Meantime it seems that the project was combined with a similar scheme for Holland.

[44] AF^{IV}1243.
[45] AF^{IV}1061, dossier 2, pièces 137 and 138.
[46] AF^{IV}1061, dossier 2, pièces 148 and 149, also pièces 144-6.
[47] Note also Napoleon's letter to Bassano (18 December) on the language to be used by French diplomats about the proposed exchange. Brotonne, *Lettres inédites*, p. 390, no. 978.

At the Conseil du Commerce of 2 December it had been decided to propose to the merchants of Holland an exportation of silks in exchange for sugars and coffees.[48] Clearly it was a device for testing how much further than the proposition of 14 November the British government could be forced. The agent selected by Montalivet was the Maître des Requêtes at Amsterdam, Baron Robert Woute. He was requested without showing his superior authority to find out whether Dutch merchants could be interested in the scheme, and whether it could be operated by the system of communications that they maintained with the English coast or ships, or whether they had influence enough with the British government to secure protection. Also he wished to know how much and what kinds of silk could be exported thus and from what ports. The object he said was to get from London the sugar and coffee of French planters of the former French colonies. Braunsberg and Company were suggested as likely to be good leaders in the project.[49]

While waiting for Woute's reply Montalivet on 9 December notified Napoleon that he had written as per instructions. He thought the silks would probably be florentines or levantines and black Lyons shawls for Spanish American trade. He did not believe the silks could be got into Great Britain unless by smugglers, but they might be left on little islets to be sent later to America. Granville and St. Malo were well placed for smuggling into the Channel Islands but not much trust could be placed in irresponsible fishing craft. Another hopeful solution, however, if the Dutch negotiation failed, seemed to be in the intimation, received on 6 December from Bonvarlet Bros. of Dunkirk, and Van Aken and Son of Ghent, that they had assurance of being able to get silk into England and to exchange silk, wines, etc., or silk alone for sugar and coffee.[50]

[48] AF^{IV}1243.
[49] F^{12}2031.
[50] F^{12}2031. Cf. Montalivet's report of 6 May 1811 on methods of smuggling silk into England.

On 20 December Woute (or Voute) replied to Montalivet's letter of the 9th. The letter is a most interesting revelation of Anglo-Dutch trade relations.[51] When contraband flourished in Holland no one, he said, had been better informed regarding it than himself who for twenty years had been fighting the English efforts to monopolize the China trade. On the basis of his former experience he had visited houses in Amsterdam, Rotterdam, Middleburg and Flushing who would be glad to engage in the proposed trade, but their connections with England were completely cut off. It was known that silk was in great vogue in England but the coast patrols against invasion made the contraband trade which had formerly flourished on every headland no longer possible. He named the former banking agents of the smugglers, including such noted houses as Hope and Company, Mailmen and Sons, Pye, Rich and Co., Melvil and Co., Isaac de Marchant of Rotterdam and others. Braunsberg & Co. had never had such dealings, their business being the handling of English paper, the importation of specie and the settling of bankrupt stocks. In short they were the bankers who fixed exchange on Paris. But they also had extensive colonial interests and might be induced to help their correspondents find an outlet for their sugar and coffee.

Woute suggested that the solution of the question would probably be found by increasing the number of supervised smuggling places to dispose of most of the silk and by granting licences to export at first innocent articles, and bring back sugar and coffee and in this way to gradually work into a trade in silks also. He figured on attaining, in the end, an exportation of 24,000,000 francs in silk. He also called attention to the movement of French silks to Prussia and North Germany, which indicated the beginning of contraband into Russia, and he thought the same channel could be used to get silks to England.

[51] $F^{12}2031$.

Montalivet answered on 9 January 1812 thanking Woute for his information.[52] However he remarked that "it is not a question of establishing in Holland a smuggling trade such as exists at other points, but of undertaking an operation which will be at least tacitly authorized by the British government. The special interest of certain merchants of that nation is susceptible of bringing about a result by means of which they will consent in England to admit some silks recognized as the sole means of finding an outlet for the sugars and coffees with which the warehouses are overloaded. It it the only condition on which these products would enter the Empire and with restrictions as to quantities." Upon this basis he therefore asked that fresh investigations should be made.

Evidently before writing this, Montalivet had had reasons to anticipate that the Board of Trade could be brought around.[53] This suspicion, indeed, is greatly strengthened by the fact that the previous day, (8 January), Montalivet had submitted for signature eight of the much debated licences for the exchange, on the compromise basis, of sugar against wine *and silks*.[54] Moreover on 13 January he presented a new report on the exportation of silks and wine against raw sugars, coffee, indigo and Pernambuco cotton by the ports of Holland, by Ostend, Le Havre and Bordeaux.[55]

The report of 13 January was prefaced with a reference to the Emperor's failure to agree with Montalivet's contention that such trade with the enemy would be prejudicial to American relations.[56] The problem of sugar having already been settled by the granting of a few licences and by the adoption of new plans for fostering the beet sugar industry, only questions connected with an importation of coffee, indigo and cotton were discussed. As to coffee

[52] F^{12}2031.
[53] Cf. AF^{IV}1243, annex 172.
[54] See F^{12}2031.
[55] AF^{IV}1243, annex 175.
[56] AF^{IV}1062, dossier 3, pièce 36.

the supply on hand was ample and importation should not be encouraged unless it were necessary to aid in disposing of French wines. Of indigo, 228,386 kilos had been on hand in November, and two rich cargoes had arrived since then, so that a year's supply was already available. The cotton supply on the other hand was only sufficient for ten months and, besides, Pernambuco cotton was highly desired by French manufacturers because of its fine quality.

Despite these preliminary recommendations, however, Montalivet did present estimates which could form the basis of a reciprocal trade with England. On the total transaction of 1,000,000 kilos of colonial goods against 2,500 tuns of wine he calculated the imports would amount to 3,461,000 francs, the exports to 6,875,000 francs, the French profits 3,414,000 francs and the imperial customs receipts 6,730,000. It would be best to grant 20 licences for this, that is, 8 for Bordeaux, 3 for Havre, 4 for Ostend, 2 for Rotterdam, and 3 for Amsterdam.

Napoleon's remarks at the Conseil of 13 January to which Montalivet brought this report were a notable revelation of the sweep of his imagination, and of his organizing genius.[57] Dramatically he summed up the results of the investigations and discussions of the preceding weeks, and revealed, if not the goal to which he had been working, at least the conclusions to which he had been brought.

"There is only a grand system to undertake," he began, "either to remain where we are, which might be sustained by good reasons, or to march *en grand* toward a different order.

"Remain as we are? We know how we are. It is necessary then to commence by establishing what his Majesty means by a grand system in order that the two states may be compared."

Then by a rapid comparison of the market prices of sugar in the states of Europe he demonstrated that in the Empire, Italy, Naples and the Confederation of the Rhine the same continental system was in force. Hence upon the government of France

[57] AF^{IV}*171, pp. 171-178; also *Cor. de Nap.*, 23:167-72.

depended·the provisioning of colonial goods for all these countries with their sixty-five millions, triple the population of ancient France. To meet this great opportunity he proposed to grant, at once, licences for the importation of 450,000 cwt. of raw sugar to be paid for chiefly with the export of wines and silks, and other products and wares of France and her tributaries. The same system would be applied to coffee, tea, cocoa, and spices, to hides, indigo, cotton and dyewoods.

This he declared would "produce a great activity in manufactures, an encouragement for navigation, the marine, the brokers, a duty of 200 millions collected by the customs during a year, a germ of activity and life in all our ports. For France the result will be a dream which will have been obtained only by the passage of the exclusion system—for how conceive that England would have been led, save for the absolute closure of the continent to an order of things so contrary to her commercial interest?" For what could England place over against all this advantage to France, against the injury to her own manufactures, the loss of brokerage and freight, against even the loss of the profit of liquidating at London the American trade to the Continent? What, in short, would have been gained but a little outlet for some colonial produce, part of which, moreover, was the property of Dutch and French planters.

The system would work a commercial revolution for England, and no less for France. It would no longer be an arrangement of pitting "sugar against silk, tariff against tariff," a consumption of thirty millions against that of ten, as in the treaty of Versailles, where the advantage to France was in the ratio of one against seven. Instead, if the proposed scheme were established it would be "by a calculation where the value is multiplied by the quantity and not appreciated by a single one of its elements,"—an advantage to France of three to one.

"If after the knowledge of this system England adheres to it, she will experience much greater hurt from the vexation and disappointment of seeing the activity of our manufacturers, and the much greater product of our customs than by the effect of the Continental System."

"His Majesty does not consider this as a change of system but as its sequence. The system has been war, the result is victory. In fact have we said that we will receive no more sugar, coffee, indigo? No, for we have contented ourselves with establishing a duty thereupon. . . . It is then the perfected system which has produced the results which one would expect only after several years. It is felt that the system which is about to be established in a permanent system which would be perpetual. . . . It is "not like the disadvantageous treaty of Versailles."[58]

From this brilliant limning of a dream comparable in its boldness—and futility—with even the more familiar products of the imperial imagination, Napoleon passed to the means of execution. Thereafter he would give but two varieties of licences. The licences of the first sort would be for importing grains, rice, etc., which would be given according to the circumstances of the year; they would be submitted to no sort of condition. The licences of the second species would embrace the permission to import a stated quantity of sugar, coffee, etc., at Nantes and Bordeaux against wines and brandies; in the North against silk for one third, cambrics, linens, and other merchandise of the sort." Each of these licences would be for a voyage.

"The system once established on these bases would be susceptible of modifications and of developments." It could comprehend not only the Empire, Italy, and the Confederation of the Rhine but also Prussia, Mecklenburg, Poland, Naples and, indeed, Austria. Austria would be included by a transit duty on goods through Trieste, the other states by special licence series from which they would receive half the proceeds. As for the states of the Rhine, Poland and other inland states they would be bound to the system by a rebate of one-third the customs duties on all colonial goods imported for them.

[58] Regarding the significant allusion to the "Eden" or Versailles treaty of 1786 see my Introduction pp. 2-4 and notes.

For these ends he conceived of eleven regular, and some three or four special series of licences to be formed as follows: (1st) Hamburg, Bremen and Lübeck; (2d) Amsterdam; (3d) Ostend and Dunkirk; (4th) Havre and Caen; (5th) Granville, St. Malo, Morlaix, Redon and Quimper; (6th) Nantes, La Rochelle, Bordeaux and Bayonne; (7th) Marseilles, Cette and Nice; (8th) Savona and Genoa; (9th) Leghorn and Civita Vecchia; (10th) Trieste; (11th) kingdom of Italy: Ancona and Venice; (12th) kingdom of Naples: Naples;* (13th) Mecklenburg, Rostock and Wismar. Also a series for Prussia and one for Poland through Danzig. The series for Naples, Prussia and Mecklenburg would be created last and upon request of those states. As to the exports and imports, that matter was left to a report which the Minister of the Interior would present the following week.

"It would be idle," declared Napoleon, "to examine whether this system will go into effect; it is necessary to try it. As we have been consistent (consequents), as we make use only of licences, when the licence has expired all returns to the ordinary law (droit commun); thus if this does not succeed the measure will be established only in the minutes of the council. Nothing will prove better the real interiority of England, and how the decrees of Berlin and of Milan, supported by the victories on the continent have led to a great result."

The minutes of the Conseil du Commerce record no event more striking than this speech of 13 January 1812. Indeed it is doubtful whether Napoleon ever expressed himself to his ministers more at length or more impressively. It was as if he had been carried away by the unexpected pliancy of the British and by the influence of long deferred hopes. It was a paean of victory— and yet, the swan's song of success. For not all the glittering colors of the deftly blown bubble could conceal the tenuousness of the Emperor's scheme, which, indeed, he himself by his actions of that very moment was preparing to prick. But this his ministers, caught by the daring possibilities of the Emperor's dream and carried along by the fervor with which he sought its attainment, probably did not realize.

"Your Majesty has developed in the last council a plan as vast as it is boldly conceived and skillfully traced in all its parts, and the great advantages of which are incontestable under whatever aspect one may wish to consider them. Its execution will open a new outlet for the productions of our soil and industry, will impart new life and movement to the great commercial ports, will feed a million workers, will employ a great number of ships and by a continual navigation will train sailors."[59] Such were the opening words of a ministerial report of 20 January upon the execution of the "grand scheme" which testify to the great impression made by Napoleon's speech. The writer was Collin de Sussy, newly appointed Minister of Manufactures and Commerce, an office just created for the purpose of realizing the vast plans by which Napoleon hoped to galvanize into new life the economic interests of western Europe.

Continuing his report de Sussy argued that there could be no valid objection to this direct trade with England since the goods imported would come from there anyway.[60] This method would provide a market for French wares "while the products of the manufactures of England encumber the warehouses of the manufacturer, while her workshops are deserted, and her industry struck to the heart is menaced with total annihilation." "Certainly such results are in an inverse sense from those which the treaty of Versailles produced when England drew from France only the products and merchandise which she needed, while under the false pretexts of an equality which could not exist in the relation of the population and of the price of merchandise, all English fabrics and chiefly those of cotton inundated France and struck a blow at our ancient manufactures." "The system of commercial war against England" would, however, by the new measures adopted "complete the ruin of England within two years."

[59] AF^{IV}1062, dossier 3, pièce 37.
[60] Note the contrast with Montalivet's report of 13 January.

The report was chiefly a mathematical demonstration of the advantages of the new scheme and added nothing to the proposed means of execution which Napoleon had already outlined. In commenting on this report, however, the Emperor himself enlarged upon this practical aspect of the question. Among other things he wished that not only should the colonial goods licences be limited to a single voyage but that the voyage should be undertaken within two months from the signature of the licence, and completed within six months. He also wished an investigation of the possibility of stipulating that the vessel should be French, with a French captain and crew. Apparently the form of licence to be used was that already adopted for the wine-sugar exchange but with the privilege for the captain to import instead of sugar, at his option, coffee, hides, indigo and medicines in proportions fixed by the licences.

A further report upon these questions was required from the Minister of Commerce, but seemingly it never was presented.[61] Sussy was absent from the immediately succeeding meetings of the Conseil du Commerce, and from 16 February to 30 December 1812, that body seems never to have met. Perhaps in the pressure of even greater issues the report was overlooked, for immediately afterward at his councils of ministers Napoleon became engrossed with questions of feeding the poor, handling the critical food supply problems, and preparing for the inevitable break with Russia and Sweden, the imminence of which had just been hastened by the occupation of Swedish Pomerania.[62] And well might these problems absorb the imperial attention for they presaged the certain failure of the Continental System in whatever garb it might be clothed.

Because of the sudden suspension of the Conseil du Commerce, and the attendant meagreness of important commercial papers

[61] AF^{IV}1243. Montalivet was also asked to prepare a general report on exports and imports which he did.

[62] Cf. *Cor. de Nap.*, 23:209, 297, 302, etc.

it is difficult to trace the *denouêment* of that consummate expression of the imperial navigation policy—the "grand system"—the unfolding of which has just been detailed. Stray bits of information, however, are suggestive of what might have been had Napoleon not crossed the Niemen.

CHAPTER XII
THE BARRIERS CRASH

A—*An Equivocal Reversal of Systems*

The impression created in England by news of Napoleon's experimental wine exchange licenes is most interestingly reflected in certain of those daily reports by which Mollien, Minister of the Treasury, kept Napoleon informed of the financial pulse beats of the Empire.[1] Thus, on 25 February, he announced significantly: "The merchants of Paris have received letters from London which seem to indicate on the part of the English government less aversion to the introduction of certain French productions such as wines and brandies; it is even inferred from these letters that the Cabinet of London expresses more moderate sentiments; that England is wearied by an unequal struggle, and that they (sic) commence no longer to dissimulate this fatigue."[2]

More striking still, however, is Mollien's report of 29 February. "Some wholesale dealers," he wrote, "pretend to have information by letters from London, *of a very recent date*, which announce that the English government will permit the establishment of a *great entrepôt* in England *for the wines of France*. Such an event would be in the rank of marvels of the age. Is it possible that England subscribes today to a condition which she admitted at the time of the pretended treaty of commerce of 1786 only to render it immediately illusory with regard to France? It is true that it is far from that epoch to this in which England finds herself exiled from the Continent from the Gulf of Biscay to the Baltic." Even the ever skeptical and critical men of commerce were rejoicing, having arrived, though "a little late," at the opinion

[1] The Mollien reports used so freely for this chapter are found in carton $AF^{IV}1089^{B}$. As the folios are not numbered where the source is quite obvious I omit its constant citation.

[2] Cf. *Writings of J. Q. Adams*, IV, 258, 261.

"that England commences at last to yield to the superior influence of your Majesty."[3]

Well could Bassano in his official report of 10 March 1812 to the Emperor, presented a few days later to the Conservative Senate, exclaim: "England flattered herself with invading the commerce of the world, and her commerce become a mere stock jobbing affair, is carried on only by means of 20,000 licences delivered each year. Forced to obey the law of necessity she thus renounces her act of navigation the first foundation of her power. She aspired to the universal dominion of the seas, and navigation is interdicted to her vessels repulsed from all the ports of the continent; she wished to enrich her funds with the tributes that Europe was to pay, and Europe has withdrawn herself not only from her injurious pretensions, but likewise from the tributes which it paid to her industry; her manufacturing cities have become deserted; distress has succeeded to a prosperity, until then increasing; the alarming disappearance of specie, the absolute privation of business, daily interrupt the public tranquility." In fact "never did an act of reprisal attain its object in a manner more prompt, more certain, or more victorious" than had the Milan decree. Therefore, he declared, the Continental System would continue to be enforced until England revoked her Orders in Council and returned to the principles of the treaty of Utrecht—and the same sentiments were re-echoed before the Senate in a report made by the Minister of War. Such were the boasts of the Emperor, forgetful that pride goeth ever before a fall.[4]

Certainly the exultation in Paris was rather premature. For Mollien and the men of the Bourse soon began to doubt the advan-

---

[3] Mollien had declared 5 October 1811 that "England would realize that the commerce of the continent is under a more skillful and powerful influence than her own." $AF^{IV}1089^B$.

[4] *Moniteur*, 16 March 1812; *Am. State Papers, For. Rel.*, III, 458. Yet Napoleon was using English licences to send wine to Danzig for his Russian campaign (*Cor. de Nap.*, 23:74; Lecestre, *Lettres inédites*, II, 197) and he was giving secret instructions to wink at the importation of colonial goods into Corsica, *Cor. de Nap.*, 23:359.

tages of that "marvel of the age"—the London wine entrepôt.[5] Moreover, the sting of the imperial boasts contributed no little at a critical moment to a less pliant attitude on the part of the British Ministry.[6] And yet, on the other hand, stronger evidence of the defeat of the British commercial policy could scarcely be desired than is afforded by the records of the Board of Trade itself, despite all its efforts to conceal the evidence of its humiliation. Thus because Napoleon insisted upon enforcing his navigation act, the Board on 25 March wrote to the Customs to forbear requiring foreign ships coming from the enemy's ports to swear to the nationality of their build, crews, etc., unless a question of national safety were at stake.[7] They also abandoned their obstinate embargo on the shipment of quinine, raw cotton, etc. to the enemy. They even consented, despite the refusal of reciprocal privileges by Napoleon, to allow enemy aliens to reside in Great Britain in order to aid in carrying on the licence trade with France.[8] Yet more striking token of abjectness, so late as the beginning of August, they considered a proposal to fortify the licence trade by protecting alien enemies engaged in it against decisions of the Court of King's Bench, which denied their right to recover insurance on their losses.[9]

Probably to all save the parties directly concerned these particular evidences of suppliance were unknown. Nevertheless enough was known, or suspected, of the state of affairs to draw forth scathing denunciations of the Orders in Council and the licence system. Particularly bitter was the parliamentary opposition led by men like Brougham and Lansdowne. When in the face of these attacks Lord Bathurst and Mr. Rose, his assistant on the Board of Trade, made the humiliating declaration

[5] AF$_{IV}$1089$_B$, 23 March, 24 March, 7 April, etc.
[6] Cf. the Proclamation of the Prince Regent, 21 April, p. 320 below.
[7] B. T. 5/21, 170.
[8] B. T. 5/21, 517.
[9] B. T. 1/67. Petition of 27 July 1812 by the "merchants trading to the continent."

that the abandonment of the Orders and licences would spell immediate ruin to all British trade, the admission was seized upon by opposition papers who taunted the ministry with being unable to move except in accordance with the imperial gesture. Nor did they fail to ring the changes upon the injustice and fatality of such a policy which was hurrying the country into war with the United States.[10]

Equally stinging were the comments of American newspapers on the development of the Anglo-French licence trade. "If Bonaparte were to grant a *licence* for the purpose," said a noted Baltimore editor, "I cannot doubt but that certain London merchants could obtain leave to supply him with *arms* and *ammunition* so zealous are they for a *trade with the enemy*. The least relaxation of his 'Continental System' is hailed as a matter of great exultation and joy. They gladly send him what *he* pleases to admit, and accept in return almost anything he pleases to give them."[11] Most galling, however, was the special activity shown at this time in seizing Americans who tried to be their competitors in the trade with France. *The blockade of Europe is violated in the Chesapeake Bay* the American journals declared. Naturally such a situation merely stiffened the demands of the American government for redress.

Nor did the French licence trade, or, in fact, the whole imperial policy toward the United States escape severe popular censure, and on the part of the government active protests. As American opposition was to actively influence the working out of the experiment of the "grand system" it is necessary at this point to take account of this influence.

The newly appointed American minister to France, Joel Barlow, had been furnished at his departure with broad instructions.[12]

[10] *London Statesman*, 20 April 1812 (given in the *Moniteur*, 29 April 1812). Cf. also the *Times*, 13 February, letter to Rose. As to Parliament see *Parl. Debates, Brougham's Works*, II, 18 ff., etc.

[11] Niles, *Weekly Register*, 25 April 1812, p. 128.

[12] *Am. State Papers, For. Rel.*, III, 509-13.

"The objects contemplated by them were 1st, the admission of our productions into France on beneficial terms; 2d, security for our neutral and national rights on the high seas; and 3d, provision for the Rambouillet and other spoliations, and these objects it was expected might be obtained by Decrees or Acts of the French Government adopted separately and independently by itself."[13]

His long and comparatively recent residence in Paris and his experience as an American diplomat and politician should have specially fitted Barlow for his new task. Unfortunately he seems to have been incautious, to have lacked the suspicious alertness of his immediate predecessors, and to have neglected the channels of confidential information which had aided them.[14] Possibly his Gallican and revolutionary sympathies proved a handicap. Perhaps his former interest in the joint adoption by France and the United States of a certain scheme for a commercial attack upon Great Britain, deterred him at first from an aggressive assault upon the Napoleonic navigation policies.[15] In any case he immediately conceived from Bassano's reassuring phrases that all pending questions could be speedily settled by a commercial treaty. Very probably Barlow misunderstood the duke. But if not, whatever Napoleon may have intended in September was vitally affected by rapid alterations of the commercial prospects of the

[13] *Writings of Madison* (Hunt ed.), VIII, 189, note, Monroe to Barlow, 23 April 1812.

[14] Cf. Adams, *History of the United States*, vol. VI, ch. 12. Also *Dept. of State, Desp. Fr.*, vol. 13 (Barlow's reports); *Cons. letters, Bordeaux*, vol. III (Wm. Lee's reports); *Writings of Madison* (Hunt), vol. VIII; *Writings of Monroe* (Hamilton), vol. V; and Todd, *Life and letters of Joel Barlow*. As the poet of the American Revolution and a warm friend of the French Revolution, in September 1792 he was elected along with Washington and Hamilton a citizen of the French republic. While residing at Paris he was appointed American agent to the Barbary States after the Tripolitan war, and served with credit.

[15] This proposal, which internal evidence would date about 1793, is found among the Barlow MSS. in Harvard Library. It is a highly interesting document, possibly connected with his unsuccessful candidacy for election to the National Convention. For other ideas credited to Barlow see the Redhead-Yorke, *Letters of 1812*, pp. 242-4.

Empire upon his return from the North in November. Moreover, in the situation that developed thereafter, it is manifest that Bassano could scarcely have devised a more effective way of *not* satisfying the United States than that of a dilatory negotiation for a commercial treaty.

Whether a negotiation, such as was expected at Washington, for obtaining redress by separate imperial decrees would have succeeded, is merely conjectural. From the character of Bassano's oral assurances of 27 and 28 December any real arrangement of difficulties looks improbable although certainly not impossible.[16] In particular the United States expected that the mode of settlement by special decree would serve for the suppression of the American permits by France. "The system of licences must be abolished," declared Madison emphatically, "if not by F. by us."[17] Had Barlow pushed this demand in obedience to his instructions he evidently would have obtained some action, for Napoleon was not oblivious of the exasperation expressed in Madison's message to Congress, and he was showing a readiness to make certain modifications in his system.[18] A significant illustration of this attitude is found in the assurances given the Russian government "that a better understanding with the United States was intended and even explicitly avowed. That the entire revocation of the Berlin and Milan decrees, so far as concerned the United States was confirmed, and that with regard to American vessels which should arrive in France, there would be little or no difficulty made as to whence they came, or as to the nature of their cargoes."[19]

---

[16] *Am. State Papers, For. Rel.*, III, 516-17.

[17] Madison to Barlow, 24 February 1812, *Writings of Madison* (Hunt ed.), VIII, 180.

[18] Letter of Montalivet to Bassano, 15 December 1811; and see a report of Sussy, December 1811, AF^{IV}1062, dossier 2, pièces 5 and 6.

[19] *Writings of J. Q. Adams*, IV, 297, to Monroe 29 February 1812, report of a conversation with Count Romanzoff. See, however, the Czernischeff despatch of 21 Feb., Sbornik, 121:158.

The basis of such assurances is found in French administrative records of the critical moment when Barlow was expected to act and did not. Thus on 6 November 1811 the influential Chamber of Commerce of Bordeaux presented a memoir urging, (1) the admission of American ships coming in ballast or with American produce without question of permits or licences; (2) the granting of American permits to French vessels for trade in colonial goods.[20] Montalivet who consistently desired better treatment of the American trade marked the memoir as *raisonable*. Moreover, he analyzed it carefully and with some modifications wrote the proposals into his notable report of 25 November and continued to advocate them persistently at every opportunity during the two following months.[21] He did not, it is true, go to the extent in these various reports of urging the suppression of American permits for importing colonial goods, indeed he presented a number for signature but he urged more liberal terms for them. Moreover he particularly advocated the granting of such permits for French ships, and he preferred to grant chiefly rice and flour permits, given without conditions, to American ships. The adoption of these ideas he secured early in December.[22]

Just at this juncture came word of Madison's message, two paragraphs of which "relative to licences seemed" to announce severe measures against those citizens of that country who should accept these foreign papers and navigate under their protection. Montalivet at once wrote to Bassano asking what changes should be made in the French licence system or in the distribution of permits to appease the United States.[23] Apparently Bassano

[20] $F^{12}2105$. Apparently the economic situation at Bordeaux was causing Napoleon uneasiness at this moment. Cf. the letter of 25 November to Montalivet, Brotonne, *Lettres inédites*, p. 385, no. 965.

[21] $AF^{IV}1243$, especially reports of 25 November, 2 and 9 December and 13 January.

[22] $AF^{IV}1243$. Cf. minutes of sessions of 2 and 9 December and licences of 5 and 11 December.

[23] $F^{12}2108$, Montalivet to Bassano, 15 December 1811. It had been published in London papers of 5 December (cf. *London Times* of that date).

could give no information. At least Montalivet merely continued advocating the changes already suggested, and using every opportunity to point out the injustice and impolicy of injuring American trade relations by adopting the British proposal of exchanging sugar for wines. He did, indeed, succeed in getting permission for American ships to enter freely and unmolested with rice and flour and to depart with such cargoes as they chose.[24] On the other hand it was evidently his continued opposition to the British proposal that contributed to the removal of commercial affairs from his charge to that of Collin de Sussy whose function had long been the urging of confiscations of American ships.[25] There is strong reason to believe that a firmer stand by Barlow supporting Montalivet would have brought better results for the United States, although it probably would not have prevented the adoption of the "grand scheme" of January 1812.

In a large sense the "grand system" of 13 January was but a new version of the omnipresent problem of colonial goods and the neutral carrier, which had dogged Napoleon's policy since the inception of the Continental System. In so far as it was based upon the reciprocity agreement with England the tendency of the "grand system" was to substitute the enemy for the neutral purveyor of colonial products. Logically this should have meant the elimination of trade under *permis americains*, and it might well be conjectured that American feelings against these licences had influenced Napoleon's readiness to accept the British proposition. But contrary to supposition and to logic, and as if to emphasize the fact that his action was due to opportunism rather than

---

Newton's report from the Committee on Commerce and Manufactures of 17 December 1811 also created some impression, (cf. *Moniteur*, 4 February 1812). It is interesting to note that the Board of Trade was worried, cf. B. T. 1/13, no. 9, and B. T. 5/22, p. 100, 12 January 1812.

[24] $F^{12}2108$. On 13 January Montalivet wrote Bassano to notify Serrurier of this decision.

[25] In March Sussy himself was reprimanded for leniency in American permits, but his resignation frightened Napoleon. $AF^{IV}1343$.

design, Napoleon continued to grant numerous fresh American permits, with stricter insistence upon enforcement of their terms, and he specifically referred to this in outlining his grand scheme.[26]

There is evidence of the arrival and admission at this time of a number of American ships with indigo and coffee.[27] In fact so much coffee arrived during February at Bordeaux and Nantes as to cause so marked a decline in prices that merchants of Nantes alone lost more than 200,000 francs on their importations.[28] Such circumstances undoubtedly, rather than unjust enforcement of the Continental System, were the cause of the long delays in admitting later arrivals under the permits, of which Lee, American consul at Bordeaux, sent home adverse reports.[29]

From the tone of such consular letters, and especially from the failure of Congress to provide the legislation against licences urged by Madison, we suspect that the refusal of permits by France might have caused more resentment in the United States than did their granting. Indeed, it is difficult to see how the United States could demand greater exemptions from the imperial navigation system than were granted to Frenchmen, or wherein the modified American permit was productive of special abuse. Moreover, in view of the publication of Monroe's, Russell's, and Barlow's recognition of the permits as French municipal regulations—not to mention Madison's own failure to execute his threatened revocation of the exequators of French consuls involved—there seems an awkward inconsistency in the American government's expectation that Napoleon could be *forced* to discontinue the permits.

In his expectation of an unequivocal confirmation of the repeal of the Berlin and Milan decrees, however, Madison was on stronger

[26] AF^{IV}1344, États des distributions des licences, for 1812. On the new conditions see AF^{IV}1243, annex 181, also AF^{IV}1343, correspondence of Sussy with Napoleon, on and about 5 March 1812, as to permits.

[27] AF^{IV}1243, annex 183, and AF^{IV}1062, dossier 3, pièce 36.

[28] AF^{IV}1089^{B}, Mollien to Napoleon, 22 February 1812, etc.

[29] *Dept. of State, Cons. letters*, Bordeaux, III, esp. letters of October.

ground. He had a right to demand energetically a less knavish and piratical treatment from the French government. The lack of a categorical statement was felt the more keenly because of the sarcastic refusal of the British government to accept the American asseverations regarding the fact of a repeal of the decrees.[30]

The matter at last came to a head in the spring of 1812, largely as a result of Bassano's report of 10 March extolling the effectiveness of the Continental System. This report suggested to the British Ministry an expedient by which to extricate itself from the situation in which it was placed by the pressure of parliamentary and economic demands at home, a situation intensified by the danger of an American war as shown in the publication of fresh diplomatic correspondence at Washington.[31] Therefore on 21 April an Order in Council and a declaration were issued citing Bassano's statements that the Continental System was still in force, but declaring that upon proof of the actual repeal of the French decrees the Prince Regent would revoke the Orders in Council.[32]

This declaration was immediately forwarded by Russell, now chargé at London, to his successor at Paris. On 1 May Barlow presented a note to Bassano asking, on the grounds of justice and urgent necessity, the immediate publication of an authentic confirmation of the repeal of the Berlin and Milan decrees with respect to the United States, and urging that this be followed by an indemnity convention covering past spoliations and by a just commercial treaty for the future. Judging from the results the note must have made a strong and immediate impression upon Napoleon, although French records are strangely silent regarding it. Barlow reported that Bassano having showed a strong reluctance to answer his note, he called upon him repeating

[30] Madison's *Writings* (Hunt ed.), vol. VIII, and cf. Adams, *History of the United States*, VI, chs. 10-12, for quotations from reports of Serrurier to Bassano.

[31] *Privy Council Register*, (George III) vol. 84, pp. 111-3, etc.

[32] *Am. State Papers, For. Rel.*, III, 429-31.

his demands and after a pretty sharp conversation was shown a mysterious decree of 28 April 1811 confirming the repeal of 1 November 1810 on the strength of the non-importation act of Congress of 2 March 1811. A copy of this newly fabricated decree, and of two other French acts, demanded by him, were sent on 11 May to Barlow, and he at once forwarded them to Russell.[33]

Just when Barlow made his personal demand upon Bassano is not known but he evidently did not wait long after presenting his note. For on 8 May the British declaration appeared in the *Moniteur* with elaborate footnotes arguing the abundant evidence already supplied to Great Britain, and citing in particular the very documents which were sent to Barlow three days later.[34] This strong article which it must have taken several days to prepare, Barlow seems not to have seen. It evidently never reached Washington, but can scarcely have failed to reach London, and have had a part in influencing the course of the British government.

Russell communicated the French documents on 21 May to Castlereagh. That minister did not reply for a month, in which time Brougham's renewed attacks upon the Orders in Council having made evident the ultimate triumph of the opposition, the Ministry on 19 June forestalled an adverse vote by surrendering at discretion and on 23 June the Orders were declared repealed on certain conditions.[35] The pretext for repeal was the French decree of 28 April 1811. The pretext, however, was as fictitious

[33] *Am. State Papers, For. Rel.*, III, 602-3, Barlow to Monroe, 2 May 1812, enclosing the note to Bassano; also Barlow to Monroe, 12 May 1812.

[34] *Moniteur*, 8 May 1812, pp. 505-7, esp. notes 5 and 12. It contains careful historical *resumés* showing considerable research. The article does not appear in any American state papers and despite its peculiar significance has been quite overlooked by historians.

[35] In Parliament on 22 May, however, Castlereagh declared the French decree fictitious and hence not to be considered by the Ministry (*Parl. Debates.* 23:286-9, and see 540, and 588). But it is interesting to find that the French decrees were sent immediately to the Board of Trade. B. T. 1/64, 0^2 29.

as was the French decree. In reality the surrender was to Brougham and the victor was the United States.[36]

The episode was a dramatic one. To Brougham it seemed the greatest triumph of his life, a victory not for himself alone, but for justice and liberal government in England.[37] For Napoleon it almost seemed the crowning triumph of his Continental System. By the United States it might have been vaunted as a signal vindication of the rights of the neutral nations. Thus, indeed, now reads the verdict upon this episode after a hundred years. And yet by the veriest irony of events, by a dramatically swift reversal of positions, it was written that the supposedly vanquished British Ministry was the nominal victor. For by a declaration of 16 June, perhaps at the very *hour* when the British Cabinet decided on surrender, the United States had begun a war against Great Britain which brought at its close neither reparation nor guarantees.[38] How then, pray, were neutral rights vindicated? The repeal of the Orders in Council being *ab initio* non-effective, wherein did Brougham and democracy triumph? And where was Napoleon's victory? For even as he made public his reluctant confirmation of the repeal of his decree he was setting out for the Russian border, across which he was to send his armies on the very day when by the formal repeal of the Orders in Council was removed the basic cause of the invasion.[39] Thus Napoleon lost his tactical victory, for when he returned from Moscow, he found a defeated Continental System.

[36] Monroe's report of 12 July 1813, *Am. State Papers, For. Rel.*, III, 609-12. Cf. *Privy Council Register*, George III, 84^2 p. 290. For the American attitude as to the "withheld" decree of 28 April 1811, see Madison's message of 12 July 1812, also his subsequent protests to France.

[37] Brougham's, *Life by Himself*, II, 7-22. Barlow to Monroe, 13 July 1812 (*Dept. of State, Desp. Fr.*, vol. 13): "I look upon the triumph of the United States as more complete than could have arisen from the most successful war."

[38] *Parl. Debates*, 23:541 ff. Cf. *Am. State Papers, For. Rel.*, III, 616.

[39] Note *Cor. de Nap.*, 23:531, no. 18857. Order for the passage of the Niemen, 23 June 1812.

B. *The Experiment of the Grand System*

Despite the significant origin and the foreign influence of that finishing touch to the French navigation acts which Napoleon had designated as the Grand System, it is difficult to trace the actual outcome of the project. This is largely due to the absence of important commercial papers owing to the suspension, from February to December, of the Conseil du Commerce. A few records of licence business for the period still remain, however, which afford at least clues as to the nature of the traffic during the year 1812.

So far as the grand system of 13 January was intended to be a reconstitution of the licence system upon new and simpler lines, it evidently never went beyond the records of the Conseil du Commerce. Instead the *actual* system of 1812 followed the bases of Montalivet's report of 25 November, as accepted in mid-December. This meant the preservation of many old licence types, somewhat revised, as well as the addition of certain new forms. Moreover, not only had the adoption of Montalivet's report been followed by the signature of more than a hundred of the licences recommended, but similar licences continued to be granted throughout the year.

Among the new types of licences granted, however, were a number for the exchange of wine for sugar, which Napoleon decided on 20 January should be the entering wedge for his grand system. A few had been granted early in January, but about 25 February were signed something like fifty such licences with terms broadened to admit other colonial goods besides sugar.[40] Thus *experimentally* the grand system actually went into effect.

The first news of the new scheme was hailed as "incomprehensible," but commercial interest was quickly stirred. On 28 February, Mollien reported to Napoleon, "the price of Bordeaux wines, and brandies obtains a sensible augmentation; this augmentation is due principally to the licences accorded by Your

[40] Cf. Niles, *Weekly Register*, II, 103, 11 April 1812, news from Bordeaux of 8 March; AF^{IV}1344, État de distribution des licences, for 25 February, licences 258-309; also AF^{IV}1343.

Majesty." The following day he reported much talk of licences at the Bourse. There was "not a word of discontent nor of censure on the manner in which they have been distributed. All trade is in a great movement of hope and activity, and, I believe, disposed to be wiser and less adventurous. One of the motives of joy is to think that England commences at last to yield to the superior influence of Your Majesty; an opinion at which it (trade) arrives a little late."[41]

About a week later Mollien began to revise his opinions somewhat for he thought he detected licence speculators buying up English paper evidently with the purpose of importing more than they exported. Then for more than a month he gave no licence news. On 11 April, he referred again to the purchase of English paper by licence speculators repeating his suspicions then, and several times subsequently, as to their purposes, and commenting adversely upon the stimulating affect of such purchases on English exchange. At the same time, however, he declared there was no great use of the new licences. Reliable merchants seemed afraid to take them being distrustful of Greeks bearing gifts. The great entrepôts of French goods on the enemy's soil did not appeal to them. Moreover, they had reason to believe that most of the goods warehoused would be merely for re-exportation. Hence another buyer must be found, and who could that be except the Americans with whom they could deal far more advantageously at Bordeaux or Nantes. Besides, the licence conditions involved risks and chances to which they did not wish to expose themselves. However, as Mollien himself intimated, his observation had probably been too limited. At any rate, the following day (14 April) he learned of the project (initiated by Montalivet in December) for sending fine wines to be exported to the British colonies.[42]

The direct evidence as to the *attitude of the seaports and industrial centers*, although regretably meagre, accords interestingly

[41] $AF^{IV}1089^B$.

[42] *Ibid.* Reports of 5 and 7 March and of 11, 13, 14, 24, and 25 April.

with information gathered by Mollien at the Bourse. It is significant of the slowness of the merchants to utilize their licences, and of the tendency to speculation upon them, that on 10-13 March a series of circulars were sent to the prefects to the effect that licence holders should be warned to make *personal* use of their licences.[43] The spirit observed by Mollien early in April is also shown in the petition from the Chamber of Commerce at Bordeaux on 1 April, asking a modification of the licences, so as to allow importation to precede exportation, and to give the right to substitute other merchandise for silk.[44] In fact, it is not until after the refusal of these changes (that is the end of April, and throughout May), that there is evidence of actual use of the licences.[45]

To properly understand the attitude of the French merchant, however, it is necessary to see what action was being taken by the English government. Thus it is found that while in February news of the French licences was favorably received yet it was late in March before the Board of Trade determined upon the new form of licence necessary for the transaction.[46] In the meantime licences for the French Empire were generally refused.

The licences which began to be granted about 25 March were founded strictly upon the French principle of a countervailing exportation. They were of two types. The first allowed the importation from France or any hostile country of a cargo of seeds, cheese, fruit, flax and linen yarn, organized, thrown and raw silk (not from East India or China), lace, jewelry, porcelains, quicksilver, bronze, drugs (not dyeing), perfumery, clinkers, rushes, bristles and books "on condition that the cargo so imported shall on arrival of the vessel in port be landed and placed under the joint Locks of the Crown and the Importer, till she has loaded and

[43] F¹²2115.

[44] F¹²2105. This was forwarded on 6 April by the Prefect of Gironde, and refused by Collin de Sussy on 21 April.

[45] F¹² 2105.

[46] B. T. 6/201—6/202, *Registers of Licence Applications*.

exported a cargo of goods permitted to be exported to the Value of not less than Five Pounds Sterling for every Ton Burden."[47]

The second type was for the importation of wine with the provision of a preliminary export of not less than £5 per ton and that the wine should be warehoused until a second exportation of colonial or other goods was made.[48] This second exportation must be of sugar, coffee, or British cotton, woolen and linen cloth at the rate of 12 cwt. of sugar or 10 cwt. of coffee for 3 hhds. of wine, or £100 value of cloths for every 3 tuns of wine. Ships also must take convoy within certain limits. This second form of licence, of course, was the one devised to meet the policy adopted by Napoleon on 13-20 January. Nominally it acceded to his conditions with the possible exception of the provisions which restricted the use of licences to ships already in the licence trade. In reality, however, the Board of Trade upon granting such licences imposed the additional heavy requirement that the exportation of English products must aggregate at least £500 per vessel.[49] This condition was made a general rule for all trade with France, Holland and Belgium, except in raw silk.

The relation of these British measures to the attitude shown by French shippers is self-evident. Thus without an English licence they could not begin their operations, and when, about 1 April, the British terms were learned, they appeared so difficult that the transaction was regarded as unprofitable and too hazardous by most reputable merchants, if not also by many speculators. When, however, Napoleon not only refused to modify his terms but declined to grant any more licences for England, the Board of Trade seem to have realized the need of altering their own system.[50] For a moment, at least, the Cabinet urged by Lord Sidmouth, who had just entered the Ministry, and hard pressed by the invincible attacks of Brougham in Parliament, would seem to

[47] B. T. 6/202; and House of Lords, *Sessional Papers*, 1812, no. 7, pp. 60-64.
[48] *Ibid.*
[49] B. T. 6/202. Cf. applications 39875, 40205, 40477, etc.
[50] F^{12}2105. Response to the Tribunal of Commerce of Calais, 10 June 1812.

have considered not only the suspension of the Orders in Council, but likewise the curtailment or abandonment of the licence trade. Thus on 15 June—the very eve of the promise to suspend the Orders—we find the export condition in licences for colonial goods changed from a total value of £500 per ship to £20 per ton.[51] This was equivalent to quadrupling the requirements, and might seem on its face a prohibitory condition. And yet there must have been some compensation as there is no evidence that it proved a serious deterrent to shippers. Be that as it may, however, the Board quickly found it necessary to grant fresh concessions. Thus among other measures—ostensibly upon the urging of the Brazil trading interests—it allowed the exportation of cotton to France.[52]

Meanwhile a few licence holders had risked chances and returned to France. On 4 May Mollien reports a strong decline in raw sugar prices due to the sale at Paris of a cargo lately arrived at Havre.[53] Then on 19 June he wonders as to the probable influence on coffee prices of news of the arrival of several cargoes of that article, although he remarks that previous arrivals of the sort had had no ill effects. Undoubtedly active operations had at last begun with these exchange licences when on 26 June came rumors of the repeal of the Orders in Council. The Bourse at once became nervous, recovering a bit the next day, and then with fresh news sending rush orders to sell old stocks of colonial goods, and to delay new purchases until at least Napoleon's future policy could be known. Mollien wrote on 2 July, urging speedy and reassuring measures, but they never were taken, for Napoleon was already at Wilna en route for Moscow.

Although in the attack upon the Orders in Council an especially sharp assault had been made against the licence trade, yet the repeal of the Orders seemed, if anything, to give a new impetus to the business. This is especially marked in the succession of

[51] B. T. 6/203, application 43149.
[52] B. T. 1/64, 0² 11, and 0² 12; and B. T. 5/21, p. 295, 25 June 1812.
[53] AF^{IV}1089^B

favors granted by the British government to encourage the direct trade with France during June and July. Indeed one cannot escape the conviction that the Ministry had deliberately deferred the date of the actual repeal of the Orders until 1 August with the purpose of reaping all possible advantages in the meantime from the reciprocity arrangement with France. It was, of course, an indirect way of nullifying the concessions forced from the Ministry by the United States. Moreover, when such favors to the enemy continued through August and September and until news of the French retreat, it lends strong color to the suspicion that the revocation of the British acts was as insincere and tricky as was that of the Napoleonic decrees.[54]

To this policy of the British, Napoleon readily lent himself although it can be said to his credit that between the first of March and the middle of July he had granted practically nothing but licences to import grain, or permits for the American trade, which being given largely to French shipping show distinctly their character as navigation papers.[55] Moreover, many of these were immediately annulled by Napoleon. Between 11 July and 12 October, however, of 299 licences signed, only three were to import American rice, and the rest were *licences diverses*, or, in other words, licences to trade with the enemy. Some fifteen of these were for the special purpose of accepting the British "favor" by which Brazil cotton could be secured from London to aid the spinners of Rouen.[56] Others were signed in consequence of a decision of 14 July approving de Sussy's plea for licences to introduce such indispensable things as hides, fish-oils, potash,

[54] From the middle of September restrictions began to be made. Some weeks earlier war had begun with America.

[55] AF^{IV}1344, bordereau of licences signed, reported 16 March 1813. Also he rigorously punished violations of licence terms, cf. Chuquet, *Inédites Napoléoniens*, nos. 637, 641, etc.

[56] Nos. 749-763, signed 20 September. See correspondence of Collin de Sussy and Rovigo, 12 to 20 November 1812, F^{12}2033.

medicines, whalebones, sulphur and raw copper, but with the condition of a counter exportation of wines, brandies and silks.[57]

As the reports of Mollien reflecting upon these later licences were destroyed on the retreat from Moscow we can not follow the effects upon French trade.[58] Some interesting information, however, is afforded for part of this period by the reports of American consuls. Thus on 2 October Lee wrote from Bordeaux: "Most of the vessels expedited under licences to England have returned to this port laden with West India produce. From forty to sixty pounds sterling per ton freight has been given by the English merchant to get his goods into France and one vessel gained five francs per pound freight on indigo. It is calculated that no less than eighty millions of francs will be paid into the treasury by means of these licences. Notwithstanding all these arrivals sugar and coffee maintain their prices which leads me to fear that the licence system will not be abandoned and that if any change takes place it will be in favor of cotton and other articles of our produce."[59] Regarding the situation of American trade under the circumstances Lee declared: "It is inconceivable that the Emperor has as yet done nothing in favor of our commerce. Our vessels coming here with licences are detained, three, four and even six months before they are permitted to enter and clear. During that time many of the cargoes remained unsold as no prudent merchant will purchase until he is certain the merchandise will be admitted."[59a]

It was within a fortnight after Lee's interesting report, that Bassano invited Barlow to Wilna in order to expedite the negotiation upon Franco-American commercial relations which since 10 May had been conducted at long range, through the medium

[57] Chuquet, *Inédites Napoléoniens*, p. 176, no. 618.

[58] Mollien's reports are existent from 9 November but do not refer to licences again until January 1813.

[59-59a] *Dept. of State, Cons. letters*, Bordeaux, vol. III.

of Duc Dalberg at Paris.[60] Barlow started north on 26 October but when he reached Wilna it was to involve himself in the great disaster which had already begun. Leaving for Paris at the beginning of December he was seized with pneumonia, of which he died in a little Polish village near Cracow, having just failed of his purpose. On 26 December (two days after Barlow's death) Lee reported conditions more discouraging than before, for news had come of the granting of eighty new licences "permitting importations from England in consequence of which West India produce has fallen in price."[61] But Lee—and Mollien, as well—was to report far more gloomy news as the weeks went by.

C—*The Outcome of Napoleon's System.*

Accurate statistics regarding the extent of the trade of 1812 by reciprocal arrangement between Great Britain and France are not available. Such data as we have, however, is interesting and suggestive. Thus records of the Secretariat of State show that Napoleon signed 799 licences and permits during the period, of which 310 were never delivered, having been annulled or lost between Russia and Paris, and evidently of the licences actually delivered a large percentage remained unused.[62] In contrast with these figures we note that during the same period the Board of Trade had 11,181 applications for licences of which perhaps a

[60] See Todd, *Life and Letters of Joel Barlow*, chapter IX; and Adams, *History of the United States*, VI, 259-65 for standard accounts. The actual significance of Barlow's negotiation is hard to determine for the affairs of the American legation fell into confusion after his death. The best information obtainable regarding the situation has lain buried in *Dept. of State, Cons. letters*, Bordeaux, vol. III. According to Consul Lee, who had acted as Barlow's secretary of legation, and was consulted by the French foreign office in January 1813, a treaty favorable to the United States had actually been secured by Barlow which France was ready to sign (with some modifications) even after his death. Moreover the papers in *Aff. Étr., Cor. Pol., États Unis*, vols. 64 and 68 seem also capable of an interpretation favorable to Barlow. Cf. also *Dept. of State, Desp. Fr.*, vol. 13.

[61] *Dept. of State, Cons. letters*, Bordeaux, vol. III.

[62] $AF^{IV}1344$. But see $AF^{IV}1356$ for other figures.

fourth were refused, but as most applications were for several vessels or voyages the actual number of licences granted would run about 20,000 for the year.[63]

As to the actual value of the business transacted between the Empire and Great Britain a report made to Napoleon on 6 January 1813 showed that under the wine vs. colonial goods arrangement sixty-five vessels had exported goods valued at 32 millions of francs (London prices) or a net return of about 26 millions after deducting for unsold silks, books, etc. Imports by these vessels amounted to 19 millions of francs (London prices), to which should be added some 3 million francs for freight and expenses.[64] Thus the net profit of the transaction was 4,000,000 francs at the arrival of the goods in France. Moreover, this was exclusive of various exports which did not figure in the licence requirements, such as clover-seed, etc., to the value of 5,000,000 francs. Nor did it include the value—14,000,000 francs—of the raw and organized silks exported under special silk licences, nor the 9,000,000 francs for the butter and cheese licences, nor 4,000,000 francs gained by the licenced smugglers; a total of 36,000,000 francs profit for French merchants and a benefit of 50,000,000 francs for the imperial treasury.

It would be impossible to harmonize such data with the British official figures which were based on artificial ratings. Besides it is highly probable that both countries deliberately "doctored" their recorded evaluations. In fact such falsification was openly charged by the opposition in England, and but evasively denied by the government. Nevertheless the British figures cannot conceal the fact that quantities of goods were coming from the French empire and apparently no corresponding amounts going thither—although it is significant to note how large a portion of the French imports figure on the records as being warehoused for re-exportation.

[63] B. T. 6/201-6/204. These figures may be compared with 14965 applications for 1810, 9862 for 1811, 5611 for 1813, and 2492 for 1814.

[64] AF^{IV}*171, pp. 231-2.

Considering the quantities of their goods warehoused in England, the goods entered but unsold, brought back unsold, or consigned to the sea, it seems questionable whether French shippers profited by the trade. Yet Collin de Sussy, like Montalivet, argued that the trade was profitable to France, and he pointed to the exceptional vigor of the silk industry at Lyons, and the cotton industry at Rouen as proofs. In a special report on the subject he also stated that there had been a total exportation during the year of 74,000,000 francs value of silk, 26,000,000 francs of woolens, 22,000,000 in linens, and 44,000,000 in cotton fabrics. The exports had exceeded the imports by 29,000,000 francs and the importation of specie had been 116,000,000 francs.[65] Even assuming the unreliability of these French calculations there still remains the significant fact that in England newspaper assertions, mercantile petitions to the government, and parliamentary debates, even including speeches by government supporters, stated that the balance of trade was against Great Britain and conducted with profit for France.[66]

Yet whether the merchants were losers or not by this interinimical trade it is clear that it was profitable both to the British exchequer and the imperial treasury. Undoubtedly this was one motive for the numerous licences of this type signed by Napoleon during the Russian campaign. Certainly the dominant idea in his policy after the great disaster was the financial aid which the licence trade would afford him for his heroic task of stemming the tide of fate which came flooding in upon him.

At a Council of Finances held on 22 December, some three or four days after his return to Paris from Moscow, Napoleon explained how, from the customs and tobacco monopoly receipts, he expected to meet the expenses of 1813 and the deficits of 1811 and 1812. Chiefly he based his estimates on an increase of the annual income due to the licence trade from the usual 24,000,000

[65] AF^{IV}*171, pp. 224-5. Conseil du Commerce, 30 December 1812.

[66] Cf. the *Moniteur*, 1 January 1813, from the *London Courier* showing by figures how unprofitable the trade was for England.

francs to 150,000,000 francs. "It is necessary undoubtedly to injure our enemies," he explained defensively, "but above all it is necessary to live."[67]

The matter was next brought before the Conseil du Commerce which assembled on 30 December for its first session in nearly eleven months.[68] Before undertaking a policy of granting licences practically without limit, an investigation was instituted. Several weeks of discussion were devoted to considering the relation of the licence business, and of the American trade, to the conditions and needs of industry. Perhaps the most important question under consideration was whether the aid extended to the silk industry could not be broadened to embrace other industries without hampering commerce. The plan suggested was the substitution of a prime or extra duty on the value of an export cargo for the conditions of exporting fixed proportions of stipulated goods.

The discussion led to the presentation of several reports highly interesting for the light thrown upon the workings of the licence trade during the previous year. Thus, reports by the Minister of Police explained how the silk manufacturers had aided shippers in placing highly inflated evaluations on the required silk shipments.[69] Other reports are even more valuable because of the detailed calculations they give of the expenses of shipments between various French ports and London, and return.[70] These calculations showed the real losses incurred because of the required shipment of one-third silks, and suggested various modes of levying an equivalent prime or surtax for the benefit of the imperial treasury.[71] Of these, the mode favored was a levy of 5% on the market value of the return cargo, fixed by the average quotations on the Paris bourse within a fixed period before and after the arrival of the ship. The actual "prime" determined upon by the decision of 18 January was 6%, which could be paid, or the silk

[67] *Cor. de Nap.*, 24:343, no. 19391.
[68] AF^{IV}171, pp. 224-5.
[69] AF^{IV}1062, dossier 4, pièces 30 and 31.
[70] *Ibid.*, pièces 45 and 46 by Portalis, maître des requêtes.
[71] *Ibid.*, pièce 47.

condition fulfilled, at the option of the shipper. This decision was embodied in a decree of 18 February 1813.[72] By it was at least partially removed the chief deterrent against which the French licenced trade had so long protested.[73] During April many cities attempted to get the 6% condition also removed but failed, although this and apparently other concessions were granted to American shippers and even privateersmen.[74]

Besides the measure granting greater freedom on the score of exportations, Napoleon planned another way to foster trade and increase customs receipts. This was by multiplying licences of existing types, and by the adoption of new forms for which a demand existed, or could be created.[75] Thus the number of wine vs. colonial-foodstuff licences which during the previous year had proved so profitable to the treasury was practically doubled at the start. Moreover, somewhat similar licences were granted for the Mediterranean ports and for Danzig. The raw silk export licences were again offered. Likewise the licences to import cotton granted at the request of Rouen factories in September 1812 were continued in 1813, both for England and for parts of Spain.[76] A notable increase was made also in the permits for the American trade.[77] Of the new licences created some half dozen

[72] Decree no. 5 bis, of 18 February 1813.

[73] Note the milder treatment given to delinquent vessels, Chuquet, *Inédites Napoléoniens*, nos. 793 and 816.

[74] F^{12}2105, Count de Sussy to Antwerp, Amsterdam, etc., 1 May 1813. Cf. Lee to Monroe, 22 April, *Dept. of State, Cons. letters*, Bordeaux, III.

[75] For details see: AF^{IV}1345; AF^{IV}*171, pp. 231-2, 6 January 1813; AF^{IV} 1062, dossier 4, pièce 14; and AF^{IV}1243, annexes 196-203.

[76] F^{12}2033, and AF^{IV}1062, dossier 4, pièces 5 and 6, 16 February 1813.

[77] Consul Lee (Barlow's secretary of legation) reported 10 January that rumor said American licences were to be given up. Later he explained their continued use as being due to Napoleon's financial necessities and his desire to get the United States to accede to less favorable treaty terms than Barlow had required. Cf. Lee's reports of 26 Dec., 10, 17, and 29 Jan. and 2 Feb. On 22 March 1813 he reported 150 American licences granted, also 120 for English trade from which the French government was expected to gain 200,000,000 francs.

were granted during January and February for importing fine tobaccos from England. A much larger number, however, were for the importation of hides and a variety of materials used for manufacturing, such as bamboo, ivory horns, whale bones, fish oil, sulphur, and potash. They were given upon conditions similar to the sugar, indigo and cotton licences, namely an importation worth £5 per sea ton and a countervailing export. The fee was 40 napoleons for regular licences, or 300 napoleons for licences of equation to balance deficiencies.

Among the measures adopted especially significant were those for the Mediterranean trade, such as new Ottoman licences for Tunis and even Persia. The most important new type of licence adopted, however, was for the exportation of mercury and the importation of colonial produce at Venice, Ancona, Trieste, and Fiume.[78] It is interesting as representing a further development along the lines of the grand system outlines in January 1812. For the licences provided for the exportation of Austrian as well as Italian and Illyrian products, and for the warehousing of imports and their transit into Austria upon paying a tax of 40 francs per quintal.[79] The trade was limited, however, to vessels of 200 tons and the licence fee was placed at the exorbitant price of 300 napoleons. Evidently, however, the restrictions seemed likely to defeat the prime object of securing income for the imperial treasury, and in March permission was given for smaller vessels to use such licences at greatly reduced fees.[80]

It is not definitely recorded whether such licenses were granted at the request of Austrian and Italian merchants, although there is eqidence that there was special pressure from both quarters at this period both upon the French and British governments.[81]

[78] AF^{IV}1345.

[79] The warehouse privilege was granted on petition of Trieste. Cf. F^{12}* 261, letter of 29 July 1813 to Consul Vigoureux at Venice.

[80] AF^{IV}1344, model of licence, April 1813, and correspondence with Cte. Prina, 20 March 1813. Lecestre, *Lettres inédites*, II, 219-20, dates it 28 March.

[81] For French evidence see the correspondence with French consuls at Venice and Ancona, F^{12}*261. For the English side of the salt trade scheme, see B. T. 1/62, M^{2}13 and 14.

In fact, the demands were spontaneous with the people themselves Yet often, undoubtedly, they were initiated and directed by the British traders whose overflowing warehouses in Malta, Sicily, Lissa and Corfu had become—like those of Heligoland, Hano, Anholt and Gottenburg in the North—indisputable proofs of the reality of the Continental Embargo.[82] By 1812 the outlook for British trade in the Mediterranean had become as alarmingly as the dire state of trade in the colonial goods which had compelled advances to France in the autumn of 1811, or like the late situation in the Baltic before the renewal of British intercourse with Sweden and Russia.[83] Under such circumstances all manner of intrigues were hatched to elude the vigilance of the imperial *douaniers* or to trick or bargain relaxations from Napoleon. Special activity was shown in this way throughout 1812 by the merchants.[84] How ably they were seconded by the British government is proved by the numerous orders in Council and Board of Trade regulations issued in favor of Malta, even when supposedly every effort was being made to end the discredited licence trade.[85] Thus, in particular, as late as 14 August 1814 was adopted a scheme of licences for Corfu, the final development of the British licence system.[86]

Hardly had the first of the new licences been issued when operations began under them. Doubtless French commerce was spurred to so speedy a response by information that although the British government upon pressure from Russia had nominally discontinued licences, yet the Board of Trade had issued a number of eleventh hour licences which were still valid for prompt use.[87]

[82] Cf. Sussy to Rovigo, 20 and 22 February 1813, F^{12}2033.

[83] B. T. 1/64, 0² 9—Resolution of Mediterranean merchants, 3 April 1812.

[84] Cf. B. T. 1/70, U² 9—Johnson's letter of 10 August 1812; and B. T. 5/22, 521-524—Letters of Brown and Goulbourn, September 1813.

[85] See *Privy Council Register*, George III, 84²:335; B. T. 5/22, 453 ff.; C. O., 136/295, numerous items.

[86] *Privy Council Register*, George III, vol. 84⁴:102, and 114.

[87] F^{12}2105, Petition of 8 January 1813 from the Chamber of Commerce at Bruges; AF^{IV}1062, dossier 4, pièce 29; and *Moniteur*, 7 January 1813, but the

The commercial effects of the licences of 1813 are strikingly revealed in Mollien's valuable daily reports to Napoleon. With the realism of a cinematographic film they develop before us the increasingly desperate situation of the imperial power in the days when Napoleon sought to withstand the embattled nations on the Pomeranian plains and by the Saxon rivers.

The uneasy optimism of Mollien's first reference to the new licences on 14 January scarcely conceals the prescience of economic ills lurking in their wake. Within three days a rapidly falling English exchange had shifted to an even more rapid rise, due largely to the purchase of English paper by licence holders. The depreciation of English credit had ever been the minister's peculiar passion, but he sought consolation in reminding the Emperor that this result had been foreseen and that "the profit of the English *by the change* is not comparable, assuredly, with the profits which the finances of Your Majesty will make from the licences." But when within five weeks the pound sterling had risen to par there were no "assuredlys" in his language, for in the meantime new causes of uneasiness were presenting themselves. Thus on 21 January he reported rumors of an approaching decline in the prices of colonial goods, while on 5 February he noticed the multiplication of "commercial engagements on the Paris exchange" which, however, he added more hopefully, had not "had an unfavorable influence upon the course of public securities."[88]

From uneasy premonitions, however, the shift was swift to unhappy confirmations. Thus the arrival of return cargoes during March and April brought to Mollien, and to Collin de Sussy as well, fresh cause for anxiety which increased to alarm as the weeks went by. On 24 March he called attention to the lower prices

---

Moniteur of 12 January reported that the Board of Trade had changed their mind and would grant more licences.

[88] $AF^{IV}1089^{B}$, cf. note 1 above. On February 3 the ships began to arrive at London for cargoes, *Moniteur*, 11 February.

for cotton, coffees, and sugars.[89] It was the keynote of a monotonous refrain about falling markets which was to run with depressive insistence through his subsequent reports. Before the end of April vessels arriving in the Channel ports and in Holland were claiming the right to warehouse their goods while awaiting a rise in prices sufficient to pay customs duties, and indemnify themselves for the costs of their adventures.[90] Then we recall with concern that weeks before at Bordeaux wines had been warehoused for government loans to finance such adventures, and that even from the first of March strenuous efforts were being made by the government to recover upon these pledges.[91]

The effects of such a commercial situation could not fail to have a speedy and most adverse influence upon general economic conditions.[92] Bankers shook their heads over the small real capital available for trade, the overbuying of colonial goods on credit, and the large amount of personal paper in circulation. Discount and interest rates grew tighter as banks grew stricter, and merchants were forced to turn to private money-lenders and brokers. Shippers began to sacrifice their purchases or to sell securities to save themselves. In May reports of failures began to come in—failures of dealers in Piedmont rice, of bankers at Venice and Milan and in the Hanseatic cities, of silk merchants, and wholesale grocers of Paris and the seaports. Protests became as numerous as in the panic of 1810. Fortunately the Bank of France by issuing notes and affording some other aid caused a rally in confidence. Yet the Bourse kept "listening to the events of the memorable days of the 20, 21, 22 and 23 May" and continued to wonder regarding those whose magazines were full of colonial produce.

[89] Compare with this Lee's reports of 23 March and 15 April (*Dept. of State, Cons. letters*, Bordeaux, III). The 15 April letter also shows the disastrous effect of the imports from England upon the sale of American shipments.

[90] $AF^{IV}1089^B$, Reports of 24 and 27 April.

[91] $AF^{IV}1062$, dossier 4, pièce 25, 3 March 1812, under a decision of 30 October 1812, AF^{12} 2034-37.

[92] $AF^{IV}1089^B$, Reports of 4, 10, 11, 13, 14, 17, 20, 21, 22, 29, and 31 May.

With the opening of June, rates began to drop and so did English exchange—but so also unhappily, did the markets for colonial goods both in France and in England, where the situation grew worse even than in 1812.[93] Moreover, what especially puzzled and worried Mollien was that the more the prices fell the less the people seemed to buy.

Yet the difficulties which commerce was experiencing were but the forecast of the more serious difficulties which confronted Mollien as he strove to finance the imperial efforts to defeat the redoubtable hosts of the uprisen nations. "I dare affirm to Your Majesty," he wrote to Napoleon at Dresden on 17 June, "that never has the service of the treasury presented such difficulties. The little available capital at Paris scarcely suffices for the needs of commerce and for the loans to which the licences have given place; the resource of negotiations with individuals has thus been closed to the Treasury."[94] Coming from the Minister who had financed all the wars and weathered all other economic crises of the Empire such a confession carried a portentous note to his imperial master.

Difficulties, however, had in reality but begun for Mollien. Almost immediately came a call for help from the armies of Spain, hard pressed by the relentless Wellington, and the Ministry of War called on Mollien for funds.[95] Even as he was seeking to float bonds upon an impoverished market, there came a new blow from the North.[96] Forced by Napoleon to buy amnesty for their brief dash for freedom, the Hanseatic cities sought to raise the merciless ransom by withdrawing all their outstanding funds through Paris, sacrificing on the Bourse all possible securities.[97] When, turning from the hopeless market place, Mollien pressed the merchants for the repayment of government loans,

[93] *Ibid.*, 2, 9, 11, 15, 17, 18, 29 June and 12 August.
[94] *Ibid.*, 17 June.
[95] *Ibid.*, 1 July.
[96] *Ibid.*, 25, 29 June.
[97] *Ibid.*, 21, 22 June, 6 and 25 July.

they sold to others or offered to the government their *caisse d' amortissement* bonds—thus forcing down this best of government securities.[98] When he called upon the Minister of Commerce for arrears from the customs, Collin de Sussy could but turn on his part to the hard pressed delinquent importers requiring the immediate removal of warehoused goods and the payment of duties. Again there were sacrifices, and failures for large sums in which the government was a heavy loser. Moreover, murmurings grew louder against the customs, an ominous sign in view of the threatening mood of Holland, of Hamburg, and the North.[99]

With such accounts coming in from Mollien, Napoleon turned anxiously to Collin de Sussy asking a full report on the status of the licence trade. For he cherished the gambler's hope that further use of this most dangerous economic device might relieve his desperate military position.[100] The Minister of Commerce replied early in August with candor, although perhaps too encouragingly. He assured the Emperor that the customs would yield the sum required of them and showed what had been the results of the licence trade up to the end of July. Thus by virtue of 104 licences for sugar and coffee given to the western ports, 90 ships had sailed and 68 returned, yielding 60 millions of francs in duties with 18 millions estimated for the 22 vessels yet to return. By virtue of 30 similar licences for the Mediterranean, 13 ships had sailed and 8 had returned with light cargoes yielding but 2,000,000 francs, with 1,200,000 yet expected. On the other hand he admitted that large quantities of goods might legally remain in entrepôt a year before paying tariff duties. Nor did he hesitate to say that more licences for France would be worse than useless as more than a year's supply of imports was already stored up without demand, not to speak of what would arrive on the large number of American vessels expected when the long autumn nights would permit blockade

[98] Note a recovery on 7 August, however. (Also see Napoleon to Cambacérès, 16 July, Chuquet, *Inédites*, no. 1114).

[99] AF^{IV}1089^B, 8 and 15 July.

[100] The letter to Sussy has not been found, but see that to Gaudin, 1 August 1813. "X—.," *Lettres de l'Empereur* no. 7, cf. also nos. 8 and 54.

running. Moreover, he pointed out that not only had the English government ceased granting licences but that a so-called Spanish cruiser was lurking in the Thames capturing, with impunity, vessels having English licences. However, Sussy suggested that it might be possible without serious effects to grant licences for Hamburg to bring in a stipulated quantity of raw sugar, coffee, pepper, tea and American cotton. Duties, he recommended, should be paid immediately upon importation.[101]

On receipt of this report Napoleon at once determined to grant not only the licences for Hamburg and Bremen at a rate which would protect French importers from competition, but he likewise proposed cotton licences for Strassburg, and if feasible other similar licences for Italy. Also he modified the licences for Perpignan and Bayonne by substituting a surtax for the former rigid export requirements. "All this," he declared, "is founded on the great needs of my finances under present circumstances."[102]

When this secret decree reached Paris the financial situation was again becoming too precarious to risk adding further to the commercial unrest. For at the beginning of September, Sussy and the customs service were engrossed in working out schemes to hasten the removal of warehoused goods, to provide outlets for an excessive grain harvest, etc., while Mollien was endeavoring to save the Bank of France from failure because of its discounts to commerce for the removal of 50,000,000 francs of colonial goods from entrepôt.[103] And with October came a new serious problem in the need to rescue from English seizure some two thousand French-owned vessels in British ports.[104] Meanwhile, Germany was fast slipping from the imperial control. And few, indeed,

[101] AF^{IV}1062, dossier 4, pièce 29 (merely dated August 1813). However Mollien's reports of 7, 14, and 21 August grow more encouraging.

[102] Lecestre, *Lettres inédites*, II, 286, no. 1082, 14 August. Note on former difficulties AF^{IV}1062, dossier 4, pièces 5 and 6.

[103] F^{12}2034-37, letters of 31 August, and 1 and 4 September; AF^{IV}1062, dossier 4, pièce 40, 15 September; and AF^{IV}1089^B, undated cipher letter supposed to be of October 1813.

[104] AF^{IV}1062, dossier 4, pièce 42.

were the soothsayers of France itself who could not see the handwriting on the wall and read the *Mene, mene, tekel, upharsin* of the Napoleonic system.

Apparently, therefore, no feature of the decree of 14 August was ever executed, unless it was the concession in favor of the Perpignan-Bayonne licences which had originally been granted at the instance of the military authorities occupying Catalonia.[105] It was speedily followed, however, by the creation of yet another form of licence for the importation of colonial goods from Spain or its colonies.[106] Thirty such licences were authorized for Bordeaux, Marseilles and Bayonne on condition of exporting French goods in exchange. It was one of the desperate moves made by Napoleon in mid-November of 1813 to mend his war-riddled finances and strengthen his Spanish policy for the supreme hour which was fast approaching. With the exception of a single licence for "Persia"—given to the Pasha of Cairo in September—these Spanish licences were the last type of licences authorized by Napoleon, and some of them, delivered at the end of February 1814, mark the final operations of the imperial licence system.

It was an appropriate coincidence that this final expression of the licence system should have come at what proved to be the last session of the Conseil du Commerce. This brief session held at Paris on 14 November 1813, was from the standpoint of its membership the most notable in the history of the Conseil, for those attending were: the Emperor, the Prince Arch-Chancellor Cambacérès, the Prince Vice-Grand Elector Talleyrand, Gaudin, Minister of Finance, Mollien, Minister of the Treasury, Montalivet, Minister of the Interior, de Sussy, Minister of Manufactures and

---

[105] No licences are recorded as having been given under the decree although a decision of 25 December 1813 might seem to indicate otherwise as to Hamburg, etc. As to Perpignan and Bayonne, Sussy on 3 September asked further instructions. See $AF^{IV}1062$, dossier 4, pièce 25.

[106] Conseil du Commerce of 14 November, and decree of 19 November, AF^{IV}*171, pp. 253-4. Cf. the demands of the Chambers of Commerce of Bayonne, Amiens, and Lyons for trade with Spain, $F^{12}1965$.

Commerce, Bassano, Secretary of State, and Counts Regnaud and Chaptal.[107] Two of these—Cambacérès and Talleyrand—had never before been present, but there was a dramatic fitness in their signalizing this closing scene by their presence, for with Napoleon himself, and perchance Chaptal, they chiefly had initiated the "navigation policy" of the Empire. It was, as it were, a typification of the brevity and the greatness of the Napoleonic régime that they who presided at the birth of one of its most momentous projects should thus together share in its obsequies.

Although the Conseil du Commerce had ceased to meet, another and final report of the licence trade was presented for the year 1813 and the first weeks of 1814. This affords no statistics for the results of the year's commerce, but it indicates clearly the number and character of all licences granted. Up to 2 June 1813, there had been granted 1419 licences of 24 types, by 25 September 1569 licences of 26 types, and by 31 December 1744 licences of 27 types, while 26 licences were granted up to 26 February 1814

Of the 1744 licences of 1813, 890 were classified as *licences diverses*, viz., for Norway 79, for San Domingo 3, for importing colonial goods from England 121, for importing hides, etc., 125, to return in ballast 154, to import tobacco 6, to export raw silk 4, licences of equation 118, licences of equation for colonial goods 11, Danzig licences for colonial goods 25, Danzig licences to export naval stores 2, Levant licences 4, colonial goods to Mediterranean ports of France 31, Illyrian licences 10, licences for hides, etc., to Mediterranean ports 90, ballast licences (Mediterranean) 3, Mediterranean equation licences 7, Sardinian licences for food-stuffs 54, Ottoman 34, and three Norway equation licences. Also there were 65 licences for mercurial products, 38 for tunny fishing, 1 for "Persia" (Egypt) and 13 for Spain. The most numerous of any type of licences, however, were the American permits of which 707 were granted prior to 30 April 1813, besides

[107] $AF^{IV}1243$, annex 204.

30 permits for vessels under the French flag. The majority of the American permits (429) were for Bordeaux; Nantes, however, had 167, Bayonne 30, La Rochelle 29, Marseilles 21, other French ports 20, Dutch ports 11, and Hamburg and Bremen one each. Of the 26 licences granted in 1814, 14 were for Spain, 9 for Sardinia and 3 for England.

As compared with previous years the licence business of 1813 was most exceptional, twice as many licences being granted as in the previous year, and perhaps quite as many as the total of the three previous years. It was still, however, not excessive in comparison with the number of British licences issued even in this hour of Britain's victory. How extensively these French licences were employed is not known, but large numbers of the American permits were never utilized, and probably of a not inconsiderable portion of the rest the same statement would be true. At least this had been the case in previous years and there was even greater cause for caution on the part of importers in 1813 than in 1812. At any rate, there was little demand for licences after the over-trading during the first semester of the year, followed as it was so speedily by the crashing down of customs barriers. For nothing could have shown more significantly the dramatic rapidity of the break-down of the Napoleonic empire during the winter of 1813, than the rush of bulletins from the north, the east and the south recording how, in countryside and city, popular wrath was demolishing the restrictions of its "fundamental principle," the Continental System. And what the populace had thus begun, the Bourbons hastened to complete, as soon as they were returned to France, by enactments which abolished the administrative organization of the system. For scarcely had the dethroned Emperor signed his act of abdication before the demolition of Napoleonic institutions began. Among the first features of the imperial régime thus hastily swept away were the famous edicts of the Continental Blockade, the extraordinary tariffs of Trianon and St. Cloud, the enforcing decree of

Fontainebleau with its additional acts, and the multifarious regulations for the licenced trade which had been the final expression of the Continental System.[108]

Of the elaborate structure of Napoleon's commercial system no part remained unrazed save those foundations laid by the men of the Revolution—the Navigation Act of 21 September 1793 and its complement the law of 18 vendémiaire An II.[109] Indeed, these laws of the Revolution (though modified and amended by the attrition of so great economic and political changes as those which have come about since 1814) remain today the constituent acts of the French navigation policy. For, being legislative enactments of the sovereign people of France, the navigation acts of the Convention were proof against annulment by another power, whereas the mere executive edicts of Napoleon fell like a house of cards, a pen-stroke undoing what a pen-stroke had created. Indeed so easy was the overturning, that it surely must have been foreseen by Napoleon who certainly realized, all the while, that much of his own navigation system was merely false work erected to meet the extraordinary commercial situation due to the war with England, and that there must be an inevitable remodelling of the fabric for the conditions of peace. Thus it has been evident throughout this study of Napoleon's system that the decrees of Berlin and Milan and the rigorous edict of Fontainebleau were primarily war measures enacted for the period of the war, while even the tariff decrees of 1810 were not expected to outlive five years. On the other hand, all the indications are that the scheme of licenced navigation of July 1810, whether in its development as the continental-wide dream of the Grand System of January 1812, or in some more tolerable guise, was to be a permanent

[108] An arrêté of 5 April abolished the Ministry of Commerce. Cf. the *Moniteur*, 5 April. Decrees of 17, 23, and 26 April suppressed the licence system, the Trianon tariffs, the cours prévôtales, etc., 5 *Bulletin des lois*, I, 50, 51, 55, and 238. See also, *Ibid.*, pp. 85, 111, 234, etc. for other measures. Cf. in general, 19 Duvergier, *Lois*, etc. and the *Moniteur*, 1814.

[109] See Charpentier, *Codes et Lois*, I, 31, 32.

policy of the Empire. But events decreed that *no* part of the imperial design should be spared. And yet it was not long before men began to doubt the failure of the Continental System as they witnessed the return of the Continent to the protective régime, and foresaw (largely as a consequence of the experiences of the Continental System) the speedy end of Britain's Acts of Navigation.[110]

[110] This change of attitude most strikingly appears in S. Millenet, *Le Blocus Continentale et les Anglais*, Paris, 1837.

CHAPTER XIII
The Administration of the Navigation System

Side by side with the evolution of policies and projects in the Napoleonic Navigation System had been developed an administrative organization whose character cannot fail to impress the student of institutions. For, though far less conspicuous than interdicts of seas and empires, crusades against coffee, and auto-da-fés for English muslins, in *reality* the adoption of commercial codes, the creation of courts and of councils, and the reconstruction of ministries was no whit less characteristic of Napoleon nor less fundamentally a part of the Commercial System which directly or indirectly dominated his Empire.

"His Majesty, the Emperor Napoleon, occupies himself much more with details of commerce than you seem to be aware of," wrote, in 1812, the keenest of American diplomatic observers on the Continent, "and if he does not exactly reason from his information as you and I might do, it is because certain motives enter into the composition of his deliberations which we should not so readily admit."[1] And he further declared: "Whatever may be the vices of France under her new system this is not among them. She at least is not governed by subalterns. The activity of all her official administrations might teach her enemies a lesson of wisdom, if luxury, sensuality and indolence could learn wisdom from either friend or foe."

The pertinency of this opinion is illustrated by the institutional aspects of Napoleon's navigation policy. How widely the administrative system of the Empire was affected by the navigation program is shown by the number of ministries involved in its execution, and by the scope of their activities.[1a]

In the first place it is manifest that the Ministry of Marine and Colonies would be especially concerned in carrying into effect

[1] Ford, *Writings of J. Q. Adams*, IV, 373, 374, to T. B. Adams, 14 July 1812.
[1a] Cf. Pichon's 1814 pamphlet—despite its brevity and animus.

a *navigation* system. During the Empire this Ministry was entrusted to Vice-Admiral Decrès.[2] His functions under the navigation acts were manifold. First, he must enforce the law as to the nationality of vessels with respect to the build and manning of vessels trading with imperial ports, the nationalizing or neutralizing of ships, and arranging simulations for those neutralized. Second, his was the surveillance of movements of shipping, namely, the protection of licenced vessels, the supervision of the *cabotage* of coasts and rivers, and the policing of fisheries. With such functions went the seizure of offending vessels, and the enforcement of embargoes decreed by the Emperor. Prior to 1810 the Minister of Marine also gave special protection papers to vessels, insuring them in certain cases against capture by French men-of-war or privateers. So largely had the functions of the marine already been determined during the period of the earlier navigation acts, that, save for the adoption of the *code de commerce* in 1807 and the establishment of three councils of marine in 1810, no important administrative reconstitution falls within the periods of our study.[3]

As a *commercial* measure the navigation system was particularly under the charge of the Ministry of the Interior, prior to January 1812. The connection was fourfold: (a) the development of commercial policies through investigations and reports; (b) the execution of regulations for external trade involving the interpretation of policies, the control of trade licences, and the keeping of commercial records; (c) the administration of the domestic system involving the encouragement of home industries—protecting and regulating them, providing raw materials for manufactures, and opening outlets for products of the soil and handicrafts of France; and, finally, (d) the popularizing of the com-

[2] He was first appointed 3 October 1801 (13 Duvergier 45.).

[3] For the Napoleonic organization of the Ministry see 12 Duvergier, 263 (26 July 1800), also the laws of 7 floréal An VIII (27 April 1800) and 7 fructidor An VIII (25 August 1800). Cf. *Moniteur*, 20 August 1810, decree of 24 July.

mercial system. The radical changes in this ministry will be considered later.[4] The most radical of these changes was due to the creation of a special Ministry of Manufactures and Commerce, 19 January 1812. This was followed by a decree of 21 September of that year reorganizing the Ministry of the Interior. During the Napoleonic régime the Ministers of the Interior were Lucien Bonaparte (25 December 1799–21 January 1801), Chaptal (6 November 1800–5 August 1804), Champagny (1804–9 August 1807), Cretet (9 August 1807–June 1809), Fouché *ad interim* (July 1809—1 October 1809), and Montalivet (1 October 1809–1814).

As a *financial* measure the administration of the imperial navigation system was chiefly intrusted to the Ministry of Finance. The connection was a peculiar one. Nominally the Minister of Finance, Gaudin, duc de Gaete, was responsible for all such affairs. In reality the Minister's personal function—aside from his participation in framing the general navigation policy—was his responsibility for funds collected and to be expended. Under him was the Director General of Customs—until 1812 Collin de Sussy a practically independent official, who from 1810 to 1812 sat in ministerial councils and reported either personally or through the Minister of Finance. The functions of Count de Sussy were manifold. He directed the administration of customs laws: inspecting imports and exports, deciding—subject to appeal—what were, or what were not permittable articles. He collected customs duties and licence fees and deposits.[5] He also controlled the acceptance of securities and hence the giving of the *acquits à caution* required for coasting vessels. Another large function

---

[4] For dates of service see the *Bulletin des lois*, the *Moniteur*, *Correspondance de Napoleon*, etc. General statements as to the Ministry of the Interior can be found in the *Almanach Impérial* for each year of the period. These general references will hold for this entire chapter, although the statements made will have been derived often from a general use of archival material which precludes specific citation.

[5] See the decree of 5 September 1810, ($F^{12}2031$).

was the detection and prosecution of customs frauds on land as well as sea frontiers. Connected with this was the laying and lifting of sequestrations of vessels, subject in each case to imperial decisions. Needless to say, the direction of the customs was vitally affected by the Continental System especially after July 1810.[6]

The Ministry of Exterior Relations was also vitally affected by the Continental System. In fact a study of the diplomacy of the Consulate and Empire furnishes incontrovertible proof that its navigation policy was the dominating element of the Napoleonic régime. As already shown Talleyrand and d'Hauterive had been drafting prototypes of the Berlin decree since 1800.[7] So, too, after its adoption Talleyrand and his successors, Champagny and Maret, had had no small share in its amplification and in its defense at home and abroad. But the connection of the Ministry with the Continental System was administrative as well as political. Even under the revolutionary navigation acts the granting of certificates of origin for neutral goods was entrusted to the consular service. This was continued under Napoleon although with various changes in the policy from time to time.[8] The adoption of the licenced navigation system in 1810 still further extended the functions of the consular service. Thus, for example, every American, Ottoman or Barbary permit had to be validated by the

---

[6] For the organization of the Ministry of Finance under Napoleon see the *Almanach Impérial*. For the *douanes*, see, in addition, Henri Bacquès, *Essai historique sur les douanes françaises*. And consult Duvergier, *Lois*, 13:439; 14:209, 512; 15:150-5, 415-32; 16:181, etc. The Direction General of the Customs was created 16 September 1801, by a law of 29 fructidor An IX (13 Duvergier 23). An interesting explanation of distinctions between the functions of the Customs, the Ministry of the Marine, and the Council of Prizes was given by Napoleon at the Conseil du Commerce of 10 September, 1810, AF^{IV}1241, annex 157.

[7] See chapter I note 12.

[8] Cf. esp. the decrees of 1 messidor An XI (20 June 1803), 22 ventose An XII (13 March 1804), and 30 ventose An XIII (21 March 1805), 15 Duvergier, 194. Decree of 11 August 1808, 16 Duvergier 351; also the Berlin and Milan decrees and the policy of 1810-11 (chapter X above).

French consul at one of the ports designated, who furnished a cipher letter for the Minister of Exterior Relations.⁹ The Minister also was concerned in the distribution of licences to allied governments. In some cases, especially in the Baltic and in Algeria, the consuls shared in the distribution of licences to local merchants.¹⁰ In the Mediterranean, as well as the Baltic and along the North Sea, the consuls also were concerned in detecting (and not infrequently in aiding) breaches of the Continental System. These enlargements of the consular functions, and Napoleon's insistence upon regular commercial and political news from his consuls naturally required an extension of the consular service. It seems also to have led in 1812 to some reorganization of the consular bureau, and to the partial transference of the service to the Ministry of Commerce.¹¹

The Ministry of War was concerned in the distribution of licences in the Hanseatic cities, and to some extent in Spain. The army also was utilized in the maintenance of the blockade laws.¹² The Minister of Police, likewise, had from the start aided in the enforcement of the blockade and the precautionary provisions of the licence system. The connection with the licence system was especially close when Fouché was acting Minister of the Interior as well as Minister of Police. He controlled the issuance of passports and the movement of persons and mails, preventing licenced ships from carrying passengers or mails without special authorization.¹³ He was concerned in the surveillance of canals and internal communications, as well as important sea coasts. Fouché and Savary also for a time controlled a limited number

⁹ Consult chapter IX above.

¹⁰ See for example $F^{12}2115$, 18 January 1811; also cf. $F^{12*}262$. As to abuses cf. chapter I, note 14, last sentence.

¹¹ See Napoleon to Cadore, 7 November 1810, Brotonne, *Lettres inédites de Napoléon*, p. 292, no. 713.

¹² Cf. 14 Duvergier 47, arrêts of 16 frimaire An XI (7 December 1802); and 7 germinal An XI (12 March 1803).

¹³ Cf. decrees of 18 September 1807, and 11 July 1810; also decree of 28 August 1810, $AF^{IV}1243$, annex 234.

of licences for the use of the secret service. The Ministry of Police was reorganized by a decree of 25 March 1811.[14] For a time the Director of Posts was concerned with the Minister of Police in the surveillance of mails, but this seems to have been chiefly before September 1810.[15]

The *legal aspects* of the navigation administration are represented by the Minister Secretary of State, and the Grand Judge, Minister of Justice. From 25 December 1799 until April 1811 when he became Minister of Exterior Relations, Maret, duc de Bassano, was Secretary of State.[16] His was the important function of drawing up, countersigning and filing all imperial decrees. He also countersigned and recorded all navigation licences received from, and returned to the Minister of the Interior. Maret was succeeded by Count Daru, who in turn was succeeded in 1813 first by Champagny, duc de Cadore, and finally by Maret himself who remained until the abdication of Napoleon. Throughout the period the Ministry of Justice was filled by Regnier, duc de Massa. Under his supervision were the prize courts, particularly the *conseil impérial des prises*, also the *cours prévôtales* and *tribunaux ordinaires des douanes*.[17]

The Conseil des Prises was constituted by virtue of a law of 27 March 1800, as the court of appeal from the officers of the administration of the marine in the local ports who passed upon captures at sea, and wrecked and stranded vessels.[18] In the case of ships of neutral or allied countries appeal lay to the Council of State, or, after its creation in 1810, to the Council of Commerce. By virtue of the Berlin decree and succeeding edicts the Conseil judged "definitively the reclamations upon prizes and seizures

[14] 17 Duvergier 365-7.

[15] Cf. Art. 11 of the Berlin decree, *Cor. de Nap.*, 13:557.

[16] 12 Duvergier 52, and 17 Duvergier 402 (17 April 1811).

[17] By virtue of a decree of 8 May 1806 (15 Duvergier 437).

[18] 12 Duvergier 189 (6 germinal An VIII), cf. also laws of 26 ventose An VIII, 7 ventose An XII, 8 May 1806, and 11 and 25 January 1807, 14 June 1806, 11 January 1808, 16 November 1809, 27 September and 8 November 1810, and 7 July 1811

made throughout the extent of the Empire and in the countries occupied by the French armies which are in contravention of the decrees of blockade."[19] This jurisdiction extended over licenced vessels violating flagrantly the terms of their licences. By virtue of a decree of 27 September 1810, it had cognizance of seizures made by the customs officers in Holland.[20] The Conseil sat at the Oratoire Saint Honoré. It was presided over by a councillor of state and was composed, besides, of eleven councillors, a procurator general and his assistant, a secretary and two bailiffs.[21] To be valid a decision of the Conseil must be signed by the president and at least four of the councillors. As usual in admiralty suits, the cases were conducted by the presentation of memorials in writing, which must be presented within a stipulated period. The court was suppressed in 1815.[22]

Of the other ministers who shared in the administration of the navigation system naturally the Minister of Manufactures and Commerce was most important. His functions can best be noted, however, in considering the creation of the office. Of the remaining ministers with portfolios the connection was largely incidental. The Minister of the Treasury, Count Mollien, merely watched the effects of the system, presenting daily reports the value of which has already been shown. The Minister of Cults and the Minister of the Administration of War, seem to have had essentially no connection with the system. Other ministers without portfolios, however, such as Chaptal, Regnaud de St. Jean d'Angely, Deferman and others had a most important influence in the framing and direction of policies, particularly in the periods of reorganization in 1810 and 1812.

[19] Lepec, *Bulletin annoté*, XI, 75-7, art. 4, notes; Brotonne, *Lettres Inédites*, 283, no. 688. After 8 October 1810 its dec'sions could not be published until after they had been announced in the Conseil du Commerce.

[20] 7 Duvergier, 191.

[21] *Almanach Impérial*, 1813, p. 252. During the whole period its president was Merlin, appointed 24 July 1800 (12 Duvergier 261).

[22] Cf. acts of 8 June, 22 July 1814, and 9 Jan. 1815, (19 Duvergier 97, 193 and 373).

From the foregoing survey it is evident that the *Ministries chiefly concerned in the administration of the navigation system as reconstituted in the summer of 1810 were those of the Interior and of Finance.* Naturally these two ministries required the most marked developments or adaptations in their organization to fulfill their enlarged functions.

In connection with the Ministry of the Interior it is needless to say that the creation of the Conseil du Commerce et des Manufactures by the decree of 6 June 1810 was a measure of the most far reaching importance.[23] Its correspondence to its prototype, the British Board of Trade, has already been pointed out. The constant reference in the preceding pages to the work of the Conseil renders superfluous any discussion here of the significance of its seventy-nine sessions. Though most closely related to the Ministry of the Interior, the status and composition of the Conseil du Commerce as an imperial state council made it the general clearing-house and governing body by which the widely scattered administration of the imperial navigation system was co-ordinated.

This Council of Commerce and Manufactures must not be confused with certain minor bodies with similar nomenclature.[24] For example there was the Conseil General de Commerce, a semi-official adjunct of the Ministry of the Interior created by a decree of 3 nivose An XII (24 December 1802).[25] This body having fallen into desuetude its reconstitution was proposed on 18 June and decreed on 27 June 1810.[26] As originally instituted this Conseil de Commerce consisted of fifteen members appointed by the Emperor from a list of nominations made by each of the Chambers of Commerce of the Empire. Once or twice a year the Conseil was expected to meet at Paris and present a report on the

[23] AF^{IV}1241. See also chapter VI, p. 166 above.

[24] M. de Lanzac de Laborie makes this mistake in his *Paris sous Napoleon,* VI, 58.

[25] 14 Duvergier 73, art. 10.

[26] AF^{IV}1241, annex 23. But the *Almanach Impérial* says 26 June.

conditions and needs of commerce. Other acts could be performed by a small quorum of members living in or very near Paris. As reorganized in 1810 the size of the Conseil was much increased, eight new members being added from Holland alone.[27] Nominally the membership was fixed at sixty, but available lists show but thirty-six for 1811, thirty-seven in 1812, and forty-one in 1813.[28] All members were required to be in active business. The lists include some of the most noted business men of the Empire such as Delessert of Paris, Mottet De Gerando of Lyons, Hottinguer of Paris, Portal of Bordeaux, Van Aken of Ghent, Voute (Woute) of Amsterdam, Mappes of Mayence, Filiechi of Leghorn. In 1813 the Hanseatic cities were represented. In 1810 the Minister of the Interior was president and the Conseil met at the Hotel Chabrillant. After 1812 the Minister of Commerce was president and meetings were held at his ministry. The vice-president was always one of the Conseil, and was appointed for a term of three months by the Minister.

Members of the Conseil who were most useful were to be rewarded at the end of five years by the title of Councillor of Commerce, conferred by an imperial brevet. Evidently this was, at least for a time, an incentive to activity by the council. An instance of this was the strong protest against the severities of the Continental System drawn up by the vice-president, Martin-fils-d'André, and presented by the Conseil to Montalivet on the eve of the crisis of 1810.[29] It made a great impression upon Napoleon, but when he found immediately afterward that Martin was deeply interested in the contraband seized in the Rhenish cities and in Switzerland, and that he had become bankrupt by

[27] 17 Duvergier 212, art 37.

[28] Cf. *Almanach Impérial*, 1807, p. 157; 1808, p. 173; 1809, p. 186; 1810, p. 188; 1811, p. 204; 1812, p. 254; 1813 p.

[29] The letter is printed in Tarlé, *Continentalnaja blokada*, p. 728. The documents relating to this episode are found in *Arch. Nat.*, AF^{IV}1061, dossier 1, pièces 92 and 93; also see F^{12}192, 28 October, 7 and 22 December, cited by de Lanzac de Laborie in his *Paris sous Napoleon*, VI, 52, 59, 60, 65, and 66.

speculations which injured many honest men, the net result was to discredit the Conseil de Commerce. On the other hand, individual members like Van Aken, Portal, Voûte, Hottinguer and Delessert rendered invaluable assistance, and the two latter were made barons of the Empire.

As already noted the Conseil General de Commerce had been originally intended as a clearing house for the chambers of commerce organized chiefly during 1803 in the important centers of the Empire.[30] Apparently the co-ordination was not successful, for after 1810 the reinvigorated chambers were brought into direct relations with the Bureau of Commerce of the Ministry of the Interior, with which the local bodies kept up a regular correspondence, particularly regarding questions of the licence trade.[31] A somewhat similar co-ordination of the Bureau of Commerce was apparently effected with the local bourses of commerce and tribunals of commerce.[32] This was necessary for, under the organization given them by the Napoleonic legislation, the bourses were rather more than stock markets, and the tribunals other than simple courts of civil law. Moreover, the tribunals of commerce as courts shared in the enforcement of licence regulations.[33]

Corresponding to the reconstituted Conseil de Commerce there was in 1810 in connection with the Second Division of the Ministry of the Interior a *Bureau Consultatif des Arts et Manufactures*.[34] This shortly became the *Conseil General des Fabriques et Manu-*

[30] Cf. 14 Duvergier, 72, 3 nivose An XI (24 December 1802) et seq.

[31] Cf. $F^{12}2105$.

[32] It is interesting to note from the *Bulletin des lois* and the *Moniteur* the renascence of these institutions after 1810. Thus the Tribunal of Commerce of Paris was organized 23 October, and that of Lyons 20 November 1810 (Cf. *Moniteur*, 1810, pp. 1171, and 1300). The tribunals were created or reorganized by a law of 28 prairial An VIII (17 June 1800), 12 Duvergier 245; and again in 1807 by the *Code de Commerce*.

[33] See $F^{12}2007$ for the organization and work of the various tribunals of commerce.

[34] Cf *Almanach Impérial*, 1810, pp. 184; 1811, pp. 200-216.

factures.[35] It was composed like the Conseil de Commerce of sixty members with the Minister of the Interior as president and a vice-president named from the membership of the Conseil by the Minister. The members had to be active manufacturers representing the various industries rather more than their local distribution, since Paris, Lyons and Rouen furnished a large share of the membership. For five years of active service a member might become a councillor of arts and manufactures. Among its noted members were Richard Lenoir, a leader in developing the cotton manufactures of France.[36] Another was Ternaux, who, as vice-president of the Conseil, having gone at the head of that body to congratulate Napoleon on the birth of the King of Rome, was greeted with the violent harangue against the merchants of Europe which astonished the world and drove Russia into preparations for war.[37] The creation of this Council of Manufactures was accompanied by a renewed attention to the various *conseils des prud'hommes* and *chambres consultatives des manufactures, fabriques, arts et metiers*, founded or reorganized by the legislation of the Consulate.[38]

The importance of these adjunct bodies in popularizing governmental regulation by co-ordinating it with individual enterprise in commerce and industry should not be minimized. Nevertheless,

[35] Cf. AF^{IV}1241, annex 23, 18 June 1810, proposal to create a conseil général des arts et manufactures. A certain Hellenc in a memoir of 10 August claims to have made the original suggestion in a former memoir.

[36] On Richard see Lanzac de Laborie, *Paris sous Napoleon*, VI, 312-4.

[37] The sensation caused by this outburst is shown by the numerous contemporary versions. Cf. Sbornik, *Imperatorskago*, 121:121; Colenbrander, VI, 131-2; *Dept. of State, Desp. Fr.*, vol. 12, Russell to Monroe, 15 and 24 April 1811; *Writings of J. Q. Adams*, IV, 12, 87; Miot de Melito, *Memoirs*, 571 and Thiers, *Consulate and Empire*, IV, 10.

[38] See AF^{IV}1241, annex 63, 7 July 1810. Cf. laws of 18 March 1806, and 11 June 1809 (16 Duvergier 434-41); and AF^{IV}1241, 27 August 1810, and 15 October 1810. See also, laws of 22 germinal—2 floreal An XI (12 April 1803), 14 Duvergier 192; 10 thermidor An XI (29 July 1803), 14 Duvergier 360; and 17 germinal An XII (2 April 1804), 14 Duvergier 539. Cf. also acts of 11 June 1809, and 15 October 1810.

like all of Napoleon's representative bodies, their functions were nominal rather than real. and the actual administration of the commercial system of the Empire was distinctly in the hands of certain bureaus of the Ministry of the Interior.

The continuous development of the functions of the Ministry of the Interior is an excellent illustration of the great interest taken by Napoleon in the peaceful development of his Empire.[39] Its organization consisted of a secretariat general, four divisions with their bureaus and subsections, a varying number of conseils, and several special branches or "directions general." In 1810 its personnel was an efficient one.[40] Count Montalivet was minister, Baron de Gerando was secretary general, under whom were Labiche, chief of the secretariat, Coquebert Montbret, director of the statistics of the Empire and Laugier, chief of public instruction. Benoist was chief of the first division which embraced the general and local administration, accounts and personnel; Fauchat, chief of the second division of commerce and industry; Barbier-Neuville, chief of the division of charities and corrections, public buildings, fine arts, science, etc., and Bohain, chief of the division of public funds and accounts. Count Molé was director general of bridges and causeways, Count Portalis of the press and publishers, and Daunou imperial archivist. The ministry proper was located in the rue de Grenelle.

Fauchat had been but newly appointed to succeed Loisel as head of the very important *second division*. He had already demonstrated his capabilities for planning and administering commercial measures, however, as chief of the secretariat general, for in 1809 there had unexpectedly devolved upon him both the duties of acting secretary of the ministry and the oversight of the experimental licence trade. The navigation legislation of June to August 1810, in preparing which Fauchat had had a considerable

[39] Cf. 13 Duvergier 123-4 (29 October 1801), with descriptions of the ministry in the *Almanach Impérial*.

[40] *Almanach Impérial*, 1810, pp. 184-198.

part, naturally involved a corresponding adaptation of the organization of the "second division." This Fauchat proposed in a series of six reports dated 9 August, predicated, as he stated, on the need for securing better and speedier results for commerce and manufactures, and to provide for the increased work entailed by the extension of the licence system.[41]

The second division had for some time consisted of the bureau of agriculture in charge of M. Sylvestre, of subsistances with Remondat as chief, of commerce and of the balance of commerce both under Arnould, and of arts and manufactures with Claude Costaz as chief, to which had recently been added a bureau of reclamation of marshes under Verneilh.[42] These bureaus and their officials were retained by Fauchat but the bureau of commerce was divided into two sections. The first section under Arnould retained the old functions of the bureau, namely, foreign commerce, trade with French colonies, re-exportation of foreign goods, reimportation of French wares, transits and entrepôts, commercial legislation, primes and encouragements for whale and cod fishing, bourses of commerce, and sanitary administration except at Toulon. The new second section under Lemoine was created to handle the business of licences, or in other words to be the central bureau of the navigation system.

The scope of the licence business administered by the Ministry of the Interior was carefully explained by Fauchat in his report to Montalivet proposing the new commerce bureau.[43] The business fell under two heads: "the instruction of demands and the distribution of licences. The first," said Fauchat, "comprehends the registration of applications, the keeping of repertoires intended to facilitate the researches of all sorts, and the verification

[41] F¹²2031. These reports in fact were for the general reorganization of the commercial sections of the ministry including the Conseil Général de Commerce, the Conseil Général des Manufactures, etc., as well as the Second Division.

[42] *Almanach Impérial*, 1806-1811.

[43] F¹²2031. Report no. 5 of 9 August.

of double uses, and the correspondence, as to details and regarding instructions, with the prefects and the merchants. The second embraces the preparation of plans of distribution, the filling out of licences; the drawing up and sending out of *lettres d'envoi* to the prefects, and of notices to the shippers; the keeping of a register of the licences delivered; the preparation and sending of *états* to the Minister of the Marine, the Director of the Customs, and the Minister Secretary of State; the sending out of safe-conducts; the accounts to be rendered to His Majesty; the keeping of registers of cargoes; the correspondence of rectification, etc."

He held that "the information as to applications should be kept continually up to date. The work of distribution requires promptness and regularity in its execution. These two duties may be confided only to assiduous and intelligent employees of proved discretion. There would be grave inconvenience in distributing the work among different bureaus, as one is forced to do at the epochs of distributions. It is proposed, therefore, to create for the licences a special section charged with this distribution. It would be confided to two or three employees. One would direct the work under the chief, the other two would make the drafts and copies. By means of this arrangement the work will move rapidly. The distributions being made more promptly will be more numerous because men will be oftener ready to make applications for licences signed by His Majesty. The licences granted will be better employed by the applicants, who will obtain them without delay; finally the registers being always up to date the Minister will be always ready to render account to His Majesty of the result of operations undertaken by favor of the licences, and to respond to all questions put to them upon this subject."

Montalivet, as usual, immediately indorsed the plan thus outlined by his efficient assistant, who in this case spoke from practical experience with the system of administering the licence business as developed under his direction during the previous fifteen months of experiments. A few weeks later the new sectional bureau composed chiefly of experienced helpers of Fauchat in the secretariat was established at the Hotel Chabrillant with Lemoine as chief. It proved its value in directing the constantly developing licence system until it became the chief bureau of the Ministry of Manufactures and Commerce at its establishment in January 1812.

Into the composition of the new Ministry of Commerce, went certain other administrative organs. These were chiefly from the Ministry of Finance which, as already seen was, after the Ministry of the Interior, most directly concerned in operating the system of licenced navigation. Until the legislation of July 1810 the relation of the Ministry of Finance to the licence trade had been largely indirect and maintained by way of directions from the Ministry of the Interior for the Director of the Customs. With the creation of the Conseil du Commerce, however, and the close linking of the Trianon and St. Cloud tariffs with the licence legislation of July, the functions of the two ministries were put upon a co-ordinate basis.

The connection of the Ministry of Finance with the licence administration was still further extended by transferring to the imperial customs service the collection of fees, formerly entrusted to the prefects and carried out usually by civil officials of the shipping ports. The new arrangement had the advantage of centralizing the financial phases of the system and hence incidentally limiting the chance of corruption and extortion while securing more efficient administration. The principle was established by the decree of 5 September 1810, which ordered licence fees as well as the usual import, consumption and harbor dues, and shipping bonds (*cautions*), to be paid to the customs officers of the port for which a licence was granted.[44] The duties of the customs service were further increased by the decrees regulating the deposits of goods, bonds, etc., required as guarantees for the balancing of imports and exports.[45] Also the warehousing services required

[44] AF^{IV}1243, annex 238.
[45] Cf. decree of 5 December 1810, AF^{IV}1243, annex 287.

under the administration of the colonial goods tariffs and in connection with certain kinds of licences entailed much additional work from the close of 1811 on, while in January 1813 the substitution of a 6% premium on the value of a cargo in place of a requirement to export silk, added greatly to the functions of the customs service.[46] For the performance of most of these duties the machinery of the *douanes* was already well adapted since it had been reorganized to meet the requirements of surveillance against infractions of the Continental Embargo. For certain functions, however, new adjunct organs were created.

By a decree of 31 August 1810 there was created a Conseil de Contentieux (administrative court) to aid the Director General of the Customs in fixing the value of cargoes exported and imported under licences.[47] The court was to be composed of two *maîtres de requêtes* and four *auditeurs rapporteurs*. Each auditor was to keep a register of licences granted for one of the four divisions: (a) Emden to Cherbourg, (b) Cherbourg to Bayonne, (c) Pyrenees to San Remo, (d) San Remo to Naples. This register must show for each vessel: the number of its licence, the date of delivery, the name of the shipper, the captain, the tonnage of the ship, its cargo, the day of departure and arrival and the decision of the Conseil de Contentieux regarding the valuation of its imports and exports. This data was secured as follows. The ship's master must send to the customs officers at the port of departure a declaration of his cargo and the value of the merchandise, signed by himself and the supercargo. This the director or superior agent of the customs at that port had to verify. In case of fraud he sequestred the vessel and reported to the Director General of the Customs who brought the case before the imperial Council of Commerce which decided regarding final confiscation. If no fraud was found the verified manifest of the cargo was sent to the Director General of Customs who referred it to an auditor

[46] Cf. $F^{12}2007$, for cases. By decision of 6 April 1813 this was kept as a separate fund.

[47] $AF^{IV}1243$ annex 237. A draft of this decree in $F^{12}2031$ is dated 31 July.

of the Conseil de Contentieux. The auditor then investigated the valuation given the merchandise exported and upon his report the Conseil officially determined the value of the cargo exported. This fixed the value of the importation to be made. On the vessel's return the procedure was repeated. If the import cargo exceeded the exports by one-third the excess was warehoused until a new export was made to balance it. If the excess was but a sixth of the whole a running account was kept and the account cleared when a new exportation was made. The decisions of the court were merely arbitral, and could not be used by the customs in collecting duties, nor cited in any judicial tribunal for any cause.[48]

Because of practical difficulties found in enforcing the decisions of the Conseil de Contentieux a decree of 5 December 1810 required that one-fifth of the value of the cargo of the first operation under a licence must be deposited with the customs until the balancing operation was carried out.[49] The work of the Conseil de Contentieux was complicated also by the decree of 31 December 1810 requiring fixed proportional exports of silks and wines under most licences and permits.[50] Another difficulty was found by the Conseil de Contentieux in adjusting their evaluations to the price current of goods which of course varied somewhat with the port concerned. At first the evaluations of the manifest apparently were accepted where possible, or else were adjusted to Paris markets. By an imperial decision of 17 April 1812, however, it was settled that in licences for England values were to be fixed at the prices current of London and Le Havre, and this decision was held to be retroactive.[51] Although at first supposed merely to report to the Director General of Customs, in practice reports of decisions of the Conseil de Contentieux were sent also to the Bureau of Licences in the Ministry of the Interior which

[48] For examples of decisions cf. $F^{12}2027$.
[49] $F^{12}2115$; and $AF^{IV}1061$, dossier 1, no. 123.
[50] *Ibid*.
[51] Cf. $F^{12}2034$-37, correspondence of Sussy and Ferrier, 17-27 October 1812.

used them in making up its weekly and quarterly reports for the Conseil du Commerce. Occasionally also *maîtres des requêtes* were called upon by the Conseil du Commerce for calculations bearing upon the licence system.

Aside from the duties of the Conseil de Contentieux the work of the general customs service was aided by the *tribunaux ordinaires* and *cours prévôtales des douanes* created by the Fontainebleau decree of 18 October 1810, and by a special court at Hamburg for the Hanseatic cities and the military districts of North Germany. The object of all these courts was the repression of contraband and the strict enforcement of the Continental System. Despite the general impression given by accounts of the Fontainebleau decree the creation of these courts was not a novel measure but merely the culmination of a long series of experiments in legislation to keep out English and colonial merchandise. They were also further amplified and modified various times until the downfall of the Napoleonic system. Originally there were 34 *tribunaux ordinaires* but certain of these were suppressed, while still others were established elsewhere.[52] Each was composed of a president, four assessors, an attorney, clerk, and bailiffs. They judged according to the forms of the correctional police subject to appeal to the *cours prévôtales*. There were seven *cours prévôtales*, or extraordinary courts located at Valenciennes, Rennes, Agen, Aix, Alexandria, Nancy and Florence. Each was composed of a grand prévôt of the customs who presided, at least eight assessors, and an attorney general and clerk. They had a definitely prescribed original jurisdiction over contrabanders, and customs officers, besides hearing appeals from the *tribunaux ordinaires*. They judged according to the criminal code, and their judgments were final where their competence was clear.[53]

[52] 17 Duvergier 207-9. *Almanach Impérial*, 1812. For their abolition see V *Bulletin des lois*, I, 55, 26 April 1814. For early legislation, interpretations and decisions see Lepec, *Bulletin annoté*, II, 341; X, 24; XII, 121-5 and notes.

[53] All these courts submitted regular reports to the Director General of Customs, according to certain prescribed forms. (See *Arch. Nat.*, F^{12}2011.)

Just as the navigation policy of 1810 was destined to undergo numerous modifications and extensions so likewise the machinery for its execution was subject to corresponding developments. The case of the Conseil de Contentieux is an example of this, but the most important illustration is found in the movement to form a special ministry for handling the business and industrial problems which were constantly becoming more troublesome and engrossing. Although doubtless a long-mooted idea, the first serious consideration of a ministry of economic interests seems to be traceable to a long memoir dated 7 May 1811, transmitted by the Duke of Rovigo, Minister of Police. This memoir "On the Situation of Commerce and the Means of Re-establishing Confidence and Credit," bore the signature of Vital Roux, Regent of the Bank of France and Member of the Paris Chamber of Commerce, and, moreover, one of the chief framers of the Code de Commerce.[54]

The memorialist protested against the tendency to attach too much importance to foreign commerce and to consider the balance of trade with its delusive figures the thermometer of prosperity. He pictured the serious economic crisis through which the Empire had been passing since the previous autumn. Then with the frankness of Nathan before David—or shall we say the bold spirit of a Republican newspaper criticizing a Democratic tariff law— he analyzed the causes of the paralysis of credit and stagnation of trade, ascribing it to the Emperor's recent commercial legislation and, above all, his decree of Fontainebleau. As correctives he proposed a number of guarantees of the inviolability of property, and a scientific and stable tariff legislation which would *ipso facto* destroy smuggling. Particularly, however, he pointed out the need of an administrative reorganization "which would

---

The *cours prévôtales* used two forms in reporting, that for original cases was under ten heads, that for appeals twelve heads—indicating the case, the parties involved, the competence of the court, and the decision, with observations. These reports are usually too laconic, however, to afford much information as to the actual extent of contraband, or the efficiency of the courts.

[54] AF^{IV}1060, dossier 1, pièces 11 and 12.

provide for business *un point d'appui* which should be able to give it an impulsion and to enlighten it upon its true interests." He especially criticized the impotent and passive councils of commerce and manufactures controlled by the Ministry of the Interior, and he urged the creation of an independent advisory council representative of manufactures, commerce, arts and sciences, and directly connected with the chambers of commerce.

On 13 May an unsigned memoir in the handwriting and style of Vital Roux carried these ideas yet farther. It was entitled *Memoire sur le formation d'un Ministère pour l'agriculture, les manufactures et le commerce.*[55] "A Ministry of Agriculture, of Manufactures and of Commerce," the writer argued, "would attract (y rattacharait) all hopes, it would produce a great impression upon public spirit (les esprits), it would assure to agriculture and to commerce an impartial and enlightened protection, it would give them a salutary impulsion. . . . As it would not have any administrative jurisdiction, its influence would never be dangerous, it would never be able to attempt any usurpation upon the other ministries to which, moreover, it could not give the least umbrage.

"Agriculture, commerce, and industry would have a *point d'appui* which they lack, a zealous protector, an impartial defender, an enlightened guide whose advice would be always respected, and whose influence could give it a wise direction.

"The Ministry of Agriculture, of Commerce, and of Manufactures would produce, besides, this happy result, that it would secure more consideration for the professions for which a sort of low esteem has been affected, it would recall the sentiments of probity and honor which alone can attract to them men of means." And particularly, as he insistently declared, it would give to agriculture that proper consideration of which it had been deprived by commerce.

Directly after the presentation of these memoirs Napoleon suddenly concluded to form a new ministry somewhat of the sort

[55] AF^{IV}1060, dossier 1, pièce 10 (18 pp.).

proposed by Roux. To be sure the Emperor did not call this ministry by the name suggested, and did not include agriculture in its jurisdiction, nor is there positive evidence that the long physiocratic disquisitions were actually the cause of the imperial determination. It is significant, however, that these memoirs carefully preserved in the papers of the Secretariat of State are, apparently, the only proposals of the sort to be found. Action in the matter was taken on 21 June, after consideration by the Council of State.[56] Unfortunately in the absence of minutes of its meetings, and because of the unexplained suspension of sessions of the Conseil du Commerce, we can not know the character of the discussions within the imperial cabinet. But a clue to the sentiment of the man at the bourse, who it would seem was cognizant of the ministerial discussion, is given us in one of Mollien's notes to Napoleon. Under date of 22 June he wrote: "Business occupies itself a great deal with the approaching creation of a Ministry of Commerce, and with the confidence that Your Majesty projects this institution only to know better the needs and interests of the trade of his great Empire."[57]

Some months later there was signed and published a decree dated 22 June 1811 which very laconically declared:[58]

"There is created a Ministry of Manufactures.

"It will have in its department manufactures, industries, commerce, subsistances, the customs, the conseil des prises.

"It will correspond with our consuls, accredited with foreign powers regarding commercial affairs."

This rudimentary decree was the *projet* accepted by the Conseil d'Etat on 21 June.[59] Evidently it was intended merely as a basis for subsequent legislation developing the embryonic ministry. Why it remained in this state, inoperative for months,

[56] Cf. AF^{IV}1062, dossier 6, pièce 3.
[57] AF^{IV}1089^A, 22 June 1811.
[58] 17 Duvergier 461, Bulletin 7603.
[59] Daru to Napoleon, 15 January 1812, AF^{IV}1062.

we do not know. Perhaps Montalivet or some other of the ministers, whose functions would be conspicuously mutilated in order to provide for a new co-laborer, intimated that he would consider the action as a marked disapproval of his own zealous services. Certain it is that later Montalivet had to be mollified by Napoleon to prevent his resignation.[60] On the other hand the creation of the proposed ministry was clearly a measure taken to encourage business to recover from the panic of the previous winter. When, therefore, it was found that business was not enthusiastic over the proposition, and was rapidly righting itself, it would seem logical that Napoleon should cast aside and straightway forget the new governmental organ.

A new situation arose in the winter of 1811-1812. From his visit to Holland in the early autumn, followed by the important 25 November meeting of the Conseil du Commerce at which he heard Montalivet's notable exposé of the workings of the system of licenced navigation, and where he discussed the humble proposal of the British Board of Trade for a reciprocal commercial arrangement, Napoleon conceived a new interest in the economic upbuilding of his Empire.[61] The culmination of this interest was the dream of the "grand system" so fervently unfolded on 13 January to his Conseil du Commerce. And he entrusted his dream to his Minister of Commerce and Manufactures.

For the appointment of this privileged official executor of imperial dreams we turn to a letter dictated three days earlier, beginning:

"Monsieur, the Count de Sussy, I have decided that there will be in the future a Ministry of Manufactures and of Commerce, and I have designated you to fill these high functions. I mean to recognize thus the good services which you have rendered in organizing the customs as they are today." After a long enumer-

[60] In January 1812 he declared there was nothing left for him to oversee but sheepfolds and sewer-systems and he preferred that some one else do that.

[61] See chapter XI above.

ation of the attributions of the new ministry Napoleon closed: "In a few days you will give me your official oath."[62]

The creation of the Ministry of Commerce was distinctly a concomitant feature of the "grand system."[63] The appointment of Collin de Sussy was a well-merited promotion for long and zealous service. Yet there surely must have been some other reasons for the sudden shifting of the oversight of business affairs from the Department of the Interior, whose functions it had so long been, to an official of the rival Ministry of Finance. Logically it would seem that if another ministry were necessary for the handling of commercial interests Fauchat, who had been Montalivet's indispensable aide in the previous years, should have had first consideration. As it was, the selection of de Sussy could scarcely have been considered in any other light than an indirect censure to Montalivet and his assistant. Indubitable evidence upon the question is, indeed, lacking but there are clues upon which to found surmises. Thus it is particularly significant that, in the day or two prior to the sudden appointment of de Sussy, Montalivet had held several conferences with Napoleon regarding the reciprocity arrangement with England which was to be the basis of the grand scheme, and that the minister persistently disagreed with the Emperor's point of view.[64] It was inevitable in the circumstances, therefore, that Montalivet should have lost countenance by his opposition. Not only must this have emphasized the need of a new administration of commerce, but it would have discredited any nominee Montalivet might put forward. Possibly Fauchat was already discredited, since some mysterious reason without apparent antecedent or sequence had caused Napoleon on 26 November to desire a secret police report as to Fauchat and his connections.[65] Yet another element, and perhaps not the least motive, determining Napoleon's change in

[62] *Cor. de Nap.*, 23:163, no. 18426, 10 January 1812.
[63] See the circular letter to the French consuls abroad. P. R. O., B. T. 5/21, 338, Q^2 23.
[64] Cf. chapter XII, above.
[65] Lecestre, *Lettres inédites de Napoléon*, II, 181.

administrators, was his feeling that Montalivet and Fauchat had misrepresented the crop situation of the Empire and hence were to blame for the serious shortage of foodstuffs and the suffering of the poor with which Napoleon suddenly found himself confronted.[66]

After the appointment of de Sussy it was necessary to formally create his ministry. Reminded of the projected decree of the previous June, the Secretary of State was instructed to hunt out the forgotten document. Daru replied on 15 January sending the desired decree and calling attention to the title of the ministry which it created and to the change in the consular service for which it provided.[67]

This decree and one naming de Sussy as minister were immediately published, together with a third decree of some length fixing "the attributions of the ministry of manufactures and of commerce" in accordance with the new plans.[68] There were still difficulties to be adjusted, however. On 27 January de Sussy had an audience with the Emperor to present plans and financial estimates for his ministry. He placed his expenses at 1,927,800 offset by a cut of 240,000 francs from the Ministry of the Interior.[69] A day or so later he received his estimates back reduced by Napoleon to 618,000 francs. The slashing strokes and haste of the Emperor's figuring speak volumes as to the consternation with which he saw the price of his new whistle. On the other hand, de Sussy was no less discomfited at the sight of his mutilated budget. He immediately protested that he could not undertake

[66] *Cor. de Nap.*, 23:209, 297, 302, etc. The Russian envoy in reporting the creation of the new ministry stated that Montalivet had been "fort mal en cour" for sometime and would be dismissed, largely because of his lack of foresight in providing grain against the dearth, Sbornik, 121:147.

[67] AF^{IV}1062, dossier 6, no. 3.

[68] 17 Duvergier 461, Bulletin 7603, and 18 Duvergier 169, Bulletin 7604 (16 January); also 18 Duvergier 172-3, Bulletin 7605, 19 January 1812. It was not until 21 September, however, that a decree, reducing the jurisdiction of the Minister of the Interior was issued, 18 Duvergier 263, Bulletin 8384.

[69] AF^{IV}1062, dossier 6, pièces 4 and 5.

his new office without funds to run it and he closed with the astonishing statement: "I just at this moment discover that I have overlooked the *bureau of licences* which of all of them is the one most charged with work."[70] Yet despite so serious a reflection upon his own calculations, thanks to Gaudin's aid, an agreement was speedily reached upon de Sussy's budget.[71] Such blunders and surprising forgetfulness or ignorance regarding his new work might, however, have augured ill for his success had not de Sussy largely retained the old administrative chiefs with the departments and bureaus taken over from the previous system. A notable exception, however, was in the case of Fauchat, who did not emigrate from the Ministry of the Interior with the commercial organization he had perfected. Possibly therein lies the explanation of the inefficient administration of commercial—especially licence—affairs for some weeks after the reorganization. For, in fact, the situation was such as to bring down upon de Sussy so severe a reprimand from Napoleon at a Council of State, that the new minister tendered his resignation in high dudgeon.[72] His excuses, however, were sufficient to bring an imperial apology, for Napoleon had no desire to lose so faithful a servant.

Directly after this episode the emperor named Baron Coquebert de Montbret as secretary general (assistant head) of the Ministry of Manufactures and Commerce.[73] By his long service in the secretariat of the Ministry of the Interior, Montbret was doubtless well trained for his new position, and it is probable that he had never ceased to repent his blunder in 1809 by which he had disdainfully thrown to Fauchat's charge the oversight of the licence trade.[74] Montbret's duties were the registration and distribution of despatches, the oversight of matters reserved by

---

[70] AF^{IV}1062, dossier 6, pièce 6.

[71] AF^{IV}1062, dossier 6, pièces 7-13.

[72] AF^{IV}1343; and Lecestre, *Lettres inédites de Napoléon*, I, 198, correspondence of Napoleon and Sussy, March 1812.

[73] *Moniteur*, 14 March 1812, decree of 8 March.

[74] See chapter III above.

the minister for his personal action, and the charge of the ministerial archives. In its order in the organization of the ministry the secretariat was preceded by a special bureau for secret and urgent matters, the headship of which was not filled until 1813.

At first there were four "divisions" of the ministry besides the secretariat and confidential bureau.[75] The chief of the *first division*, M. Tarbé, had under his charge four bureaus. In 1812 these were: (1) a bureau for the licence business under Lemoine, former chief of the similar *sub*-bureau in the Ministry of the Interior; (2) a bureau *des douanes* for the correspondence relating to the *contentieux*, to the administrative oversight and personnel of the customs service, and to affairs within the jurisdiction of the conseil des prises; (3) the bureau of the consulates, for correspondence with the consuls and the collection of treaties of commerce and foreign tariffs; (4) a bureau of *la comptabilité*, which finally had as its functions the requests for funds, the drawing up of orders, the expenses of the ministry, the accounts of the customs, the courts and tribunals of the customs, etc. In 1813 the first bureau became a division, and a "chief of payments" appears as a new fourth bureau.

The *second division* of the ministry—the administration of commerce, and the balance of commerce—was under its old head Arnould. Under him were two bureaus. The first of these had as its functions, "the movements of commerce in the ports and in the places of the interior, the nomination of *agens de change* and *courtiers*, the *conseil general du commerce*, the chambers and bourses of commerce, the establishment and changing of fairs, sanitary administration (except at Toulon), the anonymous societies of commerce, the primes and encouragements for the fisheries."[76] The second bureau gathered data regarding imports and exports, and prepared the annual tabulations of the balance of trade.

---

[75] *Almanach Impérial*, 1812, and 1813 (under Ministry of Manufactures and Commerce).

[76] *Almanach Impérial*, 1813. In 1812 the functions were less extensive.

The *third division*, also under its old chief, Costaz, was for manufactures and useful arts and for industrial statistics. The functions of its two bureaus afford an interesting review of the other side of the workings of the navigation system.[77] Under the first bureau are listed: inventions in the useful arts and improvement of manufactures; the *conseil general des fabriques*; *conseil de prud'hommes* and *chambres consultatives de manufactures, fabriques, arts et metiers*; the police of workshops and factories for the establishment of which special permission was required or those which were considered offensive or injurious to public health; the modification of customs tariffs on raw materials for manufacture, or with regard to foreign wares; delivery of *brevets* or patents for inventions, and permits for importing cotton goods into Italy; industrial statistics and the exposition of French industrial products. The second bureau had charge of the efforts to replace exotic products with indigenous ones, with the oversight of the imperial sugar factories of Chateauroux, Nantes and Sauer Schwabenheim, and of the pastel-indigo works at Florence, Toulouse and Turin.

The *fourth division*, under Remondat, had two bureaus.[78] The first of these had to do with harvests, prices of grain and the maintenance of reserves; the second aided the circulation of grains in the interior, and saw to the formalities for the export and import of foodstuffs.

The *subsidiary organs* of the Ministry of Commerce included the Conseil Général de Commerce, the Conseil Général des Fabriques et Manufactures, and in connection with the third division, a body of officials and experts to whom articles of industry were sent for examination and judgment. These were taken over from the jurisdiction of the Ministry of the Interior with few changes, except the shift in quarters to the hotel of the new ministry, No. 3

[77] *Almanach Impérial*, 1813.
[78] He had had charge of the bureau of subsistances in the Ministry of the Interior, and in view of Napoleon's criticism of the Ministry of the Interior because of the food crisis his promotion seems inconsistent.

Rue Grange Bateliere, and some necessary changes in membership.[79]

Another adjunct of the Ministry of Commerce was the Direction General of the Customs, which lost its nominal dependence upon the Ministry of Finance. Officially it was listed as a separate and minor administrative institution.[80] In reality, however, it continued under the overight of de Sussy who nominated and stood sponsor for his successor Ferrier, and who personally, or indirectly, through the bureau of the customs of the Ministry of Commerce, controlled Ferrier's policy.[81] Moreover, the new Director General seems never to have gained the prestige or influence which de Sussy had had in that office, a result, perhaps, of the decadence of the "ministerial" Conseil du Commerce.

Somewhat similar to the position of the customs administration with respect to the Ministry of Commerce was that of the consular service. From the diplomatic standpoint, indeed, the consuls remained under the jurisdiction of the Minister of Exterior Relations, who apparently still controlled their appointment, but in so far as their functions were commercial or connected with the navigation system the consuls reported directly to, and received instructions from, the bureau of consulates of the Ministry of Commerce.[82] Moreover, it was intended that they should take an active part in that program of building up French trade abroad for which the new ministry was created. Early in March 1812 this was explained to the consuls by a circular of instructions from de Sussy, who also interpreted in the same light as the purpose underlying the creation of the ministry, the various annexations made to the Empire. Several of these instructions sent to America were captured by British vessels and reached the Board

---

[79] See *Almanach Impérial*, 1811-1813.

[80] *Ibid.*

[81] See for example: AF^{IV}1062, dossier 4, especially nos. 26-28.

[82] A somewhat similar though less direct connection existed between the consuls and the Ministry of the Marine.

of Trade where their reading seems to have made considerable impression.[83]

As was inevitable, time was necessary to weld together the various units of the new ministry and to adjust them to their altered functions. The experiences of 1812 served, however, to correct initial crudities and bring to the organization an *esprit de corps*. The official description of the ministry for 1813 shows throughout a broader and more definite understanding of its functions and a number of readjustments of duties.[84] The most noteworthy change, however, was the raising of the licence bureau of the first division, to the rank of an extraordinary division with its own subordinate organization. This change was perhaps an evidence of Sussy's belated appreciation of the significance of the busiest department of his minstry. Nevertheless, the change must have been a practical necessity with the vast increase of licence business due to the reciprocity arrangements with England in 1812 and to the financial policy of 1813. This situation was accentuated also by the increased administrative burden thrown upon the directors of the licence trade because of the rare meetings of the Conseil du Commerce after the creation of the Ministry of Commerce.

The suspension of the Conseil du Commerce was largely due to the prolonged absences of Napoleon during the campaigns of 1812-14, which made the holding of administrative councils impossible. Yet it is manifest that the centralization of commercial and industrial affairs in a single ministry superseded that main reason for frequent meetings of the Conseil namely, the co-ordination of dispersed administrative organs. The chief remaining function of the Conseil was the moulding of new policies, for which under existing conditions there was little necessity and even less opportunity. The net result of this change in organization and policy is strikingly illustrated in the character of commercial records after February 1812. Instead of state papers like the

[83] B. T. 5/21, p. 338, 9 July 1812, Q² no. 23.
[84] *Almanach Impérial*, 1813.

able reports of Champagny, Montalivet and Fauchat, and the consequent broad decrees, or the striking expressions of imperial views, we find little but a mass of routine correspondence and ministerial decisions rarely of general interest or significance.[85]

The creation of a special Ministry of Manufactures and Commerce for the execution of the Napoleonic navigation policy was, as has been shown, the result of a natural administrative evolution. Such a centralization of management was doubtless inevitable and without it the system would scarcely have stood the tremendous strain of 1813 as well as it did. For such a crisis de Sussy's direction of the customs service in its *defense* of the Continental System had peculiarly fitted him, although it is an open question whether under more propitious circumstances he could have successfully directed that aggressive commercial program for which the ministry was especially created.

The sure and *faithful servant*, however, de Sussy remained to the end. The long-repressed forces of the Continent released after Leipzig burst the breastworks and crossed the dikes of the Exclusion System. He rallied his *douaniers* in new trenches. From the north, nearer and nearer, with impetuous swiftness came tales of mobs venting their pent up spite against the customs guards who so long had tyrannized over the poor man's pipe and coffee cup. Some ministers quailed and some departed. Collin de Sussy went on giving his licences and collecting his duties till the tale of the Empire was told. On 21 February 1814, he wrote to Napoleon: "Sire:

"I beg Your Majesty to permit that his Minister of Commerce should lay at his feet the respectful homage of the sentiments which animate him for his Emperor and the best of Masters.

"In these great circumstances I have seen and felt only the fatigues, the pains, and the dangers of Your Majesty; but the thought that the enemies would violate your capital has not for a single instant penetrated my heart. I found therein always that providence after giving a liberator to France could not wish

---

[85] See for example: AF^{IV}1243, F^{12}2034-37, F^{12}2164, F^{12}2105, F^{12}2115, etc.

to destroy his work and that watching over the days of Your Majesty would assure a second time the safety of the country.

"I am with the most profound respect

"Sire,

"Of your Imperial and Royal Majesty,

"The very devoted and very faithful servant and subject

[86] AF^{IV} dossier 5, unique.   Count de Sussy."[86]

* * * * *

Pages have been filled with judgments adverse, approbative or neutral, regarding the commercial policy of the first Napoleon. Almost without exception they are based upon the sandy foundations of prejudices born of personal experiences, *a priori* theories or unreliable or at least inadequate evidence. Their repetition is unnecessary here. Sufficient has already been indicated in its proper place touching each feature of the Napoleonic navigation policy. As to its actual success or failure the evidence as yet utilized or presented by students permits no generalizing verdict. The one essential fact is that though the fall of Napoleon was the fall of his Navigation System the influence of his program has affected the history of a century and still lives.

Even as the historian may not with propriety sit in judgment upon the success or failure of the Napoleonic System, much less may he hold a brief to prove, by legal rule or economic dictum, its rights or its injustice, its wisdom or its fallacy. His proper task is to witness to the facts as he has found them, to show why and how in the crucible of a bitter war of land-power with sea-power the commercial program copied from England by the idealogues of the Revolution was recast by a master opportunist, partly by the fire of his own continental visions, largely by the pressure of economic necessities at home, and especially by the cold factor of outside demands—even those of so weak and so uncertain a neutral as the United States of a hundred years ago. In thus tracing in detail the evolution of one of his greatest undertakings there has been the guiding conviction that such a study is essential to any correct appreciation of Napoleon's statesmanship.

BIBLIOGRAPHY

Explanatory Note

The preparation of an adequate bibliography for Napoleonic commercial history should be a study in itself rather than an appendix to a specialized monograph which, of necessity, is based primarily upon archival papers and a limited group of printed sources. Inasmuch, therefore, as a number of extensive bibliographical efforts are already available for the special student of the Napoleonic field it has been deemed best not to attempt a comprehensive list even of much of the material actually examined for this study. The plan followed therefore has been (1) to call attention to the various research aids, (2) to suggest the character of the archival or other manuscript sources, (3) to indicate the most important printed sources under their several classifications, (4) for secondary works, to sketch the status of special investigations pertinent to the general topic of this essay, and also, to give a partial list of the more helpful general works. Among the contemporary publications special emphasis has been laid upon the selective list of pamphlets, as this aspect of the bibliography is most likely to be of service to others interested in research in the period of this study. A final revision, though by no means exhaustive, has brought the bibliography down from the date of its preparation (1913) to the eve of its publication.

Bibliographical Aids

Of the special Napoleonic bibliographies may be cited:

Davois, G. *Bibliographie Napoléonniene Française jusqu'à 1908*. 3 vol. Paris, 1910. Poorly selected and organized.

Kircheisen, F. M. *Bibliography of Napoleon*. 171 pp. London, 1902. Scientific and useful but inadequate, as is his: *Bibliographie du temps de Napoléon comprenant l'histoire des États-Unis*, 412 pp. Paris, Geneva and London, 1908.

Lumbroso, A. *Bibliographia del blocco continentale per servire alla storia della cotta economica tra la Francia e la Gran Bretegna fine alla caduto di Napoleone I*. 52 pp. Rome, 1897. A suggestive historiographical essay, but not well organized, and contains many valueless items.

Dutcher, G. M. "Tendencies and Opportunities in Napoleonic Studies." American Historical Association, *Reports*, 1914, vol. I. An invaluable historiographical paper. Well organized and most recent.

Of bibliographies to accompany Napoleonic studies note especially: Bourne, E. G., editor, Fournier's *Napoleon the First*, 1st English edition, pp. 745–88. New York, 1903; and
Fournier, A., *Napoleon the First, a biography*, 2nd. edition, trans., A. E. Adams, 2 vols. London, 1912, I, 467–507; II, 461–505. Both bibliographies are brief but well chosen.
Cambridge Modern History, vol. IX, "Napoleon." Cambridge, 1906. Lists considerably duplicated, with much useless material, but very helpful.
For the Napoleon Correspondence and related collections the best discussion and bibliography is an article in *La Revolution Française*: 56:345-59.

For general and current bibliography should be consulted:
Caron, Pierre. *Bibliographie des travaux publiés de 1866 á 1897 sur l'histoire de la France depuis 1789*. Société d'Histoire Moderne, Paris, 1912. Excellent scientific bibliography but very weak on the economic side. Continued by other current bibliographies issued by the same society, viz:
Briére, G., Caron, P., Burnand, R., et al. *Répertoire Méthodique de l'histoire moderne et contemporaine*, Paris, 1898. An annual bibliography of publications in modern history, a compilation of the bibliographical sections of the *Revue d'histoire moderne et contemporaine*.
Dahlman-Waitz, *Quellenkunde der deutschen Geschichte*, 8th ed., Leipzig, 1912. A co-operative work of German scholars for German and Austrian history in general. Similar in character to the Société d'histoire moderne bibliographies, are the bibliographical sections of the *Jahresberichte der Geschichtswissenschaft*.
Lanson, G. *Manuel bibliographique de la littérature française moderne*, 1500–1900. 4 vols. Paris, 1912. Helpful for certain types of sources.

Besides their general notes, and summaries of current bibliography certain historical reviews at times publish historiographical articles bearing directly upon economic phases of the Napoleonic period. Especially should be noted the policy of the *Revue des Études Napoléoniennes* (1912–) as illustrated by M. Marcel Dunan's very helpful survey in the issue of January 1913, entitled "*Le Systême Continental: Bulletin d'histoire économique*," 1900–1911, in *Rev. des Études Nap*. III, 115–145. See also for similar surveys: *Ibid*, I, 5–18, 117 ff.; and *Revue de synthèse historique*, January 1903, p. 69 ff.
In English the most recent and helpful survey for the special field is by Prof. W. E. Lingelbach, entitled, "*Commercial History in the Napoleonic Era.*" (in *Am. Hist. Review*, XIX, No. 2, January, 1914). Similar in character also for those who read Russian is the critical bibliographical chapter in E.V. Tarlé's, *Continentalnaja blocada*. Moscow, 1913.

For archival research useful advice and at times valuable assistance may be gained from certain of the published guides.

For PARIS see: Schmidt, Charles, *Les sources de l'histoire de France depuis 1789 aux Archives Nationales.* Paris, 1897. Langlois, Charles V. and Stein, H. *Les Archives de l'Histoire de France.* Paris, 1891. *État-sommaire par series des documents conservés aux Archives Nationales.* Paris, 1891. This and the *État des inventaires des Archives Nationales,* Paris, Imprimerie Nationale, 1902, are indispensable and are available for consultation at the Archives,— as are also certain manuscript inventories, upon application.

For LONDON see: Paullin, C. O. and Paxson, F. L. *Guide to the Materials in London Archives for the History of the United States since 1783.* Carnegie Institution, Washington, 1914. Of incidental aid for research in European topics. Cf. my review of it in *Miss. Valley Hist. Review,* Dec. 1914.

Students will also welcome the printing (already undertaken) of the finding lists for manuscripts at the Public Record Office.

For WASHINGTON see: Van Tyne, C. H. and Leland, W. G. *Guide to the Archives of the Government of the United States in Washington,* Carnegie Institution, Washington, 1904.

Library of Congress. *Papers of James Monroe.* Washington, 1904. A chronological list of MSS.

Idem. *Handbook of Manuscripts in the Library of Congress.* Washington, 1918. A very helpful descriptive list prepared by Gaillard Hunt and assistants.

Dept. of State. *Bulleiin of the Bureau of Rolls and Library.* Nos. 2, 4, 6, 8, 10. Washington, 1894-7. Calendars of Monroe, Madison, and Jefferson papers now in the Library of Congress.

MANUSCRIPT SOURCES

A. Paris.   I. ARCHIVES

The Archives Nationales at Paris have by far the chief body of material for Napoleonic commercial history, especially in Series AF ^{IV}–AF ^{IV*}, Secrétairerie d'État Imperial, and Series F–F*, Administration general.

Series AF ^{IV} embraces the correspondence between Napoleon and his miniters (in originals or minutes), the minutes of decrees, important ministerial reports and records, and the records of various imperial councils. Papers in AF ^{IV} series bearing on the system of licenced navigation were found chiefly in the following cartons: 1060–1062, papers of the Ministries of the Interior and of Commerce, etc. (An VIII–1814); 1080–81, etc. Ministry of Finance; 1087–1089^B daily reports of the Minister of the Treasury to Napoleon; 1195-2000, papers of the Marine on movements of shipping, smuggling, etc; 1229-30, Councils of Ministers, (a few scattering papers); and 1238–43, the *procès* *verbaux* of Councils of Administration of the Interior, with most of the reports considered by the Conseil du Commerce. These last were of the highest value for this study. The registers of the minutes alone are AF ^{IV*} 169–171. Cartons 1318 ff. also contain commercial memoirs and letters of significance for the period An VIII to 1813, including papers as to prohibited English goods. Supposedly the most important licence trade papers are in 1340-5, 1355, 1356 etc., but they must be supplemented by the related documents which have got into AF ^{IV} 1060-62, 1241-3, and 1318 and various cartons of series F^{12}—"Commerce et Industrie." Likewise the usually neglected diplomatic papers of AF ^{IV} 1674–1685 and the papers of 1800–1814 still kept at the Archives des Affaires Étrangères are mutually supplementary. The same remark holds also for AF ^{IV} 1801, documents brought from the Hague in 1810.

While the cartons of AF^{IV} comprehend the selected commercial manuscripts, many rare papers of prime importance are in series F^{12}, as well as original drafts or copies of material in AF^{IV}. On the whole, however, series F^{12} consists of a vast amount of routine departmental papers not only from the central administrations of commerce, customs, and industry, but also from the seaports, local commercial courts, etc. The bulk of these papers have never been used since they were consigned to the archives. In fact a careful examination of all of them would entail many months of often unprofitable labor. As an illustration of the fullness of these records it may be stated that apparently all documents respecting the licences and the cargoes of most of the licenced ships may be found in these cartons. The inclusive citation for this material is F^{12*} 265–266, Registers of Licences (important but apparently not complete); F^{12*} 258–260, customs books for the period; F^{12} 2029–2194, licences papers; and F^{12} 1866–2028 customs papers. Of the customs papers used the most pertinent were those of the numerous cartons under 1966. Of the licence material no attempt can be made to describe specifically the cartons used. Special reference should be made to those of general importance such as 2007–11, 2031–8, 2050–3, 2057–8, 2105–9, 2112–17, 2164–5, 2175, 2192–4. A manuscript index for these cartons may be seen on application to the archivist in charge.

Another collection of departmental papers is F^7—"police générale." Of this it was possible to examine but a few of the numerous cartons in the division F^7 3643 entitled "Movement des ports; surveillance des côtes (An XI–1815)." These yielded some interesting material respecting smuggling along the English Channel, the crucial point for my study. For Holland the same material was already available for use, having been published in Dr. Colenbrander's invaluable *Gedenkstukken*. For other districts material on smuggling under the Continental System is to be found not only in F^7 3643 but especially in other divisions of the F⁷ papers such as 8008–8395, papers of the first arrondissement of police which embraced the Seine Valley. As to the licence trade, however, the use of series F⁷ yielded regrettably meagre returns.

Equally disappointing was a test examination of the most likely cartons and registers from series BB,² BB³ and BB⁴ of the Archives Modernes of the Marine (deposited at the Archives Nationales but open only by special ministerial permission). Some meagre material in the Archives de la Guerre regarding licences has been brought to light by the various recent publications of Napoleonic papers there (cf. below: Picard et Tuetey, Chuquet, etc.) For material at the Affaires Étrangères I am largely indebted to the notes of Prof. W. E. Lingelbach, as by a similar arrangement of mutual exchange I owe to Dr. Peter Hoekstra notes from the Royal Archives at the Hague. Also for the Affaires Étrangères Mr. W. G. Leland of the Carnegie Institution kindly placed at my service certain notes gathered for his forthcoming *Guide to Materials for American History in the Paris Archives*.

B. *London.*

For the study of the British side of the licence trade during the Napoleonic period the most extensive materials were found at the Public Record Office. Chief among these were the Board of Trade papers such as: B.T. 6/185–204, "Registers of licences" asked and granted; B.T. 5/15–5/24, "Journals" 1806–15; B.T. 1/26–86, "In-letters" 1806–14, often of special interest on French aspects of the traffic; and B.T. 3/8–3/12, "Out-letters," usually mere repetitions of actions recorded in the Journals. For Heligoland, (1807–14), and the Ionian Islands, (1813–1814), the papers of the Colonial Office, (C.O. 118/1–10 and C.O. 136/1-12) were used. "Malta" (C.O. 158) was closed to research but C.O. 136/295 was pertinent thereto. For Jersey and Guernsey use was made of the Home Office papers (cf. H. O. 98/12–18), and some miscellaneous licence items were found in H.O. 91/1 and 2. A very partial examination was made of the vast body of Secretary of the Admiralty papers. These are largely irrelevant but often throw light on the workings of the blockade and licence trade. Series Ad. 1, "Inletters," embraces reports from the admirals and captains on station, (such as the Baltic, Mediterranean, North Sea, and Lisbon stations, the Channel fleet, etc.); letters from Lloyds, 1/3993–94; from consuls, 1/3845, and 3854–7; intercepted letters (1750–1810), 1/3977-81; from the Customs, 1/3968–9; etc. Series Ad. 2, "Outletters," comprises replies to the various correspondents in Series 1, also Admiralty instructions, including those to admiralty and vice-admiralty courts (Ad. 2/1072–78). Series 7, "Miscellanea," includes registers of applications and of licences to sail without convoy, (Ad. 7/69–71, 1811–15). [Cf. *Camb. Mod. Hist.*, IX, 816, on this Admiralty material]. For the results of the trade such customs ledgers as have escaped destruction were used. They include import ledgers of 1807, 1809–12, (Customs 4/4–8); export ledgers: 1809–12, (Customs 10/1–4); and a bullion export ledger for 1812, (Customs 8/1).

At the Privy Council Office significant matter was found in the "Register," Geo. III, vols. 31–83,[1–5] (Mar. 1793–June 1815); in the unbound papers, filed by years, in the cellar; also in several licence minute-books, partly covering the period 1805–9, sets of fee-books for 1808–12, and "outletter" books for 1801–6, and 1812.

At the Customs House a very few minute books and miscellaneous papers remain from the fire of 12 February 1814, which incidentally indicate the method of dealing with licenced vessels. I was able also to inspect a few ledgers from the out-ports which had been sent up to London for the researches of the Librarian, Mr. Henry Atton.

C. *Washington Archives.*

At the Department of State use was made of the volume of *Instructions to American Ministers*, (vol. 7), of the *Despatches from the Ministers to France*, 1806–14, (vols. 10–13), and of the *Consular Letters*.

II. Special Collections

The Jefferson, Madison and Monroe MSS. formerly at the State Department are now in the Library of Congress, Division of Manuscripts, where are also papers of General John Armstrong, minister to France, 1804–1810; and several collections of papers of merchants of the period such as the Bourne MSS., the Ellis–Allan MSS. and the Bowker-Taylor papers. These documents have some interest but throw no important new light upon the Napoleonic Navigation System. The chief Jonathan Russell papers are at Brown University. Harvard University Library is the depositary of the Joel Barlow papers. Those Barlow papers pertinent to this essay, however, are chiefly copies of printed letters or of official dispatches to the state department, except a project (undated but evidently of 1792–3) for a joint commercial attack by the French and American republics upon England. The Pennsylvania Historical Society has one of Napoleon's American permits among other papers of the period. The manuscripts of the American Antiquarian Society were disappointing for the subject. Equally diasppointing was my research for unexploited manucripts at the British Museum especially the recently acquired papers of Lord Liverpool who was partly responsible for the British trade policy during the Napoleonic war.

Isolated documents of lesser interest were found in various autograph collections of American historical societies and several city libraries, or their publications. Considerable material of this type has been made available also by certain European journals such as: *La Révolution Française, Revue de la Révolution, Revue des Études Napoléoniennes*, A. Lumbroso's *Miscellanea Napoleonica* (Rome, 1895-98), and his *Revue Napoléoniennes* (Rome, 1901—). *Nouvelle Revue Rétrospective, Revue des Deux Mondes*, and *Revue de Paris*.

PRINTED SOURCES
I. LEGAL, DIPLOMATIC AND ADMINISTRATIVE

A. France:

Almanach impérial, Paris, published annually by Testu. After 1813, "Almanach royal."

Archives parlementaires. Paris, 1860—. Still incomplete. In series I, volume 82 (1913) reaches 1794. Series II, (1799-1860) volume 127 (1913) reaches July 1839.

Bulletin des lois. Paris, 1794—. Especially series 4 (An XII–1814), 20 vols. and series 5(1814-5), 3 vols., but consult for the full period 1800-1900.

Bulletin d'histoire économique de la Révolution. Paris, 1906—. Issued by a special commission under the Ministry of Public Instruction. Cf. especially the volume for 1912.

Charpentier, A. *Codes et lois pour la France, l'Algérie, et les colonies*. 13th ed., 2 vols., Paris, 1909. For changes in the navigation acts up to 1909 see vol. I, p. 31.

Code de commerce precedé des motifs presenté par Regnaud de St. Jean d'Angely. Paris, 1807.

Corps Legislatif, *Journal des débats et lois*. Paris, 1796-1800.

Corps legislatif, *Procès verbaux des séances*. Paris, 1795-1800. Separate series for each of the legislative councils.

Dalloz, E. *Repertoire alphabétique de legislation*. Paris, 1870 et seq.

DeClercq, R. and J. *Recueil des traités de la France*. 2d ed., 10 vols., Paris, 1880-1907. Published for the Ministry of Foreign Affairs. Volume 2 covers 1803-15.

Duvergier, J. B. *Collection complete des lois, decrets, ordonnances, etc.* (1788-1824). Vols. 12–19 cover the Consulate and Empire. Paris, 1826-7. Compiled from the *Bulletin, Moniteur*, etc.

Gerbaux, F. and C. Schmidt. *Procès verbaux des comités d'agriculture et de commerce*. 4 vols. Paris, 1906-10. Important for tracing the Revolutionary antecedents of the Continental System.

Lepec, M. *Bulletin annoté des lois, décrets, et ordonnances depuis le mois de juin 1789 jusqu'au mois d'août 1830*. 20 vols. Paris, 1834-40. Less comprehensive than Duvergier, but with a few new items and excellent notes.

Martens, C. de. *Nouvelles causes célèbres du droit des gens.* 2 vols. Leipzig, 1843.

Martens, G. F. de, and C. de., (and others). *Recueil des principaux traités d'alliance, de paix, etc.* (1761–1808). 8 vols. 1791-1835. Göttingen, 1791–1835. *Nouveau recueil des traites* etc. (1808-39). Paris, 1817-42. Later editions continue it almost to date.

Merlin, P. A. *Recueil alphabétique des questions de droit.* 3rd. ed. 6 vols. Paris, 1819-20; 4 ed., 8 vols. Paris, 1827-30.

Montalivet, J. P. Bachasson, comte de. *Exposé de la situation de l'Empire français.* Paris, July 1811.

Idem. *Exposé de la situation de l'Empire presenté au Corps Legislatif . . . . le 25 février 1813.* 138 pp., with charts. Paris, 1813.

Vandal, A. "Les instructions données par Napoléon à M. de Caulaincourt après la paix de Tilsit." (*Revue d'histoire diplomatique*, 4: 54-78. Jan. 1890.).

The old and rather dubious collections of "official" documents edited by Lewis Goldsmith, Frederic Schoëll, and Guillaume Lallemant have long been superseded.

B. *Holland*:

Colenbrander, H. T., ed. *Gedenkstukken der algemeene geschiedenis von Nederland van 1795 tot 1840.* The Hague, 1905—. Vols. 5 and 6 of Series 1, cover 1806-13. An invaluable collection of memoires, correspondence, etc., but the general organization is somewhat complicated and confusing.

C. *England*:

Debrett, J. *The Parliamentary Register.* 9 vols. London, 1797-9.

Hansard, T. C. *Parliamentary debates.* London, (1803-15).

House of Commons. *Journal.* For 1806-15, especially the appendix which contains ministerial reports, statistics, etc.

House of Lords. *Journal.* (1806-15).

House of Lords. *Sessional Papers.* For important licence trade reports, cf. 1812, vol. 4.

Parliamentary Papers. Cf. 1808-1812 for reports of testimony taken by committees of the Commons regarding the effects of the Orders in Council and the licence trade. Valuable if used with the caution necessary for such evidence.

Robinson, Christopher. *Report of cases argued and determined in the High Court of Admiralty.* 8 vols. London, 1801-12. Vol. 7 is by T. Edward and vol. 8 by Dobson. Has much material on abuses of the British licence trade.

D. *United States*:

American State Papers. Documents, Legislative and Executive. 38 vols., Washington, 1832-1861. Vol. III of the series on "Foreign Relations," although devoted primarily to American diplomatic relations incidental to the Continental System, omits much of the important material in the Department of State.

Annals of Congress, 1789-1824. 42 vols. Washington, 1834-56. A later compilation from scattering contemporary press reports of proceedings in Congress.

Richardson, J. D. *A Compilation of the Messages and Papers of the Presidents.* 10 vols. Washington, 1896-99.

State Papers and Publick Documents of the United States,—including confidential documents first included in the second edition. 3d. ed. 12 vols., Boston, 1819.

E. *Russia*:

Sbornik Imperatorskago. (*Recueil de la Société historique russe*). Petrograd. Has invaluable collections of documents upon Russo-French relations of the Napoleonic period, such as, vols. 70, 77, 82, and 88 edited by Tratchevski; vol. 89 edited by Schilder; also vols. 112 and 121. (Customarily cited simply "*Sbornik.*")

II. Correspondence and Related Documents

(N. B. Citations under this classification are cited under the editor's name but listed alphabetically according to the author's surname.)

A. *France*:

1. Writings of Napoleon I.

Regarding the status of Napoleon's writings see the critical introductions to the volumes by Brotonne, by Lecestre, by Picard and Tuetey, and by Du Casse, but especially the essay in *La Revolution Française*, 56: 296, 345-59, avril, 1909. The collections of published writings include:

Correspondence de Napoléon Ier.; publiée par ordre de l'Émpereur Napoléon III. 32 volumes. Paris, 1858-70. Of highest importance for this study. However the two imperial commissions who supervised this monumental publication for various reasons omitted numerous papers many of which have since been published.

Of the collections of additional letters the following have been found useful:

Brotonne, Leonce de, ed. *Lettres inédites de Napoléon Ier.* Paris, 1898. Note the introduction as cited above.

Ibid. Dernières lettres inédites de Napoléon Ier. 2 vols. Paris, 1903.

Chuquet, A. M., ed. *Inédits Napoléoniens.* Paris, 1913. Chiefly military orders and decisions, but contains some letters bearing upon economic matters in 1812-3. Cf., by the same editor, *Ordres et Apostilles, 1799-1815.* 3 vols. Paris, 1912. But note that Chuquet's *Lettres de 1812*, etc. are not Napoleon's letters.

Du Casse, A., ed. *Supplement à la Correspondance de Napoléon Ier.* Paris, 1887. Contents of no value for me, but note introduction. Cf. *Rev. Hist.* vol. 31-34.

Dourille, Joseph, ed. *Quarante lettres inédites de Napoléon.* Paris, 1825.

Fournier, A. *Zur Textkritik der Korrespondenz Napoleon I.* In *Archiv für oesterreiche Geschichte*, 93: 41-181. Cf. also his *Napoleon*, Adams translation, appendix, both volumes. Chiefly letters to Talleyrand and Champagny relative to Austria.

Grouchy, Vicomte de, ed. *Lettres, ordres et decrets de Napoléon Ier en 1812-13-14, non insérés dans la correspondance.* 99 pp. (Sociète de La Sabretache.) Paris, 1897.

Lecestre, Leon, ed. *Lettres inédites de Napoléon Ier. (An VIII-1815.)* 2 ed., 2 vols. Paris, 1897. Cf. the criticism by Brotonne in his introduction to his *Lettres inédites* . . . Lecestre reprints the Count de Sussy letters from *La Presse* (9 March, 1844.) where I also used them.

Loyd, Lady Mary. *New Letters of Napoleon.* N. Y. 2nd. ed., 1898. Largely a translation of Lecestre.

Picard, E. et L. Tuetey, editors. *Correspondance inédite de Napoléon Ier, conservée aux Archives de la Guerre.* 3 vols. Paris, 1912-3. Also in an English translation by Louise S. Houghton, *Unpublished Correspondence of Napoleon I.* 3 vols. N. Y., 1913.

X . . . *Lettres de l'empéreur Napoléon du 1 août au 19 Octobre 1813, non insérées dans la correspondance.* Paris, 1909. Meagre collection and contains but a little new material—chiefly from the Archives de la Guerre.

Other compilations (largely superseded or not pertinent to this monograph) will be found listed in the Brotonne introduction, as cited, in the Napoleon bibliographies, and in *La Revolution Française*, 56:345-59. That much of Napoleon's correspondence is still unpublished is shown by the recent volumes of Chuquet, Picard, and others. In fact, my own researches have shown that some significant items remain unprinted even in the much used series AF^{IV} and F^{12} at the Archives Nationales.

2. Papers of the Bonaparte family, particularly such collections as:

Du Casse, A. ed. *Mémoires et correspondance politique et militaire de Eugéne de Beauharnais.* 10 vols. Paris, 1856-60. Good.

Idem. Mémoires et correspondance politique et militaire de Joseph Bonaparte. 10 vols. Paris, 1853-4. Contains a few letters pertinent to the Continental System.

Rambaud, Jacques. *Naples sous Joseph Bonaparte.* Paris, 1911.

Duboscq, Andre. *Louis Bonaparte en Hollande d'après ses lettres, 1806-1810.* Paris, 1911.

Jorissen, T. *Napoléon I. et le roi de Hollande d'après des documents authentiques et inédits.* The Hague and Paris, 1868.

Rocquain, Felix. *Napoléon Ier et le roi Louis.* Paris, 1875. Corresponspondence between the two brothers including some important letters omitted from the *Correspondance de Napoléon.* See also letters of Louis in Colenbrander, *Gedenkstukken* (cited above) and the *Documents historiques et reflexions* of Louis, (cited below under MEMOIRES).

Du Casse, A., ed. *Jerome Bonaparte et la reine Catherine. Mémoires et correspondance.* 6 vols. Paris, 1861-5.

Idem. Les rois frères de Napoléon. Paris, 1883. Evidently a reissue of the correspondence of Joseph, Louis, and Jerome, contributed by Du Casse as "Documents inédits relatifs aux premier Empire." to the *Revue Historique,* vols. X-XXI, 1879-83.

Murat, Prince, ed. *Lettres et documents pour servir à l'histoire de Joachim Murat.* 1767-1815. Paris, 1908—. When completed will supersede the unfinished collection by Lumbroso, also the *Lettres inédites* (1813-5), in *Revue de Paris,* 1898, V: 673—.

3. Kindred documents meriting citation include:

Bailleu, P. "Fürstenbriefe an Napoleon I." *Historische Zeitschrift,* vol. 58.

Bray, F. G. de. "Mémoires sur la France en 1803." *Revue de Paris,* 1901, I: 806-15; II: 74-98. Significant reports to Montgelas.

Gentz, F. von. "Journal de ce qui m'est arrivé de plus marquant dans le voyage que j'ai fait au quartier general de sa majesté le Roi de Prusse, le 2d' Octobre, 1806, et jours suivants." Appendix, *Dropmore Papers,* VIII: 495-559. Letters, in IX; 457-79. Other published Gentz material is scarcely pertinent.

Lumbroso, A. "Le Commerce français en 1811. Conversation de Napoléon Ier avec M. Ternaux." *Revue Retrospective,* June, 1894. (See other Napoleonic documents in this periodical.)

Metternich, Prince Richard, ed. *Memoirs of Prince Clemens Wenzel Metternich.* 5 vols. New York, 1880-2.

Molé, Count. "Les Cents Jours." Documents edited by G. Bord in, *La Revue de la Revolution,* XI: 1, 85, 93; XII: 17, 69.

Montgaillard, J. G. M. *Mémoires diplomatiques, 1805-1809.* Ed., Clement Lacroix. Paris, 1896. A series of confidential resumés of the diplomatic situation, with suggested policies, by a special agent of Napoleon. Interesting, but their importance for the origins of the Continental System has been over-estimated by M. Lacroix and others.

Rose, J. H., ed. "An unpublished paper on the Continental System." *English Historical Review*, XVIII: 122-4.

Savary, A. J. M. R. (duc de Rovigo). "Rapports official à Napoléon Ier." *Sbornik imperatorskago*, vol. 83. Petrograd, 1893. Covers the period of Savary's mission as special envoy to Russia in 1807. (For Caulaincourt's mission cf. Vandal).

Stern, A. "Documents inédits sur le premier Empire." In *Revue Historique*, XXIV: 308-29; XXV: 82-107. Franco-Prussian relations partly bearing upon the Continental System.

Talleyrand-Perigord, C. M. *Lettres inédites . . . à Napoléon, 1800-1809.* Ed. P. Bertrand. 2d. ed., Paris, 1889. Pertinent for 1807. Cf. also G. Pallain, ed. *Correspondance diplomatique de Talleyrand.* 2 vols. Paris, 1889-91. Not pertinent. Also some letters in la *Revolution Francaise*, XV: 86-93.

Tatischeff, S. *Alexandre Ier et Napoléon d'après leur correspondance inédite, 1801-1812.* Paris, 1891. Complements Vandal, *Napoléon et Alexandre Ier.* 3 vols., Paris, 1891-6.

Tessier, J. "Le général Decaen aux Indes." Notes and documents bearing upon the colonial situation incident to the Continental Blockade. In *Revue Historique*, XV: 349-81.

König Friedrichs von Württemburg, *Politische und militarische Correspondenz mit Kaiser Napoleon I., 1805-1813.* Stuttgart, 1889.

B. *British*:

British correspondence of the period contributes little of pertinence for this study. However from the list of writings examined may be cited:

Therry, R.*Speeches of the Right Honourable George Canning, with a Memoir of his Life.* ed. 6 vols. London, 1836.

Stapleton, Augustus G. *George Canning and his times.* London, 1859.

Vane, Chas. W., ed. *Correspondence, Despatches and Other Papers of Viscount Castlereagh.* 12 vols. London, 1848-54.

Eden, William (Lord Auckland). *Journal and Correspondence*, 4 vols. London, 1841-2. Eden's treaty of 1786 was a prime cause of the whole Anglo-French commercial war, 1793-1814.

Fitzpatrick, W., ed. *Historical MSS. Commission, Report on the Manuscripts of J. B. Fortescue, preserved at Dropmore House.* Volumes 7-9

(1910-15) contain significant Grenville correspondence of 1801-1809. Usually cited as "Dropmore" or "Fortescue Papers."

    Hamilton, R. V. and J. K. Laughton, editors. *Recollections of J. A. Gardner*. Navy Records Society, vol. 31. London, 1906.

    Granville, Lord (Leveson-Gower). *Correspondence*. London, 1916. British ambassador to Russia prior to Tilsit.

    Horner, Leonard, ed. *Memoirs and Correspondence of Francis Horner* 2 vols. London, 1843.

    [d'Ivernois] "Documents relatifs a la correspondance secrète de Francis d'Ivernois avec la cour de Berlin." (1808 ff.) *Revue Historique de la Rev. Français et de l'Empire*. Paris, 1913, IV: 385, 577, 589; also VII: 130-3.

    Jackson, Lady, ed. *The Diaries and Letters of Sir George Jackson from the Peace of Amiens to the Battle of Talavera*. 4 vols. London, 1872-3. (British agent at Tilsit, Copenhagen, etc.)

    Idem. *The Bath Archives*. 2 vols. London, 1873.

    Laughton, J. K. ed. *Naval Miscellany*. Navy Records Society, vol. 20 London, 1907-12. Has material on the taking of Heligoland.

    Leyland, John, ed. *Despatches and Letters relating to the Blockade of Brest, 1803-1805*. Navy Records Society, vol. 14, 2 parts. London, 1899-1902.

    Sanders, L. C., ed. *Papers of Lord Melbourne*. London, 1899.

    [Malmesbury.] *Diaries and Correspondence of James Harris, first Earl of Malmesbury*. Edited by his grandson, J. H. Harris, 3rd earl. 4 vol. London, 1844.

    [*Idem*.] *A Series of Letters of the first Earl of Malmesbury and his family and friends from 1745 to 1820*. 2 vols. London, 1870.

    Markham, C. R., ed. *Selections from the correspondence of Admiral John Markham during the years 1801-4 and 1806-7*. Navy Records Society, vol. 28. London, 1908.

    Hamilton, R. V., ed. *Letters and Papers of Admiral of the fleet Sir Thomas Byam Martin*. 3 vols. Navy Records Society, vol. 12 of the series. Vol. 2 of these papers (1907) has material on the Baltic situation under the Continental System.

    Ross, Sir John, ed. *Memoirs and Correspondence of Admiral Lord de Saumarez*. London, 1838. Saumarez directed the British opposition to the Continental System in the Baltic.

    Rose, J. H. ed. *Despatches relating to the Third Coalition from the Foreign Office Correspondence*. Royal Historical Society, 1904.

    Pearce, C. F., editor. *Memoires and Correspondence of the Marquess of Wellesley*. 3 vols. London, 1846.

· [Wellington] *The Dispatches of Field Marshal the Duke of Wellington,* . . . Edited by Col. Gurwood. 8 vols. London, 1844-8.

Supplementary Despatches and Memoranda of Field Marshal, Arthur, Duke of Wellington. Edited by the Duke of Wellington. 15 vols. London, 1858-72.

Wilberforce, Robert I. and Samuel. editors. *The Life of William Wilberforce.* 5 vols. London, 1838. (Largely diary and letters).

Idem. The Correspondence of William Wilberforce. 2 vols. Philadelphia 1841.

Browning, Oscar. *Napoleon and England in 1803, being largely the Despatches of Lord Whitworth.* Camden Society. London, 1887.

C. American:

Of the writings of American leaders of the period the following have matter pertinent to our topic.

Adams, C. F., ed. *Memoirs of John Quincy Adams, comprising portions of his Diary from 1795 to 1848.* 12 vols. Philadelphia, 1874-77.

Ford, W. C., ed. *Writings of John Quincy Adams.* New York, 1912—. Vols. 3-6 (1801-18) are especially valuable for their reflection of North European as well as American views of the Continental System. See also the letters to his brother in Mass. Hist. Soc. *Proceedings,* se ies 2, vol. 10, pp. 374-92.

Donnan, Elizabeth, ed. *The Papers of James A. Bayard, 1796-1815.* Am. Hist. Assoc., *Report,* 1913. Washington, 1915. For other Bayard letters see New York Public Library, *Bulletin,* 1900, IV, 228-48.

Todd, Charles B., ed. *Life and Letters of Joel Barlow.* New York, 1886.

Smith, C. C., ed. *Bowdoin and Temple Papers, Part 2, 1783-1812.* Mass. Hist. Soc., *Collections,* 7 series, vol. 6. Boston, 1907. Largely papers of James Bowdoin and George W. Erving on Spanish relations.

Cheetham, James. *Letters.* In Mass. Hist. Soc., *Proceedings,* 41:841.

Rowland, Dunbar, ed. *Official Letter Books of W. C. C. Claiborne, 1801-1816.* 6 vols. Jackson, Miss., 1917.

Adams, Henry, ed. *Writings of Albert Gallatin.* 3 vols. Philadelphia, 1879. Volumes 1 and 2 are important for 1821-3 as well as for 1809-15.

McMaster, J. B. *Life of Stephen Girard.* 2 vols. Phila., 1918. Valuable for the large selection of material for the Napoleonic period found in the Girard commercial papers.

Gallatin, James, ed. *A Great Peacemaker; the Diary of James Gallatin secretary to Albert Gallatin, 1813-27.* New York, 1914.

Ford, P. L., ed. *Writings of Thomas Jefferson.* 10 vols. New York, 1892-1899. Note particularly volumes 8 and 9.

Randolph, T. J., ed. *Memoirs, Correspondence and Private Papers of Thomas Jefferson.* 4 vols. London, 1829.

Jefferson Papers. Mass. Hist. Soc., *Collections*, Series 7, vol. 1. Boston, 1905.

Washington, H. A., ed. *The Writings of Thomas Jefferson.* 9 vols. 1853-4, reprinted 1864 and 1884.

The Letters and Other Writings of James Madison. 4 vols. Philadelphia, 1865. Largely superseded by,

Hunt, Gaillard, editor. *The Writings of James Madison.* 9 vols. New York, 1900–10.

Idem. "Joseph Gales on the War Manifesto of 1812." Note and letters in *Am. Hist. Rev.*, 13:303—310, Jan. 1908.

Hamilton, S. M., editor. *Writings of James Monroe.* 7 vols. New York, 1898–1903. Volume V. covers 1807–16. For other Monroe letters of the period see: Mass. Hist. Soc., *Proceedings*, Ser. 3, vol. 2, pp. 318-40; New York Public Library, *Bulletin*, 4: 41–61; 5: 370–382, 431; 6: 210. Other important papers are in the Library of Congress.

King, C. R., ed. *The Life and Correspondence of Rufus King.* 6 vols. New York, 1894–1900. Other letters of Rufus King are in Mass. Hist. Soc., *Proceedings*, 49: 81–90.

Morse, E. L. C., ed. *Letters and Journals of Samuel F. B. Morse.* 2 vols. Boston, 1914. Some of the letters from England about 1812 reflect the commercial situation.

Conway, Moncure D., ed. *Writings of Thomas Paine.* 4 vols. New York, 1894–6. See his proposal for a "Pacte Maritime," vol. III, page 418 ff.

Wheaton, H., ed. *Life, Correspondence and Writings of William Pinkney.* New York, 1826.

Russell, Jonathan. *Letters.* Mass. Hist. Soc., *Proceedings*, 44: 304–21; 47: 293–310.

III. Memoires of Contemporaries

For the numerous *memoires* of the Napoleonic period consult the general bibliographies cited above. See especially excerpts of contemporary judgments of the Continental System in A. Lumbroso, *Napoleone e Inghilterra*. (Rome, 1897). This very precarious type of source material has been misused by many writers with respect to Napoleon's economic policies. My examination shows that most of these recollections are valueless for the subject. Among the few which are slightly pertinent are:

Bonaparte, Louis. *Documents historiques et réflexions sur le gouvernement de la Hollande.* 3 vols. Paris, 1820. (Rocquain testifies in its favor and it contains authentic documents).

Bourrienne, L. A. Fauvelet de. *Memoires sur Napoléon (1795–1814).* 10 vols. Paris, 1830. Many editions and translations. Has been carelessly used by many historians. Biased and inaccurate. Cf. Boulay de la Meurthe, and others, *Bourrienne et ses erreurs,* 2 vols. Paris, 1830.

Boyen, Herman von, *Erinnerungen aus dem Leben des Generals* . . . Ed. F. Nippold. 3 vols. Leipzig, 1889–90. Cf. vol. I, p. 353–4 on licence abuses.

Brougham, Henry, Lord. *Works.* Edinburgh, 1873. Cf. vol. VI for his account of the repeal of the Orders in Council, and vol. X for his speeches.

Caulaincourt, A. A. L. *Souvenirs du duc de Vicence.* Ed. Charlotte de Sor. 2 vols. Paris, 1837. Eng. trans. 2 vols. London, 1838. (Dubious value).

Caraman, le Cte. G. de. *Quelques mots sur les affaires de Hollande en 1810.* Paris, 1856.

Chaptal, J. A.C., Comte de Chanteloup. *Mes souvenirs sur Napoléon.* A. Chaptal, editor. Paris, 1892. Authoritative.

Gourgaud, General. *Saint-Hélène: Journal inédit de 1815 à 1818.* 2 vols. Paris, 1899.

Las Cases, E. A. D. M. J., Marquis de. *Memorial de Sainte-Hélène Journal de la vie privée et des conversations de l'empéreur Napoléon a Sainte-Hélène.* 4 vols. 1823.

Lavallette, Comte. *Mémoires et souvenirs du—. Publiés par sa famille et sur ses manuscrits.* 2^d edition. 2 vols. Paris, 1831.

Marbot, J. B. A. Baron de. *Mémoires.* 3^d edition. 3 vols. Paris, 1891. Considered authentic but untrustworthy.

Marmont, A. F. L. V., duc de Raguse. *Mémoires.* 9 vols. Paris, 1857.

Miot de Melito, A. F. Comte. *Mémoires,* 3 vols. Paris, 1858. Cf. vol. 1.

Mollien, F. N. Comte. *Mémoires d'un Ministre du Tresor Publique.* 3 vols. Paris, 1898. His criticisms of the Continental System are not in accord with his letters in AF^{IV} 1088–89.

Montgelas, Maximilian Graf von. *Denkwürdigkeiten.* Stuttgart, 1887. Favorable to the Continental System.

Pasquier, E. D., duc. *History of my times.* edited by d' Audiffret-Pasquier 3 vol. N. Y., 1893–4.

Pelet de la Lozère, J. *Opinions et discours de Napoléon au Conseil d'État.* Paris, 1833. (Eng. trans. *Napoleon in Council,* Edinburgh, 1837.) Of very little more value for me than: A. Gazier, *Napoléon au Conseil d'État.* (*Revue de Paris,* 1903, II; 160), or A. Marquiset, *Napoléon sténographié au Conseil d'Etat.* (1804–5). *Revue des Deux Mondes, 6e Per. Vol. IX, pp.* 359–85. Also Paris, 1913.

Richard-Lenoir, (F. Richard). *Mémoires.* Paris, 1837. Accounted spurious, but gives accurate information regarding the Napoleonic licence trade.

Richard T. B. "An unpublished talk with Napoleon," *Harper's Monthly* vol. 122, pp. 165-75. Napoleon at Elba admits the mistake of the licence trade. Cf. the Conversation with Sismondi in *Rev. Hist.* I, 238–51.

Roederer, P. L., Comte de. *Autour de Bonaparte.* Paris, 1909.

Savary, A. J. M. R., duc de Rovigo. *Mémoires pour servir a l'histoire de l'Émpereur Napoléon.* 4 vols. Paris, 1901. Cf. vol. III, chaps. XIV and XX.

Segur, P. P. Comte de. *Histoire et Memoires.* 8 vols. Paris, 1877. Cf. vol. 3, pp. 62–64 on Berlin decree—not significant.

Talleyrand–Perigord, C. M. *Memoirs.* Edited by the duc de Broglie. 5 vols. N. Y., 1891.

(Thibaudeau, A. C.) *Memoires sur le Consulat, 1799 à 1804.* Paris, 1827. *Idem. Mémoires, 1799 à 1815.* Paris, 1903.

Thiebault, Paul Charles. *Memoires.* edited by F. Calmettes. 7th. ed., 5 vols. Paris, 1894–5.

IV. Contemporary Periodicals

Magazines

The contemporary magazines consulted may be roughly classified as literary and journalistic. The first class contains articles criticizing books, pamphlets, speeches and legislation having to do with the contemporary situation. In this class belong *Blackwood's Magazine*; the *Edinburgh Review*, a chief organ of opposition to the Orders in Council (Cf. articles in vols. 11,12, 14, 19, 20, etc.); The *Monthly Review* (cf. vols. 140–4); the *Quarterly Review* (also against Orders in Council,–cf. esp. the articles against the Licence Trade in May 1811; and the *Anti-Gallican*. Of those on the Continent should be mentioned J. Peuchet's *Bibliothèque Commerciale*, Paris, 13 vols., and 1806; Posselt's *Europäische Annalen*, Tübingen, for 1806-15; *Paris, Wien, and London*, Weimar—Rudolstadt, 1797–1812; Karl Heinrich Fahneberg, *Magazine für die Handlung und Handelsgesetzgebung Frankreichs und der Bundestaaten.* (Of this I could locate only the initial number in correspondence at the Archives Nationales); and Luden's *Nemesis* (12 vols., Weimar, 1814-18) which contains the often cited articles by Dominikus entitled "Das sogennante Continental system zu Erfurt."

The "journalistic"magazines combine special articles with chronicles of the month's or year's events, (and often stock and produce market quotations) and the reprinting of government documents. Those used and *cited* in this study include the *Annual Register, The Anti-Jacobin Review and Magazine*, the *European Magazine and London Review*, the *Gentleman's Magazine*, the *Monthly Magazine*, and the *Naval Chronicle* (Joyce Gold, editor) for England; and H. Niles, *Weekly Register* for the United States.

Newspapers

The use of newspaper sources was found to be indispensable. The most important and most accessible for the full period 1806 to 1815 were the *London Gazette*, the official British Journal, *London Daily Times*, moderate ministerial, and *Gazette Nationale ou Le Moniteur Universel*, [Cited simply as the *Moniteur*], the official journal of the Consulate and Empire. For periods of critical importance such other papers were used as were accessible, such as: the semi-official *Journal de l'Empire* (i. e. the former *Journal des Debats*), *L'Indicateur*, of Bordeaux, the *Journal du Commerce*, etc., and the *Journal de Paris*, for France; British ministerial organs like the London *Chronicle*, *Sun*, and *Courier*, opposition journals like the London *Morning Chronicle*, the *Independent Whig*, *Bell's Weekly Messenger*, and the London *Examiner*, (weekly); also the pseudo-governmental *Anti-Gallican Monitor* (a virulent sheet edited by the double renegade Louis Goldsmith who having long defamed his own nation at Paris sought, after 1810, to wipe out the score by villifying Napoleon at London.) At Liverpool Public Library the files of *Gore's General Advertiser* and *Billinge's Liverpool Advertiser* were examined. Of American newspapers the *Aurora* (independent Republican) and the *American Daily Advertiser* (moderate Federalist), both of Philadelphia, were found consistently useful for both domestic and European news because of the extensive clipping service used by American newspapers of the period. Use was made also of the *National Intelligencer* (official) the *Columbian Centinel* of Boston, the *Connecticut Mirror* of Hartford, and the New York *Commercial Advertiser*. Some of these papers were used at the British Museum, Library of Congress, New York Public Library, the Mercantile Library of Philadelphia, Harvard, Yale, Cornell, Kansas, and Pennsylvania University libraries. For research in European journals of the period it is worthy of note that by far the best collection found in the United States was that at Yale University, regarding which see: *A List of Newspapers in Yale University Library*. New Haven, 1916.

V. Contemporary Books and Pamphlets

As the number of items examined, which might be included in this list, is large it has seemed best to give here only a selected list of the more pertinent brochures published in the period 1805–1815. In most cases I have indicated for the benefit of other researchers where each item was used, viz: B.M. (British Museum), B.N. (Bibliothéque Nationale), C.U. (Cornell University), L.C. (Library of Congress), U. of P. (University of Pa.), etc. Some of the items excluded from this list willl be found listed in the varous bibliographies for the field. The bibliography for the article "Commerce" in Coquelin et Guillaumin,

Dictionnaire de l'économie politique (4th ed., 2 vols. Paris, 1873.) merits special mention on this score.

Anon. *Account of the interesting island of Heligoland*. London, 1811. [B.M.]

Anon. *An Abstract of the Evidence lately taken in the House of Commons against the Orders in Council*, etc. London, 1812. (One-sided.) [U. of P.]

Anon. *An appeal to the people on the causes and consequences of a war with Great Britain*. Boston, T. B. Wait, 1811. [B.M.]

Anon. *Analysis of the three Orders in Council of November 11, 1807*. (Translation of an English work published in London, 3 December 1807. Cf. the *Moniteur*, 22 November 1810.)

Anon. *L'Angleterre considerée comme la cause des conquêtes de Napoléon sur le Continent. Reflexions adressées aux membres du Parlement. Traduit de l'Anglais sur le seconde edition*. Paris. Imprimerie impérial, 1810. [B.N.]

Anon. *An Examination of the Conduct of Great Britain respecting Neutrals*. Philadelphia, 1807. (Ascribed to Tench Coxe.) [U. of Kans.]

Anon. *Considerations on the relative state of Great Britain in May, 1813*. (Tory. Bombastic. Bears on the Continental System and the War of 1812.) [B.M.]

Anon. *Des interêts de l'Angleterre dans la Baltique*. London, 1808.) (Suggests means to control the Baltic trade.) [B.M.]

Anon. *A Discourse upon the true Character of our Late Proceedings in the Baltic, ...* London, 1808. (Condemns the Copenhagen attack.) [C.U.]

Anon. *An Attempt to elucidate the pernicious consequences of a deviation from the principles of the Orders in Council*. London, 1809. [B.M.]

Anon. *Concessions to America the Bane of Great Britain*. London, 1807. [B.M.]

Anon. *General remarks on our commerce with the Continent*. 54 pp. London, 16 April, 1806. (On securing new markets in Prussia, Russia, and especially South America.) [B.M.]

Anon. *Hints to All Classes on the State of the Country in this Momentous Crisis. By One of the People*. London, 1812. [B.M.]

Anon. *Hints to Both Parties, or Observations on the Proceedings in Parliament upon the Petitions against the Orders in Council, and on the Conduct of his Majesty's Ministers in granting Licences to import the staple commodities of the Enemy*. New York, 1808. (Against licences, for a strict blockade.) [C.U.]

Anon. *Inquiry into the state of our commercial relations with the Northern Powers*. London, 1811. (Attacks the British licence trade). [B.M.]

Anon. *Letters from Albion to a friend on the Continent.* 1810–13. 2 vols. London, 1813. (Influential but not of special merit.)

Anon. *Letters under the signatures of Senex and of a Farmer comprehending an Examination of the Conduct of our Executive towards France and Great Britain,* . . . . Baltimore, 1809. [C.U.]

Anon. *Mémoire sur la conduite de la France et de l'Angleterre a l'égard des Neutres.* Paris, Galland, 1810. Probably by Lesur (cf. below) but d' Hauterive also was writing such a work at this time, (cf. Aff. Etr., Mémoires et Documents, Angleterre, vol. 64.)

Anon. *Orders in Council, or An Examination of the justice, legality and policy of the New System of Commercial Regulations.* 2nd. ed., London, 1808. (Good.) [C.U.]

Anon. *Principles of Negotiation, and substance of the late overtures and pending discussions between England, France and Russia.* London, 1808. [B.M.]

Anon. *Thoughts on the present State of England with respect to France.* London, 1806. [B.M.]

Anon. *The Crisis.* London, 24 Sept.–4 Nov., 1807. (By the author of *Plain Facts or a Review of the Conduct of the Late Ministers.* Strong against neutral trade.) [C.U.]

Anon. *The Genius and Disposition of the French Government.* Baltimore, 1810. (Received much contemporary notice. Ascribed to Robert Walsh.)

Anon. *The License System.* In *Quarterly Review,* May, 1811. London, 1811.

Anon. *The policy and interest of Great Britain with respect to Malta.* 156 pp. London, 1805. (Military not commercial. Cf. the *Monthly Review,* vol. 47, p. 200.) [B.M.]

Anon. *The Real State of England, 1809.* 117 pp. London, [1809].

Anon. *The Reason Why. In answer to a Pamphlet entitled, "Why Do We Go to War,"* . . . . London, 1803. (Commercial reasons for the rupture of the Peace of Amiens). [C.U.]

Anon. *The Six Letters of A. B. on the differences between Great Britain and the United States of America* . . . . London. [B.M.]

Anon. *The State of Britain abroad and at home in the eventful year 1808; by an Englishman of no party.* London, 1808. [B.M.]

Anon. *Trade under Regulation Licenses.* London, 1811. (Cf. *Camb. Mod. Hist.* IX, 839.) [Could not be found.]

Anon. *Reflexions sur le Commerce.* 16 pp. Paris, 1789. (One of the first Revolutionary arguments for protection of French vs. English trade. Others noted in Gerbaux et Schmidt, *Procès-verbaux.*) [C.U.]

Anon. *War without Disguise; or, the Frauds of Neutral Commerce. Justification of Belligerent Captures With Observations on the Answer to War in Disguise and Mr. Madison's Examination, Showing that the true Interests of America Require the Rigid Application of the British Rule of '56.* Printed in America, 1807. (Striking arguments apparently by an influential New York lawyer.) [C.U.]

Antibarbaro, Amadeo. *Ueber die Handelspolitik von Grossbrittanien dem Verehrern des Vaterlands gewidmet, Aus dem Spanischen uebersetzt.* Madrid, 1811. (Apparently first written about 1804. An attack on the British Navigation System and British trade with Spanish Colonies.) [B.N.]

Arnould, Amboise. *Système Maritime et Politique des Europeans pendant le dix-huitième siècle;fondé sur leurs traités de paix, de commerce et de Navigation.* Paris, 1797. (Arnould was an authority on commercial statistics and relations and influential in the administration of the Revolutionary and Napoleonic navigation system.) [C.U.]

Aspern, J. *Public Spirit.* 104 pp. London, 1808. (Discusses the question of a mutual licence trade with France by which quinine may go to France. Claims to explain the "Ministerial" attitude.) [B.M.]

Atcheson, Nathaniel. *American Encroachments on British rights.* London, 1808. [U. of P.] New edition. 29 April 1808, in the *Pamphleteer*, vol. VI, nos. 11–12.

Atcheson, N. *Collection of Reports, etc., on Navigation and Trade*, London, 1807. [C.U.]

Atcheson, N. *A Compressed View of the Points to be discussed, in treating with the United States of America; with an Appendix.* London, 2 March 1814. [C.U.]

Baring, A. *Inquiry into the causes and consequences of the Orders in Council.* New York, 1808. (Important opposition brochure.)

Birkbeck, M. *Notes on a Journey through France, from Dieppe through Paris and Lyons to the Pyrenees and back through Toulouse.* London, 1814.

Bronson, Enos. *An Inquiry into the Origin, nature and object of the British Order in Council of May 16th, 1806.* Philadelphia.

[Broughton] = J. C. Hobhouse. *A Journey through Albania and other provinces of Turkey in Europe, and Asia to Constantinople, in the years 1809 and 1810.* London, 1813.

Brougham, H. *An Inquiry into the State of the Nations.* 6th ed. London, 1806.

Brougham, H. *An Enquiry into the colonial policy of the European Powers.* 2 vols. Edinburgh, 1803. [C.U.]

Chaptal. J. A. C. *De l'industrie françoise, 2* vols Paris, 1819.

Coessin, M. G. *De l'esprit de conquête et de l'usurpation dans le système mercantile,* . . . . Paris, 1814. [B.N.]

"Columella" [? Clement C. More.] *An inquiry into the Effects of our Foreign Carrying Trade upon the Agriculture, Population and Morals of the Country.* N. Y., 1806. [L.C.]

Courtenay, Thomas Peregrine. *Observations on the American Treaty in Eleven Letters first published in "The Sun," under the signature of Decius.* London, 1808. Interesting opposition views, written Nov.-Dec. 1807. [Harvard.]

Courtenay, Thomas Peregrine. *Additional Observations on the American Treaty, with some remarks on Mr. Baring's Pamphlets, being a Continuation of the Letters of Decius.* London, 1808. (Important.) [C.U.]

[Croker, J. W.] *A Key to the Orders in Council.* 19 pp. London, 1812. (Important.) [B.M.]

Dominikus. *Das sogenannte Continental-System zu Erfurt.* (Articles in Luden's *Nemesis.*)

Duane, W. J. *The Law of Nations investigated in a Popular Manner.* Philadelphia, 1809. (Good.) [U. of P.]

Eden, Sir. F. M. *Address on the Maritime Rights of Great Britain.* 2 ed 139 pp. London, 1808. (Three pamphlets published in Sept. 1807, Nov. 1807, and March 1808. Important in their bearing on the Orders in Council of Nov. 1807. At first published anonymously.) [B.M.]

Erskine, Lord. *Speech of, in the House of Lords (the 8th of March, 1808) on Moving Resolutions against the Legality of the Orders in Council.* London, 1808. [B.M.]

Faber. *Sketches of the Internal State of France.* From the French. Phila., 1812. [Harvard]

G———. *De l'Influence du Système Maritime de l'Angleterre sur le repos de l'Europe, son Commerce et son Industrie, par G———. membre du Conseil des fabriques et manufactures près le ministère de l'interieur.* 56 pp. Paris, 15 April, 1815. (Marks French reaction toward high protection, due to the British "dumping" program.) [C.U.]

Gaudin, M. M. C. *Notice sur les finances de France de l'an 8 (1800) au 7 avril 1814.* Paris, 1818. [U. of P.]

Georgius, G. C. O. *Finanz und Handels Pandora der neuesten Zeit.* Nuremberg, 1810. (Unimportant.) [B.M.]

Gerard de Rayneval, Joseph M. *De la Liberté des Mers.* 2 vols. Paris, 1811. (Legal exposition. Relation to Continental System indirect but significant.)

Haupt, Th. de. *Hambourg et le Maréchal Davoust, appel à la justice.* 94 pp. Paris, May, 1814. (Protest against anti-smuggling measures). [C.U.]

d'Hauterive, Comte. *Mémoire sur les principes et les lois de la neutralité, accompagné de pièces officielles justificatives.* Paris, 1812. (Jared Sparks Collection, [C.U.] Copy presented to William Duane by D. B. Warden, Consul at Paris.)

d'Hauterive, A. M. B. de L. *De l'État de la France à fin de l'an VII.* Paris, 1800. (Urges a Navigation Act against England to break down the English Navigation System.)

Hunter, William. *A Vindication of the Cause of Great Britain; with strictures on the Insolent and Perfidious Conduct of France since the signature of the Preliminaries of Peace.* London, 1802. [C.U.]

Hunter, William. *Thoughts on the Present Political State of Affairs, in a Letter to a Friend.* London, June 1811. [C.U.]

Independent American. *An Inquiry into the present State of the Foreign Relations of the Union as affected by the late Measures of Administration.* Philadelphia, N. Y. and Boston, 1806. (Opposition.) [C.U.]

Inglis, John. *Commerce as it was, is and ought to be.* London, 1811. [U. of P.]

d'Ivernois, F. *Effects of the Continental Blockade upon the Commerce, Finances, Credit and Prosperity of the British Islands.* Trans. of 3d French edition. London, Jan. 1810. (Argues that the Blockade has benefited Great Britain. D'Ivernois was a Swiss pamphleteer in the service of the British and with F. Gentz led the literary attack upon Napoleon.) [L.C.]

d'Ivernois, F. *Napoléon administrateur et financier.* 2nd ed. Paris 1814. (Of no value). [B.M.]

d'Ivernois, F. *Exposé de "l'exposé de la situation de l'émpire française . . ."* 2nd edition, Paris, 1814. [B.N.]

Jacöbsen, F. J. *Handbuch über das practische Seerecht der Engländer und Franzosen.* 2 vols. Hamburg, 1803-5. [B.M.]

———— *Bemerkungen über das Danische Prisenrecht.* Altona, 1808.

———— *Versuch eines Commentars zu den Russischen Beschwerden.*

———— *Seerecht des Friedens und des Krieges.* Altona, 1815. (Eng. trans., 1818.) [B.M.]

Lloyd, H. E. *Hamburgh in 1813, with a view of its condition in 1806-12.* London, 1813. [B.M.]

Lesur, C. L. *Mémoire sur la conduite de la France a l'égard des neutres.* Paris, 1810. (At first anonymous. As to its importance, cf. the *Moniteur*, 19-25 Dec. 1810, and *Cor. de Nap.*, 21:332.) [Cornell and B.N.]

[Lowell, J.] *An appeal to the People on the Causes and Consequences of a War with Great Britain.* Boston, 1811

[Lowell, Rev. L.] *Analysis of the late Correspondence between our Administration and France and Great Britain.* Boston and London, 1809. (See the *Moniteur,* 4 Dec. 1810. Cf. the *Columbian Centinel,* 30 Nov.-31 Dec. 1808.)

Lüders, L. *Das Continental-System.* Leipzig, 1812. [B.M.]

Le Comte de M.*** *Mémoire sur les colonies occidentales de la France.* 119 pp. Paris, 1814. (On colonial trade protection.) [C.U.]

M. le M. *Essai sur les moyens de forcer les Anglais à lever immediatement le blocus des côtes françaises.* 53 pp. Paris, 1809. (Chiefly on naval strategy.) [B.N.]

Marec (signé). *Sur le Blocus des Iles-Britanniques et l'acte de navigation d'Angleterre.* Paris, [8 Dec.] 1806. (Apparently a governmental defense of the Berlin decree. It is worthy of note also that Pierre Marec on 3 July 1793 proposed the first French Navigation Act.) [B.N.]

Medford, Macall. *Oil without Vinegar and Dignity without Pride: or, British, American and West India Interests considered.* 2nd. ed. London, 1807. (Candid, yet fair.) [C.U.]

Mill, James, *Commerce Defended.* London, 1808. (A reply to anticommercialists like Cobbett, and Spence. Contends that Bonaparte's decrees cannot hurt England.) [B.M.]

Monbrion, M. *De la prépondérance Maritime et commerciale de la Grande-Bretagne ou des interêts des nations relativement à l'Angleterre et à la France.* 364 pp., in 80. Paris, 1805. [Bib. Nat.–Binding and imprint indicates that it is from the Emperor's own library]. (Urges a continental action, under France, to combat the British Navigation System. Evidently a cause of the Berlin decree. Of the highest importance.)

[Morris, Gouverneur.] *An answer to War in Disguise.* New York, Feb. 1805. (Best known American reply. See, however, Madison's in his *Writings* ed. G. Hunt. vol. VII, p. 204.) [.LC.]

Nemnich, P. A. *Tagebuch einer der Kultur und Industrie gewidmeten Reise.* 8 bände, Tübingen, 1809–10. [Heidelberg, Universität]

Nemnich, P. A. *Reise durch die Schweiz und verschiedene Gegende Deutschlands.* Stuttgart, 1811. [B.M.]

Oddy, J. J. *European Commerce.* London, 1805. 2 vols. Phila., 1806. (Significant. Reviewed in Posselt's *Annalen* for 1809.) [U. of P.]

Penn, G. *The Policy and interest of Great Britain, with respect to Malta, summarily considered.* London, 1805. [B.M.]

M. T. D. d. P. *De la Guerre perpetuelle et de ses resultats probables pour l'Angleterre.* 60 pp. Paris, n. d. [1808] (Discusses effect of the Continental System upon England.)

Phillimore, Joseph. *Reflections on the Nature and Extent of the Licence Trade.* 100 pp. London, 1811. (Best account and criticism to be found of British licences.) [B. M. and U. of P.]

Phillimore, Joseph. *A Letter addressed to a Member of the House of Commons.* 67 pp. London, 1812. (Supports Brougham's attack on the Orders in Council and especially the licences. Supplements the "*Reflections.*") [B.M.]

Phocion (=W. L. Smith). *The numbers of Phocion which were originally published in the Charleston Courier, in 1806, on the subject of Neutral Rights. Reviewed and corrected.* Charleston, S. C. [C.U.]

Pinkerton, J. *Recollections of Paris in the Years 1802-3-4-5.* 2 vols. London, 1806. (Contains a forecast of the Continental System.)

Redhead-Yorke. *France in Eighteen Hundred. Described in a series of Contemporary Letters by Henry Redhead-Yorke.* Edited, etc. by J. A. C. Sykes. London, 1906. (Claims to be a revised reprint of the original.)

[Reimarus, J. A. H.] *Klagen der Voelker des Continents von Europa die handels sperre betreffend. Ihren fuersten dargestellt.* 15 pp. [Hamburg (?)], 1809. [L.C.]

Roscoe, William. *Considerations sur les causes, l'objet, et les consequences de la guerre presente, et sur les avantages ou les dangers d'une paix avec la France.* (Translated excerpts in London news items of the *Journal de l'Empire,* 28 Mar.-1 Apr. 1809.)

Rose, George. *A brief examination into the increase of the revenue, commerce, and navigation of Great Britain during the administration of the Rt. Hon. William Pitt.* London, 1806. (Rose largely directed the British attack on the Continental System.)

W. P. R. *A Few Valuable Hints for the New Ministry,* etc. London, 1806. (Urges peace with France.) [B.M.]

Schlegel, A. W. de. *Sur le Système Continental et ses rapports avec la Suède.* Hamburg, 1813. (Clever contemporary criticism of Napoleon's system.)

Sheffield, Lord. *The Orders in Council and the American Embargo beneficial to the political and commercial interests of Great Britain.* London, 1809. [U. of P.]

Spence, William. *Britain independent of commerce.* London, 1807. (Argues that British prosperity would not suffer if her trade were annihilated.)

Staël-Holstein, Mme. de. *An appeal to the Nations of Europe against the Continental System.* Stockholm, 1813. (Doubtful authenticity. Mere denunciations.)

[Stephen, James.] *War in Disguise; or, the Frauds of the Neutral Flags.* London, 1805. (A cause of the Orders in Council, the Napoleonic Decrees, and the War of 1812. Any question of the authorship is removed by remarks of Stephen in presenting a copy which is now in the University of Pennsylvania library.)

Stephen, James. *The Dangers of the Country.* London, 1807. (Urges retaliation for the Berlin decree. Is directly connected with the Orders of November, 1807.) [B.M.]

[Stephen, James]. *Observations on the speech of the Hon. John Randolph . . . . by the Author of War in Disguise.* (London, 1 May 1806.) New York reprint. 43 pp. (Significant relationship with Fox's Order in Council of 16 May 1806. Bears on licence trade.) [C.U.]

Sturt, Chas. *The Real State of France in the Years, 1809-10 . . . .* 6th ed. London, 1810. (Bad effects of Continental System.) [C.U.]

[Ternaux, Baron G. L. *Mémoire en faveur de la liberté du commerce contre les licences.* Paris, 1808. (Not found).]

Thornton, Edward. *Observations on the report of the committee of the House of Commons on the high price of bullion, ...* London, 1811. (Bad effect of the Continental System on England.)

[Weiler, J.] *Que deviendra le monde si l'Angleteere* (sic) *succombe dans sa lutte contre la France. Traduit de l'Allemand avec des notes par J. Weiler.* 32 pp. Paris, 1806. (Discussed in chapter I, above. Cf. Posselt's *Annalen*, 1806, article entitled, "Was wird aus der Welt werden wenn England in seinem Kampfe mit Frankreich unterliegt?")

[Walsh, Robert.] *A Letter on the Genius and Disposition of the French Government, including a View of the Taxation of the French Empire. Addressed to a friend by an American recently returned from Europe.* Philadelphia, 1810. (Introduction dated 2 Dec. 1809.)

Williams, W. T. *State of France during the years 1802, 1803, 1804, 1805 and 1806: comprising a description, ...* 2 vols. London, 1807. [C.U.]

Wilson, Robert. *Observations on the depreciation of money, and the state of our currency.* Edinburgh, 1811. (Well argued, shows clearly the effects of the Continental System.) [Univ. of Ill.]

[Yelin, J. K. von.] *Deutschland in seiner tiefen Erniedrigung.* n. p., 1806. [C. U.]

Young, Arthur. *An Inquiry into the Rise of Prices in Europe during the last Twenty-five Years, compared with that which has taken place in England; with Observations on high and low prices.* London, 1815. (Cf. the *Pamphleteer*, vol. VI, no. xi.) [C.U.]

SECONDARY WRITINGS

I. Special Studies
A—THE CONTINENTAL SYSTEM:
General, Political and Economic Aspects

Leaving out of account the writings of Chaptal, Verneihl, Tooke and others who were either active participants in the economic history of the first decades of the last century or else keen contemporary observers thereof, the first account of Napoleonic commercial polices to be noted here is S. Millenet's *Le Système Continental et les Anglais*, (34 pp., Paris, 1837). Written in a protectionist atmosphere this brochure is a sympathetic though fairminded account of the Continental System, the lasting results of which are well stated. A different period saw the publication of *Die Kontinentalsperre in ihrer Ökonomisch-Politischen Bedeutung*, by W. Kiesselbach (Stuttgart, 1850), with its trenchant treatment of the weaknesses of the blockade program. Considering the paucity of sources available for research prior to the publication of Napoleon's correspondence and the opening of archives it is a creditable study. Though an unusually rare book today it is still significant because of its influence upon later writers, many of whom, indeed, have slavishly used it. However except for its notice by those contributors to the economic dictionaries, etc. of the later 19th Century who touch upon the Continental System, the influence of Kiesselbach's study would seem to have been slight for more than forty years. [Cf. the dictionaries of Coquellin et Guillaumin, Say, Cons, Rotteck und Welcker, Palgrave, etc.]. Of course the Continental System was noticed also by general historians like Beer (*Geschichte des Welthandels*, Vienna, 1884); Thiers (*Consulat et Empire*, Paris, 1845-62), etc.

The revival of interest in the Continental System came about 1893 when Dr. J. Holland Rose published his article on "Napoleon and English Commerce," (*Eng. Hist. Review*, VIII, 704–25). This article has been expanded, and recast by Dr. Rose for his chapter on the "Continental System" in the *Cambridge Modern History* (vol. IX, pp. 361–389); also for his essay entitled, "England's Commercial Struggle with Napoleon." (*Lectures on the History of the Nineteenth Century*. Kirkpatrick, editor. Cambridge, 1902, pp. 59–78); in his *Life of Napoleon I*. (4th ed., London, 1910); and in his *Napoleonic Studies* (London, 2nd ed., 1906), which includes several other earlier magazine articles such as "Britain's Food Supply in the Napoleonic War" (cf. the *Monthly Review*, March, 1902). Although in the preparation of these various essays on the British economic contest with Napoleon the use of much printed material of doubtful value seems to have been preferred to an examination of the mass of pertinent material in the London archives, nevertheless a few papers from the Foreign Office and Admiralty have been well exploited. Indeed the exploitation of these selected papers has been the chief contribution made by Dr. Rose aside from the very felicitous and suggestive presentation of his subject. Almost coincidently with the original essay by Dr. Rose appeared the late Admiral A. T. Mahan's study of the *Influence of Sea Power upon the French Revolution and Empire* (2 vols., London and Boston, 1893; N. Y., 1898, etc.). It involved a treatment of the Continental System from the naval and neutral standpoint which, despite the inadequacy of the sources used, still remains in many respects the best available account of the Napoleonic program.

The renewed interest in the Continental System was shared also by the compatriots of Kiesselbach, for in 1894 at Naumburg appeared a Leipzig dissertation by P. Rocke on *Die Kontinentalsperre und ihre Einwirkungen auf die französische Industrie*, which needs mention not for its own merits but as forecasting the chief lines of later monographic work in the field, namely, either local studies or else studies of special aspects of the Continental System. Both tendencies are shown, for example, in the careful study by Albin König on *Die sächsische Baumwollenindustrie am ende des vorigen Jahrhunderts und während der Kontinentalsperre* (Leipzig, 1899), while the local interest accounts for the gymnasium program by K. A. H. Hitzigrath entitled *Hamburg und die Kontinentalsperre* (30 pp., Hamburg, 1900), based partly on source material.

Meanwhile largely inspired, it would seem, by the work of Rose and Mahan, Baron Alberto Lumbroso had published his *Napoleone e Inghilterra, saggio sulle origini del blocco continentale*, (361 pp., Rome, 1897). This comprehensive and suggestive study was based upon secondary material, but it was significant because with its accompanying bibliography it demonstrated that the Continental System was already an important subject of research. It evoked a number of historiographical articles, among them one in the *Quarterly Review* for 1898, and another entitled, "The Continental System of Napoleon" in the *Political Science Quarterly* (XIII, 213–231, June 1898) by Professor W. M. Sloane whose own interest in the subject had appeared in his *Life of Napoleon Bonaparte* (N. Y., 1894–7. Rev. ed., 4 vols., N. Y., 1910). A further recognition of the significance which the subject had assumed was the appearance in 1904 of the seventh volume of A. Sorel's *L'Europe et la Révolution Française, 1789-1815* (8 vols., Paris, 1885–1904) entitled "Le Système Continental, Le Grande Empire," being chiefly a political interpretation of Napoleon's policy.

Studies involving various aspects of the Continental System have multiplied since 1904 and have improved in scholarship with the more extensive use of archival sources. Pioneers in this respect were Dr. Paul Darmstädter, M. George Servières, M. Charles Schmidt, and M. de Lanzac de Laborie. Dr. Darmstädter's *Das Grossherzoglum Frankfurt. Ein Kulturbild aus der Rheinbundzeit* (Frankfurt, A. M., 1901) contains a short but careful account of the Continental System. His excellent *Studien zur Napoleonischen Wirtschaftspolitik* in the *Vierteljahrschrift für Sozial und Wirtschaftsgeschichte*, II, 559–615, III, 1–31, (Berlin 1904-5), treat, on the basis of documents at the Archives Nationales, Napoleon's protective tariff policy for French industries. He later published *Studien zur bayerischen Wirtschaftspolitik in der Rheinbundszeit*, a discussion of Napoleon's trade treaties with Bavaria, Naples, etc. for which he used Bavarian and Italian archives. M. Servières in his *L'Allemagne française sous Napoléon I.* (Paris, 1904) gives special attention to the Hanse towns, in which connection he devotes much of a chapter to a hasty account of French licences. *Le Grande-Duché de Berg, 1806-1813: Étude sur la Domination Française en Allemagne sous Napoléon Ier* (Paris, 1905) by M. Charles Schmidt includes a discussion of the operation of the Continental System. As archivist in charge of modern material at the Archives Nationales, M. Schmidt has also greatly encouraged research in the Napoleonic field. His most recent article, "Anvers et le ·Système continental, 1792-1814" (*La Revue de Paris*, 1 Feb. 1915, pp. 634-52), however, is an interesting *Tendenzschrift* rather than a study of the Continental System. For the treatment of Belgian aspects of the Continental System we would turn instead to *La Domination Française en Belgique* (2 vols., Paris, 1895) by M. de Lanzac de Laborie. More recently in his *Paris sous Napoleon* (8 vols., Paris, 1905–1913), vol. VI, "Le Monde des Affaires et du Travail" (Paris, 1910) the same writer has given the best account we have of the effect of the Continental System on financial and industrial conditions.

The tendency to localized treatments of the Continental System has been most pronounced with respect to Germany. In most cases, however, such accounts are merely incidental chapters in local histories, and for this reason and because of the number of such histories no attempt can be made to discuss them here. [Cf. Marcel Dunan, "Le Système Continental" in *Revue des Études Nap.* III, 115-145 for an extended list of such works.] There may be mentioned, however, two little monographs distinctly on the Continental System, viz: (1) Anton Schmitter, *Die Wirkungen der Kontinentalsperre auf Frankfurt am Main: Ein Beitrag zur Geschichte des Kontinental-Systems* (Frankfurt, A. M., 1910, 44 pp.), a Giessen Ph. D. dissertation whose new results are not commensurate with its elaborate title, despite a use of various local archives; also, (2) Walther Vogel, *Die Hansestädte und die Kontinentalsperre* (64 pp., Munich and Leipzig, 1913) consisting of well organized gleanings from good secondary material. But all these studies illustrate the entire inadequacy of so minute a method of treating so large a subject unless there be a broad system of coöperation in such researches.

The Germans have gone also to the other extreme, however, with certain slight monographs intended to "cover the field" of Napoleon's commercial system. There may be noted for example: Robert Hoeniger, *Die Kontinentalsperre und ihre Einwirkungen auf Deutschland* (Berlin, 1905), a very suggestive political address before the Volkswirtschaftlichen Gesellschaft; (2) Gerhard Drottboom, *Wirtschaftsgeographische Betrachtungen über die Wirkungen der Napoleonischen Kontinentalsperre auf Industrie und Handel* (Bonn dissertation, 1906, 100 pp.), ambitious in plan but very inadequate in execution; and (3) Alexander von Peez und Paul Dehn, *Englands Vorherrschaft*, vol. I, "Aus der Zeit der Kontinentalsperre" (381 pp., Leipzig, 1912), a superfluous "popular" repetition of secondary materials, with an anti-English animus.

For Switzerland the plan of regional studies has proved more feasible than elsewhere largely because of the greater unity and simplicity of the problem and probably also because of more active research by local scholars. Even ten years ago the compilation of results for the whole field was undertaken by Bernard de Cérènville, as a Zurich dissertation entitled "*Le Système Continental et la Suisse,*" *1803-1806* (345 pp., Lausanne, 1906) a well organized monograph although criticized for the faults of over-hasty production. A somewhat better received study is' E. Chapuisat's *Le Commerce et l'industrie à Genève pendant la domination française* (337 pp., Paris, 1908). Its central problem like that of Cérènville's monograph has been the question of contraband on the French land frontier. In fact this emphasis of these Swiss monographs might warrant their being considered topical as well as geographical studies.

Though far less numerous than the local investigations the topical studies touching the Continental System have been the broader and more significant. In this class properly belong certain monographs already cited such as König's study of the Saxon cotton industry, de Lanzac de Laborie's contributions touching general finance and industry as well as treating the Parisian situation in particular, and Darmstädter's brief but valuable *Studien* with respect to certain large aspects of Napoleon's industrial policy. With these should be grouped Audrey Cunningham's *British Credit and the Last Napoleonic War* (146 pp. Cambridge, 1910, Girton College Studies, No. 2.), and E. V. Tarlé's *Continentalnaja Blocada*, (739 pp., Moscow, 1913). The former is a creditable study of limited source material, primarily of Parliamentary reports, and of several rare pamphlets of the period for the reprinting of one of which the study serves as an introduction. The opportunity remains, then, for a more thorough investigation of the same question based on a comprehensive use of the body of pamphlet literature and contemporary newspapers, and an examination of Treasury and Exchequer papers which should prove as valuable as the Mollien reports exploited by M. de Lanzac de Laborie. Professor Tarlé's large volume is in some ways the most notable monograph yet written on the Continental Blockade and should be a distinct contribution to Napoleonic literature. It represents extensive archival research in France, England, Holland and elsewhere although most regrettably not in Russia, despite the fact that the book is written in the Russian language. The emphasis of the work is upon industrial development, thus continuing the author's earlier studies for the Revolutionary period, and also complementing Dr. Darmstädter's *Studien* already mentioned. Indeed it is believed that Professor Tarlé might well have limited his study to his special interest, thereby avoiding various surprising errors of fact and of citation, the results either of too comprehensive a plan of treatment or of over-hasty writing. (For other reviews of Tarlé, cf. *Rev. Hist.*, Jan. 1914, *Rev. des Études Nap.*, May 1914, etc.)

B—*The Blockade*: *Legal and Strategic Aspects*

Besides the economic studies thus far discussed the Continental Blockade has naturally evoked much interest in the legal problems involved. Of recent special treatises on the subject, for example, we have the suggestive *Essai sur le Droit de Gens Napoléoniens, d'après la correspondance, 1800-1807* by E. Chevalley (190 pp., Paris, n. d.), and the well organized and perspicuous doctoral dissertation of Fernand Bertin for the Faculty of Law of the University of Paris, entitled *Le Blocus continental*: *Ses origines*; *ses effets. Étude de Droit Internationale*, (219 pp., Paris, 1901). The question however has been recognized by writers on international law for a century as one of special significance. Among the best of these numerous discussions are counted: Paul Fauchille, *Du blocus maritime, Étude de droit international et de droit comparé* (Paris, 1882), and Hautefeuille, *Des droits et des devoirs des nations neutres en temps de guerre maritime* (3 vol. Paris. 1868, vol. II, p. 177 ff.). As to the legal aspects of the license trade perhaps the most useful accounts are: H. W. Halleck, *International Law* (3rd ed., 2 vols., London, 1893); H. Wheaton, *Elements of International Law* (8th ed., Boston, 1866); Wildman, etc.

In so far as the blockade and neutrality problems affect naval strategy Mahan's *Influence of Sea Power upon the French Revolution and Empire* is still the best authority. There seems room, however, for a good study of the efficiency of the British blockade despite the various histories of the French and British marine, which have been written of late, for a mass of interesting material remains to be exploited both in the British and French archives.

The application of the lessons of the Continental System to contemporary problems has not been neglected by alert students and publicists. The warnings of Mahan, Rose, and other students of the Napoleonic blockades have emphasized the vulnerability of Britain in case of a starvation blockade. At the same time German writers like Hoeniger, Peez and Dehn have found in the System arguments for the German naval and commercial propaganda. Similarly in England naval increase has been aided by tracts like John T. Danson's *Our Commerce in War, and how to protect it* (London, 1897).

The recourse to the weapon of general blockade with the outbreak of the World War in 1914 has evoked much discussion of precedents, particularly those of the Napoleonic period. While a comprehensive list of such literature can not properly be included here, a few typical articles merit special notice, such as:

Lingelbach, W. E. "England and Neutral Trade." In *The Military Historian and Economist*, Vol. II, No. 2, April 1917. A significant study.

Murray, Gilbert. "Great Britain's Sea Policy." *Atlantic Monthly*, Dec. 1916.

Piggott, Sir Francis. "Belligerent and Neutral from 1756 to 1915." In *The Nineteenth Century and After*, Sept.–Nov. 1916. (See his kindred articles in the May and July issues and others in 1915.) Justice Piggott's position gives special interest to these well-presented summaries, despite their bias.

Scott, W. R. "Mercantile Shipping in the Napoleonic Wars: with Some Statistics of Shipping Losses of a Hundred Years Ago." *Scottish Historical Review*, April, 1917. Slight but of interest.

Stockder, Archibald H. "The Legality of the Blockade instituted by Napoleon's Decrees and the Orders in Council." *Am. Journal of Int. Law*, X, 492-509, July, 1916. Trite.

II. BOOKS AND ARTICLES OF MORE GENERAL TYPE

From the standpoint of *international relations* as affected by the Napoleonic Navigation System, and the Continental System in general, the following have been among those used:

Adams, Brooks. "The Convention of 1800 with France." Mass. Hist. Soc., *Proceedings* 44: 377-428.

Adams, Henry. *History of the United States. 1801-17*. 9 vols. New York, 1889–91. Especially volumes V and VI. A scholarly work based on wide archival research, although too great dependence upon certain materials has affected the exactness of the account of American relations with Napoleon.

Ahnfelt, A. "La diplomatie russe à Stockholm en 1810." *Revue Historique*, 37: 68 ff.

Caumont de la Force, Mis. de. "La Hollande sous Lebrun, 1812-3." *Revue de Paris*, 1897, I, 573–605.

Channing, E. *History of the United States*. Vols. I-IV. New York, 1905-17. Volume IV contains the most recent treatment of the American aspects of the Continental Blockade. In view of the materials exploited this account is dissappointing, but it is clearly more cautious and accurate than the account in Channing's *The Jeffersonian System* (*The American Nation*, volume 12, N. Y., 1906).

Coquelle, P. "La Mission d'Alquier à Stockholm." In *Revue d'Histoire Diplomatique*, XXIII, 196–239. Paris, 1909.

Coquelle, P. *Napoléon et Angleterre. 1803–1813*. Paris, 1904. (English translation, London, 1904). Prejudiced against Napoleon.

Driault, J. E. *Napoléon et l'Europe*; *La Politique exterieure du premier consul, 1800–3*. Paris, 1910.

Driault, J. E. *Napoléon en Italie*. Paris, 1906.

Ibid. *Études Napoléonienes*; *La Politique Orientale de Napoléon, 1806–1808*. Paris, 1904.

Ekedahl, W. "The Principal Causes of the Renewal of the War between England and France in 1803." Royal Historical Society, *Transactions*. N.S. VIII, 181–202.

Fish, C. R. *American Diplomacy*. 2d ed. New York, 1916.

Fisher, H. A. L. *Studies in Napoleonic Statesmanship in Germany*. London, 1903.

Ford, G. S. *Hanover and Prussia*. New York, 1903.

Hardman, Wm. *History of Malta, 1798-1815*. London, 1909.

Hall, Major Sir John. "A New Clue to the Mystery of Tilsit." In, *Nineteenth Century and After*, August 1916, pp. 322-36. Adds the latest guess to the controversy. For earlier discussions see Rose, *Napoleonic Studies* (supra); H. W. V. Temperley, *Life of George Canning*, (London, 1905); also various articles or communications in, *Notes and Queries*, the *Athenaeum*, *Edinburgh Review*, and *Quarterly Review*. For a fair summary of the issue see Fitzpatrick's introduction to volume IX of the *Dropmore Papers*, (*Hist. MSS. Com. Rept.*, 1915).

Johnson, R. M. *The Napoleonic Empire in Southern Italy*. New York, 1904.

Levy, A. "Napoleon à Berlin." In *Revue de Paris*. 1895, VI, 597 ff.

McMaster, J. B. *History of the People of the United States*. 8 vols. New York, 1883–1914. Gives an invaluable picture of American aspects of the economic war of England and Napoleon.

Mahan, A. T. *Sea Power in its Relation to the War of 1812.* 2 vols. Boston, 1905. Good.

Moore, J. B. *International Arbitrations.* 6 vols. Washington, 1898. Note especially chapters on French spoliation claims.

Idem. *Digest of International Law.* 8 vols. Washington, 1906. Significant because of its official acceptance.

Robertson, C. Grant. *England under the Hanoverians.* London, 1911. Has a very brief but good statement as to the Continental System.

Tatischeff, Serge. *Alexandre Ier et Napoléon, d'après leur correspondance inédite, 1801–12.* Paris, 1891.

Updyke, F. A. *The Diplomacy of the War of 1812.* Baltimore, 1915. The Albert Shaw lectures on Diplomatic History, 1914. Scholarly.

Vandal, A. *Napoléon et Alexandre Ier; l'Alliance Russe sous le premier Empire.* 4th ed. 3 vols. Paris, 1900.

Works bearing upon general economic questions and special or local interests: a very partial list of those examined follows.

Amé, M! *Étude sur les tarifs de douane et sur les traités de commerce.* Paris, 1876.

Atton, H. and H. H. Holland. *The King's Customs.* 2 vols. London, 1910.

Bacquès, Henri. *Essai historique sur les douanes françaises.* 108 pp. Paris, 1852. Has an interesting chapter on customs organization under Napoleon.

Ballott, Chas. "Les Prêts aux Manufactures sous le premier Empire." In *Revue des Études Nap.*, II, 12 77. (1912).

Bloch, Camille. *Études sur l'histoire économique de la France, (1760-1789).* Paris, 1900. Cf. on Eden treaty of 1786.

Bourne, H. E. *The Revolutionary Period in Europe.* New York, 1914. A scholarly text-book; chapter XXI is an excellent presentation of the Continental System.

Butenval. *Précis historique et économique du traité de commerce entre France et la Grande-Bretagne, signé à Versailles le 26 Septembre 1786.* Paris, 1869.

Chatterton, E. K. *King's Cutters and Smugglers, 1700-1855.* London, 1912.

Dumas, F. *Étude sur le traité de Commerce de 1786, entre la France et l'Angleterre.* 197 pp. Toulouse, 1904. Interesting but neglects certain material of value.

Gouraud, Chas. *Histoire de la politique commerciale de la France.* 2 vols. Paris, 1854. Meagre.

Hasse, Ernst. *Geschichte der Leipziger Messe.* Leipzig, 1885.

Levasseur, P. E. *Les traités de commerce entre la France et l'Angleterre sous l'ancien régime.* Paris, 1901.

Idem. *Histoire des classes ouvrières et de l'industrie en France de 1789 à 1870.* 2d ed. 2 vols. Paris, 1903. Cf. vol. I ch. vi, (brief).

Idem. *Histoire du commerce de France.* 2 vols. Paris, 1911–12. Disappointing.

Norway, Arthur H. *History of the Post Office Packet Service between the Years 1793 and 1815.* London, 1895.

Pariset, E. *Histoire de la fabrique lyonnaise; Étude sur la régime social et économique de l'industrie de la soie depuis le XVIe siècle.* Lyons, 1901.

Pasquini. *Histoire de la ville d'Ostende et du port.* Brussels, 1842.

Poulet, Prosper. *Les institutions françaises de 1795 à 1814; Éssai sur le origines des institutions Belges contemporaines.* Paris, 1907.

Roloff, G. *Die Kolonial Politik Napoleons I.* 257 pp. Leipzig, 1899. A much overrated *Tendenzschrift*.

Rose, J. H. *Pitt and National Revival.* London, 1912. Contains a fresh study of the Eden treaty.

Sassenay, Marquis de. *Napoléon I et la fondation de la Republique Argentine.* Paris, 1892.

Scheurman, Albert. *Itinèraire général de Napoléon Ier.* 2d ed. Paris, 1911. Useful but not yet definitive.

Schmidt, Charles. "Napoléon et les routes balkaniques." In *Revue de Paris*, 1912, vi, 325. Note also his article, "Les Francais a Raguse." *Ibid.* 1912, ii, 150. (Cf. his other studies, cited above.)

Scott, Ernest. *Terre Napoleon. A History of French Explorations and Prospects in Australia.* London, 1910. Good.

Stourm, R. *Les Finances de l'ancien régime et de la Revolution.* 2 vols. Paris, 1885. Cf. vol. II, pp. 11-60 on the Eden treaty of 1786.

Tooke, Thomas. *Thoughts and Details on High and Low Prices of the Last Thirty Years.* London, 1823.

Weeden, W. B. *Early Oriental Trade in Providence (R. I.).* In Mass. Hist. Soc., *Proceedings* 41: 236–78.

BIBLIOGRAPHY ADDENDA

Omissions from page 388, under "3"

Boucher Crèvecœur de Perthes, Jacques. *Sous dix rois. Souvenirs de 1791 à 1866.* 8 vols. Paris, 1863. For a critical discussion with copious excerpts see, Baron Oscar de Watteville, "Souvenirs d'un douanier du premier Empire, Boucher de Perthes," in *Revue Napoléonienne*, April 1908–May 1909. Although Boucher's extensive and very confidential services in connection with the enforcement of the Continental Blockade make his letters (especially volume II) of particular value to the student of the Napoleonic System—quite aside from their unusual literary and personal interest—yet they have been so generally neglected that the present writer discovered them too late to utilize them for quotation or general citation. However no statements or conclusions of this study would have been changed by their earlier use.

Dunan, Marcel. "Un adversaire du Systéme Continental." *Revue des Études Napoléoniennes*, vii: 262-275. Largely critically presented excerpts from pamphlets of Stephen Pichon.

Fiévée, Joseph. *Correspondance et relations de, avec Bonaparte, premier Consul et Empereur, pendant onze années (1802 à 1813)*. 3 vols. Paris, 1836. Contains a few points of actual interest.

Omission from page 402

Pichon, Stephen. *De l'état de la France sous la domination de Napoléon Bonaparte*. Paris, 1814. Sharp criticism of the administration of the Continental System. (Extensive excerpts given by M. Dunan in *Rev. des Et. Nap.*, vii: 262-275).

Omission from page 411

Blanc, A. E. *Napoléon Ier, Ses institutions civiles et administratives*. Paris, 1880. Has significant judgment (pp. 157-8) respecting the enduring economic effects of Napoleon's commercial measures.

INDEX

Abel, ———, Hanseatic minister at Paris, 102, 148, 242

Adams, Henry, 103n, 156n, 158n,184n.

Adams, John Quincy, American minister at St. Petersburg, 141, 182; opinion of, on Trianon tariff, 227, 229–230; notifies Smith of adoption of the Trianon tariff, 228n, 231n; opinion of, on licence system, 246, 254; notifies United States of secret negotiations between France and England, 267; opinion of, of Napoleon, 347

Admiralty courts, British, 39n, 87n, 150n

Adour, 110

Adriatic Sea, 17, 33, 276

Agadir crisis, i

Agde, 201, 238

Agen, 364

Agriculture, Napoleon's solicitude for, 78, 89, 124, 125, 235; licence trade as an outlet for products of, 78–96, 112–114, 120–121, 125, 128, 133, 140, 176, 199, 204, 250, 258–259, 262; condition of, in England, 81–82, 292; administrative oversight of, 348, 359, 366, 373

Aix, (en Provence), 364

Ajaccio, 258

Albania, licences for, 249, 259, 262

Albrecht and Delbrück, 137n

Aldini, Count, 294

Alexander I, of Russia, Napoleon's alliance with, 17, 140, 232, 233n; refusal of, to adopt a licence system, 246

Alexandria, 364

Algeria, exempted from Continental System, 67–70; licence trade between France and, 251n, 351

Algerines, 70

Algiers, exempted from Continental System, 68, 69; licenced trade with 238, 250, 259

Allan, ———, 272n. *See* Ellis and

Alost, 133n

Alps, 188

Altenberg letter, 104, 151–152, 154, 156, 157

Altona, 35

America, *see* United States, Latin America, Spanish America, South America

American Embargo, one cause for, 39; effect of: on French West Indies, 55; on France, 58, 71–76, 79, 113; on England, 81, 84, 101–102; repeal of, 142, 146, 182

American Revolution, 315n; French aid in, 2; effect of, in France, 3

Americans, *see* United States

Amiens, Peace of, 4; demands trade with Spain, 342n

Amsterdam, Bourne, American consul at, 39, 142, 154; insurance at, 57; Napoleon's orders to attack, 145; licences for, under Navigation System, 209, 252, 296, 304; tariff rates of, 215; Woute from, 301,

415

355; smuggling carried on from, 302; licences for, under Grand System, 307, 334n
Ancona, 18, 203; licences for, under Navigation System, 248; licences for, under Grand System, 307, 335
Angoulême, 114
Anholt, 336
Antwerp 35, 56; licence trade from, 133n, 137; Napoleon at, 161, 163; confiscated American property in, 170; need of American raw products in, 173; licence port under Navigation System, 201; licences for, under Navigation System, 238, 268, 286; licences for, under Grand System, 334n
Archipelago, Aegean, 48
Archives, French National, iii, iv, 1, 87n, 92n, 118n, 380–382
Aremberg, 104
Armand, Delessert and Co., *see* Delaroche, Armand etc.
Armed Neutrality, *1800–1801*, 4
Armstrong, General John, 29n, 34n, 76, 160, 272; protests against need of certificates of origin for American trade with Hanse ports, 21n; American minister at Paris, 30; transmits interpretation of Berlin decree, 37–39, 42, 43n; Napoleon informs, of the elimination of neutrals, 47n; protests against Milan decree, 71; protests against Bayonne decree, 72–73; protests against licences for American ships, 86, 101; reports on creation of neutrals for licence trade, 102; failure of negotiations for repeal of Berlin decree, 103–104, 151–159; fails to secure passports, 164–165; reports June 6, *1810*

decree, 166n; disapproves trade permit *projet* of May, 29–30, *1810*, 174–175, 179–180; inaction regarding decrees of July *1810*, 180–182; August 5 letter to, regarding repeal of Berlin-Milan decrees, 183–186, 207, 218–219, 221–222; information of, about smuggling trade, 191n; knows of secret negotiation between France and England in *1810*, 265n
Arnould, Amboise, 359, 372, 398
Atton, H. H., 150n
Auckland, Lord, *see* William Eden
Austria, 233; accepts Berlin decree, 17, 33, 34; Council of Interior classifies as a neutral, 50; Napoleon at war with, 85, 103, 104; Napoleon marries Marie Louise of, 160; Trianon tariff and, 226, 227, 231, 232; issued coffee licences, 247; included in Grand System, 306, 335
Austrian Netherlands, 160
Avignon, 260

Baden, 227
Baltic Sea, 48, 276; Continental Blockade for, 35, 90; British licence trade in, 84n, 247, 293, 311, 336; French licence trade in, 110, 129, 135n, 148; trade in, under Navigation System, 204, 222, 228, 244, 252, 290, 351; American ships sequestered in, 284
Baltimore, 62n, 177, 242, 257, 314
Barbary States, accept Berlin decree, 17; secure exemption from Milan decree, 69–70, 100n; trade permits for, 203, 249–250, 253, 350; Barlow minister to, 315n. *See* Algiers, Algeria, Morocco, Tripoli
Barbé-Marbois, François, marquis de, 71

Barbier-Neuville, ——, 358
Barcelona, 53
Barère, Bertrand, de Vieuzac, 3n, 200
Baring, Alexander, 1st. Baron Ashburton, 282, 398
Baring, house of, 83
Barlow, Joel, 271n; advocates commercial attack on England, 3n; presents demands of America, 284-285, 314-322, 329-330, 334n; secures acknowledgment of America's claims, 320-322, 330n; death of, 330
Basel, 215
Bassano, *See* Maret, duc de
Basse Bretagne, 52, 78-80, 131
Basses Alpes, Department of, 63
Bastia, 258
Batavia, 219, 220, 251
Bathurst, Henry, Lord, 45n; interviewed regarding trade concessions to France, 266, 267; policy of, criticized, 282, 313
Bavaria, Trianon tariff and, 226, 227, 231, 232
Baylen, 85
Bayonne, 175, 180; seizures at, 46; results of Napoleon's visit to, 51, 54, 55, 70, 162, 257; petition from, for coast trade privileges, 52; colonial trade with, 60; quinine shipped to, 65; Napoleon issued decree from, 72; licence trade of, under Continental System, 114, 133n; licence port under Navigation System, 201; licences for, under Navigation System, 209, 238, 296, 362; licences for, under Grand System, 307, 341, 342, 344, 362
Beauharnais, Eugène de, 211; to enforce Berlin decree, 18; Napoleon asks, for tariff report, 22n; admonished for non-enforcement of Berlin decree, 33; notified of new tariff, 211, 223-224; Napoleon explains new system to, 248n, 254n
Begouen, ——, 27
Belgium, 27, 165, 284, 286, 326
Benoist, ——, 358
Berg, Grand Duchy of, 227, 406
Berlin, 12n, 29, 43, 221. *See* decrees
Bernadotte, General, Jean-Baptiste Jules, 18, 31
Bigot-Premeneau, F. J. J., 27n
Bilbao, 52
"Biscay, Gulf of," 311
Black Sea, 259
Board of Trade, British, notes from, 35; method of, in securing initiation of French licences, 82, 84; refuses licences to United States, 102; grants special privileges to Holland, 141; result of Van Aken's negotiations with, 164; prototype of French *Conseil du Commerce*, 166, 354; effect upon, of French grain restrictions, 189, 205; attitude toward new navigation policy of France, 209; concessions of, for trade with France, 265-270, 291-296, 300, 301, 303, 313, 368; regulations for new licence policy, 281-283; criticisms of, 282; attitude toward American situation, *1812*, 318n; receives French *1812* decrees, 321n; decides upon new form of licences, 325; alters new system, 326-327; number of licences signed by, 330; regulations for Mediterranean trade, 336-337; reads instructions to French consuls, 375
Bohain, ——, 358
Boissè, Philippe, 137n
Bonaparte, (Buonaparte), *see* Napoleon I

Bonaparte, Jerome, 79, 84; notified of Trianon tariff, 211, 226n; Fontainebleau decree and, 231
Bonaparte, Joseph, King of Spain, 147
Bonaparte, Louis, 6, 104; King of Holland, 30; evades Continental System, 32–33, 452, 141–145; abdicates, 161–162, 224
Bonaparte, Lucien, Minister of Interior, 349
Bonifacio, 258
Bonvarlet Brothers, 301
Bordeaux, 57n, 355; protests against Berlin decree, 13; Lee American consul at, 39n, 48, 329; trade of 51, 79; British blockade of, 53; stock company for colonial trade at, 55, 56, 58, 60; American trade with, 70–72, 74, 152; English buying flour at, 90n; chief exports of, 91; Prussia buying wine from, 103; licence trade of, 114, 117, 120, 124, 128, 129, 133n, 135n, 137, 149, 188; port for American permit trade, 173, 175, 177, 178, 240, 241, 259, 290, 297, 319, 324, 344; Napoleon at, 162; licence trade of, under Navigation System, 198, 297, 300, 303, 304; port for trade with Hanseatic cities, 242; English licences for, 266n; French licences for, under Grand System, 306, 307, 323, 325, 338, 342; desires American trade, 317
Boston, 177; Jarvis from, 152; ships from, engaged in licence trade, 153n; shipping port under Navigation System, 242, 257
Boucher de Perthes, 9n. 12n, 191n, 230n, 233n
Boulogne, 191, 265n, 272n; army concentrated at, 33; licences for, 133n, 271n, 274, 275; Napoleon visits, 163, 264; English licences for, 266n
Bourbons, the, 234, 344
Bourbon, Isle of, 270n
Bourbon Archambault, 73
Bourne, Sylvanus, American consul at Amsterdam, 39, 142, 143, 154
Bourrienne, L. A. Fauvelet de, 11n, 12n, 18
Bourse, the, plans for, 19; effect of Trianon decree on, 221, 226n; effect of Grand System on, 312, 324, 325, 327, 333, 338
Bowker, see King and
Brabant, 163
Brandy, United States purchases, 20; Baltic import, 35; advantages of exportation of, 80; Bordeaux's trade in, 91; licenced article of export, 94, 95; licenced trade in, under Continental System, 109, 110, 122, 125, 134, 137, 188; permit for Americans to export, 172, 173; smugglers export, 191; licences for, under Navigation System, 238, 241, 243, 260, 261, 264, 266, 267, 268, 278–279, 288, 295, 296, 298; licences for, under Grand System, 306, 311, 323, 329
Braunsberg and Company, 301, 302
Brazil, orders to capture ships of, 61n; Regent of, ally of England, 81; French need of sugar from, 172; Trianon tariff and, 217; France accepts colonial goods from, 286; cotton from, to be exported to France, 327, 328
Bremen, American trade with, 21n; licence trade under flag of, 102; licence trade of, 104, 105, 148; licence trade of, under Navigation

INDEX 419

System, 203, 242, 245; licences for, under Grand System, 307, 341, 344
Brest, English blockade from Elbe to, 8; trade between Bordeaux and, blocked by British, 53; plans for colonial trade with, 60, 61; licences for, 133n
Bretons, 82
British, see England
British East India, see East India
British India, 300
British Isles, see England
Brittany, 52, 131. See Basse Bretagne
Broadbent, ——, 147
Brougham, Henry Peter, baron Brougham and Vaux, attacks Orders in Council and licence system, 282, 313, 321, 322, 326
Bruges, 133n, 163, 261, 336n
Brussels, 163, 280n
Buenos Ayres, 54, 176, 253, 299
Bureau Consultatif des Arts et Manufactures, see Navigation System
Burton, l'aine, 280n

Cadiz, 65
Cadore, duc de, see Champagny
Caen, English licences for trade with, 114; licence trade from, 133n, 137, 153, 289, 294; licences for, under Grand System, 307
Cagliari, 246n, 249n
Cairo, 342
Calais, 163, 326n. See Pas de Calais
Cambacérès, Jean-Jacques Regis de, 19, 118, 342, 343
Cambrai, 163
Campbell committee, 39n
Campion, ——, 137n
Caprara, 249n
Caracas, 176
Carcassone, 250
Carlsham, 135n

Carnegie Institution, iv
Cassel, 226
Castlereagh, Robert Stewart, Viscount, 321
Catalonia, 223, 342
Caulaincourt, Armand-Augustin-Louis de, duc de Vicence, 233n; connection of, with licence system as French ambassador to St. Petersburg, 140–141, 260n; instructions to, for American minister, 182n
Cayenne, plans for trade with, 56, 58, 59, 60; American proposals to carry products from, 172
Central America, 54
Cette, licences for, 133n, 248, 307
Chamber of Assurance, 57
Chamber of Commerce, 57, 87n, 112, 113, 151, 155
Chamoulard, Joseph, 271, 273
Champagny, J. B. Nompere de, duc de Cadore, 233n; Minister of Interior, 14, 349; action of, in economic crisis of *1807*, 14; views on neutral trade, 19–21, 29, 30; reports and suggestions of August *1807*, concerning expansion of Continental System, 23–26, 27n, 28; Cretet succeeds as Minister of Interior, 28n; Minister of Exterior Relations, 29, 38, 91, 155, 350; Armstrong's negotiations with, regarding execution of Berlin-Milan decrees, 38, 39, 40, 42, 43n, 70–74, 76, 101n, 155–158, 160, 164, 179; orders of, for trade with Spain, 52; buys quinine in Spain, 65; August 5 letter to Armstrong regarding repeal of Berlin-Milan decrees, 71n, 183, 184–185, 207, 221, 256; connection of, with licence trade, 91,

98, 102–103, 116, 127n, 139–141, 145, 236, 244n, 269; correspondence of, with Abel, 102; member of *Conseil du Commerce*, 167, 170n; receives copy of July 3 decree, 202n; reply to Armstrong's August 20 letter, 218; sends Trianon tariff decree to European princes 226–227; instructions to, for American permits, 241, connection of, with Italian licences, 248; Barlow presents America's case to, 284–285; Secretary of State, 352; able reports of, 376

Channel Islands, 265, 278, 279, 301. *See* Jersey and Guernsey

Chaptal, J. A. C., comte de Chanteloup, 78; Minister of Interior, 23, 287, 349; influence of, on textile industries, 125; favors licence system, 132n, 353; member of *Conseil du Commerce*, 167, 343; opinion of, on Continental System, 234

Charente, 110; licence trade from, 133n, 135n, 137, 238

Charente Inferieure, 238, 279

Charles, the, 143n

Charleston, shipping port for American permit trade, 173, 176, 177, 241

Chataud, *see* Imbert and

Chateauroux, 373

Cheminant and Kerkhove, 90

Cherbourg, 284n, 362

Chesapeake affair, 34

Chesapeake Bay, 314

China, 302, 325

Civita Vecchia, 18, 307

Clarke, General H. J. G., duc de Feltre, 244n

Cloths, need of raw material for French, 19; trade with Italy in French, 22, 24; advantages of exportation of, 80; licenced article of importation under Continental System, 121; permits for Americans to export, 173, 175; licences for Silesian, 245; licences for French under Navigation System, 250; exportation of British, 291, 326

Cobbett, William, 89n

Coblentz, 217

Code du Commerce, 19, 26–28, 225n, 234, 348, 365

Code Napoleon, 26–27, 225n

Coffee, 7, 14; importation of, considered, 22, 59; supply of, in France, *1808*, 62; Holland imports, 143; *Conseil du Commerce* to discuss supply of, 168; Americans not permitted to import, 176, 177; trade in, under Navigation System, 199, 239, 250, 267, 269, 270, 278, 291, 293, 297, 300, 301, 302, 303; Trianon tariff duties on, 217, 226; Austrian licences for, 247; licences for, under Grand System, 305, 306, 309, 319, 329, 340, 341; English licences for, 326, 327; lower price of, 338

Cognac, 133n

Colbert, Jean-Baptiste, marquis de Seignelay, 26, 235

Collin de Sussy, count, 38, 210, 319n, 325n; customs report of, *1807*, 22n, 23; proposes modification of customs legislation, 27; member of Conseil du Commerce, 49; reply of, on quinine inquiry, 64–65; report on and policy toward American trade, 74–76, 318; attitude toward licence system, 77–78; connection with licence system as Director General of Customs, 97, 99, 112, 123, 124, 135n, 239, 243, 244, 268n,

INDEX 421

275, 349–350; Napoleon calls, to Antwerp, 163; is notified of smuggling trade, 190; receives copy of July 3 decree, 202; Trianon decree sent to, 216, 217; favors inclusion of Holland in licence system, 251; report of January *1812* on Grand System, 308–309; asks for licences, 328; Grand System and, 328, 334n; reports on licence trade, *1812* and *1813*, 332, 340, 341; anxious about licence system, 337; pressed for funds, 340, 341; attends last session of Conseil du Commerce, 342; Minister of Manufactures and Commerce, 368–377
Cologne, 217
Colonies, connection of England with loss of French, 2, 62; Napoleon's plans for use of war ships in trade with, 16; efforts to increase French trade in produce of, 20–21, 23n, 25, 35, 48n, 49–50, 55–70; Napoleon's dreams of, *1808*, 54; trade with, in Algerian ships, 67–70; Napoleon denies he gives licences for produce of, 140; Trianon tariff and, 214–221; licences for, under Navigation System, 219–221, 240, 250–253, 290; Fontainebleau decree and, 230; licences for, under Grand System, 323, 331, 334, 343; overbuying of produce of, 338, 339, 341. See separate listing of chief commodities of; also particular regions
Colonies, Ministry of Marine and, *see* Navigation System, and Decrès
Columbian Centinel, 39n
Commerce, Conseil Général de, see Navigation System
Commerce, Ministry of Manufactures and, *see* Navigation System, and Collin
Commercial Intercourse Act, *see* Macon Bill No. 2
Compiègne, 160, 284
Confederation of the Rhine, commerce with, 22, 23n, 24, 27, 34; Trianon tariff sent to, 226, 227; Navigation System and 232, 304; licences for, under Grand System, 306
Congress of the United States, 75, 222n; passes Macon Bill No. 2, 165; proposed measures against permit trade urged by, 180, 181; threatens to declare war on France, 183; inaction of, after Madison's message relative to licences, 316, 319; passes Non-Importation Act, 321
Conseil de Contentieux, see Navigation System
Conseil des Prises, connection of, with Berlin decree and United States, 37, 38, 152; decisions of, in licence system, 115; American property condemned by, 171, connection of, with Navigation System, 244, 350n, 352–353
Conseil du Commerce et des Manufactures, creation and work of, 135, 166–210, 212, 213–214, 218, 219, 220, 223, 224, 228, 235, 242, 244, 250, 256, 260, 269, 271n, 276, 284, 285, 286, 287–291, 294, 295, 296, 300, 301, 304–309, 350n, 352, 353n, 354, 361, 364, 368; suspension of, 309, 323, 367, 368; December 30, *1812* session of, 332n, 333; last session of, November *1813*, 342–343. *See* Navigation System
Conseil Général de Commerce, see Navigation System
Conseil Général des Fabriques et

Manufactures, see Navigation System

Constantinople, 238

Consulate, the, 3, 9

Contentieux, Conseil de, see Navigation System

Continental Blockade, *see* Continental System

Continental System, international aspects of, i–ii, 12, 139–159; connection of, with Napoleon's downfall, ii–iii, connection of, with Navigation System, 1–2; Berlin decree of November *1806* inaugurates, 5–14; England retaliates with Orders in Council, January and February *1807*, 14–16; Europe assents to, 16–18; reports and discussions relative to expansion of trade under, 18–29; Denmark secures exemption from, 29–32; enforcement of, and Fontainebleau decree, 34–37; America and other neutrals object to strict enforcement of, 37–40; English November Orders, 40–41; Milan decrees, November and December *1807*, extending, 41–47; consequences in France of, and attempts to relieve, 48–70, importation of quinine in exception to, 65–66; England tries to break, 66–67; Bayonne decree and result of discussion of American trade, 70–76, Economic conditions, in *1808*, lead to beginning of trade by licences, 77–91; inauguration of licences and the problems of execution, 91–108; Non-Intercourse Act, Altenberg letter, and American participation in licence trade, 102–104; administration and growth of licence experiment under Cretet, Fouché, and Montalivet, 109–138; licence trade reports, 133–137; participation of European states in licence trade, 139–151; Franco-American negotiations of *1809-1810* resulting in Rambouillet decree, 151–159, 164–165; conditions leading to change of, 160–164; Macon Bill No. 2 and July 5, *1810* decree for American trade permits, 165, 171–179; creation and work of *Conseil du Commerce*, 166–173; American reception of July 5 decree and revocation of Berlin-Milan decrees, 179–186; Napoleon's Navigation System supercedes, July 3, *1810*, 187–200. For administration of, *see* Navigation System

Convention, the National, 9, 200, 211, 345

Convention of 1800, Negotiations for reviving or superseding, 156–158, 164

Convention of Versailles, *see* Versailles, also Eden treaty

Coolidge and Co., 153n

Copenhagen, 247; attack on, 12, 31–33, 38

Corfu, 34, 259, 290, 336

Corn, Portugal's trade in 51; French supply to England, 88, 90, 263, 265, 282, 291; licenced trade in, 112, 259; exportation of, forbidden, 187, 188, 189

Corps Legislatif, 26, 27

Corsica, 52; licences for, 249, 258, 290; colonial goods imported into 312n

Corvetto, ———, 27n

Costaz, Claude, 359, 373

Cotton, 80; petition for tariff protec-

INDEX   423

tion on, 5; importance of neutrals furnishing, 20, 24; Napoleon considers importing, 22, 78; duties on, in Regnaud's proposals, 27; proposed importation of, from North Africa, 54; French factories need, 58, 62, 172; England prohibits exportation of, 64; prohibited article of importation in French licence trade, 123, 125; Russia seeks to import into France, 139; Holland imports, 143; backers of cotton industries desire American trade in, 155; *Conseil du Commerce* to discuss manufacture of cloth from, 168; American ships to import, 172, 173, 203; proposed exemption of, 215, 235; tariff duties on, 217, 220, 226; licences for, under Navigation System, 239, 241, 248, 250, 262, 287, 296, 303, 304, 373; English desirous of importing into France, 263; licences for, under Grand System, 305, 308, 328, 329, 332, 334, 335, 341; England withdraws embargo from, 313; English licences for, 326, 327, 328; cotton industry at Rouen, 332, 334; lower price for, 338; development of manufactures of, 357

Council of Administration for the Interior, creation and work of, 48–52, 71

Council of Five Hundred, 9n, 57n

Council of State, *see* Navigation System

Court of King's Bench, 313

Cracow, 330

Cretet, Emmanuel, comte de Champnol, 58, 101; report of, defending Continental System, August *1807*, 27n, 28–29; succeeds Champagny as Minister of Interior, 28n, 349; orders to, relative to Milan decree, 45; member of Council of Administration, 48–49; corresponds with Napoleon regarding colonial trade, 55, 56, 57, 58; action regarding quinine need, 63–66; confronted by requests for exceptions, 66–70; intercedes for America, 71; attitude toward licence system, 77–78; Loyseau's memoir to, 78–81; drafts Napoleon's licence plan, 86–87, 91, 93; Montbert sends, criticism on licence system, 90–91, 93; author of circular of April 14, *1809*, 94–96, 97n, 98n; report of, May *1809* on flags for neutral trade, 103; growth of licence trade under, 105, 109–111, 112, 116, 117, 118, 237n

Cromwell, Oliver, 2

Cults, Ministry of, *see* Navigation System

Customs, Director General of, *see* Navigation System Collin, Ferrier Cunningham, Audrey, 88, 407

Customs tariff, England's effective use of, 2; French, legislation aimed at England, 4–5; decree of February 22, *1806*, 5, 125; Collin's report on, *1807*, 22n, 23; Champagny's views on, 24–26; Regnaud's proposed legislation for, 27; for colonial produce, 59; revisions of, under Trianon decree, August *1810*, and its supplements, 66, 126, 185, 207, 212, 213–218, 220, 260; connection of licences with, 99, 123n; decree affecting, February 8, *1810*, 125, 131, 215; execution of Trianon tariff, 126, 221–228, 231–234; creation of customs courts, 169; Fontainebleau decree, 228–230,

260; Bourbons do away with system of Napoleon's, 344–346; Collin directs administration of laws for, 349–350; connection of Ministry of Finance with, 361–362; work of *Conseil de Contentieux* for, 362–365; connection of Ministry of Manufactures and Commerce with, 372–374. *See* Navigation System, licence system, decrees, and *douanes*

Czernischeff, General, 232, 233n, 246n, 256, 316n

Dagneau, ——, 274, *See* Loriol and
Dalberg, Emmerich-Joseph, duc de, 330
Dalmatia, 262
Dangibau, Captain, 279n
Danish East India Company, 277
Danzig, Licence trade with, 135n; petitions for licence privileges, 139; licence trade of, under Navigation System, 203, 204, 242, 244, 245, 246; licences for, under Grand System, 307, 334, 343; English licences used to send wine to, 312n
Darmstadt, 227
Darmstaedter, Paul, 1, 221n, 232n, 406
Daru, Pierre-Antoine, count, Secretary of State, 246n, 352, 370
Daunou, Pierre-Claud-François, 358
Davout, Louis Nicolas, Marshal, 66
Deal, 280
De Clercq, R., 130, 137n, 242

Decrees, *1793:* October 9, 4; *1800:* July 16, 77; *1802:* December 24, 354; *1806:* February 22, 5, 125, March 4, 5, July 15, 79, Berlin, November 21, 5, 6–47, 70, 75, 76, 103, 165, 171, 181n, 182, 183, 194, 199, 201, 207, 208, 213, 215, 218, 221, 222, 227, 228, 230, 254, 256, 257, 292, 307, 316, 319, 320, 328, 345, 350, 352; *1807:* August 28, 32, 33, 36, 45, Fontainebleau, October 13 or 14, 35, 36, 37, 44, 45, Dutch, October 17, 35–36, 45, Milan, November 23, 36, 42, 43, 45, Milan, December 17, 12, 13, 41–42, 44–47, 50, 67, 70, 71, 76, 79, 80, 103, 165, 171, 181n, 182, 183, 194, 199, 201, 207, 208, 213, 215, 218, 221, 222, 227, 228, 230, 254, 256, 257, 292 307, 312, 316, 319, 320, 328, 345; *1808:* Tuileries, January 11, 44, 48, 201, March 2, 102, Bayonne, April 17, 55n, 72; *1809:* February 16, 86, March 15, 86–87, July 13, 104; *1810:* February 8, 125, 215, February 14, 125, 126, 127, Rambouillet February 18–25, 158, 165, 170, 171, 180, 183, 184n, 185, 315, May 29–30, 172–173, St. Cloud, June 6, 166–167, 170, 354, June 12, 187–188, June 15, 187–188, 191–192, June 27, 354, July 3, 87, 197–202, 205, 206, 208, 236, 237, 240, July 5, 87, 174–181, 202, 206, 208, 218, 236, 237, 240, July 22, 205, July 25, 205–206, 219, 236, 237, 249, 250, July 31, 212, Trianon tariff August 5, 66, 87, 126, 213–218, 220, 221–228, 231–234, 235, 236n, 251, 253, 260, 267, 344, 361, August 10, 188, August 28, 249, August 31, 352, September 5, 361, St. Cloud, September 12, 219, 220, 235, 260, 344, 361, September 27, 353, Fontainebleau, October 18, 228–230, 235, 260, 282, 345, 364, 365, November 1, 219, 251, 321, December 5, 275, 363, December 31, 363;

INDEX 425

1811: March 18, 252, March 25, 352, April 28, 321, 322; *1812:* January 19, 349, 370, April 17, 363, September 21, 349, 370; *1813:* February 18, 334, August 14, 341–342.

Decres, Denis, Vice Admiral, opposes Napoleon's plan of using war ships for colonial trade, 16; attitude toward neutrals, 29, 101; secures Denmark's exemption from Berlin decree, 29–30; negotiations between Armstrong and, 30, 37, 38, 73; orders regarding Milan decree, 46; member of Council of Administration, 49; Napoleon writes, regarding protective measures for trade, 51–53, 58–61; orders to, regarding colonial trade, 56; Cretet writes, regarding exceptions for Algeria, 67–70; attitude toward America and neutrals 73–76, 77, 100, 101; connection with licence system as Minister of Marine and Colonies, 97–98, 100, 105, 119, 269, 348; member of *Conseil du Commerce*, 167; receives copy of July 3, decree, 202

Defermon des Chapelières, Joseph, member of *Conseil du Commerce*, 167; influence of, on Navigation System, 353

De Gerando, Mottet, 111n, 355

Delaroche, Armand, Delessert and Co., 137n

Delbrück, *see* Albrecht and

Delessert, François-Marie, 355, 356

Delessert and Co., *see* Delaroche, Armand etc.

Delmotte, ——, 137n

Denmark, 134, 222, 237; Berlin decree and trade with, 17, 18, 33, 34; secures exception from Berlin decree, 29–32, 70; not regarded as a neutral, 40; Milan decree and, 45; Council of Interior classifies as an ally, 50; American trade under flag of, 74n; engaged in grain trade with France, 79; condition in, as result of Continental Blockade, 86; use of flag of, for licence trade, 103, 104, 105, 113,139; licence trade and 149–150, 236–237; American shipping excluded from, 154; supports demands of United States, 155n; Trianon tariff and, 226, 227, 228, 231, 232; trade of, under Navigation System, 241, 244, 245, 246, 247, 249n, 276, 281n, 290. *See* Copenhagen

Desyeux, ——, 63

De Villiers du Terrage, ——, 265n

Dieppe, proposed opening of, for quinine importation, 63–65; licence trade from, 137; Napoleon in, 163

Directory, the, 3, 9, 77

Director General of the Customs, *see* Navigation System, and Collin

Douanes, 27, 228, 362, 364, 372. *See* customs tariff

Doysié, Abel, iv

Dixmude, 133n

Dollart, Gulf of, 35

Dover, 90, 149. *See* Straits of

Dresden, 22, 339

Dryer, ——, 29

Ducher, ——, 3n

Dunkirk, 56, 271, licences for, 133n 137, 273, 274–275; Napoleon in. 163, 264; smuggling port, 190–192, 274, 280; licence trade of, under Navigation System, 198, 242, 294, 301; trade with England through

272n; licences for, under Grand System, 307
Dutch East India Company, 277
Dutch West Indies, *See* West Indies
Dyewoods, importance of, to French manufactures, 24; licenced article of importation under Continental System, 124, 125, 128, 137; permits for Americans to import, 175; Trianon tariff duties on, 217, 226; licences for, under Navigation System, 238, 239, 241, 289; licences for, under Grand System, 299, 305

East Indies, 325; licence trade with, 125; customs duties on goods from, 220; merchants of British, desirous to sell to France, 263, 267; certificates of origin required in trade with, 277
Eden, William, Lord Auckland, negotiator of Convention of Versailles, 2; criticism of, 41n. *See* Holland-Auckland note
Eden treaty, *see* Versailles treaty
Edward III, 2
Egypt, 42, 343
Elba, 52, 90
Elbe River, English blockade from Brest to, 8; opened to commerce, 27; enforcement of Berlin decree on, 35; Hamburg outlet for, 203; licences for trade from, 290
Ellis, Charles, 272n. *See* Ellis and Allan
Ellis and Allan, 271-272
Eliza, Bonaparte-Baciocchi, Grand Duchess of Tuscany, 116, 139
Emden, 40, 286, 362
Emmery, ———, 137n
Ems River, 35, 223
England, 1; general navigation policy of, 2; effect in France of commercial negotiations of *1786*, 2-5; Barlow advocates attack on, 3n; French Navigation Act of *1793* aimed at, 4; Napoleon inaugurates commercial policy against, by Berlin decree, November *1806*, 5-44; effects of blockade of, 14-16, 52-70, 77, 113; passes retaliatory Orders in Council of January and February *1807*, 15-16; effect of Copenhagen attack on Napoleon's commercial policy, 31-32; European countries agree to Berlin decree against, 33-34; stricter closure of North Sea coast against, 34-36; Fontainebleau decree and, October *1807*, 35-36; neutrals affected by relations of France with, 37-47; retaliatory Orders in Council, November *1807*, adopted by, 39, 41; attitude of, toward neutral flags, 40; retaliatory Milan decree directed against, 36, 41-47; French coast trade affected by blockade of, 52-53; policy of, toward quinine for Europe, 63-65; simulates French ships in trade with colonies, 66-67; question of neutral trade with France and interference by, 68-76; critical situation in, leads to efforts to get corn from France by licence trade, *1808-1809*, 81-91; inauguration of French licence trade with 91-108; workings of this trade during *1809*, 109-138; Russia's interest in licence trade between France and, 109-141; licence trade between Holland and, 141-145; bearing of Dutch crisis upon Anglo-French-American relations, 142-145, 158-159; trade of, with Naples, 146-147; licence trade with Hanse cities and

Denmark, 148–150; influence of relations with America upon Anglo-French measures, *1809-1810*, 150–160, 164–165, 171, 176, 180–186; circumstances affecting Napoleon's policy toward, 151–165; Fouché's secret negotiations with, 161–162; France curtails grain export to, 187–189; French-supervised smuggling with, 190–192, 277–281; decree of July 3, *1810* initiates new Navigation System affecting, 198–200, 202, 204; Trianon tariff affects, 212–214, 221–222, 225; effect of Fontainebleau decree on, 229–230; regulations of French licenced Navigation System and, 237–255; Berlin and Milan decrees not repealed for, 256; Napoleon seeks to further war between United States and, 256–257, 285; conditions leading to negotiations with, to extend licence trade, 258–283, 287; Montalivet summarizes the licence trade with, 287–291; economic conditions in, lead to concessions in licence trade, 291–296; Napoleon's proposals and negotiations for futher licence trade with, 296–304; contemplated effect of Grand System on, 305, 307, 308; acceptance in, of Napoleon's proposals, 311–314; repeals Orders in Council, 320, 321, 322, 327, 328; America' declares war on, 322; trade regulations for, under Grand System, 323–329; statistics regarding licence trade with, under Grand System, 330–332; alterations in and downfall of Grand System, 332–346. *See* Orders in Council

English Channel, 129, 229, 263, 265, 286; lack of commercial activity in French ports on, 79; French fishing in, at night, 163; smuggling across, 190–191, 277; British licences for French ports on, 293, 294; overstocking in French ports of, 338

English West Indies, *see* West Indies
Erfurt, interview at, 61, 76
Erskine agreement, 102, 104
Erving, George William, 38
Este of Caen, Baron d', 130
Etruria, 7
Eudel, 242n
Eugène, *see* Beauharnais
Executive Directory, 9n
Exterior Relations, Ministry of, *see* Navigation System, Talleyrand, Champagny, and Maret
Eyder, the, 268, 269
Eylau, 230

Faber, Richard, 280n
Fauchat, ——, 106, 242; connection of, with licence system, 94, 106, 111n, 119, 265n, 269; report of August 17, *1809*, on effectiveness of licence system, 113–115; report defending licence system, May 25, *1810*, 127–130, 132, 154, 172, 173, 192; author of report presented by Montalivet to the *Conseil*, November 25, *1811*, 287; chief of division of commerce and industry of the Interior, 358; proposes new commerce bureau in report of August 9, *1810*, 359–361; Collin appointed Minister of Commerce in preference to, 369, 371; able reports of, 376

Falmouth, 90, 268
Fencés, Guérin de, 268

Ferrier, ———, Made Director General of Customs, 374
Fiévée, Joseph, 58n
Filiechi, ———, 355
Finance, Ministry of. *See* Navigation System, Gaudin
Finisterre, 150n, 279
Fish, 27; Champagny advocates no duty on, 25; American permit to import, 173; question of night fishing, 163, 168, 190; licences for, under Navigation System, 238, 240, 241, 242, 249, 253, 261, 262, 271, 290; licences for, under Grand System, 299, 343
Fiume, 335
Flanders, 82; British trade with, 134; Napoleon's visit to, 163, 286
Florence, 364, 373
Flour, need of, in French colonies, 55, 56, 58, 59, 60; British licences for, 82, 90n, 282; licence trade in, under Continental System, 114; exportation of, forbidden, 188, 189; licences for, under Navigation System, 243n, 259, 266, 290; imported from United States, 317, 318
Flushing, licences for, 133n; Napoleon in, 163; smuggling port, 190, 302
Folkestone, 280
Foncia, *see* Fencés
Fontainebleau, 43n. *See* decrees.
Forbes, Consul, 30n
Ford, Guy Stanton, ii
Fouché, Joseph, duc d'Otrante, 86n, 136, 273; seeks concessions for America, 71, 155n; licence trade under, as acting Minister of Interior, 97–99, 109, 111–119, 140, 151, 351; intrigue of, with England, 161–162; Minister of Interior, 349; Minister of Police, 351
France, Napoleon's program for economic reconstruction of, iii; American relations with, iv; effect of England's commercial power in, 2–5; passage of Navigation Act of *1793*, 3–5; Berlin decree and economic crisis in, 13–14, 16; British blockade affects trade of, 14–16, 48–54, 112; attempts to overcome effect of blockade on trade with colonies, 16, 54–70; treaty of *1800* with United States, 37; reception of Milan decree in, 45–46; effect of American Embargo on trade of, 55; quinine crisis in, 63–66; American trade with, 70–76; crop conditions lead, to negotiations with England regarding licence trade, *1808*, 77–91; inauguration of licence trade with England, 91–101; status of American trade with, passage of Non-Intercourse Act, and Altenberg offer, August *1809*, 101–109; workings of licence trade during *1809–1810*, 109–133; statistics for *1809* regarding licence trade, 133–137; interest of European states in licences of, 139–151; American negotiations with, relative to licence trade results in Rambouillet decree March *1810*, 151–159; result of Napoleon's *1810* trip through northern, 160–165, 187–192; effect of Macon Bill No. 2 upon, 165–166; Conseil du Commerce to reconstruct licence system for, 166–170, 187–197; decree of July 5, *1810* for American trade permits, 170–179; America threatens to declare war on, 183; Cadore's August 5 letter revoking Berlin-

INDEX 429

Milan decrees for United States, 183–186; grain exports of, curtailed, 187–189, 258; supervised smuggling trade with England, 190–192, 277–281; decrees of July *1810* inaugurate licenced Navigation System for, 197–210; tariff decrees of July and August *1810*, 211–228, 233–234; effect of Fontainebleau decree, October *1810*, in, 228–232; licenced navigation established by, 235–255; equivocal position of, on revocation of Berlin-Milan decrees, 256–257; economic conditions in, lead to negotiations with England to extend licence trade, *1810-1811*, 258–283; Barlow's negotiations with, 284–285; result of Napoleon's tour to northern, *1811*, 284, 286–287, 294; Montalivet summarizes the licence trade of, 287–291; Napoleon's proposals and negotiations for further licence trade of, with England, 296–304; Napoleon's plans for the Grand System of trade, 304–310; Barlow's negotiations with, lead to proof of repeal of Berlin-Milan decrees, 314–322; regulations for trade under Grand System, 323–329; statistics regarding licence trade of, under Grand System, 330–332; report of licence trade of, for *1813*, 343–344; alterations in and downfall of Grand System, 332–346; economic conditions in, after Moscow defeat, 338–341

Frankfort, 64; effect of Trianon decree at, 221, 227; protests against Fontainebleau decree, 230

Frederick II, the Great, of Prussia, 6
French India, 27

French Revolution, 20, 315n; commercial policies of, 3, 5, 9n, 10, 195, 200, 211, 345
French West Indies, *see* West Indies
Friedland, 19

Gaëte, duc de, *see* Gaudin
Gallatin, Albert, 39n
Garnier and Ransom, 137n
Garonne river, 53
Gaudin, M. M. C., duc de Gaëte, 11n, 36, 68, 69, 155, 371; duties as Minister of Finance, 34, 349; member of Council of Administration, 49; notified of Bayonne decree, 72; recommends enlarging list of licenced articles, 120–121; member of *Conseil du Commerce*, 167, 168; recommends sale of condemned American cargoes, 171; June report of, preceding Trianon decree, 185; note to, regarding smuggling 190-191; receives copy of July 3 decree, 202; Napoleon writes, regarding licence system, 340; attends last session of *Conseil du Commerce*, 342
Geneva, 289
Genoa, protection for trade of, 52; licences for, 248, 250, 258, 261n, 307
General Washington, the, 38n
Georgia, 172, 217
Gerando, Josèphe-Marie, Baron de, secretary general of Ministry of Interior, 111n, 358
Germany, 1, 8, 24, 202, 212, 364; trade of Bordeaux with, 13; new trade routes in, 27; Napoleon attends Erfurt interview in, 76; licence trade with, 114, 134; sale of manufactures in, 168; Trianon tariff and, 226, 233; silk trade with north, 302; slipping from French

control, 341. *See* Confederation of the Rhine

Ghent, 127; Napoleon in, 128n, 163, 264; Van Aken merchant in, 128n, 137n, 164, 189n, 263, 266, 269, 295, 301, 355, licences for, 133n; American raw products needed in, 173, 176

Gibraltar, 34, 69, 268

Gironde, department of, Prefect of, notified of licence system, 94–95; licences for, 110, 114n; letter from Prefect of, regarding licences, 116, 118, 325; smuggling trade in, 279

Glasgow, 295

Glückstadt, 149

Godoy, Manuel de, 18, 38

Goldsmith, Lewis, 89n

Gottenburg, 286, 336

Grains, need of, in French colonies, 58; neutral trade in, 75; licences for trade in, between France and England, 78–96, 263; licenced article of export, 95, 106; licenced trade in, under Continental System, 110, 113, 114, 116, 120, 121, 122, 125, 128, 129, 131, 133, 134, 137, 140, 141, 142, 146, 147, 153; exportation of, forbidden, 187–188, 203, 205, 258; trade in, under Navigation System, 201, 204, 238, 242, 243, 244, 245, 248, 249, 258–259, 266, 282, 290, 297; licences for, under Grand System, 306, 328, 341; Montalivet blamed for shortage of, 370; oversight of, by *Conseil du Commerce*, 373

Granville, stock company in, for colonial trade, 55, 56, licences for, 133n, 289, 307; smuggling from, 301

Gravelines, 192

Gray, William, 178

Greece, 250, 259

Greffulke Brothers, 83, 270n, 293

Grenville, William Wyndham, 15, 16.

Guadeloupe, affected by American embargo, 55; Napoleon's plans for trade with, 56, 58, 59, 60, 61; trade with, in Algerian vessels, 69; Hanse cities trade with, 148; American proposal to carry products from, 172; licenced trade with, under Navigation System, 199, 251; England issues licences for French trade with, 269–270, 293

Guérin de Fencés (Foncia), 268

Guernsey, French ships trading with, 68n; English licences for, 114; petitions for trade with France, 263, smuggling in, 278. *See* Channel Islands

Guianas, 217

Guillot and Co., Phillibert, 106

Haley, Captain, 73–76

Hall, Hubert, iv

Hamburg, 50, 63, 130, 232; American trade with, 21n; postal facilities for, 27; Berlin decree and, 30; Fontainebleau decree enforced at, 36n; vessels of, to be sequestered, 102; licence trade under flag of, 102, 103, 104, 105; licence trade with, 129, 137, 148, 149; English trade with, 131, 137n; licence trade of, under Navigation System, 203, 242, 274, 286; licences for, under Grand System, 307, 341, 342n, 344; complains about customs, 340, customs, court at, 364

Hamilton, Alexander, 315n

Hano, 336

Hanseatic cities, 36, 40, 282, 339; smuggle from England, 11n; en-

forcement of Berlin decree in, 18, 33, 35; regulations for American trade with, 21n; proposed use of ships of, for neutral trade between France and England, 83; ships of, released for licenced trade, 102, 105, 139; licenced trade of, 137n; licences for, under Navigation System, 204, 205, 242–247, 253, 261, 268, 289, 351; Trianon tariff and, 224, 227; failure of bankers in, 338, 339; represented in *Conseil Général de Commerce*, 355; customs court for, at Hamberg, 364. See Kniphausen, Pappenburg, Oldenburg, Aremberg, Hamburg, Bremen, Lübeck, Mecklenburg, Danzig
Harlem, 253
Harwich, 90, 189, 263n
Hauterive, A.M.B. de L.d', 103, 104, 155n, 350
Havre, 74; plans for colonial trade with, 55, 56, 58; Loyseau from, 78; licences for, 133n, 137, 275n; Napoleon visits, 163; licenced trade at, under Navigation System, 198, 294, 295, 296, 303, 304, 363; licences for, under Grand System, 307, 327
Heligoland, English seize, for entrepôt, 35, 40, 81; importance of, as smuggling center, 148, 229, 259n, 336
Hellespont, 17
Hibernia, the, case of, 37
Hodder, Frank Heywood, v
Hoekstra, Peter, v, 142n, 382
Holland, 2, 66n; enforcement of Berlin decree in, and trade with, 7, 27, 30, 32–33, 35, 36, 38, 40; Louis, king of, 30; Milan decree and, 45; French Council of Interior classifies as ally, 50; insurance in, 56; English get colonies of, 62; British desire trade with, 82; sailors of, used on neutral vessels, 84; annexes Kniphausen, 102; use of flag of, for licenced trade, 104, 105; English licences procurable in, 115; English trade with, 134, 141; Louis evades Continental Closure, 141–145, 158, 159; American shipping excluded from, 154; supports Armstrong's views, 155n; Louis abdicates and Napoleon annexes, 161–162, 219; Napoleon visits, 161, 284, 286, 368; issue regarding American property confiscated in, 170–171; restricted grain exportation to, 187, 188n; smuggling in, 191; licences for, under Navigation System, 205, 209, 210, 243, 244, 251–253, 259, 261, 263, 264, 289, 290, 297, 300, 301, 344, 353; trade policy for colonies of, 219; Trianon tariff and, 217, 224, 228, 236; benefits to trade of, 286; project of trading with England via, 295–303; English trade with, 326; warehouses overstocked in, 338; complains about customs tariff, 340, member from, in *Conseil Général de Commerce*, 355
Holland -Auckland note, 15n
Holstein, 36, 232, 247
Hope and Company, 302
Horizon, the, case of, 39
Horstman, I, 267n
Hottinguer, ——, 293, 355, 356
Hottinguer & Co., 270n
Hundred Year's War, 2

Ile de France, plans for colonial trade with, 58, 59, 60; Hanse cities petition for trade with, 148; American proposal to carry products of, 172; licence trade of, under Navigation System, 206, 251; customs duties on goods from, 220; English licences for, 270

Ile d'Oléron, 133n

Illinois, University of, ii

Illyria, reconstruction of customs of, under Trianon tariff, 224; licences for, under Navigation System, 248, 249, 259, 261; licences for, under Grand System, 335, 343

Imbert and Chataud, 68

Independent Whig, the, quoted, 32

India, 27

Indigo, licenced import under Continental System, 124, 125; Americans not permitted to import, 176; Trianon tariff duties on, 217, 234; licences for, under Navigation System, 239, 250n, 289, 300, 303, 304; licences for, under Grand System, 299, 305, 306, 309, 319, 329, 335; works for manufacture of, 373

Interior, Ministry of, *see* Navigation System, Lucien Bonaparte, Champagny, Cretet, Fouché, Montalivet, Chaptal

Ionian Isles, 34, 147

Istria, 262

Italy, 1, 147; powers of Prize Court in, 7; Berlin decree and, 22, 23n, 24, 27, 28, 33, 34; Napoleon in, 42, 43; Council of Interior classifies as an ally, 50; need of protection of trade with, 52; licenced trade of, under Continental System, 124; sale of French manufactures in, 168; licence trade of, under Navigation System, 203, 205, 289, 373; new tariff for, 211; Trianon tariff and, 212, 223–224, 294; trade with under Navigation System, 240, 247–249, 253, 258, 260, 289, 294, 295, 304; licences for under Grand System, 306, 307, 335, 341

Jackson, F. J., 31n
Jarnac, 133n
Jarvis, Leonard, 152–154
Java, 143, 219, 251
Jefferson, Thomas, 39, 45n
Jena, 6, 13
Jerome, *see* Bonaparte
Jersey, English licences for, 114, petition of, for trade with France, 263; smuggling in, 278. *See* Channel Islands
Joseph, *see* Bonaparte
Josephine, Empress, 11n, 160
Joy, George, 247
Journal de Paris, publishes item concerning licence system, 97, 98
Juist, Island of, 268, 269
Junon, the, 74
Junot, Andoche, duc d'Abrantes, 18, 20, 34
Juries, ——, 100
Justice, Ministry of, *see* Navigation System, Regnier

Kenny, ——, 274
Kerkhove, *see* Cheminant and
Kiesselbach, W., 1
King and Bowker, 143n
Kniphausen, Council of Interior supresses French ocean trade of, 50; licence trade under flag of, 102, 103, 104; annexed to Holland, 102
Kolberg, 244n
Königsberg, 135n, 244n

Labiche, ——, 358
Labouchére, Pierre-César, 158

INDEX 433

Lafayette, M.-J.-P.-R.-Y.-Gilbert Motier, marquis de, 71
La Fortuna, case of, 149
La Franchise, case of, 62n
La Liebe, case of, 30
Lallemand and Co., 137n
La Marie, case of, 279n
Lannion, 133n
Lansdowne, Henry, Petty-Fitzmaurice, marquis of, 313
La Plata, 54
Larochefoucauld, ——, 55n
La Rochelle, plans for colonial trade with, 55, 56, 58, 60; licenced trade with, 133n, 137; licences for, under Navigation System, 198, 238; licences for, under Grand System, 307, 344
Las Cases, Emmanuel-A.-D.-M.-J., marquis de, 89, 136, 281
Latin America, see Spanish America, Spain, colonies, and special regions or ports
Lauenburg, 227
Laugier, ——, 358
Lavallette, Marie Chamans, comte de, 34
Lebrun, Charles-François, duc de Plaisance, 4n, 224, 236, 251, 254n
Lee, William, American consul, 39n, 48, 52n, 70, 142n, 152n, 153n, 319; reports on licence trade, 329, 330, 334n, 338n
Leeward Islands, 56, 60. See Guadeloupe, Martinique, Marie Galante
Leghorn, Berlin decree and, 17–18; protection of trade of, 52; request for blank licences from, 116; Trianon tariff and, 223; licences for, under Navigation System, 250, 258; licences for, under Grand System, 307; member of Conseil Général de Commerce, 355
Leland, Waldo G., iv, 382
L'Esperance, case of, 63
Leipzig, 13, 221, 376
Lemoine, ——, 359, 361, 372
Lenoir, Richard, 357
Les Sables, 133n
Les Saintes, 61
Levant, the, plans to resume French trade with, 19; regulation of trade with, 27; proposed improvement of trade with, 28; no exceptions for trade with 69; permits for, under Navigation System, 203, 232, 238, 239, 248, 249, 250, 276, 287, 299; customs duties on cotton from, 217, 220; licences for, under Grand System, 343
L'Hirondelle, see the Swallow
Licence System, Significance of the Napoleonic, ii; relation of, and Continental System, ii;
Commercial situation prior to adoption of, by Napoleon: English licence trade order, February 4, 1807, 15; Champagny advocates exceptions to Berlin decree, 19–20, 24–26; Denmark secures relief from Berlin decree, 29–31; Lubbert warns of danger from British, 43, 45; need of quinine not cause of French, 65–66; passports to Algerine ships step toward French, 67–70; Americans trade under English, 74; 75; effects of English, 77, 80, 82, 87, 96;
Ancien systéme, 1809-July, 1810: economic conditions causing adoption of, 77–84; establishment of, 84–91; administration of, 91–106, 109; administrative problems under 104–107; Cretet's administration

of, 109–111; Fouché's connection with, 111–119; developments under Montalivet, 119–126, 133–138; arguments for and against, 126–133; foreign interest in, 139–159; Dutch aspect of, 142–145; Naples and, 145–148; American attitude toward, 151–155, reasons and events leading to reconstruction of, 160–186, permits for United States considered, 172–185;

Nouveau système, under Navigation System, July *1810*-January *1812*: reconstruction of system under decrees of July *1810*, 187–210; inauguration of, 235–255; modification of, to meet economic pressure, 256–262; Franco-English negotiations for special, 262–275; abuses of, 275–283; Montalivet's *1811* report on, 287–291; English concessions in, 291–293; reclassification into first, second, and third groups, 299–300; amount of business done under, 330; Fauchat's August *9, 1810* plan for, 359–361;

Kinds of, under nouveau système: *licences simples*, 209, 238–239, 253, 261, 288, 290; *licences diverses*, 209, 239–240, 253, 289, 290, 328, 343; sugar licences, 209, 239, 240; American permits, 240–242, 253, 257, 259, 261, 287, 290, 299, 316, 317, 319, 328, 334, 343-344; Channel Island, 265; Hanseatic licences, 242–245, 246, 643, 261, 268, 289; Prussian licences, 245; Italian licences, 247-249, 253; Ottoman-Barbary permits, 250, 253, 259, 261, 290, 299, 335, 350; colonial trade licences, 250–251, 253, 290; Dutch licences, 251–253, 259, 261;

Grand System: Napoleon outlines, 304–306; varieties of licences under, 306–309; new English policy, 325–328, 336; workings of, 323–324; new forms adopted by Napoleon, 334–343; final report on, *1814*, 343–344; Bourbons do away with, 344. For administration *see* Navigation System; also, cutstoms tariff

Liberation, War of, *see* War of,

Lignum vitae, licenced import, under Continental System, 121, 124, 125; licences for, under Navigation System, 238

Liguria, 27

Lille, 133n, 163

Lingelbach, William Ezra, iv, v, 379, 382

Lissa, 336

Loire river, 53, 110

Loisel, ——, 358

Loison, General Louis-Henri, 152

London, 40, 56, 182, 241, 271n, 273, 275n, 282, 290, 293, 295, 300, 305, 321, 331, 337n; trade center at, 19; attitude in, toward Copenhagen attack, 32; effect in, of enforcement of Berlin decree, 33; Monroe in, 37; American opinion regarding treatment of neutrals printed in 39n; plans in, to break Continental blockades, 67; letter regarding French foodstuffs, from a merchant in, 83, 100; market at, for licence trade, 129, 131, 363; Danish ship makes trip to, 149; rumors in, about changes in Continental System, 163; hears of American permit trade, 175; Pinkney American minister at, 184; effect of Trianon decree in, 221; effect of Fontainebleau decree in, 229; permits from,

INDEX 435

for Baltic trade, 247; merchants of, desire trade with France, 263; Van Aken, French agent in negotiations with, 264; 265, 266–268; colonial produce stored in, 270; announcement in, of trade with France, 291; Napoleon's proposals for trade with, under Grand System, 299, 301; effect in, of Napoleon's wine licences, 311, 313, 314; Madison's *1812* message on licences published in 317n; Russell, American chargé at, 320; sends Brazil cotton to France, 328; trade between France and, 333

London Times, 181n; protests against Fontainebleau decree in, 229

London Morning Chronicle, 282

L'Orient, plans for colonial trade with, 60, 61; licences for, 133n, restricted grain exportation from, 187, 188, licences for, under Navigation System, 209, 238

Loriol and Dagneau, 137n, 274

Louis, *see* Bonaparte

Louviers, 163

Loyseau, Charles Auguste, agricultural memoir of, 78–81, 82, 84, 96n, 100

Lubbert, ——, 130, author of *Sur le Commerce de l'Angleterre*, 42–43

Lübeck, Berlin decree and policy toward, 30; licence trade with, 148; licence trade under flag of, 102, 103, 104, 105; licences for, under Navigation System, 204, 242, 244, 245, 246, 290; licences for, under Grand System, 307

Lubinski, ——, 139

Lumbroso, A., 1

Lyons, silk industry at, 20, 260, 262, 332; licences for, 133n, 289, 301,

342n; represented on *Conseil Général de Commerce*, 355; Tribunal of Commerce of, 356n; represented on *Conseil Général des Fabriques et Manufactures*, 357

Macedonia, 168

Macon Bill No. 2, passage and results of, 165, 171, 173, 180, 181, 182, 183, 185, 194, 218, 256. *See* Non-Intercourse Act

Madison, James, 142n; Napoleon ready to free seamen for, 30n; instructions of, to Armstrong, 73, 76; Armstrong writes, regarding Napoleon's attitude toward America, 73; Armstrong's letter to, regarding change of French policy, 101n; attitude toward licence system, 153, 179, 180, 186n, 316, 317, 319, 322n; Armstrong's August 5 letter to, 183n, 222n; *not* deceived by Napoleon, 185; accepts conditions of August 5 letter, 256; notified of negotiations between France and England, 265n

Madrid, 38, 65

Magastre and Company, 67, 68, 69

Mahan, Admiral A. T., 1

Mailmen and Sons, 302

Mainot, ——, 106

Mainz, 217, see Mayence

Malaga, 287, 296

Malta, Algerian ships not to stop at; 69; English entrepôt, 81, 146, 217, licenced trade with, 238, 248, 250, 268, 276, 336

Manche, department of the, 119, 265, 279

Manufactures and Commerce, Ministry of, *see* Navigation System, Collin

Mappes, ——, 355
Marans, licences for, 133n, 137, 188, 238
Marbois, ——, see Barbé-Marbois
Marbot, Jean – Baptiste – Marcelin, General, 11n
Marchant, Isaac de, 302
Marennes, 133n
Maret, Hugues-Bernard, duc de Bassano, 103, 123, 127, 160, 167n, 300n; connection of, with licence trade, 107, 133n; proposes enlarging list of licenced articles, 120; draws up July 3 decree, 197; and American situation, 257n, 285, 315–318, 320, 321, 329–330; report of, on England's commercial position in *1812*, 312; attends last meeting of *Conseil du Commerce*, 343; Minister of Exterior Relations, 350, 352
Maret, Jean-Philibert, councillor of state, 187
Marie Galante, 61
Marie Louise, Napoleon marries, 160, 163
Marine and Colonies, Ministry of, see Navigation System, Decrès
Marmont, A.-F.-L. Viesse de, duc de Raguse, 224
Marseilles, petitions for measures against England, 46n; colonial trade with, 67, 68; licences for, 133n, 248, 258, 261; Americans ships at, 152; port for American permit trade, 175, 178, 241; licences for, under Grand System, 307, 342, 344
Martin-fils-d'André, 355
Martinique, 66; Napoleon's plans for trade with, 56, 57, 58, 59, 60, 61; use of Algerian vessels in trade with, 68–69; American proposals to carry products from, 172; Navigation System and, 199; English licences for French trade with, 269–270, 293
Massa, see Regnier, duc de
Massachusetts, 178
Massonda, the, 68n
Mayence, 355
Mauritius, see Ile de France
Mecklenburg, French occupation of, 17n; Council of Interior suppresses French ocean trade of, 50; licence trade under flag of, 102; Trianon tariff and, 226, 227, licences for, under Navigation System, 246, licences for, under Grand System, 306, 307
Medicine, Champagny advocates no duty on, 25; licenced article of import under Continental System, 95, 124, 125, 128, 133; Holland imports, 143; exempted from customs duty, 220; licences for, under Navigation System, 238, 253, 289, 296; licences for, under Grand System, 299, 309, 329. *See* Quinine
Mediterranean Sea, 188; problems of coast trade in, 52–53; British control of, 70, 336; American trading in, 146; Naples' trade on, 146, 147n; licenced trade on, under Navigation System, 201, 203, 206, 208, 209, 210, 246n, 247–249, 253, 261, 269, 290, 351; relation of Trianon tariff to, 223, 228; need of grain incountries of, 258–259; trade on, under Grand System, 334, 335–336, 340, 343, 351
Melvil and Company, 302
Memel, 244n
Merlin, de Douai, P.-A., 353n

INDEX 437

Meuse river, 168, 201
Mexico, 54
Meyer, Daniel C., 137n
Middleburg, 163, 302
Milan, Prize Court at, 7; decree issued from, 36, 41, 42; failure of bankers in, 338
Mining, licences for products of, 262
Ministries, for various, *see* Navigation System
Miranda, Francisco, 270
Mocha, 250
Molé, Louis-Matthieu, count, 358
Molitor, G.-J.-J., 242, 268
Mollien, Nicolas-Francois, count, disagrees with Fouché, 112; reports against licence system, 130–132, 154; reports on effect of Trianon tariff decree, 221, 222n, 226n; reports to Napoleon on English conditions, 292, 311–312; reports on Grand System, 323–325, 327, 328–330, 337, 339; presses for funds for war, 339–340; tries to save Bank of France from failure, 341; present at final session of *Conseil du Commerce*, 342; reports of, as Minister of the Treasury, 353, 367
Monbrion, M., 8
Moniteur, the, publishes: Berlin decree, 13; results of Berlin decree, 18; American opinion regarding treatment of neutrals, 39n; Milan decree, 41, 45; allusions to British Orders of November, 42; comments on trade between France and West Indies, 59n; England's prohibition of cotton and quinine exports, 64; information regarding Neapolitan trade, 147; August 5 letter, 184; acceptance of Trianon tariff by Rhine Confederation, 227; acceptance of Fontainebleau decree, 230, 231; item on postal service between France and England, 273; British criticisms of Board of Trade, 282; British declaration regarding repeal of Continental System, 321
Monroe, James, 37, 271n; Russell protests to, regarding American permits scheme, 257n; recognizes American permits, 319
Montalivet, J.-P. Bachasson, comte de, 236, 286, 293, 332, 355; Minister of Interior, 109, 119, 349, 358; in charge of licence trade, *1809*, 106, 109, 119–126, 147, 150; Fauchat's May 25, *1810*, report to, defending licence trade, 127–130, 132; reports of, on licence trade, 132–137; report on licence trade November 25, *1811*, 135–137, 259n, 287–291, 293, 295, 298, 317, 323, 368; reply to Russian petition for licences, 139–140; connection of, with American relations, 155, 157, 257n; Van Aken agent of, in negotiations with England, 164, 264–275; member of *Conseil du Commerce*, 167; July 30 report on trade, 183n, 204, 207–208, 215–216; attitude toward smuggling, 190, 224, 279; June 11, *1810* report on licence policy, 170, 193–194, 224; influence of, on decree of July 5, *1810*, 172–174, 176–178; report of July 17 on American ships, 182, 183, 213; presents *projet* for new licence policy, June 18, 194–197; Napoleon's letter to, regarding new navigation policy, 202–204, 212; influence on July 25 decree, 204–206, 242, 248; presents plan revising licence policy, July, 207–10; August 5 tariff report of,

216, 217, 219–220; proposes new Hanse licence, 244, 245n; urges colonial trade licences, 250–251, favors Holland in general licence system, 251–252, advocates silk export requirement, December 31, 260–261; secret negotiation between England and France, 264–275, December 31 report on certificates of origin, 276–278; December projects of, 296–300, 324; Woute Holland agent of, for silk trade, 301–303; report of January 13, *1812*, 303–304, 308n; to report on imports and exports under Grand System, 307, 309n; urges liberal terms for America, 317–318; Collin made Minister of Commerce in preference to, 318, 368, 369–370; attends last meeting of *Conseil du Commerce*, 342; indorses Fauchat's August 9 report, 359–361; able reports of, 376

Montbret, Coquebert, report of, on licence system, 87n, 90–91, 93, 94, 103; director of trade statistics, 358; duties as assistant to Collin, 371–372

Montgaillard, J.-G.-M. 8, 389

Moore, Sir John, 84

Morlaix, English licences for trade with, 114; French licences for, 133n; negotiations with England at, 162, 164; licenced trade at, under Navigation System, 198; licences for, under Grand System, 307

Morocco, 34, 54

Moscow, Campaign of, 12n; Napoleon's return from, 322, 332; Napoleon in, 327, 329

Moustier, Clément-Edouard, marquis de, 164

Muhl, ——, 139n

Murat, Joachim, King of Naples, 58, 146–147

Nancy, 364

Nantes, 53, 106, 137n; stock company for colonial trade at, 55, 56, 60; grain exported from, 79; licences for, 133n, 135n, 137n; port for American permit trade, 173, 175, 177, 178, 241, 259, 290, 319, 324, 344; licence trade of, under Navigation System, 198, 209, 248, 289; port for Hanse trade under Navigation System, 242; English licences for, 266; licences for, under Grand System, 306, 307; sugar factory at, 373

Naples, notified of Berlin decree, 7; British blockade affects, 14n; accepts Berlin decree, 34; trade privileges of, as French ally, 50; evades Continental System, 145–147; American shipping excluded from, 154; cotton from, 168, 215, 217; licences for under Navigation System, 205, 206, 217, 220, 240, 248, 249, 261, 304, 362; Trianon tariff and, 226, 227; ordered to capture Ottoman ships, 228; Grand System and, 306, 307, 362

Napoleon I, statesmanship of, i, iii-iv, 1-6, 9, 347; connection of Navigation System with downfall of, ii-iii, commercial policies of, prior to Continental System, 3–5, inaugurates Continental System by Berlin decree, 6–37; negotiations with United States relative to Berlin and Fontainebleau decrees, 19–21, 35–37; exempts Denmark from Berlin decree, 30–31; issues

INDEX 439

Fontainebleau decree in October *1807*, 36; actions toward United States and neutrals, 37–40, 44–47, 72; issues Milan decree following English November Orders, 41–47; attempts to mitigate effects of his System, 48–76; results of visit to Bayonne, 51–52; colonial dreams of, 54; plans for colonial trade, 55–63; action regarding quinine crisis, 64–66; grants Algerian exception, 67-**70;** effect of American Embargo upon, and resulting Bayonne decree, 70–76; conquers Spain and defeats the English, 81, 84–85; inaugurates licence system *1809*, 84–106; opinion of, on licence trade, 89–90, 91; makes Altenberg offer to America after passage of Non-Intercourse Act, 102–104; growth of licence trade and attitude of, toward it in first half of *1810*, 109–138; dealings with European nations regarding licence trade, 139–150; attitude toward America as seen in licence trade and Rambouillet decree, 150–159, 164–165; marries Marie Louise and makes a tour of northern France *1810*, 160–164; negotiations with America resulting in decree of July *1810*, 164–167, 170–181; effect of Macon Bill No. 2 on, 165; begins program of reconstruction in creation of *Conseil du Commerce*, 166–170; forced to American concessions in August 5 letter, 183–186, 207–10; inaugurates Navigation System by decrees of July *1810*, 186–210, letter of to Montalivet setting forth commercial program, 202–203, works out and inaugurates Trianon tariff, 211–228, 230–234; issues Fontainebleau decree October *1810*, 228–230; "continentalizes" Navigation System, 235–255; issues trade permits to United States, 240–242; modified licence system, 256–262; negotiations between England and, for extended licence trading, 262–283; tour of, in the north, *1811*, 284–286; conditions leading to change in Navigation System of, 286–304; presents his Grand System, January *1812*, 304–310; effect on England of Grand System of, 311–313; American demands of *1812* and invasion of Russia, 314–322, 327; workings of the Grand System, 323–332; revises licence system of *1813*, 332–343, Bourbons do away with Navigation System of, 343–346; administration evolved by, for Navigation System, 347–377

Nassau, 227

National Industry, *see* Society for the Encouragement of

Naval stores, need of, in colonies, 56; French need of, 172; Montalivet opposes exportation of, 204; licences for, under Navigation System, 238, 242, 243, 246, 253, 294; licences for, under Grand System, 343

Navigation Acts, England's effective use of, 2; connection of, and English negotiations of *1786*, 2; French: September 21, *1793*, 3, 4, 200, 211, 345; July 3, *1810*, 200–202; July 5, *1810*, 175–176; July 25, *1810*, 205–206. *See* Continental System and Navigation System.

Navigation System, international aspects of, i–ii; connection of, with

Napoleon's downfall, ii–iii; connection of, with Continental System, 1–2; relation of *projet* of May 29–30, to, 173; decrees of July 3, 5, 25, *1810* inaugurate, 200–210; enactment and reception of Trianon and Fontainebleau decrees, 313–234; continentalization of July decrees, 237–255; actual operation of, 256–283; resumé and prospects of, 284–304; Napoleon's Grand System of January *1812*, 304–310, 313, 318; actual workings of the Grand System, 323–344; Bourbons do away with Napoleon's, 344–346 administration of, by: *Bureau Consultatif des Arts et Manufactures*, 169, 356; *Conseil de Contentieux*, 169, 362–365; *Conseil Général de Commerce*, 169, 269, 354–356, 359n 373; *Conseil Géné al des Arts et Manufactures*, 169, 356; *Conseil des Prises*, 352–353; *Conseil du Commerce et Manufactures*, 166, 354; Council of State, 352, 367, 371; Council of Administration for the Interior, 48–52; Director General of Customs, 97, 99, 243, 349, 360, 361, 362, 363, 374; Director General of Posts, 7, 352; Minister Secretary of State, 92, 93, 107, 352, 360; Minister of the Treasury, 353; Ministry of Administration of War, 353; Ministry of Cults, 353; Ministry of Exterior Relations, 7, 97 172, 243, 350–351, 374; Ministry of Finance, 7, 99, 167–169, 171, 206. 349–350, 354, 361, 369, 374; Ministry of Interior, 91–96, 98, 99, 105–106, 107, 127, 132, 167–169, 206, 235, 286, 348–349, 352, 354, 355–361, 363, 366, 369, 370, 373; Ministry of Justice, 352; Ministry of Manufactures and Commerce, 94, 170, 308, 349, 351, 353, 355, 361, 367–377; Ministry of Marine and Colonies, 7, 97, 99, 105–106, 206, 243, 347–348, 360, 374n; Ministry of Police, 7, 97, 98, 106n, 351–352; Ministry of War, 7, 243, 351

For details *see Conseil du Commerce et des Manufactures*, Council of Administration for the Interior, *Conseil des Prises*. See also table of contents, Navigation Acts, decrees, customs tariff and licence system

Niemen river, 310, 322n

Nerac, ——, (Nairac), 57

Netherlands, *see* Holland

Neutrals, affected by Napoleonic System, ii, iv, 4; influence of United States as chief of, iv–v; 150–159; do not protest against British licence trade Order of February *1807*, 15; Champagny favors exceptions for, from Berlin decree, 19–21, 24–26; Napoleon's reaction to Champagny's recommendation, 21, 29; Napoleon exempts Denmark from Berlin decree, 30–32; affected by Continental System, 37; stricter interpretation of Continental System for, 37–40, 41; Napoleon eliminates, by Milan decree, 44–47, 48; Council of Interior redefines allies and, 50; and quinine importation, 64–66; negotiations relative to seizures of American ships under Milan and Bayonne decrees, 70–76; failure to find substitute carrier for, 77; trade of, in grain of northern France, 79; trade of, between England and

INDEX 441

France, 83–84, 90, 140n, 266; Napoleon inaugurates licenced trading through medium of, 86–106, 110, 118, 123n, 130; *Conseil du Commerce* to discuss relations of, 170; consideration of complaints of United States results in August 5 letter, 171–186; use of, in licence trade recommended, 194, 196–197; case of United States results in permit scheme for America, 198, 199, 200, 206, 211, 215, 240–242, 256–258, 259; effect of Trianon tariff on trade of 227; status of, after July *1810* decrees, 236; use of, in Mediterranean trade, 248; abuse use of certificates of origin, 276–277; United States demands rights of, in *1812*, 315; position of, in the Grand System 318, 322; connection of Ministry of Exterior Relations with trade of, 350

New England, 54, 153n

Newton, ——, 318n

New York, seizure of goods for Holland from, 143n; shipping port for American permit trade, 173, 176, 177, 241

Nice, 307

Niles, H. 89n

Nimwegen, 201

Non-Importation Act, 321

Non-Intercourse Act, passage of, 101, 102, 113, 151, 152, 158; provisions of repeal of, under Macon Bill No. 2, 165, 171, 173, 180, 181, 182, 183, 194, 218, 256. *See* Macon Bill No. 2

Normandy, 3n, 52, 63

North Africa, 54, 259

North Sea, 148, 282; Continental Blockade in, 35, 36, 43, 202; French licence trade in, 111, 247, 351

Norway, licences for, under Navigation System, 245, 246, 290; Danish licences for, 247; licences for, under Grand System, 343

Nussbaum, F. L., v

Oder river, 244

Oils, advantages of exportation of, 80; licenced article of importation under Continental System, 121; licenced article of exportation under Continental System, 124, 134n, 146, 147; Licences for, under Navigation System, 238, 241, 267, 289; licences for, under Grand System, 328, 335

Oldenburg, 17n; Napoleon suppresses flag of, and seizes ships of, 50, 102; licence trade of, under flag of, 102, 103

Orders In Council, connected with British blockade policies, *1806:* May 8, 14, 152, 165, 171; *1807:* January 7, 15–16, 41; February 4, 15–16, November 11 and 25, 41–42, 44, 45, 47, 74, 79, 80, 171, 182, 183, 292, 312, 313–314, 320, 321, 322, 327, 328; *1809:* April 26, 102, 104; *1812:* April 21, 320

Oxford, 87n

Oudinot, Charles-Nicolas, duc de Reggio, 145

Ostia, 201, 238

Ostend, 271, 272; licences for, 133n, 137; Napoleon visits, 163, 264; smuggling at, 190–192, 274; licence trade at, under Navigation System, 198, 261, 264, 265, 268, 274, 275,

279n, 296, 303, 304; licences for, under Grand System, 307
Orleans, 51
Orestes, the, 59, 61n
Page, Richard, 83
Pappenburg, Napoleon suppresses flag of, and seizes ships of, 50, 102; licence trade of, under flag of, 102, 103
Paris, iv, 48n, 50, 57, 63, 65, 106, 151, 155, 172, 176, 181, 183, 190, 223, 266n, 270n, 271, 292, 293, 294, 295, 330, 333, 337, 365; Prize Court at, 7; plans for trade center at, 19; Armstrong, American minister at, 30, ·165; Louis in, 32; Napoleon in, 41, 70, 84, 165, 190, 332; Haley in, 73; Loyseau in, 78, 79, 81; Abel Hanseatic minister at, 102, 148, 242; petition from, regarding licences, 112; market prices in, compared with London, 131–132, 363; licences for, 133n; Lubinski Russian consul at, 139; Murat in, 146; Napoleon marries Marie Louise in, 160; Collin called from, 163; protests in, regarding American permit scheme, 179; protests against Fontainebleau decree, 230; central licence administration at, 238, 243, 288; grain needed in, 258; Barlow American minister in, 284, 315, 320; Maret returns to, 285; news in, of England's acceptance of Napoleon's *1812* demands, 311, 312; sale of sugar in, 327; failures of merchants in, 338, 339, 341; Hanseatic cities withdraw securities from, 339; last session of *Conseil du Commerce* held in, 342; *Conseil Général de Commerce* in, 354–355; Tribunal of Commerce of, 356n; represented in *Conseil Général des Fabriques et Manufactures*, 357
Parliament, British, 101n
Parrish, David, 152n
Pas de Calais, 265, 278, 279. See Strait of Dover
Peace of Amiens, *see* Amiens
Peace of Tilsit, *see* Tilsit
Pennsylvania, University of, iv, v; Historical Studies, v
Perceval Ministry, 42, 292, 293
Permits, American, Ottoman-Barbary. See licence system, kinds of
Pernambuco, 303, 304
Perpignan, 341, 342
Persia, accepts Berlin decree, 17; licences for, 335, 342, 343
Pétry, M., 155, 157, 164
Philadelphia, v, 173, 177
Phillimore, Judge Joseph, 87
Pichon, Stephen, 42n, 348n
Piedmont, 24, 52, 338
Pinkney, William, 184
Plymouth, 268; French ships in harbor of, 118; Danish ship stops at, 149; corn ships arrive at, 189
Poe, Edgar Allan, 272n
Poland, 34, 140; Napoleon's campaign of, 13; trade with, 13, 24; new trade routes in, 27; trade advantages for, under Navigation System, 203, 232; licences for, under Grand System, 306, 307; Barlow dies in, 330
Police, Ministry of, *see* Navigation System, Savary, Fouché
Pomerania, *see* Swedish
Pontoise, 133n
Portal, Pierre-Barthélemy, baron, 355, 356
Portalis, Jean-Etienne-Marie, count, 358

INDEX 443

Porte, the, *see* Turkey
Portsmouth, 90
Portugal, 43n, 49, 81; accepts Berlin decree, 17, 18, 32–33, 34; question of improvement of trade with, 20–21, 22, 23n, 29, 30; not regarded as a neutral, 40; Milan decree and, 45; coast trade with, 51, 53; Napoleon occupies, 53, 54; orders to capture ships of, 61n; quinine to be imported from, 65; trades in French grain, 79; ships of, excluded from the north, 228; licence trade with, 134, 241; English licences for, 270
Privy Council, British, 92n; action of, regarding licence trade with France, 84n; policy of, regarding licences, 96n; creates licences for Holland, 141; petitions to, for trade with France, 263, 266; criticized, 282; archival material at, iv, 383
Prize Court, powers of, under Continental System, 7
Public Record Office, British, iv, 382
Prussia, 91; Napoleon's campaign against, 6, 13; British blockade affects, 14n; accepts Berlin decree, 17; signs treaty of Tilsit, 17, 29; Berlin decree and, 30, 34, 86; use of flag of, for licence trade, 103, 104, 105, 113, 139, 149, 153; licence trade with, 134; American shipping excluded from, 154; Trianon tariff and, 226, 227, 228, 231, 232; licence policy for, 244, 245, 246n, 276; issues own licences, 247; silk trade with, 302; Grand System and, 306, 307
Pye, Rich, and Co., 302
Pyrenees, the, 223, 362

Quai d'Orsay, 165
Quimper, 307
Quingamp, 133n
Quinine, 78; special action regarding need of, 62–66; licenced article of import under Continental System, 95, 125, 128, 137, 140; licences for, under Navigation System, 238, 253, 296, 298; English withdraw embargo from, 313

Rambouillet, 83; seizures, 46; decree issued at, 158. *See* decrees
Ransom, *see* Garnier and Redon, 307
Reggio, duc de, *see* Oudinot
Regnaud de St. Jean d'Angely, count, proposes customs legislation, 26n, 27; member of Council of Administration, 48, 49; member of *Conseil du Commerce*, 167, 343; influence of, on Navigation System, 353
Regnier, Claude-Antoine, duc de Massa, Minister of Justice, 38, 40n, 352
Remondat, ——, 359, 373
Rennes, 114, 364
Reunion, Island of, 60
Revolution, American, *see* American
Revolution, French, *see* French
Rhine, *see* Confederation of
Rhine river, 168, 201, 284
Rhone river, 110
Rich, and Co., *see* Pye, Rich, and Co.
Riga, 135n
Rochefort, 60, 61, 133n
Romanzoff, Count Nicholas, 229, 267, 316n
Rome, 357; licences for, 133n, 147, 148
Rose, George, 313
Rose, J. Holland, 1, 88

Rosengarten, Joseph G., v
Rostock, 307
Rousset, Mme., 63
Rotterdam, licences for, 252, 296, 304; smuggling carried on from, 302
Rouen, 97; plans for colonial trade for, 58; Napoleon in, 163; need of American raw products in, 173, 176; industries flourish in 262; licences for, 294, 328; cotton industry in, 332, 334; represented on *Conseil Général des Fabriques et Manufactures*, 357
Roux, Vital, 230n, 234n, 285n, 365, 366, 367
Rovigo, *see* Savary, duc de
Royal Commission on Public Records, iv
Russell, Jonathan, 321; protests against American permits scheme, 179n, 257; recognizes American permits, 319; American chargé at London, 320
Russia, 254, 276, 316, 357, 370n; invasion of, 1n, 259, 309, 312n, 322, 327, 329, 330, 332; Berlin decree and trade with, 13, 17, 24, 34, 48n; signs peace of Tilsit and threatens England, 17, 18, 31n, 33, 45; Council of Interior classifies as ally, 50; ukase against England, June *1808*, 81; at war with Sweden, 81; wants modification of Continental System, 86; flag of, used in licence trade, 113; licenced trade with, 114, 116, 139–141; American shipping excluded from, 154; supports demands of the United States, 155n; Trianon tariff and, 226, 228, 231, 232; tariff ukase of, 232, 233, 260, 261n, 284; licence trade with, under Navigation System, 238, 290; never adopted licence system, 246; contraband trade with, 302; renewal of British intercourse with, 336

St. Cloud, 22, 160, 162, 205, 219, 286. *See* decrees
St. Helena, 90, 234
St. Jean de Luz, 52
St. Malo, plans for colonial trade at, 55, 56, 58; licence trade at, 133, 198, 307; smuggling from, 301
St. Petersburg, licence trade with, 135n; petitions from, for participation in licence trade, 139–140; Adams American minister at, 141, 182, 227, 246
St. Quentin, 163
St. Valéry, 163
Saintes, 133n
Salt, licenced article of export, 95; licenced trade in, 114, 142n, 144, 335n
San Domingo, 60, 172, 219, 343
San Remo, 362
San Sebastian, 59
Sansom, the, case of, 39n
Santander, 65
Sardinia, 344; Berlin decree and, 17–18, 34; licence trade with, 134, 238, 249, 258–259, 290, 343
Sauer-Schwabenheim, 373
Savary, Anne-Jean-Marie, duc de Rovigo, police licences and, 271, 272, 273, 274, 275, 351; silk reports of, 333; Minister of Police, 351; presents memorial of May 7, *1811*, 365
Savona, 307
Saxony, Trianon tariff and, 226, 227; licences for, under Navigation System, 245
Scheldt river, 110, 168, 201

INDEX 445

Schiedam, 191
Schmidt, Charles, iv, 1, 87n, 118n
Schoenbrunn, 112
Schoewen, 187, 188
Schroeder and Schuyler, 137n
Scott, Sir William, Lord Stowell, 39n
Seaman, J. E., 143n
Secretary of State, Minister, *see* Navigation System, Maret, Daru
Secretary of State, of the United States, 222. *See* Robert Smith, James Monroe
Seeds, advantages of exportation of, 80; licence trade of, under Continental System, 114, 134n; licence trade of, under Navigation System, 238, 252, 267, 280, 288, 296, 298; licences for, under Grand System, 299, 331; English import, 325
Seesperre, i, 29
Seine river, 110
Senegal, 60
Serrurier, ——, 318n, 320n
Serruy, Joseph, 268
Serruys and Co., 137n
Ships, Napoleon considers trading in foreign, 22; Collin reports on trading with foreign, 23n; orders covering, in Fontainebleau decree, 36–37, 38; American ships seized by Spain, 38; regulations for, under Milan decree, 44–46; regulations for, outlined by Council of Interior, 49–50; kinds of, for speculative colonial expeditions, 55–63; proposed insurance for, 57; English simulate colonial commerce in French, 66–67; colonial trade in Algerian, 70; regulations for licence trading in neutral, 86, 90, 94–96, 99–106, 111–112, 114–118, 120, 121, 122–123; sequestered in France, 130; *Conseil du Commerce* to discuss new measures for, 167; papers for, engaged in American permit trade, 176; regulations for smuggling, 191; regulations for, under Navigation System, 200, 201, 206, 238, 239, 243, 250; regulations for, under Grand System, 309; surveillance of Minister of Marine and Colonies over, 348; surveillance of *Conseil du Commerce* over, 352; surveillance of *Conseil de Contentieux* over, 362–363
Ship papers, Algerian ships secure exception passports, 67–70; for American ships engaged in permit trade, 176; for ships engaged in colonial trade, 220; Napoleon abolishes certificates of origin, 228; under July *1810* decrees, 236, 243, 248; practice of forging, 276; issued by Minister of Marine, 348; issued by Minister of Exterior Relations, 350
Sicily, Algerian vessels not to stop at, 69; English entrepôt, 81, 146, 147; licence trade with, 238, 248, 249, 259, 336
Sidmouth, Lord, 326
Silks, American demands for, 20; duties lowered on Italian, 27; dyes imported for, 124; licenced article of export, 134, 147; *Conseil du Commerce* to discuss manufacture of, 168; permits for Americans to export, 172, 173; Trianon tariff and, 212, 223; licences for under Navigation System, 241, 243, 250, 252, 253, 260–262, 278, 279–281, 286, 288, 289, 290, 293, 294, 296–299, 300, 301, 363; licences for under Grand System, 299, 305, 306, 325,

329, 331, 332, 333, 334, 343; plans for silk trade with England, 293, 296–304, 325, 326; industry at Lyons, 260, 262, 332; failure of silk merchants, 338

Skins, proposed licenced export, 121, 137; American permit to import, 173; customs duties on, 220; licences for, under Navigation System, 238, 241, 243n, 253, 262, 289; licences for, under Grand System, 299, 305, 309, 328, 335, 343

Smith, Robert, American Secretary of State, 222; notified of Trianon decree, 228n, 231n; Russell protests to, regarding permit scheme, 257n; informed of secret negotiations between France and England, 267n

Smuggling, for Empress Josephine, 11n; Collin reports on activity of, 23; in Italy, 24; England employs system of, 77; Napoleon considers northern ports for, 163–164; *Conseil du Commerce* to consider, 168; government control of, and results, 187, 190–192; Trianon tariff and, 224, 225, 227, 228; police licences and, 273–275; extent of, 277–281, 331; methods of silk smuggling, 301–303; proposal to destroy, 365

Smyrna, 67, 238, 250

Society for the Encouragement of National Industry, 18

Solberg and Co., 137n

Sorel, A, 1, 7

South America, 81, 269–270, 271n. *See* Latin America and Spanish America

Spain, 43n, 91, 147, 152; 241; revolt in, 1n; Berlin decree and trade with, 7, 22, 23n, 27, 30, 34, 38, 49; Milan decree and, 45; Council of Interior classifies as ally, 50; coast trade with, 52, 53, 249; Napoleon covets colonies of, 54; Napoleon conquers, 54, 61, 76, 81, 84, 85; trade of colonies of, 55, 58, 61n, 176, 197; orders to capture ships of, 61n, quinine from, 63–65, 66; British trade with, 84n; American shipping excluded from, 154; customs duties on cotton from, 212, 215, 220; French licences for, 238, 239, 249, 253, 262, 265, 334, 342, 343, 344, 351; colonies of, issued licences, 247; English licences for, 265; defeat of Napoleon's armies in, 339

Spanish America, 219, 247, 257, 269, 285, 301. *See* Latin America

Spices, proposed importation of, 59; Trianon tariff duties on, 217; licences for, under Navigation System, 239, 289; licences for, under Grand System, 305, 341

State, Council of, *see* Navigation System

Stettin, 244n

"Strait of the Sound," 17

Strait of Dover, 273. *See* Pas de Calais.

Strassburg, 217, 341

Stuarts, 2

Sugar, 7, 19, 253; Napoleon considers importing, 22, 78; Collin's and Champagny's *1807* reports concerning, 23; Portugal to bring in, 51; proposed importation of, from North Africa, 54; proposed importation of, from Martinique, 59, 60; *1808*, supply of, in France, 62; Holland imports, 143; *Conseil du Commerce*, to discuss supply of, 168; French need of, 172; Americans not permitted to import, 176, 177,

179; trade in, under Navigation System, 199, 235, 239, 240, 241, 250n, 267, 269, 270, 278, 291, 293, 295, 296–300, 301, 302, 303, 304; Trianon tariff duties on, 217, 226, 234; rise of price of, in England, 221; licences for, under Grand System, 305, 306, 309, 318, 323, 335, 340, 341; English licences for, 326, 327, 329; lower price of, in France, 338; factory for manufacture of, 373

Sur le Commerce de l'Angleterre, 42

Swallow, the (*L'Hirondelle*), 62n

Sweden, 241; Berlin decree and, 17, 18, 33, 34, 35; orders to capture ships of, 61n; English ally, 81, 90, 336; American shipping excluded from, 154; Trianon tariff and, 226, 228, 231, 232, 233; trade with, under Navigation System, 241, 244, 245, 246, 290; independent trade of, 247; Napoleon's break with, 309

Swedish Pomerania, 246, 309

Switzerland, trade of, with Italy, 24; proposed improved trade with, 28; accepts Berlin decree, 34; proposal to check commerce of, 168; Trianon tariff and, 226, 227, 232; licence trade with, 261, 355

Sylvestre, ——, 359

Tarbé, ——, 372

Ternaux, Baron, 87, 357

Terveere, 163, 191

Thainville, Dubois, 69

Thames river, 341

Thomas Jefferson, the, 153n

Tiber, department of, 127n, 147

Tiber river, 223

Tilsit, peace of, 12, 17–18, 29, 31n, 32, 41, 46, 232

Toulouse, 373

Tours, 260

Trafalgar, 6

Treasury, Minister of, *see* Navigation System, Mollien

Trianon tariff, *see* decrees and customs tariff

Tripoli, 248

Tripolitan War, 315n

Tuileries, 8, 255, *see* decrees

Turin, 373

Turreau de Gambrouville, General Louis-Marie, 179

United States, influence of, on Napoleonic System, iv–v; France aids, in American Revolution, 2, Barlow advocates attack on England *1792*, 3n; influence of, on commercial policy of the French Revolution, 3n; resents British blockade measures, 15, 34; Champagny urges importance of trade with, 19–21, 28, 30, 40; attitude toward Copenhagen attack, 32n; strict interpretation of Berlin decree given to, 21n, 37–40, 44–47; trade of *1800* with France, 37; ocean trade of France open to, 50, 64; French coast trade not open to, 51; French orders to capture ships of, 61n; ships of, sequestered, 63, 72, 218, 284; as a quinine carrier, 63–64; trade in colonial goods with, 68; negotiations after Milan and Bayonne decrees, 70–76; effect of American Embargo on Napoleon, 71; engaged in grain trade in northern France, 79; effect of Embargo on England, 81, 82, 84; use of, in neutral trade between France and England, 83–84; connection of licence trade, *1809*, with the, 101, 105, 122, 123n, 134, 140, 142–144, 145–147, 150–158; trade with France passage of Non-Intercourse Act and Altenberg offer, 101–109, 151; negotiations relative to trade result in Rambouillet decree, 126, 151–159, 164; legation at St. Petersburg, 140–141; comments in, on Napoleon's visit to the north, 163; passes Macon Bill No. 2, May *1810*, 165–166; *Conseil du Commerce* considers question of, and decree of July 5, *1810* for trade permits, 170–179, 194, 195, 202, 203, 206, 218; resents "permits" plan, 179–182; threatens to declare war on France, 183; Champagny's August 5 letter promising revocation of Berlin-Milan decrees, 183–186, 194, 207–208, 218, 221; flag of, used for French smuggling trade, 191n; Trianontariff and, 213, 214, 218–219, 222–223, 225, 226, 228, 232; permits for, under Navigation System, 240–242, 247, 257–258, 259, 261, 262, 287, 290, 291, 297, 299, 316–319, 328, 334, 343–344, 350; Napoleon hopes to see war between England and, 256–257; protests of, against equivocations in repeal of Berlin-Milan decrees, 256–258; gets results from Barlow's negotiations, 284–285, 314–322, 330; Montalivet on trade with, 290, 297, 299, 303; War of *1812*, 314, 320, 322, 328n; trade with, under Grand System, 318–319, 324, 329, 343, 344; passes Non-Inportation Act, 321. *See* American Embargo Act, Non-Intercourse Act, and Macon Bill No. 2

United States Gazette, 175

University of Illinois, *see* Illinois

University of Pennsylvania, *see* Pennsylvania

Utrecht, French camp at, 145; treaty of, 284, 312

Valencia, 296
Valenciennes, 364
Valladolid, 84
Van Aken, ———, agent in Franco-English licence negotiations, 128n, 137n, 164, 189n, 263–273, 281, 295, 301; refused licence not including silk, 261n; member of *Conseil Général de Commerce*, 269, 355, 356
Van Aken and Son, trade of, with England, 268, 301
Van der Heyden, 137n
Vannes, 133n
Venice, smuggling at, 23n; licences for, under Navigation System, 203, 248; licences for, under Grand System, 307, 335; failures of bankers in, 338
Verneilh, ———, 359
Versailles, treaty of (Eden treaty), 2–4, 5, 305, 306, 308, 311, *See* Auckland
Vicence, duc de, *see* Caulaincourt
Vienna, 154, 221
Vigoureux, ———, 335
Vincent, ———, 106
Viollette, Dubois, 106
Virginia, 271
Vistula river, 203
Vittoria, 65
Voute, *see* Woute

INDEX 449

Walcheren, 85, 117
Waltentorf, de ——, 245n
War Ministry of, *see* Navigation System
War, Ministry of the Administration of, *see* Navigation System
War of 1812, 185, 314, 320, 322
War of Liberation, 1n
Warsaw, Napoleon in, 15n; *Code Napoleon* adopted for, 225n; Trianon tariff and, 226, 227; licences for, under Navigation System, 245
Washington, George, 315n
Washington, D. C., 158, 182, 316; archives at, iv, 380, 383; Armstrong's instructions from, 156; France plans to send negotiator to, in *1810*, 164; reception in, of French permit scheme, 179; rumors of war with England in, 320; British declaration regarding repeal of Continental System does not reach 321
Weiler, M J, 8
Wellesley, Richard Colley, marquis of, 256
Wellington, Arthur Wellesley, duke of, 339
Wesel, 201
Weser river, 36; enforcement of Berlin decree on, 35; Bremen outlet for, 203; licences for trade on, 290
West Indies, British prohibition on products from, 42; Napoleon dreams of exploiting, 54; American embargo affects French, 55, 71; attempts to keep up trade with, 59n; American embargo affects British, 81; licence trade with, 125;
tariff provisions on goods from, 220; Spanish licences for trade with, 247; licence system and, 286; English concessions for French trade with, 293, 329, 330
Westphalia, 211; adopts Trianon tariff, 226, 227
William the Silent, 179
Wilna, 327, 329, 330
Wimereux, 191, 192
Wine, 188; Baltic import, 35; Portugal's trade in, 51; need of, in French colonies, 55, 56, 58; neutral trade in, 75; Bordeaux's trade in, with the north, 79, 91, 103; advantages of exportation of, 80; licenced article of export, 94, 95; licenced trade in, under Continental System, 109, 110, 116, 120, 121, 122, 125, 133, 134, 137, 140, 149, 153, 188; British forbid importation of, 124; permits for Americans to export, 172, 173, 175; licence trade in, under Navigation System, 238, 239, 241, 243, 252, 258, 260, 261, 263, 264, 265, 266, 278, 279, 288, 289, 291, 295, 296–300, 303, 304, 363; licences for, under Grand System, 299, 305, 306, 309, 311, 312n, 318, 323, 329, 331, 334, 338; English licences for, 326
·Wismar, 307
Woute (Voute), Baron Robert, 301–302, 355
Wundt, Captain, 149
Würtemburg, 226, 227

Ypres, 133n

Zealand, 191